GERMAN NATIONALISM AND
RELIGIOUS CONFLICT

GERMAN NATIONALISM AND RELIGIOUS CONFLICT

CULTURE, IDEOLOGY,
POLITICS, 1870–1914

Helmut Walser Smith

PRINCETON UNIVERSITY PRESS   PRINCETON, NEW JERSEY

Library of Congress Cataloging-in-Publication Data

Smith, Helmut Walser, 1962–
German nationalism and religious conflict : culture,
ideology, politics, 1870–1914 / Helmut Walser Smith.
p.   cm.
Includes bibliographical references and index.
ISBN 0-691-03624-1 (CL)
1. Nationalism—Germany—History—19th century.   2. Germany—
Politics and government—1871–1918.   3. Catholic Church—
Germany—History.   4. Kulturkampf—Germany.   5. Church
and state—Germany.   I. Title.
DD204.S57   1994
320.5′4′0943—dc20   94-16983

To my mother
and the memory of
my father

Contents

Figures and Tables _____

Figures

Tables

Acknowledgments

IN THE COURSE of writing this book, I have incurred many debts, which I am now pleased to acknowledge. The book began as a Yale dissertation directed by Henry A. Turner. For his encouragement, for his close reading, and for his continual support, I am very grateful. I am likewise indebted to Peter Gay, for his insight and criticism, and for the standards he sets. Paul Kennedy read the dissertation with meticulous care and gave valuable advice for its improvement. On the subject of nationalism, I have benefited from the criticisms of Ivo Banac, who also read the dissertation in its final form. At this point I should also like to thank the late Hans Gatzke, who taught me much about what it is to be a German historian.

The research for this book would not have been possible were it not for the generous financial support of a number of scholarly institutions and foundations. I should like, therefore, to offer my gratitude to the Council for European Studies at Columbia University, the Yale Center for International and Area Studies, and the University of Karlsruhe. The writing of this book was supported by a Mellon Fellowship in the Humanities given by the Woodrow Wilson National Fellowship Foundation, by a fellowship granted by the Berlin Program for Advanced German and European Studies of the Social Science Research Council and the Free University of Berlin, and by a summer fellowship of the Vanderbilt University Research Council.

In my first year of research in the German archives, the History Department of the University of Karlsruhe provided me with a home base. For the hospitality of that department's faculty and staff, I am very grateful. I would especially like to thank Professor Rudolf Lill, who directed my research in Germany, and Dr. Wolfgang Altgeld (now of the University of Würzburg), who shared his vast knowledge of religious conflict with a generosity hardly self-evident in German university circles.

The research for this book is based on work in a number of archives and libraries throughout Germany and the United States. For their helpfulness and patience I should like to thank the archivists and librarians of the Geheimes Staatsarchiv Preußischer Kulturbesitz in Berlin-Dahlem, the Archiv des Diakonischen Werkes der EKD in Berlin, the Evangelisches Zentralarchiv in Berlin, the Politisches Archiv des Auswärtigen Amtes in Bonn, the Erzbischöfliches Archiv in Freiburg, the Bundesarchiv/Militärarchiv in Freiburg, the Generallandesarchiv in Karlsruhe, the Landeskirchliches Archiv in Karlsruhe, the Bundesarchiv in Koblenz, the Landeshauptarchiv in Koblenz, the Stadtarchiv in Cologne, the Stadtarchiv in Ludwigsburg, the Bayerisches Hauptstaatsarchiv in Munich, the archive of the Pfälzische Landesbibliothek in Speyer, the Hauptstaatsarchiv in Stuttgart, the Landeskirchliches Archiv in Stuttgart, the Bistumsarchiv in Trier, as well as the Badische Landesbibliothek in Karlsruhe, the Württembergische Landesbibliothek in Stuttgart, the Bayerische Staatsbibliothek in Munich, the Universitätsbibliothek in Cologne, the Germania Judaica in Cologne, the Staatsbibliothek Preußischer Kulturbesitz in West Berlin, the Deutsche Staatsbibliothek in East Berlin, and, especially, the staffs of Sterling Memorial Library at Yale and the Jean and Alexander Heard Library at Vanderbilt.

I should, at this point, like to give special acknowledgment to the Konfessionskundliches Institut des Evangelischen Bundes in Bensheim in Hessen for allowing me to use its rich archive and library, for offering me a place to stay, and for the hospitality that its members and their families extended to me in the winter and spring of 1989. I should especially like to thank Dr. Heiner Grote, who shared with me his profound knowledge of confessional matters with an ecumenical spirit that I am not sure his Wilhelminian predecessors would have fully understood.

I wish I had written this book in one place. As it turns out, I wrote parts of it in New Haven and Tübingen, other parts in East and West Berlin, and still others in Nashville. I would not advise this approach to historians, but it did bring me a wide range of friends and critics, many of whom commented on drafts of chapters or patiently listened as I explained to them more about Catholics and Protestants than they cared to know. For their comments on my work, I should like to thank Susan Crane, Gabriel Finkelstein, David Patton, Cele Bucki, Ulrike Baureithel, and Pieter Judson. In the Department of History at Vanderbilt, my colleagues Michael Bess, Simon Collier, Joel Harrington, Jim Epstein, Leon Helguera, Arleen Tuchman, and Frank Wcislo have all read parts of the manuscript and, through their support and critical engagement, have much improved it. At Princeton University Press, two anonymous readers reviewed the book with care and critical acumen. One of them, Margaret Lavinia Anderson, has followed the development of this project from its earliest stages, offering insight and encouragement from the start. For the maps and charts, I should like to acknowledge the work of Christopher Brest. Remaining faults and deficiencies are, of course, my own.

Finally, I thank Pater Alexander Walser, my uncle, for first introducing me to the world of history, and am sorry that he could not live to see this book completed. I thank my friends Sönke Seifarth, Judith Forrest, Pamela Rothstein, and Steve Dowden for going out of their way when I needed their support. And I thank Norman Kutcher and Meike Werner—for their help and for their considerable influence on me.

Notes on Usage and Translation ─────────────

IN MOST CASES I have translated *Volk* as nation. The usual English translation, "folk," makes the German word more peculiar than it is. To avoid confusion, I have made it a point never to use "nation" where I mean state.

The German word *Konfession* has been translated, depending on the context, either as confession or as religion. Strictly speaking, "confession" refers to religious groups within Christianity. "Denomination," the standard translation of *Konfession*, refers to religious groups within Protestantism and is, therefore, too narrow a translation for our purposes.

The Evangelischer Bund zur Wahrung deutsch-protestantischer Interessen has been translated as the Protestant League and not, as the *Oxford Dictionary of the Christian Church* suggests, the Evangelical League. The reasons are that "Protestant" has retained more the ring of anti-Catholicism and, at least in the English language, "evangelical" still suggests strict adherence to scripture as well as missionary zeal. Conversely, the term "Evangelical movement in Austria" has been retained precisely because this movement tried to convert Catholics on a mass scale.

Unless stated otherwise, all qualifications in brackets are my own. Conversely, all italicized words are emphasized (italicized or underlined) in the original documents.

I have retained the German when referring to east-central European place names simply in order to render towns and cities in the east more accessible. Thus, the historical capital of Silesia is referred to as Breslau and not as Wrocław.

GERMAN NATIONALISM AND
RELIGIOUS CONFLICT

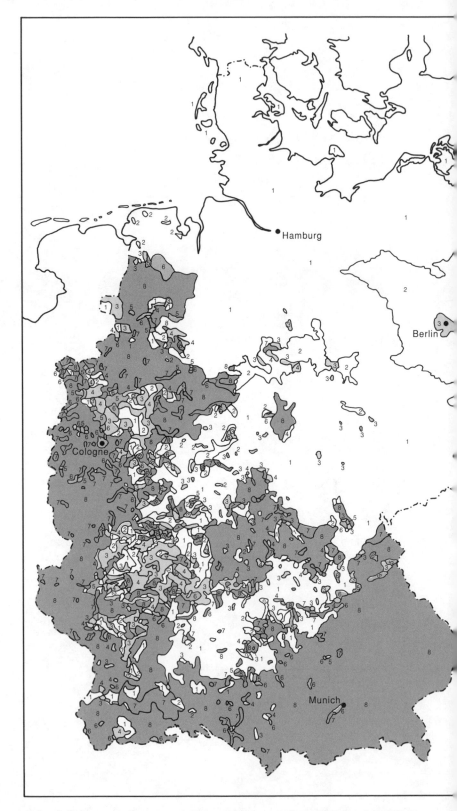

Source: *Meyers Kleines Konversationslexikon* (Leipzig and Vienna, 1908), vol. 2, 332–33.

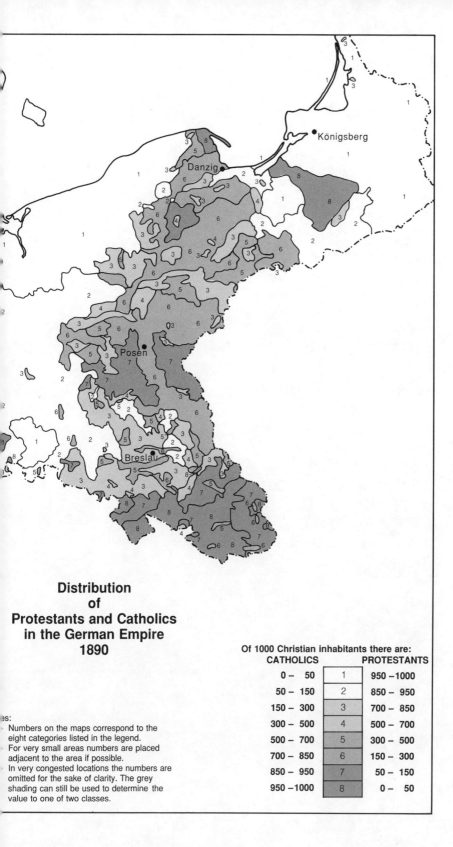

Distribution
of
Protestants and Catholics
in the German Empire
1890

Königsberg

Danzig

Posen

Breslau

Of 1000 Christian inhabitants there are:

CATHOLICS		PROTESTANTS
0 – 50	1	950 –1000
50 – 150	2	850 – 950
150 – 300	3	700 – 850
300 – 500	4	500 – 700
500 – 700	5	300 – 500
700 – 850	6	150 – 300
850 – 950	7	50 – 150
950 –1000	8	0 – 50

es:
Numbers on the maps correspond to the
eight categories listed in the legend.
For very small areas numbers are placed
adjacent to the area if possible.
In very congested locations the numbers are
omitted for the sake of clarity. The grey
shading can still be used to determine the
value to one of two classes.

Introduction

NATIONS DEPEND on a certain amount of fellow feeling, on a sense, however contrived, that fellow citizens represent kith and kin. Typically this sense derives from a common history, a common memory. Yet while that memory may evoke heroic acts and legendary figures of the distant past, it may also recall civil war and religious intolerance, hatred and persecution, betrayal and subterfuge. "The essence of a nation," wrote the nineteenth-century French social philosopher Ernest Renan, "is that all the individuals have many things in common and also that they have already well forgotten some of them." Memory is a blessing but also a burden to nations. Renan believed it the duty of French citizens to "have already forgotten" the great massacres—of the Albigensians in the thirteenth century, and of the Huguenots on Saint Bartholomew's Day, 1572—that haunted the collective memory of the French with the trauma of fratricide.[1]

Across the Rhine, in the land of the Reformation, in a country more deeply divided and more visibly scarred by wars of religion, the burden of memory rested with still greater weight upon the national consciousness of patriotic citizens. When nineteenth-century German Catholics imagined their Protestant counterparts, they recalled a rebellion replete with iconoclasm and violence that destroyed the great *Una Sancta* of the medieval empire. Conversely, Protestants saw in the past and the present of their Catholic brethren the source of great intolerance, which in turn led to great bloodshed; they remembered the massacre by Tilly's armies of the Protestant population of Magdeburg, and they argued that for centuries Catholics had worked to ensure the division and debilitation of the German nation.

Forgetting, easy for individuals, has always been difficult for nations and religious groups. In Germany, the effort to "have already forgotten" was rendered still more Sisyphean by the degree to which religious division had for centuries been an immutable part of the old order. The principle *Cuius regio, eius religio*, formally introduced at the Peace of Augsburg in 1555, asserted that subjects of states should, for purposes of inner-state cohesion, remain unified confessionally. Reli-

---

[1] This passage has been called to the attention of historians by Benedict Anderson, *Imagined Communities: Reflections on the Origin and Spread of Nationalism*, 2d ed. (London, 1991), 199–201. Here, and throughout, my argument has been profoundly influenced by Anderson's work. On the subject of forgetting, see also Yosef Hayim Yerushalmi, *Zakhor: Jewish History and Jewish Memory* (New York, 1989), esp. 105–17.

gious and political identity should, according to this principle, ideally be one. For the next two hundred years, this idea remained axiomatic to the politics of the Holy Roman Empire; it survived the devastation of the Thirty Years War and the long peace, at first uneasy, then increasingly settled, that followed. By the eighteenth century, it had become an attribute of early modern Germany as self-evident, if also as contrary to enlightened reason, as the empire itself. "Nature," wrote Immanuel Kant in *On Everlasting Peace*, "employs two means to separate peoples and prevent them from mixing: differences of language and of religion." Kant expressed optimism that with the passage of time these differences, "which involve a tendency to mutual hatred and pretexts for war," would diminish in their divisiveness. "The progress of civilization," he thought, "finally leads to peaceful agreement."[2]

The historical experience of succeeding generations of Germans was to demonstrate the inaccuracy of this sanguine prediction. In the nineteenth century, progress both aggravated and ameliorated traditional divisions of religion and nationality. As men liberated themselves from what Kant called their "self-imposed tutelage," they also came to understand and appreciate their differences. Midway into the nineteenth century, Wilhelm Heinrich Riehl, a German folklorist with a discriminating sense of the mentalité of his countrymen, still found it necessary to speak of two Germanies, one Protestant, the other Catholic.[3] And with an eye to the turn of the century, to the Wilhelminian period, the historian Thomas Nipperdey observed that despite a certain amount of "cooperation and coexistence . . . , confessional division and tension was one of the fundamental, vital facts of everyday life in Germany."[4]

This book is an attempt to understand the influence of these "fundamental, vital facts of everyday life" on the formation of German national identity, on the construction of German national politics, and on the thought and expression of German nationalism. Specifically, it focuses on imperial Germany in the years 1870 to 1914 and addresses the reasons for the recrudescence of religious conflict between Protestants and Catholics in these years. The history of the struggle between these two groups, the waxing and waning of their conflict, will then be used as a window on the larger problem of nation-building and nationalism in Germany.

[2] Immanuel Kant, *Zum ewigen Frieden*, ed. Theodor Valentiner (Stuttgart, 1954), 49.
[3] Wilhelm Heinrich Riehl, *Die Naturgeschichte des deutschen Volkes*, 8th ed., vol. 1, *Land und Leute* (Stuttgart, 1883), 370.
[4] Thomas Nipperdey, *Religion im Umbruch. Deutschland 1870–1918* (Munich, 1988), 155.

This study is, then, primarily about ideas of nation and nationalism—protean, sprawling categories that require provisional definition. Nationalism is predicated on a concept of nation, and nation, though it may in the words of Hugh Seton-Watson "have no scientific definition," nevertheless has a history of attribution.[5] Common language is its most important attribute. Although there are polylinguistic nations (Switzerland), and though there have been successful national movements not based on linguistic unity (as with many anticolonial movements), common language remains, especially for the European conception of nationalism, the elementary prerequisite of nationhood. Common language is not, however, a sufficient condition; it must first be made into an object of "cultural value" by a group existing in solidarity. For Max Weber, nation meant that "it is proper to expect from certain groups a specific sentiment of solidarity in the face of other groups."[6] This solidarity may be formed as a consequence of common experiences of oppression, a sense of shared political destiny, economic centralization, or confessional unity. Although commonality in a national community must be rooted in material or historical reality, the resulting solidarities are, as the political scientist Benedict Anderson has argued, imagined.[7] A nation is therefore primarily a matter of culture. It will be defined here as a coherent culture based on a common language that binds its members into a political community, if not necessarily into a state.

National consciousness, it follows, is the sentiment associated with an awareness of belonging to such a community. It should be distinguished from nationalism, in its purest expression "a political principle which holds that the political and the national unit should be congruent."[8] European Socialists, as became agonizingly clear in August of 1914, possessed national consciousness in good measure; but this revealed little about the ideological content of their nationalism. Nationalism, writes Ivo Banac, "seeks to change the world," and it does so by saturating even everyday aspects of social and political life with national criteria, by demanding that the world, as well as the world order, be ruled by its premises.[9] It is, therefore, a theory of praxis; and if its prescriptions for action may diverge in order to account for the distinctiveness of each national struggle, nationalism is, neverthe-

---

[5] Hugh Seton-Watson, *Nations and States* (Boulder, Colo., 1977), 5.

[6] Max Weber, *Economy and Society*, ed. and trans. Günther Roth and Claus Wittich (New York, 1968), vol. 2, 922.

[7] Benedict Anderson, *Imagined Communities*, 6–7.

[8] Ernest Gellner, *Nations and Nationalism* (Oxford, 1983), 1.

[9] Ivo Banac, *The National Question in Yugoslavia* (Ithaca, N.Y., and London, 1984), 27.

less, programmatic and grounded in a tradition of political philosophy.

Following the work of Hugh Seton-Watson and Benedict Anderson, this study will divide nationalism into two categories: official and popular.[10] Official nationalism is a strategy of domination; it refers to the attempts of European dynasties in the late nineteenth century to co-opt and put forth certain demands of popular nationalism while, in fact, resisting the principle of popular sovereignty. The efforts of the Hohenzollerns to Germanize their Polish and Danish subjects would fall into this category, for, like the Russification policies of Alexander III, such efforts were accompanied by profoundly antidemocratic intentions. Ultimately this "willed merger of nation and dynastic empire" attempted to exploit the former in order to save the latter.[11] Although usually restricted to the nationalities policies of empires, the term "official nationalism" will be stretched, in this study, to fit a wider range of nationalist activity organized by the state—to wit, the official attempt to create a homogenous national culture across lines of confession (the Kulturkampf) as well as the officially directed mobilization of national consciousness known to German historians since Eckart Kehr as *Sammlungspolitik*. By binding together the economic interests of agriculture and industry, the architects of *Sammlungspolitik* sought to rally the "bourgeois" parties around an imperialist, protectionist, antisocialist, and anti-Polish political program centered, after 1897, on the buildup of the kaiser's (not the people's) navy. Official nationalists, they attempted to mobilize national consciousness without endangering the dynastic status quo or threatening power relations already in existence. But, as with the government's nationalities policies, the logic of *Sammlungspolitik* sometimes forced the government to assume political positions incompatible with the dynastic-conservative intent of its own official nationalism.[12] In such cases, the government found itself impelled by popular nationalism.

Popular nationalism refers less to a strategy of rule than a tradition of sentiment and ideology. In modern German history the compass of popular nationalism extended wide and far: from the romantic nationalism of Johann Gottfried von Herder to the social-Darwinist universe of the integral nationalist Heinrich Class—and ultimately to Na-

[10] Seton-Watson, *Nations and States*, 148. See also Benedict Anderson, *Imagined Communities*, 83–111; Oscar Jaszi, *The Dissolution of the Habsburg Monarchy* (Chicago, 1929), 328.

[11] Benedict Anderson, *Imagined Communities*, 88.

[12] Geoff Eley, *Reshaping the German Right: Radical Nationalism and Political Change after Bismarck* (New Haven and London, 1980), 166.

tional Socialism. The common property of popular nationalism lies in its appeal to the people as the last and highest instance of legitimation. That does not, however, make it democratic, for "*das Volk*" may be an idealized conception of the people or it may be represented by a charismatic leader. On the other hand, it does not follow that, because popular nationalism may be undemocratic, it necessarily serves the status quo in authoritarian polities. From the perspective of dynastic empires, the logic of popular nationalism, when thought through, almost always represents a challenge. It does so for three reasons. First, it defines national objectives in terms often at odds with classical concepts of raison d'état; the interest of the people, considered as a collective, is placed logically above the demands of the dynasty or the requirements of the royal house. Second, it transforms the subjects of the dynasty into citizens of a nation; commonality with compatriots therefore replaces fealty to superiors as the most important form of social cohesion. Finally, the logic of popular nationalism insists that the delicate system of intermediary loyalties and cultural attachments (church, village, kin) so important to social control in dynastic empires be dissolved, and in their stead a unified national culture formed.

The conceptual difference between romantic and integral traditions of popular nationalism lies not so much in their respective ideas of sovereignty, or in the challenge they pose to dynastic empires, but in the similes they choose to explain the world. For romantic nationalists, nations—communities of language and culture—could be cultivated like separate and distinct flowers in a garden, each with its own hue. Every nationality, in Friedrich Schleiermacher's words, represented "a certain side of the divine image."[13] Integral nationalists viewed the world quite differently. For them, nations and states were like species struggling amongst one another before the hour of their extinction. The national state was exalted as the perfect political form because it insured the survival of powerful, vital nations. Only nations that could draw strength from the common bonds of language, high culture, tradition, and blood could sustain themselves. Moreover, integral nationalists insisted on the absolute purity of the citizen's commitment to the nation. They therefore attempted to extirpate provincialism, for provincialism, whether cultural, economic, or political, represented intermediary attachment between the individual citizen and the nation. Consequently, integral nationalists also attacked the church, especially the Catholic church. In nineteenth-century Germany, the repeated diatribes against ultramontanism derived, in

---

[13] Quoted by Elie Kedourie, *Nationalism* (New York, 1981), 75.

large measure, from the desire of integral nationalists to create a unified national culture based on common national symbols and on one
indivisible loyalty. The most embittered invective of integral nationalists was reserved, however, for ethnic minorities: in Germany's
Second Empire for Poles, Danes, French, and, though here the matter
is more complex, for Jews.

Romantic and integral nationalism represent ideal types to be plot-
ted on opposite poles of an axis. Concrete expressions of national
ideology usually fell between the two poles and often shared elements of both positions. In the German empire few nationalists
pushed their assumptions to the logical end points. The reason for
this is partly to be found in the ideological consequences that nationalists drew from the unfinished character of the empire. The Kaiserreich was a national state, but not in a pure sense. There were both
Germans outside the empire and non-Germans within it. The German empire therefore possessed characteristics of a "matrix state" on
the one hand, a state with a dominant nationality and peripheral nationalisms on the other.[14] To integral nationalists in German-speaking
areas of the Austro-Hungarian Dual Monarchy, the German empire
constituted the locus of their national aspirations. In this sense, and
for this group, the empire was a matrix state, like Hungary for
Magyars living in Rumania, or Albania for its nationals in Kosovo.
The status of the empire as a state with a dominant nationality and
peripheral nationalisms was, however, of far greater significance,
whether for the formulation of state policy or for the development of
German national consciousness. It meant, above all, that the German
state was forced to make choices about its periphery: choices about
autonomy versus control, freedom versus repression, and about national language. There were also other characteristics of the German
state that made it—from the German nationalist standpoint—an "unfinished nation."[15] The confessional division meant that a cultural rift
ran straight through the empire, the historical consciousness of each
side burdened by enduring memories of mutual intolerance. The
unity of Germany's national culture also suffered from the persistence
of particularist loyalties, whether to Prussia, to Bavaria, or to an even
narrower *Heimat*. Finally, as class conflict became acute—as it did in
the late phase of the empire—the German middle classes redefined
the terms of class struggle, using the vocabulary of nationalism as
mask and shield against a potentially revolutionary working class.

[14] The term "matrix state" comes from Banac, *The National Question in Yugoslavia*, 22.
[15] Theodor Schieder, *Das deutsche Kaiserreich von 1871 als Nationalstaat* (Cologne and
Opladen, 1961).

The empire was, then, a national state easily divisible. The fault lines that divided society defined the terms with which Germans expressed their national consciousness and thought through their nationalist assumptions. And as the German Kaiserreich was an unfinished nation, so the nationalisms of Germans remained discordant, rarely sounding sonorous notes.

Currently, there are two preeminent scholarly approaches to the study of nationalism in the Kaiserreich. The first analyzes nationalism by describing its function and delineating the interests it served. In *The German Empire*, Hans-Ulrich Wehler argued that "rather than picture this nationalism as a force in its own right, it would make more sense to inquire at the outset what Germany's rulers actually stood to gain from allying themselves with it."[16] For Wehler, modern German nationalism constituted the ideological reaction of threatened groups to social strains caused by rapid, uneven industrialization in an essentially premodern polity. A deus ex machina for social and political cohesion, nationalism functioned as a force for integration when traditional ties unraveled. It also diminished social conflicts by directing attention away from them. An instrument of the empire's dominant elite, nationalism was noteworthy because it was pliable, significant because it served the status quo.

The weaknesses of Wehler's analysis lie in the general inadequacies of a functionalist approach to the study of nationalism. The research agenda of functionalism, ultimately concerned with the stability of polities, encouraged an overemphasis on concerns of the center over those of the periphery, state power over civil society, the ideologies of dominant cultural groups over ideologies formed in regional, religious, ethnic, or class subcultures.[17] Nationalism can indeed be functional from the standpoint of rulers—that is, after all, the point of official nationalism. But nationalism can also represent competing ideologies and conflicting passions, can, in fact, be acutely divisive and profoundly destabilizing. Wehler had at best a weak sense for this. Rather than analyzing German nationalisms as ideologies with various intellectual and symbolic contents, he described ideal types and, in the process, reduced the study of nationalism to a taxonomic elaboration of terms, which were then fit into a theoretical (and teleological) model of society.

It might make more sense to reverse this procedure. Rather than

---

[16] Hans-Ulrich Wehler, *Das deutsche Kaiserreich 1871–1918*, 4th ed. (Göttingen, 1980), 109.

[17] See the critique of functionalism in Anthony D. Smith, *Theories of Nationalism* (New York, 1983), 49–57.

assume the malleability of nationalist ideology, it may be more accurate to picture it as a force in its own right. And rather than inquiring, at the outset, into the interests it served, it may be of greater utility to comprehend how different nationalist pronouncements made sense to diverse groups with disparate life experiences.

In part this suggestion coincides with Geoff Eley's criticism of Wehler's functionalism. In *Reshaping the German Right*, Eley argued that German society was neither particularly malleable nor its central power structure seamless.[18] If Wehler defined groups and ideologies by plotting their relation to a central power structure, Eley insisted that historians of imperial Germany should recognize the indeterminate and volatile character of nationalist ideology. Radical nationalism, he correctly maintained, rarely played obedient servant to the power elite.

As a theoretical alternative to functionalism, Eley proposed the Gramscian theory of hegemony. For Eley, hegemony is "negotiated consent," in which "the dominance of a ruling class is constructed ideologically through a continuous process of resistance and intervention."[19] The "scene of domination" in the German empire was ideology itself; the forum of struggle, civil society. Nationalism, in this model, remained an instance of class control, but the composition of the ruling class changed, as did its strategy for domination. Not the aristocratic elite but the bourgeoisie increasingly occupied the leading positions of civil society, and it was the latter who set the tone of the national debate. Nationalist ideology was not, in Eley's view, controlled from the center. Rather, it was constructed in the process of middle-class ("grass roots") mobilization. Hegemony—the ultimate function of nationalism—was, for this reason, always unstable.

Eley's use of Gramsci's concept of hegemony, though certainly a conceptual advance over functionalism, nevertheless brings theoretical difficulties to the study of nationalism in the Kaiserreich. It is, for one, problematic to appropriate a theory grounded in class conflict, designed to explain disjunctures between base and superstructure, in order to analyze an ideology—radical nationalism—which, by Eley's own admission, cannot properly be understood as simply a function of class. "Hegemony," if we follow its theoretical injunctions closely, induces us to look behind the mask of culture and ideology and to perceive the true visage of nationalist conflict as ultimately a conflict defined by class interests. We are thus prevented from taking the ideological contents of nationalism seriously—on their own terms.

[18] Eley, *Reshaping the German Right*, 7–19, 160–67, 203–5.
[19] Ibid., 163–64.

Yet much of what makes nationalism a divisive and at times un-predictable ideology has less to do with class antagonism, with the vertical field of the ruling and the ruled, than it does with the hori-zontal field of antagonisms, animosities that run along ethnic, lin-guistic, regional, or religious frontiers. The horizontal field may be as constitutive of ideology as the vertical field, and to nationalism, as well as to the ruling apparatus of a national state, every bit as important.[20]

Both Wehler and Eley appropriate theoretical traditions that oper-ate within metaphors emphasizing the primacy of vertical conflicts. This study focuses on the horizontal field of affinities and antago-nisms in the Kaiserreich. It does not deny the importance of class conflict in the making of German nationalism, but rather insists that horizontal scissions in society also be taken seriously in the theoreti-cal models that historians develop to understand this nationalism. Cultural divisions between regions, nationalities, and religious groups often influenced daily life as much as, and sometimes more than, class inequality. They also shaped the categories Germans used to articulate ideas about the nation, and, consequently, they affected the function of nationalism in German society.

Division and conflict between Protestants and Catholics constituted a case in point. Few lines of division so clearly cut to the quick of people's identities, so self-evidently defined their cultural horizons, and so deeply determined their political loyalties as the line that sepa-rated the two major religious groups. As Adolf Harnack, one of Ger-many's most perspicacious Protestant theologians, put it in 1908:

> In numerous and important questions of life and of the common weal, our nation is at the outset divided into two camps, and this state of affairs, starting from the center, works its way into the periphery of our existence, deep into the smallest and most everyday aspects of our lives. Everywhere one confronts confessional prejudice; everywhere one encounters the fence, indeed the wall of confession.[21]

Although central to German life and politics in the imperial period, this division, until recently hardly acknowledged by historians focus-

---

[20] For earlier suggestions to focus research on the segmentation of German society, see M. Rainer Lepsius, "Parteiensystem und Sozialstruktur: zum Problem der Demo-kratisierung der deutschen Gesellschaft," in *Deutsche Parteien vor 1918*, ed. Gerhard A. Ritter (Cologne, 1973), 56–80; and Vernon Lidtke, *The Alternative Culture: Socialist Labor in Imperial Germany* (New York and Oxford, 1985), 10–12.

[21] Adolf Harnack, "Protestantismus und Katholizismus in Deutschland," *Preußische Jahrbücher* 127 (1907): 295.

ing exclusively on issues of class, remains largely unexplored.[22] Yet as historians begin to focus on people's identities, and how these identities are constructed and expressed, issues of confessional identity, and therefore of confessional conflict, will become an increasingly prominent part of our understanding of the Second Empire. Working from close studies of voting behavior, Karl Rohe, one of the most sophisticated historians of electoral behavior in the Kaiserreich, has already concluded that "religious division was the deciding reality of life, of thought, of self-perception, and of politics in Germany."[23]

This study is an attempt to explain the dynamics of this division. What follows is neither a comprehensive examination of Protestants and Catholics in the empire nor a thorough survey of religious politics, but rather a study of what set Protestants and Catholics apart. Pastors and priests more concerned with the baleful effects of class society than with the curse of confessional division have remained largely outside my analytical scope. Moreover, by focusing on Catholics and Protestants as antagonists, I do not wish to slight tensions within the respective camps. But in this book, I am primarily interested in the reasons for conflict across the major confessional divide. Friedrich Meinecke once described his method of intellectual history as wandering among the peaks. Here I am more concerned with measuring the depths of a mutual antagonism.

The conflict between Protestants and Catholics is examined as a cultural, ideological, social, and political phenomenon. Divided into four parts, the book begins with a discussion of the Kulturkampf. Often perceived as a misguided passion of intolerant liberals or as a maladroit manipulation by Bismarck, the Kulturkampf is (in chapter 1) considered as a strategy for nation-building, as an ultimately unsuccessful attempt to create a common national culture across confessional lines. When that attempt failed, confessional conflict did not cease, but rather was cast anew. The two principal groups involved in the post-Kulturkampf confessional conflict included the Protestant League and the Catholic Center party. Founded in 1887, the Protes-

[22] Given the centrality of this issue, the paucity of research on confessional conflict in its late nineteenth century setting is surprising. Two studies address the problem in its regional context, but, partly for this reason, neglect the problem's national dimension. See Alfred Wahl, *Confession et comportement dans les campagnes d'Alsace et de Bade (1871–1939)* 2 vols. (Metz, 1980); Christel Köhle-Hezinger, *Evangelisch-Katholisch. Untersuchungen zu konfessionellem Vorurteil und Konflikt im 19. und 20. Jahrhundert vornehmlich am Beispiel Württembergs* (Tübingen, 1976). Marjorie Lamberti, *State, Society and the Elementary School in Imperial Germany* (New York, 1989) goes some way to remedy this deficiency, but her study is limited to one aspect of the problem.

[23] Karl Rohe, *Wahlen und Wählertradition in Deutschland: Kulturelle Grundlagen deutscher Parteien und Parteiensysteme im 19. und 20. Jahrhundert* (Frankfurt a.M., 1992), 114.

tant League intended to raise Protestant consciousness in imperial Germany and to purge German national culture of ultramontane Catholic influence. By 1914, it had become the largest Protestant lay organization in the empire and, with a membership of roughly 500,000 adherents, one of the most popular voluntary organizations in German society. The Catholic Center party, the Protestant League's chief opponent, was neither a single-issue pressure group nor a specifically anti-Protestant party, yet it continually addressed the challenge posed to it by the Protestant League as well as the larger dilemmas involved in Catholic integration into a national culture defined primarily by Protestantism. This study investigates the ideology (chapter 2) and the social bases (chapter 3) of the mutual antagonism between these two groups; it then attempts to discern the impact of their conflict on national politics between 1897 and 1914 (chapters 4 and 5). Confessional conflict was also germane to the problem of peripheral nationalism within the empire and to the struggles of irredentist Germans outside it. Religious categories greatly influenced the nationality conflict between Germans and Poles in Prussia (chapter 6) as well as the ideology and politics of "Los von Rom," a movement to achieve a "spiritual Pan-Germany" by converting German Catholics in Cisleithanian Austria to Protestantism (chapter 7).[24] Largely organized and funded by the Protestant League in imperial Germany, the Los von Rom movement attempted to "free the German spirit from the shackles of Rome forever."[25] As such, it represented the logical conclusion of an important, if neglected tradition of German nationalism that envisioned German history as a centuries-long struggle over the confluence of religious and national identity.[26]

[24] AKIEB S185.810.60 Paul Bräunlich, "Streng vertraulicher Reisebericht 'Zur Evangelisierung in Böhmen,'" 6.11.1898.

[25] AKIEB PL Friedrich Meyer, "Mitteilungen vom Ausschuss zur Förderung der evangelischen Kirche in Österreich," Nr. 12, 11.10.1901.

[26] To understand the intellectual background of this tradition, see the important new work of Wolfgang Atltgeld, *Katholizismus, Protestantismus, Judentum. Über religiös begründete Gegensätze und nationalreligiöse Ideen in der Geschichte des deutschen Nationalismus* (Mainz, 1992). For the role of this tradition in the visions of three German nationalists, see Fritz Stern, *The Politics of Cultural Despair: A Study in the Rise of Germanic Ideology* (Berkeley, 1961).

Part One

CULTURE, IDEOLOGY, SOCIETY

1

The Kulturkampf and German National Identity

"THE Kulturkampf," Otto Pflanze has written, "was a kaleidoscope, altering its shape with each angle of observation."[1] Generations of scholars, when observing this event, took primary cognizance of the church-state conflict, a struggle fought between Bismarck and the Vatican, and carried out by Catholic bishops and Prussian ministers. Thus defined, the conflict commenced with the pulpit paragraph of 1871, which forbade "the misuse of the pulpit for political purposes" and concluded, depending on the political proclivities of the historian, either in 1878, when Bismarck first entered into negotiations with Pope Leo XIII, or in 1887, when the most onerous Kulturkampf laws were finally struck from the books.[2] In both cases, the 1870s represent the high-water mark of the conflict, a political storm centered on a series of repressive measures directed mainly against the Catholic church.

Germany was not the only country to weather such a storm. "Cultural struggles" between modern states and the Catholic church occurred throughout Europe in the second half of the nineteenth century. Between 1860 and 1890, Kulturkampf legislation was passed in Austria, Spain, Switzerland, Belgium, the Netherlands, and in France—in Catholic as well as in Protestant countries.[3] In Germany itself, not just Protestant Prussia but also Catholic Bavaria and confessionally mixed Baden promulgated antichurch measures. Yet German particularities did exist. Divided by confession, the rhetoric of Germany's conflict was reinforced by the vocabulary of religious antagonism, the fronts between the two adversaries hardened by a history

---

[1] Otto Pflanze, *Bismarck and the Development of Germany*, 2d ed., vol. 2, *The Period of Consolidation, 1871–1880* (Princeton, 1990), 179.

[2] Some historians place the beginning of the struggle earlier still, with the dissolution in the summer of 1871 of the Catholic Department of the Prussian Ministry of Culture. See Rudolf Lill, "Der Kulturkampf in Preußen und im Deutschen Reich (bis 1878)," in *Handbuch der Kirchengeschichte*, ed. Hubert Jedin (Freiburg, 1973), vol. 6, no. 2, 35.

[3] For a concise, analytically sharp comparison, see Winfried Becker, "Der Kulturkampf als europäisches und als deutsches Phänomen," *Historisches Jahrbuch* 101 (1981): 422–46.

of civil wars between Catholic and Protestant powers, their antipathy tempered by a long and tenacious memory of mutual intolerance.

This particular heritage, shared only by Switzerland and the Netherlands, informed the ideological justification for the Prussian and for the German Kulturkampf, the object of which was not to further divide the nation but rather to unify it. Constantin Rössler, one of the most articulate defenders of the "cultural struggle," imagined a future in which "the German people will arrive at the point where they draw their national and religious life from the same source, both streams of life in innermost harmony."[4] The German nation, he believed, would then become a "model . . . for the spiritual life of civilized peoples [Kulturvölker]."[5] Central to Rössler's Kulturkampf vision was the creation of a national high culture, based on common religious assumptions, which would be the well of German national identity, its waters healing divisions within the body politic, providing sustenance to a vital German nationalism.

With Rössler's vision in mind, it may be opportune to turn the kaleidoscope through which we view the Kulturkampf, not with the intention of reversing previous interpretations, but in order to reconsider the context of an episode central to the course of modern German history. Rather than seeing the Kulturkampf exclusively as a church-state affair, it might also be instructive to consider it as part of the general trajectory of German nation-building, as an attempt to consolidate German national culture, to create—by force of state coercion—a cultural unity, a coherent nation, across confessional lines. The official Kulturkampf, in this way of seeing it, was a strategy of nation-building, supported by the state and centered on an attempt to create a common high culture in which national values, largely synonymous with those of enlightened Protestantism, would be shared.

Protestantism and Kultur: Constructing a National Canon

Nationalism is often conceived of as a force welling up from below, as the surfacing of oral traditions and peasant folkways long submerged. Yet in late nineteenth-century Germany, it makes more sense to view nationalism as an ideology imposed from above, sometimes from the state, but more fundamentally from the cultural activity of nationalist intellectuals—lexicographers, folklorists, philologists, historians, men

---

[4] Constantin Rössler, *Das deutsche Reich und die kirchliche Frage* (Würzburg, 1876), 439.
[5] Ibid.

of letters—who not only propagated, but also imparted shape and form to a collective sense of what it was to be German. In scholarly books and popular pamphlets, in lecture halls and in schoolrooms, they propounded not the vision of the people but rather their own visions—intricately tied to their own middle-class understanding of German identity—to the people. It is in this sense that Ernest Gellner, looking more to the experience of Asian and African nations, argues that "nationalism is essentially the imposition of high culture on society where previously low cultures had taken up the lives of the majority."[6] Nationalism, in this analysis, is not the amicable union of popular and elite culture, the world of folklore with the world of print, but rather an ideology of elites propunded in the name of the people.

In the late nineteenth century, German nationalists certainly appealed to the spirit and culture of the "German people." How else could they have legitimized national claims and assertions? Yet closer inspection often revealed ambivalence. For despite their periodic panegyrics to the culture of the folk, nationalist intellectuals such as Constantin Rössler and Heinrich von Treitschke were, in fact, embarrassed by it. For folk culture was still in good measure religious culture, and this culture, filled as it was with superstitions, eccentric devotional rituals, pilgrimages to miraculous objects, and kitsch-ridden novellas, was especially visible, and therefore especially embarrassing, when Catholic. In this way, religious conflict became part of a struggle over the terms of culture and, in a deeper sense, identity—national identity.

The national dimension of high culture was already implicit in the German idea of Kultur. As Norbert Elias showed in *The Civilizing Process*, Kultur conveyed three associations for the German bourgeoisie. It evoked a sense of national identity, because it placed "special stress on national differences."[8] Kultur also suggested specific class values, for the origins of the word lay "in the polemic of the strata of the German middle-class intelligentsia against the ruling courtly upper class."[9] Finally, the concept of Kultur possessed a historical connection to the struggle for German unity: "it was this learned middle class who first attempted to create . . . models of what German is,

[6] Gellner, *Nations and Nationalism*, 57.

[7] On the relationship between liberalism and Catholic piety, see David Blackbourn, "Progress and Piety: Liberals, Catholics and the State in Bismarck's Germany," in Blackbourn, *Populists and Patricians: Essays in Modern German History* (London, 1987), 143–67.

[8] Norbert Elias, *The Civilizing Process* (New York,1978), 5.

[9] Ibid., 9. Kultur was also defined against the lower classes. See Peter Uwe Hohendahl, *Building a National Literature: The Case of Germany* (Ithaca, N.Y., 1989), 274.

and thus to establish at least in the intellectual sphere a German unity which does not yet seem realizable in the political sphere."[10]

Kultur also came to be associated with the values of Protestantism. Daniel Schenkel, a founding member of the liberal Protestantenverein (Protestant Association) echoed a wide consensus when he wrote in 1862: "We say with the deepest conviction: the entire cultural progress of peoples in our century is based upon the foundation of religious, moral and intellectual freedom, and for that reason, upon Protestantism."[11] Schenkel's assumption informed the relationship not only between Catholics and Protestants but also between Christians and Jews. It created an idea about national style—about what it was to be German—and therefore set cultural criteria for national authenticity. In *Christians and Jews*, Uriel Tal has demonstrated how this assumption forced an enlightened bourgeoisie, steeped in Kantian ethics, to insist on the complete cultural assimilation of Jews in Germany.[12] Although the relationships between Catholics and Protestants and Christians and Jews were in very many respects predicated upon different assumptions, on this issue—cultural assimilation in the new national state—the problems were similar.[13]

But in the case of Protestants and Catholics the assimilationist assumptions of German high culture were buried beneath the rhetoric of confessional peace and, often enough, the force of unspoken assumptions. The construction of a national literary canon, an act of considerable national importance, illustrated this problem.[14] The canonization of German high literature was, and was consciously conceived to be, an act by which German identity could be defined. Wilhelm Scherer, who in 1877 became the first scholar officially to hold a chair of German literary history, conceived of his task as "constructing a system of national ethics." For Scherer, the rise of German literature represented "a complete picture of what we are and signify," and offered the historian of literature "an inventory" of "national values and duties."[15] So defined, the canon of national literature would then

[10] Ibid., 11.

[11] Daniel Schenkel, *Die kirchliche Frage und ihre protestantische Lösung* (Elberfeld, 1862), 12.

[12] Uriel Tal, *Christians and Jews in Germany: Religion, Politics, and Ideology in the Second Reich, 1870–1914*, trans. Noah Jonathan Jacobs (Ithaca, N.Y., and London, 1975), esp. 31–80.

[13] On the relationship between Catholics, Protestants, and Jews from the late eighteenth century to 1880, see Altgeld, *Katholizismus, Protestantismus, Judentum*.

[14] On the relationship between German nationalism and German literature in the nineteenth century, see Hohendahl, *Building a National Literature*.

[15] Wilhelm Scherer, *Zur Geschichte der deutschen Sprache*, 2d ed. (Berlin, 1878), xi. On this aspect of Scherer's work, see also René Welleck, *A History of Modern Criticism: 1750–*

become the foundation for both a common national culture and a unified national state. As Rudolf Gottschall, a contemporary of Scherer, wrote in the preface to the 1871 edition of his *German National Literature of the Nineteenth Century*, building a national literature "does not merely accompany the rise of national life, it helps to create it."[16]

Yet among the major literary historians of the *Gründerzeit*, the aesthetic form and ideal content of this literary canon remained an object of contention. Julian Schmidt, the literary editor of *Die Grenzboten*, pleaded for the virtues of literary realism; while Rudolf Gottschall, writing for *Die Gegenwart*, urged more introspective, idealistic verse closely tied to national sentiment. Hermann Hettner, the author of the monumental, six-volume *History of German Literature in the Eighteenth Century*, advanced the aesthetics of the German Enlightenment; William Scherer, a positivistic approach to literary studies. Despite their considerable differences on aesthetic and methodological questions, the literary historians of the *Gründerzeit* shared important assumptions. They assumed, as Peter Uwe Hohendahl has shown, that "the Germans possessed a corpus of classic authors and works which gave them legitimacy as a 'civilized people' [*Kulturvolk*]"[17] When political rivalries threatened to tear Germans apart, their identity as a *Kulturvolk* bound them together; and if German political history was marred, especially in the recent past, by fratricidal warfare, its literary history was well defined, coherent, centered on the German classics.[18]

But this was not always so. And religious disunity counted as one of the principal reasons for the unfortunate fragmentation of cultural life in the past. With near unanimity, the literary historians agreed that Germany's century-old confessional division impeded the growth of a national literary culture and, as a consequence, forestalled political unification. But rather than treating the literary products of Protestantism and Catholicism with analytical parity, they concurred that national literature and national culture must be built on the foundation of Protestantism. As Scherer put the matter: "Luther's Bible was the decisive act toward the establishment of a unified German culture and language. It was the act of creation of that which we now call our nation. We attribute to Luther our national unity as Italy attributes its unity to Dante. Luther's Bible is our Divina Commedia. It

---

1950, vol. 4, *The Later Nineteenth Century* (New Haven and London, 1965), 300; and Hohendahl, *Building a National Literature*, 227–28.

[16] Rudolf Gottschall, *Die deutsche Nationalliteratur des 19. Jahrhunderts*, 4th ed. (Breslau, 1875), vol. 1, xxx (foreword to the 3d ed., 1871).

[17] Hohendahl, *Building a National Literature*, 196.

[18] Ibid., 196.

is the foundation stone of the temple which surrounds us."[19] In the typical way of plotting German literary history, it was not the Reformation itself but the reaction of Rome that destroyed German unity.[20] The ensuing confessionalism, religious warfare, and dismemberment of German politics sounded the death knell of German literary life. "In the time after the Thirty Years War," wrote Julian Schmidt, "German literature had a period in which the old spirit wearied and atrophied."[21] This period of atrophy, concurrent with the ascendancy of baroque poetry, lasted until the beginning of German classicism. Classicism was then interpreted as a continuation of the Reformation. Julian Schmidt asserted that "the literature of that time was with few exceptions produced by Protestants, and in keeping with the Protestant spirit."[22] In his *History of German Literature in the Eighteenth Century*, Hermann Hettner also advanced this argument: "at least for Germany, it is completely correct to characterize the eighteenth century as the conscious resumption and continuation of the great ideas of the Reformation."[23]

The classical period, as it became the foundation for German national claims to a great literary tradition, represented the rebirth of German national consciousness. That national consciousness was, however, defined within a highly charged field of affinities and antagonisms. Julian Schmidt began his *History of German Literature since the Death of Lessing* by opposing German classicism to French Enlightenment: the former developed nature by felicitous cultivation, the latter, in its Voltarian passion to "eradicate the infamous," extirpated Christian tradition.[24] In Germany, it was Protestantism, synonymous with a more reasonable Christianity, that created the conditions of spiritual continuity between the old world and the new, the present Germany with its past. That continuity was still precarious, however. Rudolf Gottschall worried that in the course of the nineteenth century the coherent voice of the German literary tradition would dissolve into "literatures" segregated "by the narrow-minded parties who weave their own laurels, by severe provincial isolation, and by the deep divi-

[19] Wilhelm Scherer, "Die deutsche Spracheinheit," in Scherer, *Geschichte des geistigen Lebens in Deutschland und Österreich* (Berlin, 1874), 55.

[20] Ibid, 56.

[21] Julian Schmidt, *Geschichte der deutschen Literatur von Leibniz bis auf unsere Zeit* (Berlin, 1886), vol. 1, vii.

[22] Ibid., viii. The other important social fact of German classicism was that, in contrast to the literature of the old nations, the German poets had to form a nation through their literature.

[23] Hermann Hettner, *Geschichte der deutschen Literatur im achtzehnten Jahrhundert*, 2d ed. (Braunschweig, 1872), vol. 1, 2.

[24] Julian Schmidt, *Geschichte der deutschen Literatur seit Lessings Tod* (Leipzig, 1866), 1.

sion between north and south."[25] A chorus, once singing in unison, would collapse into the clamor of cacophonous voices.

Although the necessity of maintaining a coherent voice stemmed in part from political imperatives, it also influenced aesthetic taste. René Welleck, an important authority on modern criticism, has written of Scherer's *History of German Literature* that its "ethos is nationalistic, Prussian, and Protestant," and of Hettner that "he has no use for materialism, mysticism, or Catholicism."[26] Especially in their treatment of the Romantics, the literary historians of the empire betrayed their confessional sensibilities. Just as it became commonplace to praise Romantic poets for their insight into the soul of the people, so it became a cliché to perceive their attraction to Catholicism as something mannered, "a purely artistic preference," in any case an aberration from the much more fundamental tradition of German *Innerlichkeit*.[27] Consequently, the attraction of leading Romantics to Catholicism—Novalis, Brentano, Friedrich Schlegel—spelled the end of their literary genius. Of these poets Hettner wrote: "The aesthetic themes recede ever more into the background. Pure Catholicism steps naked and unconcealed into the foreground. It is displayed, as is naturally the case with converts, for show, pointed, yet equivocal. In other words, this romantic Catholicism is *Jesuitismus*."[28] Generally, the effect of this confessionally informed interpretation of the German literary tradition was not necessarily to exclude the individual contributions of Catholic authors. Rather, it was to identify the spirit of the literary tradition as Protestant and to marginalize the specifically ultramontane influences on it.

Still, the literary canon did exclude writers whom Catholic critics considered worthy of inclusion, and the gulf between the two camps seemed only to widen as the nineteenth century wore on. Friedrich Wilhelm Weber, an ultramontane author of epic poems, a poet whom Catholic critics compared now to Shakespeare, now to Homer, did not, for example, find his place in the late nineteenth-century pantheon of the German literary tradition.[29] The same fate befell Oskar

[25] Gottschall, *Die deutsche Nationalliteratur*, vol. 3, 8.

[26] Wellek, *A History of Modern Criticism*, vol. 4, 300, 297. Scherer, however, was by birth an Austrian.

[27] Hermann Hettner, "Katholizismus und Mittelalter," in Hettner, *Schriften zur Litteratur*, ed. Jürgen Jahn (Berlin, 1959), 138. See also Gottschall, *Die deutsche Nationalliteratur*, vol. 2, 6.

[28] Hettner, "Katholizismus und Mittelalter," 142–43.

[29] For the Catholic reception of Weber, see Heinrich Keiter, *Zeitgenössische Katholische Dichter Deutschlands* (Paderborn, 1884), 184–224, and Peter Norrenberg, *Allgemeine Litteraturgeschichte*, 2d ed., ed. Karl Macke (Münster i. W., 1898), vol. 2, 423–34.

von Redewitz, a Westphalian aristocrat whose epic verse "Amaranth" belongs with Weber's "Thirteen Lindens" among the most widely read poems of the nineteenth-century Catholic milieu. Yet Rudolf Gottschall, not without reason, dismissed "Amaranth" as wooden, without subtlety, a study in dramatic, but unconvincing, contrasts—and too full of religious ardor.[30] When included, authors close to the ultramontane worldview were typically denigrated, usually for their sentimentality and pathos, sometimes for their intolerance toward members of other religious communities. Ida Hahn-Hahn, a lyricist whom Catholic critics praised for the richness of her language and the depth of her religious sensibility, Rudolf Gottschall dismissed as a poetess whose verse was overwrought, florid, "mellifluous but meaningless."[31]

In a basic sense, then, the two cultural milieus did not share meaning; their literary traditions were not congruent, their German national identities not the same. Yet for national intellectuals in the liberal tradition, a common high culture defined national identity; it represented—in the literal and literary meaning of the word—the nation, imparting, not only coherence and form to a nation long politically divided, but also legitimacy to a national state recently founded. With an eye to the experience of new states in the postcolonial world, Clifford Geertz has argued that in new national states efforts to define identity, and ensure legitimacy, tend to revolve around two principles: "the indigenous way of life" and "the spirit of the age."[32] The first looks to customs, habits, national character and traits, and therefore to popular culture to legitimate the new nation. The second centers on the idea of high culture and historical destiny. It conceives of culture in developmental stages and posits a relationship between the historical development of a high culture and the power and status of a nation. Although nationalist intellectuals in new national states usually draw from both principles, the question of emphasis is decisive. It determines the kinds of ideological conflicts that will occur as well as the nature of the social and political strain on the new nation.[33]

In imperial Germany, in the 1870s, nationalists placed great emphasis on the second principle and little on the first. In the liberal public sphere, which was largely coterminous with the national public sphere, class conflict, conflicts between center and periphery,

---

[30] Gottschall, *Die deutsche Nationalliteratur*, vol. 3, 244–48.

[31] Ibid., 223.

[32] Clifford Geertz, "After the Revolution: The Fate of Nationalism in the New States," in Geertz, *The Interpretation of Cultures* (New York, 1973), 240.

[33] Ibid, 234–54. See also Geertz, "The Integrative Revolution: Primordial Sentiments and Civil Politics in the New States," in ibid, 255–310.

dominant nationality, and peripheral nationalism were recast, in popular as well as theoretical literature, as cultural and therefore national problems. In *Debit and Credit* (Soll und Haben), the favorite novel of the empire's educated classes, Gustav Freytag justified the repression of Polish subjects by the assumption that high culture was the foundation of nationhood and that the Poles, unlike the Germans, were stuck in the backward ways of popular culture. A merchant says of the Poles: "As if the nobility and bonded peasants could make their own state!" Anton, one of the main characters, agrees, replying: "They have no bourgeoisie." To which the merchant responds, "that means they have no culture."[34] In 1896, Max Weber expressed a similar sentiment, though with a violence characteristic of a later age. The Poles, he argued, have not been made into "second-class German citizens," rather "the opposite is true: we made the Poles into humans."[35] This way of perceiving national states, of positing a relationship between the high culture of the bourgeoisie and the legitimate claims of nationalism both to civilize popular cultures and to build a state congruent with the boundaries of nationality, also shaped the imagination of the empire's major historians. Like their colleagues in philology and German literature, the historians wove a culturally and confessionally determined sense of the German historical experience into their peculiar pattern of the German past.

The historians of the so-called small-German school of historiography, foremost among them Johann von Droysen, Heinrich von Sybel, and Heinrich von Treitschke, have been the subjects of a prodigious number of scholarly studies. The view that has emerged—of a historical tradition marked by a one-sided emphasis on power over principle, by an ahistorical projection of the national mission of the Prussian state into the distant past, and by an uncritical veneration of Prussian values—sheds much light on the political attitudes of these historians. But it also renders their cultural assumptions and confessional presuppositions difficult to discern, and, in the case of Sybel and Treitschke, it obfuscates the importance of their specifically Protestant narration of the recent German past.

Johann von Droysen, the patriarch of the small-German school, celebrated for his fourteen-volume *History of Prussian Politics* and for his lectures on historical methodology, saw the nation not just as a power-political force but also as a moral and cultural institution, an

---

[34] Gustav Freytag, *Gesammelte Werke*, 2d ed., vol. 4, *Soll und Haben* (Leipzig, 1887–88), 382–83. On this passage, see Jeffrey L. Sammons, *Imagination and History: Selected Papers on Nineteenth-century German Literature* (New York, 1988), 201–3.

[35] Max Weber, "Zur Gründung einer national-sozialen Partei," in Weber, *Gesammelte politische Schriften*, 2d ed., ed. Johannes Winckelmann (Tübingen, 1958).

agent of the forward motion of history.[36] Though secure in his belief that Prussia represented the iron wheel of progress, Droysen often worried that the Catholic revival would put a severe brake on its potential. In his letters, he wrote of the seamy side of Prussia's present, of the persistence of superstition in an enlightened age, of the cultural degradation of the common people—a malady that especially afflicted the Catholic population. In 1844—on the eve of the revolution but also at the dawn of the ultramontane movement—Droysen pondered whether the nineteenth century did not, in fact, represent a period of political Counter-Reformation, the Congress of Vienna a "political Tridentinum," the approaching conflict between church and state "a new Thirty Years War with all its horror."[37] For Droysen, political Catholicism was synonymous with unfreedom, the rituals of the church with idolatry. And idolatry he considered a form of worship fit only for the plebeian mob.[38] Part of the mission of the Prussian state was then to combat these tendencies, weeds in a robust garden.

The idea that ultramontanism vitiated the power of Prussia and retarded the growth of the German nation constituted a central axiom of Droysen's historical thinking. It also informed his political positions. In the 1870s, he, like almost all other university historians, not only praised the commencement of the Kulturkampf but also situated the struggle within the stream of Prussia's historical destiny. On 1 October 1872, he wrote an impassioned letter to his son Gustav (himself the author of a two-volume work on Gustav Adolf as well as a critical account of the Counter-Reformation) in which he recounted the recent history of Prussia, from Frederick II to the victory over the House of Habsburg in 1866. "With this victory," Droysen wrote, "we finally became master of the miserable situation of 1519" (when Charles V became emperor).[39] The war against France, "which established the importance of Germany as the heartland of Europe, as the ruling middle power," was, by the necessity of Droysen's historical

[36] Günther Birtsch, *Die Nation als sittliche Idee* (Cologne and Graz, 1964), 90–91.

[37] Johann Gustav Droysen, "Deutsche Briefe," in Droysen, *Politische Schriften*, ed. Felix Gilbert (Munich and Berlin, 1933), 3.

[38] Johann von Droysen to his brother Karl Droysen, 17.9.1852. In Johann Gustav Droysen, *Briefwechsel*, ed. Rudolf Hübner (Berlin and Leipzig, 1929), vol. 2, 130. For Droysen's view on Catholic religiosity, see also Droysen to Heinrich von Sybel, 12.12.1854, in Droysen, *Briefwechsel*, 299–300.

[39] In a similar statement, he called 1866 "the triumph of the true German spirit of 1517 and 1813 over the Latin (*Romanischen*) spirit." Cited in Adolf M. Birke, "Zur Entwicklung und politischen Funktion des bürgerlichen Kulturkampfverständnisses in Preußen-Deutschland," in *Aus Theorie und Praxis der Geschichtswissenschaft*, ed. D. Kurze (Berlin, 1972), 268.

logic, followed by the Kulturkampf, the struggle against Rome, "a campaign of greater importance and difficulty than the one in 1870." Yet Droysen felt certain that the Roman church, like the French nation before it, would soon meet its Sedan. "It is," he added, "a pleasure to imagine this great development before one's eyes."[40]

His colleagues shared his enthusiasm. Theodor Mommsen, the historian of ancient Rome whose scholarship was as impeccable as his reputation universal, cast, in a Landtag debate in 1877, aspersions at ultramontanism that were sufficiently acerbic to induce the speaker to call the historian to order.[41] Hermann Baumgarten, the Strasbourg historian best known for his contributions to the political theory of German liberalism, also penned a three-volume work on modern Spanish history in which he painstakingly revealed the debilitating effects of Catholic influence on the fate of the Iberian nation. Ardent in his support of Germanization measures in Alsace-Lorraine, zealous in his advocacy of the Kulturkampf, Baumgarten seriously considered whether after 1870 Protestant Germany was not the sole bearer of human culture, though he thought this burden would be too much for the young nation.[42] If Germany was the source of light, Rome represented the provenance of darkness. It was Baumgarten's considered historical judgment that "almost all of the great catastrophes of our century have been brought about by reliance on Rome: the fall of the Second [French] Empire, the fall of the last Bourbons in Spain and in Naples, the destruction of the conservatives in Switzerland, the defeat of Austria."[43]

In Heinrich von Sybel, editor of the prestigious *Historische Zeitschrift* and author of the official history of *The Foundation of the German Empire*, Baumgarten possessed a comrade in ideological arms. In 1874, Sybel and his colleagues at the University of Bonn founded the Deutscher Verein (German Association), an organization dedicated to combating ultramontane influence on the state and in civil society. The association counted nearly twenty thousand members, most of them from the ranks of the Rhineland intelligentsia. Its express purpose

---

[40] Johann von Droysen to his son Gustav, 1.8.1872. In Droysen, *Briefwechsel*, 903–4.

[41] Alfred Heuss, *Theodor Mommsen und das 19. Jahrhundert* (Kiel, 1956), 191.

[42] Hermann Baumgarten to Heinrich von Sybel, 1.4.1871. In Paul Wentzcke, *Im neuen Reich 1871–1890. Politische Briefe aus dem Nachlaß liberaler Parteiführer*, (Bonn, 1926; reprint Osnabrück, 1970), vol. 2, 16. For an excellent illustration of the confessional coloring of the national story, see Hermann Baumgarten, "Wie wir wieder ein Volk geworden sind (1870)," in Baumgarten, *Historische und politische Aufsätze und Reden*, ed. Erich Marcks (Strasbourg, 1894), 241–316.

[43] Hermann Baumgarten to Heinrich von Sybel, 1.1.1881, in Wentzcke, *Im neuen Reich*, vol. 2, 373.

was to monitor the movements of ultramontane fellow travelers among the Rhineland's state employees and to expose district magistrates and public schoolteachers whose black sympathies were manifest, if only to denounce them.[44] The association also hoped to raise public consciousness concerning the danger of the Roman Catholic menace.[45] For Sybel, such public engagement was not new. Since the 1840s he had been writing tracts and polemical works directed against the pretensions of Catholic revivalism. With his colleague Johannes Gildemeister, an orientalist at the University of Bonn, Sybel applied the critical historical method (*Quellenkritik*) to what he perceived to be a monument to Catholic superstition: the display in 1844 of the holy, seamless robes of Christ in the chapel of the Liebfrauenkirche in Trier.[46] Forbidden by enlightened Catholic bishops at the beginning of the nineteenth century, the display of the seamless robe attracted the largest procession of pilgrims (over 500,000) in German memory. To Sybel and the enlightened mind, it was a cynical manipulation of superstition in the service of clerical power. But to believing Catholics, especially from the lower and from the rural classes, the robe, which Christ was said to have worn his whole lifetime, constituted a relic of highest symbolic and religious significance.[47] Sybel, the Protestant professor whose sympathies with the great unwashed were not especially pronounced, coolly and scientifically debunked its authenticity.

As a nationalist intellectual, Sybel did not perceive his historical scholarship as separate and distinct from his ideological engagement. Impeccably modern, he ruthlessly reconstructed the German past to fit the demands of the national present. The principal sacrifice was the medieval period so dear to Catholic and Romantic historians alike. In a letter to Hermann Baumgarten, Sybel conceded his antipathy. In his view, the Middle Ages represented an arid period of German history, a time when the soul of the German people languished. "Essen-

[44] Margaret Lavinia Anderson and Kenneth Barkin, "The Myth of the Puttkamer Purge and the Reality of the Kulturkampf: Some Reflections on the Historiography of Imperial Germany," *Journal of Modern History* 54, no. 4 (1982): 658.

[45] Sybel attempted, for example, to get Gustav Freytag to write a popular almanac for the German Association "against the Reichsfeind." See Heinrich von Sybel to Gustav Freytag, 3.4.1875, in Wentzcke, *Im neuen Reich*, vol. 2, 120.

[46] J. Gildemeister and Heinrich von Sybel, *Der Heilige Rock zu Trier und die zwanzig andern heiligen ungenähten Röcke* (Düsseldorf, 1844). On Sybel's engagement in this issue, see the detailed analysis of Volker Dotterweich, *Heinrich von Sybel. Geschichtswissenschaft in politischer Absicht (1817–1861)* (Göttingen, 1978), 72–81.

[47] On the pilgrimages to Trier in 1844, see Wolfgang Schieder, "Kirche und Revolution. Sozialgeschichtliche Aspekte der Trier Wallfahrt von 1844," *Archiv für Sozialgeschichte* 14 (1974): 141–170.

tially all of our medieval culture between 800 and 1500 was imported ware, in philosophy, in literature (except for the Niebelungen), in architecture, and our own creativity did not begin until the reform movements."[48] In 1859, in a polemic against Wilhelm von Giesebrecht and Julius Ficker, Sybel argued that the Romantic vision of the medieval Germanic Kaiserreich was fundamentally flawed, that the Middle Ages were not a period in which, as Giesebrecht had argued, "the German man counted most in the world and the German name sounded farthest and widest."[49] Far from supporting a strong German nation, the medieval Kaiserreich drained it of vitality. The imperialist politics of the early Hohenstaufens, especially of the emperors Otto I and Heinrich VI, inexplicably ignored the centrality of German nationality to German history: their southern conquests to Naples and Sicily in the tenth and twelfth century squandered national strength while suppressing the instinctive national mission of the Germans: to colonize the east.[50] The polemic raged at many levels: whether each epoch was entitled to its own values or whether the historian should home in on such world-historical principles as nationality; whether the first Kaiserreich was a national or a universal state; whether the medieval Reich could count as a model for German national life in the nineteenth century; and whether Germany's close ties to the Roman episcopate were compatible with its growth and well-being as a nation.[51] On this last point, Sybel, against the background of emerging confessional conflict, argued that the tie was not compatible, that there lay, at the very basis of German history, an inherent tension between Catholicism and German nationalism.

Perhaps no historian advanced this last point as vigorously, and with as much influence on the historical imagination of German nationalists, as Heinrich von Treitschke. Considered by the literary editor Alfred Dove as the "prophet of our new empire," Treitschke tirelessly churned out tracts on Prussian politics and history defend-

[48] Heinrich von Sybel to Hermann von Baumgarten, 16.4.1871, in Wentzcke, *Im neuen Reich*, vol. 2, 16–17.

[49] The essays of the controversy have been collected by Friedrich Schneider, ed., *Universalstaat oder Nationalstaat. Die Streitschriften von Heinrich v. Sybel und Julius Ficker zur Kaiserpolitik des Mittelalters* (Innsbruck, 1941). Giesebrecht is cited by Schneider in the introduction, p. xvii. By reissuing these polemical works, Schneider hoped to show that Catholic, Greater-German conceptions of nationalism were compatible with National Socialism and that the First Reich was a forerunner of the Third Reich. See Schneider's introduction, p. xxxvi.

[50] See especially Heinrich von Sybel, "Über die neueren Darstellungen der deutschen Kaiserzeit," in Schneider, ed. *Universalstaat oder Nationalstaat*, 11–18.

[51] A terse summary can be found in Heinrich Ritter von Srbik, *Geist und Geschichte vom deutschen Humanismus bis zur Gegenwart* (Munich and Salzburg, 1951), vol. 2, 33–36.

ing the verities of the small-German school of historical writing.[52] His *German History in the Nineteenth Century*, best known as a paean to the power of the Prussian state, also contained insightful, but biting, chapters that dripped vitriol on national minorities, especially the Poles, on the cultural still-life of the Prussian provinces, and on the development of nineteenth-century German Catholicism.

In Treitschke's history, Catholicism inevitably clashed with the spirit of the German nation. On the Middle Ages his views were at one with von Sybel's. Consequently Luther, far from being a purely religious figure, "attempted to liberate the whole fatherland from Roman domination."[53] The ensuing confessional division, which resulted from the resistance of the Latin world to German unification, remained a centuries-long nightmare weighing on the conscience of German patriots. In the nineteenth century, when national unity seemed within grasp, Catholicism, in league with particularism, resisted it. Cologne, "long the bulwark of the Roman party," constituted the center of this resistance, the Rhineland its outer walls.[54] Here "the Catholic principle stood against the Protestant principle": the latter represented progress and German national unity, the former spiritual and material poverty, intolerance, disunity.[55] Treitschke recounted such historical shibboleths with rhythmic regularity—but also with exceptional narrative verve. "With deft hands the small, but silently growing ultramontane party stoked the flames of Rhenish particularism," he wrote of the early resistance to the imposition of Prussian rule. In order to render Catholicism, Treitschke evoked images of surreptitious agitation, of long-fingered, unprincipled clerics undermining the fragile, as yet still incomplete, temple of national unity.

In Treitschke's epic nineteenth-century confrontation between ultramontane Catholicism and Protestant Prussia, the "Cologne Troubles" of the 1830s constituted a central turning point. The manifest issue was the refusal of the archbishop of Cologne, Baron Klemens August von Droste zu Vischering, to accept the legal validity of confessionally mixed civil marriages. Treitschke interpreted the Catholic position not only as an affront to the principles of parity and tolerance (which it most certainly was) but, with a view to Germany's precarious religious history, also as a peril to a nation still divided and struggling for a unified voice. He imagined the recrudescence of "all the

---

[52] On Dove, see Heinrich von Treitschke, *Briefe*, ed. M. Cornicelius (Leipzig, 1913), vol. 3, pt. 2, 348, fn.

[53] Heinrich von Treitschke, *Deutsche Geschichte im Neunzehnten Jahrhundert*, 4th ed., 5 vols. (Leipzig, 1890), vol. 3, 215.

[54] Ibid., vol. 2, 235.

[55] Ibid.

passions of the Thirty Years War" and charged Catholic intolerance and intransigence with gravely threatening "to destroy the most precious property of the nation, the confessional peace for which we have paid dearly."[56] The Cologne Troubles, with their arrests and violence, created an unbridgeable caesura between the Protestant and Catholic camps.[57] Protestant Prussia had now to enforce the religious peace with the blunt end of the billy club. And as a consequence, Catholic intellectuals, foremost among them Joseph Görres, no longer appealed to the nation as a whole but to "Catholic Germany."[58] For Treitschke, however, there could be only one Germany, and the whole of his history made it clear that it could not be Catholic.

The historical appeal made by Sybel and Treitschke was not to a generalized and inclusive notion of German history and German nationhood but rather to a privileged group within the nation, a group that could imagine itself as partaking in Treitschke's narrative, as accepting his normative standards and intuitive judgments of value. This group—in the main the men of the Protestant middle classes—could situate themselves in Treitschke's oeuvre, could with ease project present concerns into the distant past, could conceive of Treitschke's historical characters as a collective to which they too belonged. It is difficult to envision other groups doing the same. Catholics who took their Catholicism seriously, or Jews whose ties to their religious and ethnic community remained tight, did not belong to the groups historically privileged by Treitschke. Nor, for that matter, did Poles, particularists, or women. But it would be wrong to see the work of these historians as merely reflecting relations of power or documenting affinities and antagonisms already in existence. Rather, their histories, precisely because they claimed to be general and not particular, because they represented German history without an attribute, created a reading public for whom this particular narrative—with its blindness as well as its insight—represented historical realism.[59]

Here realism refers less to the literary genre than to the propensity to perceive given relations of power as the natural order of things—as realistic. History, so conceived, lends legitimacy to privilege and authority in the present.[60] But the historians of the small-German school

[56] Ibid., vol. 4, 683.

[57] Ibid., 683–728.

[58] Ibid., 718.

[59] Hayden White, *The Content and the Form: Narrative Discourse and Historical Representation* (Baltimore, 1987), 86–88.

[60] On the relationship between historical narrative and present authority, see Marshall Sahlins, *Islands of History* (Chicago, 1985), 47–49.

did more than that, for their history was also oriented to the future, to a *telos* already set.[61] Their historical writing, essentially organicist, attempted to reveal the genesis of the German national state and to uncover the myriad historical forces supporting it.[62] Following Droysen, they argued that a strong state was necessary to create a cohesive nation—and that groups which did not support the state or assimilate to the values of the nation would be marginalized, not just by the historian, but by history itself. In a revealing passage of his *German History in the Nineteenth Century*, Treitschke wrote that the ideals of clericals and democrats "ran counter to the eternal development of history, and were therefore impossible."[63] Conversely those who possessed history, as opposed to those to whom history was denied, could legitimately claim to define the spirit of the age, to place their imprint upon historical identities—in this case that of the new national state.

The idea that the new national state represented the natural order of history, and Prussia's dominance a natural law, imparted a strong sense of destiny to those who unconditionally supported the new empire and to those who, like the monist Ernst Haeckel, now believed that the "modern cultural state" must combat "the black international."[64] This struggle appealed to a wide political consensus, a chorus of the like-minded whose voices, despite differences in pitch, were in unison precisely because almost all liberal and conservative politicians came from the same confession. With the exception of the SPD (the Social Democratic Party of Germany) and the Center, the confessional composition of the leadership of all other political parties was, with few exceptions, Protestant. The National Liberal party, which considered itself to be the voice of the nation, a party that stood above the many divisions—class, region, religion—that marked and marred German society, had only 51 Catholic (but 569 Protestant) Reichstag deputies between 1867 and 1917.[65] Of the 51 Catholics, most (36) were born before 1840 (they therefore made their

[61] See especially George Iggers, *The German Conception of History* (Middletown, Conn., 1968), 95–96.

[62] Hayden White, *Metahistory: The Historical Imagination in Nineteenth-century Europe* (Baltimore and London, 1973), 16.

[63] Treitschke, *Deutsche Geschichte im Neunzehnten Jahrhundert*, vol. 5, 303.

[64] On the importance of the idea of natural law to the liberal idea of the new Reich and of the Kulturkampf, see Birke, "Zur Entwicklung und politischen Funktion," 267–68, 272.

[65] Information on the confession of National Liberal parliamentarians can be found in Hermann Kalkhoff, ed., *Nationalliberale Parlamentarier 1867–1917 des Reichstages und der Einzellandtage* (Berlin, 1917).

political careers before the reconfessionalization of German life that accompanied the Kulturkampf), and many (22) held positions as civil servants. The story was similar in the state diets—only in Baden did Catholics constitute a significant proportion of National Liberal Landtag deputies (101 as against 153 Protestants). In all the other states with significant Catholic populations, Protestant National Liberals far outnumbered Catholics—in Bavaria 78 to 33, in Hessen 117 to 20, in Württemberg 60 to 4.[66] The degree of this confessional imbalance is best illustrated by the case of Prussia. In 1874, there were 153 Protestants and 3 Catholics in the National Liberal party in the Prussian Landtag. In 1913, the party counted 91 Protestant deputies and not one Catholic. In the other parties, Catholics were also severely underrepresented. The left-liberal parties had 60 Protestant deputies in 1874 and 2 Catholics; by 1913, that ratio was 29 to 3. The Conservative party counted 26 Protestants and no Catholics in 1874; in 1913, 147 and 2. The Free Conservatives were in this respect hardly different: in 1874 they had 25 Protestant and 6 Catholic deputies; in 1913, 54 Protestant deputies and not one Catholic.[67]

All of this meant that German political life was palpably divided along confessional lines. It also meant that the poets and polemicists of this cultural struggle could appeal to an understood "we" and "they." In his poem "Whom Are We Fighting Against?" written for the *Gartenlaube* in 1874, Ernst Scherenberg insisted "it is not against the church or the altar / but against that hypocritically sanctimonious crowd."[68] Replete with images of light and darkness, of modern idealism combating medieval obscurantism, of forces of movement against defenders of stasis, the crusade against ultramontanism became a crusade against aspects of Catholic culture perceived to be inimical to German identity: Catholicism's claim to universalism, its reliance on superstition and popular prejudice, its catering to the crowd, its inveterate confessionalism, and its turn away from rational religion.[69]

In its bifurcated vision, the figurative language of Kulturkampf verse revealed a German identity informed by tension between elite and popular culture and constructed within a tradition of confessional antagonism. This antagonism, though self-evidently a post-Reformation phenomenon, was projected back through a timeless history and situated in an ancient narrative. In "Against Rome," Felix

[66] Ibid.

[67] Bernhard Mann et al., *Biographisches Handbuch für das preußische Abgeordnetenhaus, 1867–1918* (Düsseldorf, 1988), 21.

[68] Ernst Scherenberg, "Wem gilt unser Krieg," *Die Gartenlaube* (1874): 64.

[69] For a revealing collection of Kulturkampf verse, see Ernst Scherenberg, ed., *Gegen Rom. Zeitstimmen Deutscher Dichter* (Elberfeld, 1874).

Dahn, the bard of popular patriotic verse, painted images of *Kulturkämpfer* emerging from "the dark forests of our ancestors" to slay Roman lies and defeat clerical deceit. "Rise joyous Teutons," he called out, "rally from tribe to tribe and march on Rome."[70] It would be a mistake to consider the language of such poetry, though dripping with allusions to Germanic mythology, to be regressive, backward-looking. The struggle was, and was perceived to be, for light, for progress, for modernity, and for the new, and still young, German empire. As one writer put it, "no train will ever bring us to Canossa."[71]

The dichotomies that underlay Kulturkampf verse and that informed national identities were indeed stark. In the nationalist imagination, German patriots were loyal, steadfast, honest; in the Kulturkampf they struggled for light and for truth; and they were men. "Only he who has courageously sworn upon the truth / Counts as a man in the German Fatherland," insisted one balladeer.[72] Gendered language, central to the German nationalist tradition generally, was especially important to the religious component of that tradition. Typically, German men saved confessing Catholic women from the peering and probing eyes of their priests.[73] Or, in another motif, the poets dreamed of rescuing young women—"a pale child . . . the last ladylike rose"—from the "silence and death," from the twisted and gnarled branches, from "the dark madness" of the monastery.[74] Against the world of Teutonic heroes and templar knights, the ultramontane Catholics, the "enemy within," emerged from the Reich of darkness. Dishonest, weak and aged, conniving, the inner enemy furtively stalked the fatherland bringing death and decay, and, in one poem, even supplying a shroud to envelop the nation—depicted as a corpse—caught in the icy ultramontane grip.[75]

The Manichaean vision of the poets and the polemicists of the Kulturkampf contained as its counterpart an ethos of complete assimilation to the values of the new national state.[76] This ethos, demonstrably shared by the vast majority of German liberals, insisted that if

---

[70] Felix Dahn, "Gegen Rom," in ibid., 17.

[71] A. T. Brück, "Die Männer zu Fulda," in ibid., 14–15.

[72] Hermann Lingg, "Aufruf," in ibid., 62.

[73] See, for example, Ernst Scherenberg, "Am Beichstuhl," in ibid., 87.

[74] Bernhardt Endrulat, "Die Nonne," in ibid., 21–22.

[75] Rudolf Gottschall, "Wie ein Leichnam sollt ihr werden!" in ibid., 30–32.

[76] On the assimilationist assumptions of German liberalism, see the trenchant analysis of Margaret Anderson, *Windthorst: A Political Biography* (Oxford, 1981), 193–98. On the dualities that haunted the political imagination of German liberals, see also Blackbourn, "Progress and Piety," in Blackbourne, *Populists and Patricians*, 149.

Catholics were to be recognized as true Germans, they must rescind
the weight of their dark, intolerant, and un-German past, a weight
that bore down heavily not just on the Catholic religious community
but on the development of the German nation as a whole. Once freed,
the German nation would then experience a new dawn, a second
spring. Only then, opined one balladeer, "can the German cathedral
of unity / Rise in its full beauty."[77]

Force, Freedom, and Cultural Disunity: The Role of the State

The nationalist dream of spiritual unity, evidently frustrated by the
reality of cultural heterogeneity within the national state, could be
achieved only by severing the fetters of Germany's feudal and particularist past. Here German nationalists insisted that naïveté vis-à-vis
the power of the Roman church would have a deleterious effect on the
young empire. Roman Catholicism, they believed, threatened a unified German identity with an institutionally supported web of cultural
attachments opposed, in so many ways at once, to a progressive and
modern and therefore Protestant conception of that identity. Though
partly a matter of images and representation, of literary canons and
historical traditions, this was also an issue of high politics. In order to
combat the influence of ultramontanism on German culture, nationalist intellectuals considered it necessary to destroy church power, especially in the schools but also in parliament, in social life, and in the
press.

In the struggle against this religious culture, for which nationalist
intellectuals had little understanding and even less patience, the in-
terventionist state, and not the people, constituted the most reliable
ally. Treitschke observed: "For us the state is not, as it is for the Americans, a power to be contained so that the will of the individual may
remain uninhibited, but rather a cultural power from which we expect
positive achievements in all areas of national life."[78] Heinrich von
Sybel also urged state intervention. The "most essential tasks in the
struggle against the clerical system could be mastered," he argued,
"only through the positive influence of state power."[79] Although

[77] Wilhelm Osterwald, "Den Geistesstreitern," in Scherenberg, ed., *Gegen Rom*, 71–72.

[78] Heinrich von Treitschke, "Die Maigesetze und ihre Folgen," in Treitschke, *Zehn Jahre deutscher Kämpfe* (Berlin, 1879), 440.

[79] Heinrich von Sybel, "Klerikale Politik im 19. Jahrhundert," in Sybel, *Kleine Schriften* (Stuttgart, 1880), vol. 3, 450.

Treitschke and Sybel both tended to the conservative side of the Liberal party, it would be a mistake to consider these views as somehow in opposition to a more principled German liberalism. Eugen Richter, the leader of the Progressive party, much to the left of Sybel and Treitschke, and considerably more suspicious of the state, also realized that "it was not possible for the state to liberate itself from clerical domination without interfering in the course of the events."[80]

To German liberals, of both the left and the right, the state represented, at least in its potential, an agent of modernization; the church, by contrast, a bulwark of backwardness. But German liberals, whose relation to the vox populi had always been equivocal, did not necessarily equate a more modern with a more democratic polity. Indeed, German liberals worried deeply about the implications of a democratically mobilized Catholic dissent. Treitschke feared that universal suffrage, "which grants to the powers of custom and stupidity such an unfair superiority" would be "an invaluable weapon of the Jesuits," while von Sybel argued that Catholics did not simply constitute a minority religion but rather "a militarily organized corporation, which in Germany contains more than 30,000 agents sworn to absolute obedience."[81] Democracy, far from hindering the malicious influence of the church, fortified Catholic power anew. "The more democratic the current of the times," Sybel thought, "the more important will be the party that controls one and a half million voters with military command."[82] The very existence of a large religious culture that did not necessarily share the values of the new national state posed a dilemma to the democratic sentiments of German liberals—even to those whose commitment to the parliament and to constitutionalism was otherwise unimpeachable. Rudolf Virchow, the left-liberal pathologist, in every sense a bearer of enlightened values and civic responsibility, pondered the necessity of a "dictatorship of ministers" to combat Catholic resistance to the Kulturkampf.[83]

It is typically assumed that the German-liberal appeal to state power represented a distortion of true liberal values, that in the universal conflict between force and freedom German liberals exalted the former at the expense of the latter. But, in fact, many did not perceive the tension.[84] Force, argued Treitschke, would be harnessed in the

[80] Cited in Tal, *Christians and Jews in Germany*, 83.

[81] Sybel, "Klerikale Politik," 450; Treitschke quoted in Margaret Lavinia Anderson, "The Kulturkampf and German History," *Central European History* 19, no. 1 (1986): 93, fn. 22.

[82] Sybel "Klerikale Politik," 452.

[83] Virchow is cited in Tal, *Christians and Jews in Germany*, 82.

[84] Leonard Krieger, *The German Idea of Freedom: History of a Political Tradition* (Boston, 1957), 4–5.

service of freedom. Indeed, given the spiritual poverty of the people (as they actually existed), force was necessary in order to create a common high culture, the precondition for the development of liberal values. "Many precious benefits of freedom are given to peoples only through state coercion," Treitschke maintained.[85] Freedom from clerical bondage constituted one such benefit. Constantin Rössler argued that should the clergy continue to resist the Kulturkampf measures of the state, then "the state will have no choice but to deny its citizens, regardless of confession [sic!], the guidance of the Roman clergy."[86] The school issue, mercury by which one could measure the intensity of the conflict between nationalist intellectuals and ultramontane Catholics, provided another example of what liberals imagined as a happy marriage between force and freedom. Compulsory education in secular, confessionally mixed schools was, they believed, the best means by which to integrate the confessions while recasting an ignorant and apathetic populace into a respectable, responsible citizenry. But Catholics, mired in their own backwardness, feared such schools as institutions that taught children to criticize their traditional beliefs, that exposed them to blasphemous works, and that indoctrinated them in the materialist beliefs of an increasingly godless age. The resistance of Catholics to compulsory education was particularly tenacious in the countryside and in small towns, where, especially during harvest season, school alarms rarely rang in consonance with time marked out by the requirements of rural life.[87] Nevertheless, argued German liberals, the age demanded change. "The German State," declared Treitschke, "forces parents to have their children educated; it does not give them 'the right to their Catholic stupidity.'"[88]

Not freedom from state coercion, but rather the creation of a national state in which culture and values were shared, in which there was a common commitment to a common destiny, constituted the precondition for a truly, not just a formally, free polity. The state, which "fights on the side of freedom," was to carve out the cultural contours of the new empire, to give form to an emerging national consensus of values.[89] Here too national intellectuals across the liberal spectrum shared common assumptions. Both Treitschke and the public-minded pathologist Rudolf Virchow expected the state to give

---

[85] Treitschke, "Die Maigesetze und ihre Folgen," in Treitschke, Zehn Jahr deutscher Kämpfe, 437.

[86] Rössler, Das deutsche Reich und die kirchliche Frage, 437.

[87] Geoff Eley, "State Formation, Nationalism and Political Culture in Imperial Germany," in Eley, From Unification to Nazism (Boston, 1986), 69.

[88] Treitschke, "Die Maigesetze und ihre Folgen," in Treitschke, Zehn Jahr deutscher Kämpfe, 437.

[89] Ibid., 442.

shape to the "incomplete form of our young German empire."[90] The emerging profile, both men hoped, would be progressive and modern—free of particularism, parochialism, feudal privilege, and fanatical religion. It is with this vision in mind that German liberals pursued the Kulturkampf with a sense of newfound idealism. The left-liberal historian Theodor Mommsen saw the Kulturkampf as "a momentous turning point in which the German state . . . attained self-knowledge, that is, its full freedom."[91] The alternative to the Kulturkampf was not, within the reference of this worldview, toler-ance, but rather absolutism. His gaze fixed on the nationality and reli-gious struggles of the Austro-Hungarian Empire, Treitschke ob-served: "Absolutism is without doubt the natural form of government for such a mixed empire (*Mischreich*).[92] And, it should be added, he thought Germany should have no part of it.

German liberals, it should be clear, urged the repression of ultra-montanism, not in opposition to, but rather in consonance with, their basic principles. And these principles served not as a brake on Bis-marck's "illiberal" attack on the Catholic church but rather as its ideo-logical justification.

Bismarck's repressive measures struck deep into the Catholic church's sphere of influence.[93] In 1872, soon after Bismarck's appoint-ment of Adalbert Falk as minister for education and cultural affairs, Prussia passed a school inspection law that arrogated to the state the sole right to inspect public and private schools. Bismarck directed this law, harmless enough on the surface, against what he perceived to be "un-German" clerical and Polish influence in public education. The Jesuit law of the same year, passed by the Reichstag, was more mani-festly repressive: it expelled the Jesuit order, as well as the Re-demptorist and Lazarist orders, from German soil; it ordered their monasteries to be dissolved and stipulated that, in the case of individ-ual German Jesuits, their citizenship rights be restricted and, in the

---

[90] Treitschke, "Bund und Reich," in ibid., 556.

[91] Cited by Tal, *Christians and Jews in Germany*, 84.

[92] Treitschke, "Österreich und das deutsche Reich," in Treitschke, *Zehn Jahre deut-scher Kämpfe*, 367.

[93] The literature on the official Kulturkampf is immense. For a concise chronological summary with a rich bibliography, see Lill, "Der Kulturkampf," 28–48. For a more detailed account, see Christoph Weber, *Kirchliche Politik zwischen Rom, Berlin und Trier 1876–1888* (Mainz, 1970). Erich Schmidt, *Bismarcks Kampf mit dem politischen Ka-tholizismus. Pius der IX. und die Zeit der Rüstung 1848–1870* (Hamburg, 1942), and Erich Schmidt-Volkmar (the same person), *Der Kulturkampf in Deutschland 1871–1890* (Göt-tingen, 1962), are infected with National Socialist positions, which, however, manifest themselves mainly in the uncritical reproduction of anti-Catholic shibboleths concern-ing the status of Catholics as "enemies of the empire."

case of foreign-born Jesuits, that they be driven from the empire. Despite its affront to civil liberty (as an exceptional law, it deprived a class of citizens of equality before the law), the bill received enthusiastic support from German liberals.[94] Yet the most incisive laws directed against the church were still to come. In May 1873, Bismarck introduced, and the Prussian Landtag passed, a series of bills that ensured state control over the appointment and education of priests. These laws, known as the May laws, required of Catholic priests that they possess German citizenship, a certificate of German higher education, and that they pass an exam in philosophy, history, and German literature. The May laws also gave the state the right to veto the appointment of a priest to a particular parish as well as the power to relieve him of his position if he proved politically unacceptable.

But rather than subordinating the church to the state, these measures encouraged Catholic resistance. Bismarck responded to this resistance, which was largely passive, by sharpening the instruments with which the state could cut into the traditional sphere of the church. In 1874, the Reich passed an expatriation law that allowed the government to exile priests who resisted the May laws. In the same year, Prussia made the exercise of an ecclesiastical office contingent on conformity with the laws of the Kulturkampf. When conformity was not forthcoming, the state appointed commissars to control ecclesiastical affairs. Bishops who resisted were arrested and incarcerated. The Vatican, for its part, declared the May laws invalid and excommunicated those responsible for them. But Prussia parried with still sharper laws. In April 1875, the Landtag passed the so-called breadbasket law, which withheld state financial support for bishoprics that resisted the May laws. In the following month, Prussia expelled the remaining monastic orders and congregations from its territory—left were only the Catholic orders who cared for the sick.

These, in the main, constituted the laws of the Kulturkampf. In theory they represented an impressive intrusion of the modern state into the traditional sphere of the church; in practice the incursion was more modest, the sword rather an épée that bent and blunted when it came into contact with the popular resistance of the Catholic population.[95]

[94] Noteworthy dissidents included Ludwig Bamberger and Eduard Lasker. See Lill, "Der Kulturkampf," 38.

[95] Ronald Ross, "Enforcing the Kulturkampf in the Bismarckian State and the Limits of Coercion in Imperial Germany," *Journal of Modern History* 56 (September 1984): 456–82.

The Kulturkampf and the Catholic Community

If Kulturkampf laws were meant to unify the new nation culturally, they effected the reverse. Rather than assimilate the Catholic population, the repressive measures of the Kulturkampf deepened the cultural rift, already existent, between Catholics and Protestants. The rationalization and homogenization of German cultural and political life revived and politicized, rather than repressed and rendered harmless, the attachment of Catholics to their religious culture and to its rich, if to outsiders archaic, world of rituals and symbols. This clash, which took place concurrently with Germany's rapid industrialization and modernization, was in the 1870s easily as severe as conflicts determined by differences of class. Yet the form of this struggle was different. The scenes of conflict were not, as with class conflict, union halls and factory floors, but rather churches, schoolrooms, monasteries, and charitable foundations; the issues involved were not wages and working conditions but religious instruction and history books; the weapon of struggle was not the strike but the public procession and the power of the ballot box.

Perceiving the decrees of the Kulturkampf to be an affront to constitutional freedom, the Catholic popoulation resisted them, disobeyed them. Priests, traditionally pliant, refused to take the required cultural exams. When the state subsequently revoked their certification, they remained at their pulpits, preaching in defiance of the law. Bishops, hitherto a pillar of order, now refused to consult the state in order to accredit their seminars or confirm their clerical appointments. Deposed by the state, they directed their dioceses from afar, or, through commissars, from the prisons in which they were kept. Catholic organizations, forbidden to gather, did so despite the police. Dutiful and law-abiding, Catholic men and women now held the authorities in contempt.[96]

The Prussian police cracked down on the people perceived to be the primary agitators. Of the eleven bishops in the state of Prussia, seven were imprisoned for inciting resistance; the other four were in exile. Persecuted by the state, they were celebrated as martyrs by the pious. In the bishoprics of Paderborn and Münster, the faithful from outlying villages streamed into the cities in support of their persecuted prelates: they carried banners and torches and papal flags; the dwellers of Münster and Paderborn decked their houses; and many covered the streets with flowers.[97] Though less exalted, the parish

[96] Margaret Lavinia Anderson, *Windthorst*, 173; Ross, "Enforcing the Kulturkampf," 461.

[97] Jonathan Sperber, *Popular Catholicism in Nineteenth-Century Germany* (Princeton, 1984), 227–28.

priests shared their bishops' lot. It is difficult to estimate how many were actually incarcerated for disobeying Prussian laws, but one register for the diocese of Trier lists 251 cases of clerical disobedience of the May laws. For most of these impertinent priests, a few weeks behind bars became de rigueur, almost a qualification for the confidence of their parishioners.[98] Very often, the priests were simply harassed. Forbidden by the police to preach from the pulpit of one parish, they moved to another. In the countryside of Fulda, in Hessen, one priest thus avoided the police for eight years. In another village, this time near the border of Luxembourg, a priest rebuked Prussian magistrates by declaring that he respected only the authority of his bishop. The magistrates imprisoned him nonetheless.[99] The long arm of the Prussian state reached out for Catholic journalists as well, principally with the clutching hand of censorship but also through harassment, arrests, and searches of dubious legality. Between 1872 and 1874, the vast majority of Prussia's 610 press censorship cases and convictions involved Catholics, not socialists.[100] Between January and April 1874 alone, 136 Catholic editors were convicted for the alleged crimes of their contumacious pens.[101]

Yet the reach of the Prussian state was not always the same as its grasp. Despite its impressive apparatus, the state neither broke nor rendered permeable the resistance of the Catholic population. One magistrate complained that "it is very difficult to apprehend these people [the priests who resisted the May laws] . . . because the locals are always informed about the whereabouts of the police officers."[102] Not only did the locals hide their priests, but they also intimidated informers or anyone else involved in carrying out Kulturkampf laws in the densely Catholic provinces.[103] In Münster, a crowd stoned and vandalized the house of a workman hired by the state to impound the bishop's belongings.[104] In Freiburg, Catholic women threatened with their umbrellas anyone who placed bids at the state auction for the furniture of the deposed auxiliary bishop.[105] Resistance, as the historian Jonathan Sperber has shown, sometimes took a tumultuous turn,

---

[98] LHAK 403/15716 diocese of Trier, "Verzeichnis der auf Grund des Par. 22 und 23 des Gesetzes über die Vorbildung und Anstellung der Geistlichen vom 11. Mai 1873 beantragten und eingeleiteten gerichtlichen Untersuchungen und erfolgten Bestrafungen." For the diocese of Münster, which had only 34 such cases, see LHAK 403/15717.

[99] LHAK 403/7558 Report of the district magistrate in Bitburg, 25.6.1874.

[100] Ross, "Enforcing the Kulturkampf," 473, fn. 57.

[101] Margaret Lavinia Anderson, Windthorst, 178.

[102] LHAK 403/7558 Report on the regency of Trier, 5.4.1875.

[103] Ibid.

[104] Vividly portrayed in Margaret Lavinia Anderson, Windthorst, 174.

[105] Ibid.

much to the dismay of state authorities.[106] In the Rhineland between 1872 and 1877, eleven clashes between the Prussian police and the Catholic populace ended in violence.[107] Similarly, a number of demonstrations in Polish-Catholic areas of Prussia's eastern provinces devolved into small-scale jacqueries. When resistance in confessionally homogenous areas turned violent, demonstrators typically focused their wrath on a symbol of the state—a gendarme or local magistrate; but in mixed areas, they tended to single out members of another confession: wealthy Protestants, Jews, or "Old Catholics."[108]

The experience of persecution and resistance created the conditions for the formation of a Catholic community that transcended, at least in part, differences of class and status, a community that shared a common, emotive rhetoric, and that was bound by a dense, tightly woven network of Catholic organizations. In the governmental district of Düsseldorf, the police counted 389 Catholic organizations at the height of the Kulturkampf, in 1874; in the district of Cologne, there were 139 organizations; in the district of Trier, 160; in Koblenz, 147.[109] This constituted an organizational web considerably more intricate than could be found in competing parties or subcultures, whether liberal, socialist, or conservative. Moreover, the thematic diapason of these Catholic organizations was very wide, ranging from reading clubs to charitable organizations, from choruses to confraternities devoted to the cult of the sacred heart; they included men's as well as women's organizations; devotional, instructional, trade, and a number of political organizations—indeed far too many political organizations for the taste of the Prussian police. In the district of Düsseldorf, the gendarmes targeted, with the intention of disbanding, 51 Catholic organizations alleged to have a political bent: Catholic reading clubs, citizens' clubs, Catholic veterans' organizations, Christian workers' clubs, and, most prominently, branches of the Mainz Association, officially known as the Association of German Catholics, an important and powerful Catholic organization dedicated to "defending the freedom and rights of the Catholic church and bringing Christian principles to bear on all aspects of public life."[110] If the range of Catholic organizations testified to the breadth of the Catholic public

---

[106] See the excellent analysis in Sperber, *Popular Catholicism*, 229–33.

[107] Ibid.

[108] Ross, "Enforcing the Kulturkampf," 474.

[109] LHAK 403/6695 "Zusammenstellung der Katholischen Vereine im Regierungsbezirk Düsseldorf," 15.8.1874. See similar reports, all completed in August, for Cologne, Trier, and Koblenz.

[110] LHAK 403/6695 "Nachweisung über die erfolgte polizeiliche Schließung, die vorläufige gerichtliche Aufrechterhaltung dieser Schließung, sowie die Definition gerichtliche Schließung der katholischen Vereine in dem Regierungsbezirk Düsseldorf," 5.10.74. On the Mainz Association, see Sperber, *Popular Catholicism*, 211.

sphere, local support for the Mainz Association bore witness to its depth. In the district of Düsseldorf, an estimated 20 percent of adult Catholic men belonged to the association; its mass rallies drew throngs of thousands to the center of Düsseldorf; and its enthusiastic gatherings, part revivalism, part politics, utterly captivated the Catholic faithful.[111]

Politics also affected piety, a phenomenon especially visible in the discernible increase in pilgrimages, especially in those to sites of the alleged apparition of Maria. During the Kulturkampf, there were at least four reported apparitions of Maria in the German empire: she was said to have appeared in the villages of Krüth and Issenheim in Alsace in 1872–73, in Dietrichswalde in West Prussia in 1877, in Marpingen in the Saarland in 1876, and once near the Benedictine monastery of Metten in Lower Bavaria in 1878.[112] Her apparitions in Germany never received episcopal sanction, yet she always seemed to proclaim a turn in political events. Speaking French, she assured the Alsatians freedom from the pressures of Germanization; in "beautiful Polish," she promised a homeland to the Poles of Posen and West Prussia; and in Marpingen, according to one contemporary observer, her presence gave German Catholics both "satisfaction of patriotic feeling, since now the beloved Mother of God seems also to have come to our Fatherland," and hope, since "such a visible supernatural intervention in the natural order foretold a prompt turn in the Kulturkampf."[113] In fact, however, it prefigured the deployment of Prussian troops. "To maintain order" in the midst of devotional fervor, Prussian troops stormed a crowd of pilgrims in Marpingen, injuring a number but, more importantly, revealing the deep distrust, even hostility, of the state to the "devotional revolution" taking place among the Catholic population.[114] Similarly, though without violent incident, the army stood guard over the annual pilgrimage to the cathedral in Aachen, again to "maintain public peace and order" but also as "open intimidation to prevent excesses."[115]

[111] Sperber, *Popular Catholicism*, 212.

[112] Margaret Lavinia Anderson, "Piety and Politics: Recent Work on German Catholicism," *Journal of Modern History* 63, no. 4 (December 1991): 695.

[113] Wilhelm Cramer, *Die Erscheinungen und Heilungen in Marpingen*, 3d ed. (Würzburg, 1879), 1. On the apparition in Dietrichswalde, PAAA R4063 Memorandum of the provincial governor of West Prussia, Gustav von Gossler, 6.9.1896. See also Gottfried Korff, "Kulturkampf und Volksfrömmigkeit," in *Volksreligiosität in der modernen Sozialgeschichte*, ed. Wolfgang Schieder (Göttingen, 1986), 143–45; and Blackbourn, "Progress and Piety," in Blackbourn, *Populists and Patricians*, 164–66.

[114] On the military intervention, see Julius Bachem, "Militär-Excesse und Militärgerichts-Verfahren," *Historisch-politische Blätter für das Katholische Deutschland* 84 (1879): 517–26.

[115] LHAK 403/13687 Report on the district of Aachen, 31.5.1874.

The rise of ultramontane piety, a process that began in the 1830s, seemed to accelerate dramatically during the Kulturkampf. In 1873, a Protestant observer in the town of Uedingen in the district of Aachen complained that he had never seen such a swarm of pilgrims "as in this year." He considered it "a sad sight to see these people drawing near in long columns"—"stupid and dull . . . peasant men and women and shop girls . . . singing their monotonous prayer without interruption," following their young chaplain to the site of "yet another miracle performed by the Mother of God."[116] The scene, and the sentiments it evoked, were increasingly typical of the Kulturkampf years; the gulf separating the educated Protestant merchant from the pious Catholic underclasses had widened and, more importantly, had become politicized. Catholic piety expressed this politicization. The cult of the heart of Christ, perhaps the most popular devotional cult of the period, served, in the words of the Catholic journal *Stimmen aus Maria Laach*, as a "secure haven of salvation . . . from the Kulturkampf."[117] This resistance, as David Blackbourn has argued, "possessed highly developed iconographical forms": club banners, garlands, the papal flag, religious art (lithographs, votive paintings, devotional prints, glass paintings), devotional figures (especially Maria), relics and elaborate reliquaries (for which there was now vastly increased demand), and, in every parish, a crucifix—the symbol, especially on Corpus Christi Day, of suffering, but also of strength.[118] The ultramontane movement of the 1870s possessed a good deal of rhetorical richness as well. "The Catholic church, particularly in Germany, bleeds from many wounds," wrote a Catholic author, appealing to the image of Christ on the cross.[119] In 1874 *Der Katholik*, the newspaper of the bishopric of Mainz, compared Catholics of the present to the martyrs of the distant past: "Especially in our era of the Kulturkampf the conditions of the first Christian century are reproduced in so many ways."[120]

The image of an embattled church—wounded, bleeding—constituted a powerful symbol, one that placed a claim on the devout, demanding sacrifice and self-abnegation. Indeed, here is what, follow-

[116] LHAK 403/16005 Louis Herbertz (local merchant) to the Prussian minister for education and cultural affairs, 19.9.1873.

[117] Cited by Korff, "Kulturkampf und Volksfrömmigkeit," 148–49, fn. 42. Original source is *Stimmen aus Maria Laach* 12, no. 5 (1877): 122.

[118] See, again, Blackbourn's seminal essay, "Progress and Piety," in Blackbourn, *Populists and Patricians*, 153. See also Helena Waddy Lepovitz, *Images of Faith: Expressionism, Catholic Folk Art, and the Industrial Revolution* (Athens, Ga., and London, 1991).

[119] *Der Katholik* 50, no. 1 (1870): 2.

[120] *Der Katholik* 54, no. 1 (1874).

ing the anthropologist Victor Turner, we might call the "root metaphor" of political Catholicism in the period of the Kulturkampf, the image from which moral suasion, political analysis, exhortations for behavior proceeded.[121] In *Writing Hand on Wall and Sand*, Alban Stolz, one of the few Catholic authors to reach a truly national audience, told parables of modern martyrdom taking place now in Baden, now in Silesia—Catholic shoemakers or smiths defending the sanctity of the cross or the integrity of saint's relics against hostility and desecration. He alternated these stories with negative parables about Catholics who had fallen from the faith and now despised the clergy and mocked pilgrims. Stolz invited Catholic readers to mirror themselves in these stories, to reflect on their own moral conduct, and to see in local struggles, universal ones.[122] Herein lay the power of popular Catholic culture: it patterned proximate events as universal struggle. The act of defending local saints or apparitions of Maria against modern science and the logic of Protestant professors was at the heart of this essentially defensive, if also intolerant, way of etching meaning onto a world rapidly, all too rapidly, changing.

In addition, a strong element of social drama infused Catholic exhortations to defend the church, its persecuted bishops and priests, its desecrated saints, its violated Maria. This drama, whether acted out in street demonstrations or passively supported from the pews of the parish church, imparted form, meaning, and sense to Catholic politics in a way that the usual debates over taxes and tariffs never could; it politicized the Catholic population; it bound Catholics into struggle, into conflict, the obverse of which was confessional cohesion, in Victor Turner's vocabulary, "communitas." Turner defines "communitas" in opposition to "structure": the former binds, the latter differentiates; "communitas" refers to subcultural cohesion that may well transcend class and status distinctions; "structure" connotes dominant hierarchies, prevailing vocabularies, from which groups in communitas may dissent, but always at the penalty of becoming outsiders or marginals. From this outsider, "liminal" position, the popular culture of political Catholicism developed a common language, a vocabulary in opposition to the dominant culture of Germany, which when seen through Catholic eyes seemed to be elite, liberal, enlightened, Protestant, and German national.

This deep division antedated the Kulturkampf but became wider as

[121] Victor Turner, *Dramas, Fields, and Metaphors: Symbolic Action in Human Society* (Ithaca, N.Y., and London, 1974), 25–29.

[122] Alban Stolz, *Schreibende Hand auf Wand und Sand*, in Stolz, *Gesammelte Werke*, vol. 16 (Freiburg, 1894).

a result of this conflict, a tendency one can discern through the popularity of Catholic dictionaries for newspaper readers. These dictionaries, such as August Reichensperger's *Phrases and Slogans* or Alban Stolz's *ABCs for Grown-ups*, redefined the "key words" of the dominant culture, captiously giving each of them a Catholic inflection.[123] Reichensperger, for example, defined a constitutional state (*Rechtsstaat*) as a state that advances the "idea of unconditional progress at any cost," but noted that to Catholics it suggested a state in which "the poorest are sure to be safe from oppression and the weak need not tremble before the strong."[124] These authors demonstrated that the same words of the same language implied different meanings to different groups, and that the two cultures did not necessarily share meaning.

To Catholics socialized in the ultramontane milieu, dissent from German national culture therefore concerned basic values; it manifested itself at the level of vocabulary; and it involved the sacred. In a secular age, it is easy to forget the political power of institutions considered sacred. Yet as late as 1890, after some of the passions of the empire's Kulturkampf had already cooled, priests in Württemberg still had no difficulty gathering 100,000 signatures (there were only slightly more Catholic voters) on a petition imploring the state to allow its expatriated monks to return. When the state refused, citing as an argument the sensibilities of its Protestant subjects, the "spontaneous" Catholic movement vowed to pressure the state so that in Württemberg, "Catholic things will be done in Catholic ways, not measured by the views of those who believe differently."[125]

Here was the crux of the matter. The Kulturkampf was meant to culturally unify the new national state, but instead it aggravated the division between Protestants and Catholics; it created not one nation, but two; it sent worlds, already apart, into a deeper antagonism, an antagonism all the more rigid because it was in part the product of the universal struggles of the nineteenth century: the struggle between elite and popular culture, between city and country, modernity and older ways of life. It is perhaps for this reason that Constantin Rössler began his popular and learned polemical work, *The German Empire and*

---

[123] August Reichensperger, *Phrasen und Schlagwörter. Ein Noth- und Hülfsbüchlein für Zeitungsleser*, 5th ed. (Paderborn, 1872); Alban Stolz, *ABC für große Leute. Kalender für Zeit und Ewigkeit 1864*, 3d ed. (Freiburg, 1884).

[124] Reichensperger, *Phrasen und Schlagwörter*, 115–16.

[125] On this petition, see the correspondence and press clippings in StAL E211/VI/2079. For the response of the Württemberg Ministry of Religion and Education, see State Minister of Religion and Education Sarvey to Bishop von Hefele, 10.3.1891.

the Church Question, with the assurance that "the struggle in which the German empire finds itself pitted against the empire of the Roman pope is unquestionably the greatest event of the political world of our day."[126] Perhaps an exaggeration, it was nevertheless a sentiment widely shared.

[126] Rössler, *Das deutsche Reich und die kirchliche Frage*, 1.

2

Visions of the Nation: The Ideology of Religious Conflict

LIKE THE WORLD of T. S. Eliot's "hollow men," the struggle that Constantin Rössler considered the greatest event of the age ended "not with a bang but a whimper." In 1878, Bismarck began gradually to repeal the measures most odious to the Catholic church while retaining legislation especially dear to Protestants and liberals. By 1887, the state had relinquished some of its control over the appointment of parish priests, had exempted Catholic theology students from cultural examinations, and had repatriated select monastic orders as well as Catholic priests who had actively resisted Kulturkampf legislation. But state supervision of schools remained, as did obligatory civil marriage, the pulpit paragraph, and the anti-Jesuit law.[1] A number of German nationalists registered the close of the official Kulturkampf in 1887 with resignation. Not only had ecclesiastical power not been broken, but the Catholic Church had emerged from the struggle with its organizational edifice intact and its ideological buttresses sturdier than ever before. As one Protestant publicist grudgingly conceded: "In the old, fragile man in the Vatican, Bismarck has found his master."[2]

The passing of the official Kulturkampf did not, however, herald a new age of confessional peace and harmony. The social conflicts and the structures of mentality that underlay religious antagonism persisted. In the period after 1887, confessional conflict was of a different order, marked less by the separateness of what one scholar has called the "two nations" than by the dilemmas accompanying the integration of two groups with competing visions of the German national state, its history, and its political destiny.[3]

---

[1] On the dismantling of the Kulturkampf, see Rudolf Lill, *Die Wende im Kulturkampf. Leo XIII., Bismarck und die Zentrumspartei 1878–1889* (Tübingen, 1973), and Christoph Weber, *Kirchliche Politik.*

[2] Richard Adelbert Lipsius, *Zehn Jahre preußisch-deutscher Kirchenpolitik* (Halle, 1887), 7.

[3] The term "two nations" comes from Margaret Lavinia Anderson, *Windthorst*, 164.

The Ideology of the Protestant League

Ideologies are often closely constructed precisely when they seem no longer to assert self-evident truths. The idea that Roman Catholics somehow constituted inauthentic Germans, though very old, was advanced most vigorously when German Catholics began their gradual reconciliation with the German national state. As Bismarck moved to make his final peace with the Vatican, the newly founded Protestant League prepared to continue the struggle against Rome—not with the repressive measures of the state, but with the force of ideological conviction.

In the spring of 1886, Willibald Beyschlag, the founder of the Protestant League, envisioned a mass organization in which "all available and willing forces in Protestant Germany could come together."[4] German national sentiment and antagonism toward Rome could, he thought, unite Protestants otherwise divided. As professor of theology at the University of Halle, and as the leader of the Evangelical Middle Party, a theological group in the Prussian Synod that attempted to mediate between liberal and conservative Protestants, Beyschlag believed that only in unity could German Protestantism find strength. Thus he proposed to "awaken the living Protestant spirit in all areas of our national life" by waving "the flag of resistance against the Roman flood."[5]

On 26 May 1886, he invited a group of twenty theologians to Halle to consider the nation's confessional fate. Like Beyschlag, these men, most of whom were from Saxony and Thuringia, were convinced that the time had come for Protestants to take matters into their own hands. They formed a committee of five theologians, which was soon expanded to seven, to consider the shape and form of the new Protestant organization. The committee, consisting of Eduard Riehm, Richard Bärwinkel, Albert von Bamberg, Friedrich Nippold, Richard Adelbert Lipsius, Coelestin Leuschner, and Beyschlag himself, represented a wide range of theological positions within German Protestantism from the rationalist left to the theological positivists of the right, though the decisive weight was in the middle with Beyschlag and the mediation theologians.[6]

[4] Willibald Beyschlag, *Zur Enstehungsgeschichte des Evangelischen Bundes*, posthumous (Berlin, 1926), 12–13.

[5] Ibid.

[6] On Beyschlag and his milieu, see Walter Fleischmann-Bisten and Heiner Grote, *Protestanten auf dem Wege. Geschichte des Evangelischen Bundes* (Göttingen, 1986), 9–25;

The committee charged Beyschlag with the task of writing a "confidential memorandum" on the purpose of the Protestant League. In this memorandum, written in the summer of 1886, Beyschlag proceeded from the assumption that the Kulturkampf had achieved the opposite of its intended effect. Rather than subordinate the Catholic church to the Prussian state, the Kulturkampf had "refined the power of the Roman system on German soil." Catholic unity and power now stood over and against Protestant disunity and political powerlessness. Already divided into territorial churches, German Protestantism suffered still more for being torn by theological disputes. As liberals and conservatives debated how much hierarchy should be allowed in ecclesiastical constitutions or whether biblical truth resided in revelation or reason, the ultramontane challenge went unmet. It was necessary, wrote Beyschlag, "to strike a new way," to establish an organization that could "break the power of Rome on German soil."[7]

Yet this organization, the Protestant League, was itself internally divided. Conservatives insisted on a confessional statute that would require members to recognize "the fundamental principles of the Reformation" and to see in Jesus Christ "the sole intercessor of salvation." Liberals opposed this idea and advocated instead "a union of all religious groups in Germany free from Rome."[8] The one group wanted the league to emphasize positive, Protestant Christianity; the other, cultural resistance to ultramontanism. This dispute, which ended with the inclusion of the confessional paragraph, revealed the depth of ideological division within the league. Had Beyschlag not compelled a final compromise, the league may well have broken apart. But with messianic certainty, he insisted: "I see in this moment the balancing-scale of Germany's future shaking and trembling before God's throne."[9]

On 15 January 1887, fortuitously the day that Bismarck dissolved

---

Gottfried Maron, "Willibald Beyschlag und die Entstehung des Evangelischen Bundes," in Maron, ed., *Evangelisch und Ökumenisch. Beiträge zum 100jährigen Bestehen des Evangelischen Bundes* (Göttingen, 1986), 19–45; Armin Müller, "Der Evangelische Bund im Kaiserreich. Entstehung, Struktur, Programm und politisches Verhalten einer protestantischen Sammelbewegung, 1886–1914" (Staatsexamensarbeit, Universität Hamburg, 1985), 14–26. On the theological positions of the original committee, the most detailed source is still Friedrich Nippold, *Die Anfänge des Evangelischen Bundes und seiner Pressthätigkeit* (Berlin, 1897), 8–28.

[7] The memorandum is conveniently reprinted in Beyschlag, *Zur Enstehungsgeschichte*, 16–26.

[8] This position was represented most forcefully by Albert von Bamberg. See Nippold, *Die Anfänge des Evangelischen Bundes*, 13–14.

[9] Cited in Müller, "Der Evangelische Bund," 20.

the Reichstag and declared the oppositional Catholics "enemies of the Reich," the Protestant League issued its summons: "Fellow Protestants and Germans! The Kulturkampf is coming to a close. But the struggle with Rome continues. It will continue 'so long as a heretic is still in the land,' or, as we intend, until the truth of the Evangelium forces its way to victory in all Germany."[10] In the main, the proclamation reiterated the central points of Beyschlag's confidential memorandum: the resurgent power of Rome, the divided and debilitated state of German Protestantism, the necessity of consolidated action, and the need to go on the offensive in the confessional struggle.[11]

Initially, this struggle was more a matter of propaganda than of politics. The league's first chairman, Wilko Levin Graf von Wintzingerode-Bodenstein, believed that political activity divided rather than unified the league.[12] Moreover, the pastors, who made up 30 percent of the league's ten thousand members in 1887 and who held almost all the important leadership positions, tended to distrust political activity.[13] But if the pastors disagreed on politics and theology, or even on the degree to which politics and theology should be discussed, they could all agree on basic assumptions concerning the influence of religion, and religious discord, on the German nation.

The pastors believed that German antagonism toward Roman Catholicism was conditioned by "over a thousand years of acquired experience"[14] It began not with Luther but with the emergence of a specifically Germanic piety in the early Middle Ages. Characterized by individuality and conscientiousness, Germanic piety had resisted Roman influence from the start. Kurt Schindowski, the editor of the *Deutsch-Evangelische Korrespondenz*, the Protestant League's news wire service, argued that "a harmonious relationship between [the church]

[10] AKIEB S500.9.125 "An unsere Glaubensgenossen in ganz Deutschland!" 15.1.1887.

[11] Ibid.

[12] Wilko Levin Graf von Wintzingerode-Bodenstein, *Der Evangelische Bund in Frankfurt, 2, Eröffnungsrede* (Leipzig, 1887), 3.

[13] In its organizational structure, the league was divided into two tiers: the national committee (*Bundesvorstand*) and the provincial branches (*Hauptvereine*). The national committee consisted of a central committee of eight to ten members and a joint committee (*Gesamtvorstand*), which included the leaders of all the provincial branches. The central committee, which usually met in Halle on a monthly basis, directed the league's affairs and prepared the annual general assemblies. It also organized the major special committees of the league, the most important of which—at least in the first decade—was the press committee. For more detail, see Müller, "Der Evangelische Bund," 34–36.

[14] Willibald Beyschlag, *Der Friedensschluß zwischen Deutschland und Rom* (Leipzig, 1887), 6. Friedrich Meyer attributed a "nearly 2,000 year" history to this antagonism. See "Bismarck in der Walhalla," in Meyer, *Heroldsrufe und Hammerschläge. Ein deutschevangelisches Vermächtnis* (Berlin, 1929), 41–47.

and the educated, individual spirits of the German race" never existed.[15] Unfit to be a lasting religion among "young, vital, manly tribes," medieval Catholicism was, according to Schindowski, designed for "womanly peoples."[16] Luther's challenge thus laid bare a "previously instinctive conflict between Germanism and Romanism."[17] From this perspective, the Reformation represented national emancipation; its principal protagonist, Martin Luther, the first truly "German Christian."[18]

The pastors of the Protestant League appropriated the language of race, yet at least in the early years their historical vision was influenced less by Herbert Spencer and Houston Stewart Chamberlain than by ideas concerning the habits, customs, and ethics of peoples. They imagined the German character to exist in timeless contrast to the Catholic peoples "beyond the mountains." The ultramontanes, thought Carl Fey, were "Roman through and through, hardened for centuries in Latin racial darkness [*Rassendunkel*]."[19] Where Germans were historically free and independent, Latins were traditionally slavish and obsequious. In this Manichaean view of history, light contrasted with darkness, vigor with atrophy, youth with age, and manliness with femininity.

The pastors of the Protestant League posited an idea of national character, based on an idea of German national culture, and supposed that groups which did not contribute to the formation of this character or share in the values of this culture could not be considered properly German. Thus they quarreled with Catholics less about theology than about moral life and custom; less about the meaning of Christian ritual than the fate of national culture; less about God than the inner life of nations. In short, they quarreled with Catholics about history.

The nation, argued Coelestin Leuschner, the conservative secretary of the league, could have "rejuvenated" itself had not "an alien [*Fremdling*] rather than a German regent held the scepter in the days

---

[15] Kurt Schindowski, "Christentum und deutsche Eigenart," *Deutsches Wochenblatt* 11 (March 1899): 436.

[16] Ibid.

[17] Ibid., 438. For a similar view see Adolf Schmitthenner, *"Wisset ihr nicht, wes Geistes Kinder ihr seid?"* (Leipzig, 1891), 1–3.

[18] See especially Hermann Kremers, *Martin Luther, der deutsche Christ* (Leipzig, 1895), but also F. Haberkamp, *Protestantismus und nationale Politik* (Halle, 1909), 13. And for this theme in German nationalist thought generally, see Hartmut Lehmann, "Martin Luther als deutscher Nationalheld im 19. Jahrhundert," *Luther. Zeitschrift der Luther-Gesellschaft* 55, no. 2 (1984): 53–65.

[19] Carl Fey, *Ultramontanismus und Patriotismus* (Leipzig, 1891), 2. Here Fey approvingly quotes Wolfgang Menzel, *Roms Unrecht* (Stuttgart, 1871).

of Luther."[20] Instead, Charles V condemned German history to run a tragic, because divided, course. "Germany was already almost completely Protestant," wrote Leuschner. "Not the Reformation but the Jesuit reaction tore it internally and externally apart."[21] Of the two halves, only one was legitimately German. "Only in the Protestant half," argued Willibald Beyschlag, "did the life of the whole, insofar as it was a life, continue to pulse."[22] The Catholic rest lived on, but under the rule of a spirit alien to the German character. It followed that Protestant interests were not special interests but rather the interests of the nation, and national history was not the history of the constituent groups that made up the nation but rather the history of the Protestant half.[23] In a speech before the general assembly of the league in 1892, Beyschlag proclaimed:

> all that is great in our history, the rise of the Brandenburg-Prussian state, the monumental literature of the eighteenth century, the patriotic and religious uprising of the Wars of Liberation, came from the Protestant side, but redounded to the benefit of Catholics as well; therefore it is a just outcome of history that the German empire, with its Protestant majority, should have a Protestant kaiser at the head.[24]

The consummate nation, Beyschlag assumed, consisted in a community shorn of religious or ethnic diversity. This assumption informed not just the national ideology of the league but also the political views of some of the empire's leading historians, many of whom were league members.[25] Max Lenz, for example, argued in 1907 that "national unity is not complete so long as our worship of God is not on common ground."[26] The league gave this peculiarly German version of Whig history messianic force. Coelestin Leuschner preached that

[20] Coelestin Leuschner, *Die unserer Kirche gebührende Stellung im öffentlichen Leben* (Leipzig, 1981), 6.

[21] Ibid.

[22] Beyschlag, *Der Friedensschluß*, 6. For a similar view, Hermann Baumgarten, *Römische Triumphe* (Halle, 1887), 13.

[23] Leuschner, *Die unsere Kirche gebührende Stellung*, 1. "In truth, Protestant interest is not a special interest. It is the interest of the whole German nation, indeed the whole world."

[24] Willibald Beyschlag, *Deutsch-evangelische Blätter* (1892): 68 (hereafter *DEB*).

[25] Leading historians who were also members of the league included Hermann Baumgarten, Hermann Oncken, and Dietrich Schäfer. Heinrich von Treitschke, who was not a league member (most likely because of his age), was nevertheless considered by the league to be "the greatest Protestant historian of the modern era." See AKIEB S500.9.60 Jahresbericht der Generalversammlung des Evangelischen Bundes, 1897.

[26] Cited in Altgeld, *Katholizismus, Protestantismus, Judentum*, 67.

"God had ordained a time for Germany to become one empire with one church."[27]

Initially, the league's aim was less to convert Catholics than to civilize them, though the pastors developed more polite idioms to express their intentions. They argued that a core of enlightened Catholicism existed beneath layers of Jesuit obscurantism. Criticism of ultramontanism could thus be conceived as a positive act, pursued for the sake of Catholics. Beyschlag, for example, urged the league to support the Old Catholics, a dissident group that split from the Roman church in 1870 on the occasion of the First Vatican Council. Unlike the ultramontanes, the Old Catholics resisted papal infallibility. Nationalist in sentiment and rationalist in theology, they approximated Beyschlag's ideal of Catholics with whom he could coexist. Although their numbers were small, their ethics were grounded in the higher ideals of German Kultur.

Roman Catholicism, on the other hand, sapped the spiritual substance of nations. The leaders of the league fixed their gaze on the cultural development of Catholic countries—Poland, Italy, France, Spain, and Belgium—only to see low literacy rates, mass superstition, chronic poverty, and political disunion. "We have France and we have Spain before our eyes," wrote Beyschlag, "both of which have been ruined by the same system."[28] Victims of a "cancerous affliction," these lands suffered from the influence of "papacy, monasticism, and clericalism."[29] In Belgium, ultramontanism allegedly encouraged militant socialism; in Italy, atheism supposedly coexisted with bigotry and hypocrisy.[30] While these countries paid for Catholicism with their decline, Germany owed its ascendancy to Protestantism. "The true greatness of our nation stems from the spiritual power that resides in Protestant culture," resolved the league in 1905.[31] But the "cancerous growth" of ultramontanism threatened Germany as well, for it divided the nation into two alien and antagonistic parties. "After God's mercy unified our people politically," proclaimed Leuschner, Roman advances threaten "to tear it even more terribly apart inwardly, even to the point of endangering our existence."[32] The vast web of Catholic organizations appeared to the league as a fifth column working qui-

---

[27] Leuschner, *Die unsere Kirche gebührende Stellung*, 16.

[28] Beyschlag, *DEB* (1899): 3.

[29] Beyschlag, "Der Krebsschaden Spaniens," *DEB* (1898): 362.

[30] Ludwig Weber, *Wer soll und muß dem Evangelischen Bund beitreten* (Barmen, 1888), 5.

[31] AKIEB S500.9.60 "Jahresbericht der Generalversammlung des Evangelischen Bundes in Hamburg, 1905," 48.

[32] Coelestin Leuschner, *Römische Angriffe und Evangelische Abwehr* (Leipzig, 1893), 4.

etly to divide the nation in every imaginable aspect of community life. Beyschlag worried that neither army nor constitution would be able to hold the two antagonistic parties together. Instead, a new Thirty Years War threatened. Between Protestantism and Catholicism "a final battle" would have to be fought.[33]

The pastors believed that they lived in an age of counterreformation; if the form of Catholicism had changed, its content remained the same; and if Catholic organizations had become modern, they still served "a fantastic, wide-ranging, medieval worldview."[34] Intolerance, in the opinion of the league, was essential to Roman Catholicism. The source of Catholic intolerance was, on one level, the hierarchical structure of the church; on the other, Catholicism's concessions to popular religiosity. To the Protestant mind, the hierarchical structure of the church assured Catholics that they would be spared the onerous burdens of independent reasoning, the prerequisite to true tolerance. Instead, Catholics slavishly followed the dictates of the pope, who, as everyone knew, had listed tolerance among the many modern errors damned in the Syllabus of 1864. The counterpart of Catholic intolerance decreed from above was a deeper intolerance that welled up from below, from the murky underworld of superstition and strange religious practice. Beyschlag considered exorcisms, ritual murder accusations (a form of anti-Semitism peculiar to Catholic areas), veneration of the sacred heart, Maria apparitions, pilgrimages to the cloak of Christ in Trier, and fanatical displays of devotion to be typical of modern Catholicism, not relics of the past, but harbingers of a dark future.[35] He was not alone. "The age of the Counter-Reformation is not yet over," warned the prominent church historian Adolf Hausrath. "The tendency of Catholicism is completely the same."[36] Wary that history might repeat itself, the pastors of the Protestant League alerted the nation to the dangers posed by the renaissance of Catholic religious life. Like sentinels surrounded by foes, they anxiously observed the spread of Catholic hospitals, the renewed popularity of female orders, the revival of monastic devotion, and the portentous proliferation of Catholic organizational life. They also cautioned against repeated Catholic calls—necessarily hypocri-

---

[33] Beyschlag, *Der Friedensschluß*, 17.

[34] Beyschlag, *DEB* (1897): 278–79.

[35] Beyschlag, *DEB* (1892): 430, 561. For a thoroughgoing critique of Catholic practices from the perspective of the league, see Leopold Witte, *Der Protest gegen die römisch-katholische Einstellung des Christentums, eine Pflicht christlicher Frömmigkeit* (Halle, 1889), and Schmitthenner, *Wisset ihr nicht*, 7.

[36] Approvingly cited by Karl Bauer, *Carlo Borromeo und seine Zeit. Ein Spiegelbild für unsere Gegenwart*, (Halle, 1910), 21.

tical—for tolerance and parity.[37] And they proved their premonitions by pointing out that once again, as in previous centuries, Rome had emerged as an "important ally of the enemies of Germandom," whether Polish or French.[38] From this perspective, the ascendancy of the Center party, alarming enough on its own, represented a historical process considerably larger and more ominous: the re-Catholicization of German national life.[39] As the Counter-Reformation had brought the dawn of a century of national division and decline, the influence of the Center would bring the dusk of German unity and power. "If we continue to place our public life under the aegis of the Center party," warned Kurt Schindowski, "we will renounce the masculine ideal of independent morality and individual national character; we will show ourselves to belong to the degenerating nations."[40]

It followed that the league's principal task was, as Beyschlag had put it in his confidential memorandum, "not just to defend our spiritual property, but to break the power of Rome on German soil."[41] The end of the Kulturkampf, far from making this task superfluous, convinced league leaders of its renewed importance. Beyschlag, who lamented the decade between 1878 and 1887 as one long, weary march to Canossa, now hoped for "a new era."[42] With Bismarck departed, the heads of state could pursue "Protestant politics in a free spiritual and moral sense."[43] This, thought Beyschlag, should be the "highest end" of German statesmanship.

Yet what constituted Protestant politics? The pastors could all agree that the state of Prussia was a Protestant state and that this fact was belied by the principle of parity, which asserted that the state should grant equal rights and equal status not only to both churches but also to the individual members of both religious communities. This "unholy principle," declared Leuschner, ignored the "essential differences between the two churches" and disregarded "their fundamentally opposite relationship to the state."[44] Conservative in both the

---

[37] For an examples of this way of thinking, see Leuschner, *Römische Angriffe*, 4.

[38] J. Neumeister, "Das Papsttum als Feind des Deutschtums in der frühen Neuzeit," *DEB* (1899): 778. See also Schindowski, "Christentum und deutsche Eigenart," 438.

[39] See, for example, *Württembergische Bundesblätter* 15, no. 2 (1902): 21–25.

[40] Schindowski, "Christentum und deutsche Eigenart," 439.

[41] Beyschlag, "Denkschrift," in Beyschlag, *Zur Enstehungsgeschichte*, 16–26.

[42] Beyschlag, *DEB* (1890): 281.

[43] Beyschlag, "Die gegenwärtige deutsch-preußische Kirchenpolitik und der Evangelische Bund," *DEB* (1890): 375.

[44] Leuschner, *Die unsere Kirche gebührende Stellung*, 12. Similarly, Beyschlag polemicized against parity in government hiring because it "undermined the Protestant character of the Prussian state even further." *DEB* (1896): 278.

theological and political sense, Leuschner emphasized the Protestant character of the monarchy and the state as opposed to the people and the nation. The "essence" of the Prussian state was, he thought, "its calling as an independent carrier of the ethical ideas of Providence."[45]

The preeminent political conservatives of the league—Willibald Beyschlag, Leopold Witte, Richard Bärwinkel, and Count Wintzingerode—shared Leuschner's vision of a dynasty whose ultimate aim should be to follow divine ordinance. Between 1887 and 1898, they also controlled the league's central committee. From here they marked out the terrain of confessional conflict, often choosing issues for debate that were symbolic of parity: whether it was acceptable to introduce Corpus Christi Day processions in Protestant towns with Catholic minorities, whether the state should treat Protestant and Catholic missions in the colonies equally, whether the Jesuits should be allowed back into the empire, or whether particular pontifical pronouncements should be considered incompatible with basic tenets of tolerance. In this first period the Protestant League still hoped for the return of a state-directed Kulturkampf (though they no longer called it that) fought in the name of the Prussian state and the Hohenzollern dynasty. In 1894, the general assembly in Bochum resolved: "The day will come when the state must once again take up the struggle against the [Catholic] church . . . Our task is to prepare the Protestant people for this decisive struggle, to put the Protestant church in order and consolidate its strength."[46] The Bochum resolution betrayed a certain trust in the state, a hope, however misguided, that the alliance of throne and altar would take up the struggle against ultramontanism.

Yet for some members of the league, this hope proved an illusion. As the Center party assumed an impervious position in parliament, as the government made one concession to the Catholics after the next, the full extent of this illusion became evident. Within the league, a younger, more progressive generation of Protestant intellectuals emerged around the turn of the century. Not the static alliance of throne and altar, but the dynamic world of industrial civilization and great-power imperialism determined their political horizon. Deeply influenced by the work of Houston Stewart Chamberlain, this younger generation gave place and priority to the power of Protestant culture and to the spiritual calling of the German race. Within the coordinates of political Protestantism, the turn to nation and race made them, at least in their own eyes, modern, experimental, abreast

[45] Coelestin Leuschner, *Das deutsche Reich und die kirchliche Frage* (Leipzig, 1893), 10–11.

[46] AKIEB S500.9.60 "Jahresbericht über die Generalversammlung des Evangelischen Bundes zu Bochum, 1894," 16.

of the latest theories (some would say mendacities) of their age. The "progressives" of the Protestant League included Otto Everling, who became director of the league in 1906, Johannes Hieber, leader of the Württemberg branch of the league, Paul Bräunlich, organizer of the Los von Rom movement, Hermann Kremers, director of the powerful Rhineland branch, and Friedrich Meyer, who, despite his advanced years, showed enough enthusiasm for Chamberlain's ideas to place him among the Protestant intellectuals of the newer ilk.[47] His language shot through with the vocabulary of racism and with visions of a final confrontation between Protestants and Catholics, Germanic peoples and other peoples, Meyer conceived of the Reformation as the period of history in which God revealed himself to the Germans (die Germanen).[48] Otto Everling, the most influential of the young generation, opened the general assembly of the Protestant League in 1908 by claiming: "Protestantism is the rock on which the German tribes [Stämme], the Germanic race is built. Protestantism is the basis of [the race's] power, of its moral uprightness, of its unflinching, victorious science, of its powerful artistic creativity."[49] This ideological shift from scripture to culture, from state to nation, even to race, and from Conservative to National Liberal redefined the terrain of confessional conflict. Although questions of parity and tolerance remained important, the central issues of the younger generation revolved around nation-

[47] The generational rift in the Protestant League was acute. The birth dates of the founding generation, who assumed a more cautious political role, tended to cluster around the 1830s. Among this generation one may count Beyschlag (1823), Friedrich Nippold (1838), August Wächter (1840), Gustav Warneck (1834), Leopold Witte (1836), Count Wintzingerode (1833), Coelestin Leuschner (1829), Paul Wurm (1829), and Karl Lechler (1820). Most of them came of political age at the time when Bismarck unified the empire, and many of them were well established when the Kulturkampf began. Conversely, the young generation of Protestant League leaders were in their teens or early twenties when the Kulturkampf was at its apex. The prominent members of this generation included Johannes Hieber (1862), Otto Everling (1864), Hermann Kremers (1860), Carl Mirbt (1860), Albert von Hackenberg (1852), Paul Bräunlich (1866), and J. F. Lehmann (1864). The birth date of Kurt Schindowski, who also belonged to the younger generation, could not be ascertained. Paul Hoensbroech, who was born in 1852, constitutes an exception, since he experienced the Kulturkampf as a Catholic. Friedrich Meyer (1840) should be counted among the older generation, but in worldview he was closer to Bräunlich and Everling than to Beyschlag or Wintzingerode.

[48] AKIEB PL Friedrich Meyer, "Mitteilungen vom Ausschuss zur Förderung der evangelischen Kirche in Österreich," 19 (1903): 13; 29 (1906): 2. Hermann Kremers, who had in 1896 described Martin Luther as the first "German Christian," would later, in October 1933, claim his earlier work to have been a forerunner of a Christian-influenced National Socialist ideology. See Hermann Kremers, Sammeln und Zerstreuen! Bericht und Rede bei der 44. Versammlung des rheinischen Hauptvereins des Evangelischen Bundes in Bonn am 23. u. 24 Oktober 1933 (Bonn, 1933), 7.

[49] Cited by Müller, "Der Evangelische Bund," 61.

ality problems in Germany's ethnic borderlands, both within the empire and outside it, and around the question of whether Germany could survive the Spencerian struggle of nations when the burden of ultramontane influence still weighed heavily upon German culture and politics.

Catholics, the Nation, and the Roots of Antagonism

The national and confessional ideology of German Catholics, quite unlike that of German Protestants, was born of resistance to the integrative potential of the new national state. Catholic intellectuals, whether exiled Jesuits or hardened particularists, imagined a different Germany—one rooted in past traditions, not future destinies, a nation that drew strength from diversity, not from a progressive march to higher cultural unity.[50] They argued for the political legitimacy of identities anterior to the national state—kinship, region, religious community—affiliations experienced as given, self-evident, and timeless.

In a wider cultural context, Clifford Geertz and Ed Shils have defined such affiliations as "primordial attachments": though rooted in identities of the past, primordial attachments became objects of political discourse and political mobilization precisely during periods of cultural modernization, usually as a reaction to forced centralization in the new states. In Germany, these affiliations—at once stubborn and volatile—stood in steadfast opposition to the political and cultural centralization that German liberals perceived to be necessary for the growth of a dynamic, modern state.[51]

[50] On Catholics and the German national state, there is now a rich and differentiated literature. See Altgeld, *Katholizismus, Protestantismus, Judentum*, 65–83; Nipperdey, *Religion im Umbruch*, 46–50; Rudolf Lill, "Die deutschen Katholiken und Bismarcks Reichsgründung," in *Reichsgründung 1870/71*, ed. Theodor Schieder and Ernst Deuerlein (Stuttgart, 1970), 345–65; George G. Windell, *The Catholics and German Unity, 1866–1871* (Minneapolis, 1954); Hans Maier, "Katholizismus, nationale Bewegung und Demokratie in Deutschland," *Hochland* 57 (1965): 318–33; Ernst Deuerlein, "Die Bekehrung des Zentrums zur nationalen Idee," *Hochland* 62 (1970): 432–49; Horst Gründer, "Nation und Katholizismus im Kaiserreich," in *Katholizismus, nationaler Gedanke und Europa seit 1800*, ed. Albrecht Langer (Paderborn, 1985), 65–88; and the classic statement, Rudolf Morsey, "Die deutschen Katholiken und der Nationalstaat zwischen Kulturkampf und Erstem Weltkrieg," *Historisches Jahrbuch* 90 (1970): 31–64. Nevertheless, we still lack a sophisticated cultural study of this problem. For a beginning, see Werner K. Blessing, *Staat und Kirche in der Gesellschaft. Institutionelle Autorität und mentaler Wandel in Bayern während des 19. Jahrhunderts.* (Göttingen, 1982).

[51] See Geertz, "The Integrative Revolution," in Geertz, *The Interpretation of Cultures*, 255–64; Ed Shils, "Primordial, Personal and Civil Ties," *British Journal of Sociology* 8 (1957): 130–45.

This was the heart of the matter—not whether Catholics wished to live in Großdeutschland or Kleindeutschland, a Germany that included Catholic Austria or one that did not, but what kind of state they were to live in, and how that state was to be defined. Georg Michael Pachtler, S.J., a prolific, if forgotten, Catholic political theorist, argued against a centralizing liberal state that strove to efface historical institutions.[52] For Pachtler, the "historical" included not only the church but also the "old division according to the venerable provinces" as well as a corporate social order, which "laid chains on the omnipotence of the state."[53] Similarly, the bishop of Mainz, Wilhelm Emmanuel von Ketteler, appealed in his pamphlet *Germany after the War of 1866* to "German freedoms," by which he meant the freedom of a man's conscience from the intrusion of state power.[54] He opposed "German freedom" to "French freedom," which he considered merely formal. And he argued that only when Germany returned to its peculiar form of freedom, best preserved in a society of estates, could "a new, healthy, vital, domestic political life on a Germanic foundation be developed."[55]

To the Catholic publicists who wrote for the journals *Stimmen aus Maria Laach* and *Historisch-politische Blätter*, the centralized, bureaucratic state was both cause and unfortunate consequence of an atomized, liberal, capitalist order characterized by inner strife. When Catholics looked to Spain, Italy, and Belgium, they did not, like the Protestant pastors, see poverty and illiteracy but rather a world breaking apart, marked in its outward manifestation by an endless succession of anticlerical violence, plundered monasteries, and despoiled holy sites. When viewed through Catholic eyes, the conflict between church and state, a Europewide phenomenon of the 1860s and 1870s, seemed a consequence of modern, liberal ideas of state- and nation-building.[56] It represented the intrusions of the "all-powerful state" into the hallowed domain of house and family, and, according to one pamphleteer, would end by dividing the German nation.[57] Similarly,

---

[52] Georg Michael Pachtler, S.J., "Das Nationalitätsprincip," *Stimmen aus Maria Laach* 4 (1873): 563.

[53] Ibid.

[54] Wilhelm Emmanuel von Ketteler, *Deutschland nach dem Kriege von 1866*, in *Sämtliche Werke und Briefe*, ed. Erwin Iserloh et al., vol. 1, pt. 2, *Schriften, Aufsätze und Reden 1867– 1870* (Mainz, 1978), 1–127 esp. 60–61, 64.

[55] Ibid.

[56] See "Der moderne Staat als Urheber des Verfalls der katholischen Staaten," *Historisch-politische Blätter* 70 (1872): 225–81. On the European dimension of the Kulturkampf, see Winfried Becker, "Der Kulturkampf."

[57] *Was lehrt das Christenthum über Patriotismus, und sind nach dieser Lehre die Katholiken "Vaterlandslose"?* vol. 7, pt. 12, in *Broschüren-Cyclus für das Katholische Deutschland* (Soest, 1872), 28.

Prussian militarism, an extreme manifestation of a general European problem, appeared to Catholic publicists as the modern state's answer to the social anomie created by a liberal, capitalist order and by the centralizing impulse of the national state itself.[58] The new German empire of 1871 was not therefore on a special path to modernity, a peculiar German *Sonderweg*. Rather, Catholics thought Germany to be characteristic of European countries marked by liberal, nationalist ascendancy.

It is in this context that we must understand the resistance of Catholic Germany to claims of the modern national state and not conflate this resistance, as historians often do, with pro-Austrian feeling or—though here the matter was more complex—with Catholic universalism.[59] Although these sentiments existed as well, one would have to look very far in the Second Empire before finding a German Catholic priest who truly believed a Catholic in Passau to be more akin to his coreligionist in Avignon than to his Protestant conational in Bayreuth, or for that matter, in Erfurt. As one ultramontane pamphleteer put it: "we too are German in word and deed, we are true to kaiser and Reich, we think and feel German"—but, he added with a dash of defiance, "we do not have to betray our religion in order to be patriots."[60]

The sense of Germanness cultivated in the Catholic subculture was conceived in a comparative, competitive field. Ketteler, the most influential Catholic author on questions of German national identity, affirmed "we can little forget that Germany was once the first nation of Europe and that it held the royal crown which represented the highest temporal power on earth."[61] In this assertion, he was echoed by countless Catholic writers, each cultivating his own peculiar combination of Catholic and German chauvinism. Bonifacius thus became the "apostle of our fatherland."[62] The Middle Ages, when there were no Protestants in Germany, were presented as a period of infinite

[58] Georg Michael Pachtler, S.J. [pseud. Annuaris Osseg], *Der Europäische Militarismus* (Amberg, 1875), 19–20. See also Philipp Wasserburg, *Gedankenspähne über den Militarismus* (Mainz, 1874).

[59] This is not to suggest that German Catholics did not have special ties with Austrian Catholics but that these special ties do not go far in explaining the ideological reaction of German Catholics to the new national state. For somewhat contrary views, see Windell, *The Catholics and German Unity*, and Rudolf Lill, "Großdeutsch und Kleindeutsch im Spannungsfeld der Konfessionen," in *Probleme des Konfessionalismus in Deutschland seit 1800*, ed. Anton Rauscher (Paderborn, 1984), 29–47.

[60] *Bonifacius-Broschüren*, vol. 2, pt. 1, *Katholische Kirche oder deutsche Nationalkirche* (Paderborn, 1871), 310–11.

[61] Ketteler, *Deutschland nach dem Kriege vom 1866*, 47.

[62] Preface to *Bonifacius-Broschüren*, Matthias Eberhard, bishop of Trier (Paderborn, 1873), 1.

German wealth and power.[63] Florian Riess, a Jesuit author who wrote for *Stimmen aus Maria Laach*, even argued that "Rome is not the enemy but the mother of the German nation."[64] That the German national identity of German Catholics was not, like that of German Protestants, closely bound to a specific political solution to the national question did not prevent Catholics from appealing to an exclusive idea of what it was to be German. In his polemic against Berthold Auerbach (the Jewish author of *Village Stories of the Black Forest*), Alban Stolz informed his Catholic readers that "a Jew can never become a native of the Black Forest even if, right after the destruction of Jerusalem, his ancestors moved to the Feldberg or settled in Todtnau."[65]

Initially, the foundation of the new empire with its Protestant majority did little to alter the national consciousness of German Catholics—quite the opposite. On Sedan Day, the first national holiday, the Catholic newspaper *Germania* reminded its readers of the "victory bells that sounded over to us from France last year" and insisted "ultramontane or not—we are all Germans, and we ultramontanes are Germans despite those who call us unpatriotic [*vaterlandslos*]."[66] It was not the foundation of the new empire as such but the manner in which liberal nationalists sought to confer legitimacy on the German national state that aroused the opposition of German Catholics. "How quickly it came to be," discerned one Catholic with dismay, "that the victory at Sedan was not celebrated as the triumph of the whole nation against the threatening enemy but rather as the conquest of the liberal party over the suppressed minority."[67]

Under the impact of the Kulturkampf, Catholics attempted to offer symbolic alternatives to what seemed to them a liberal, and in many respects Protestant, monopoly on national discourse. In this spirit *Germania* called on its readers in 1874 not only to desist from further celebrating Sedan Day but, in a juxtaposed article, to rally for the building of a Mallinckrodt monument to commemorate the recently deceased Center leader.[68] Symbolic battles over what could be counted as properly German spilled over into history, arts, and letters. For every treatise from a Protestant hand eulogizing King Gustav

[63] *Bonifacius-Broschüren*, vol. 4, *Macht der katholische Glaube die Leute arm?* (Paderborn, 1873), 7.

[64] Florian Riess, S.J., "Rom und die Anfänge Deutschlands," *Stimmen aus Maria Laach* 1 (1871): 405.

[65] Alban Stolz, *Kleinigkeiten, gesammelt von Anfang bis 1872* in *Gesammelte Werke*, vol. 8, 291.

[66] *Germania*, 1 September 1871.

[67] Ibid., 2 September 1876.

[68] Ibid., 1 September 1874.

Adolph of Sweden as the religious and military savior of Germany, there was a Catholic countertract on the destruction he wrought; for panegyrics to the "German Renaissance" in painting and in architecture, there were tributes to the Gothic style, not as a Catholic style, but as the most authentic German style, which however owed its expressive power to Catholicism; for volumes written on Goethe, there were books on Walter von der Vogelweide and, for the modern period, pamphlets on Görres and Droste-Hülshoff.[69]

Of the historical issues, the evaluation of the Middle Ages proved most contentious. Typically, Catholic historical pamphlets took the form of crassly uncritical apologetics. In a book entitled *Historical Lies*, Paul Majunke, the editor of *Germania*, defended the inquisition as well as the role of the church in late-medieval witch-hunting by smothering them in a warm blanket of sympathetic historicism.[70] There were, however, more serious attempts to reconsider the role of the Middle Ages for the course of German history. Against the prevailing and predominantly Protestant view that the period prior to the Reformation represented a long, dark age, Catholic historians, such as Johannes Janssen, argued that the late fifteenth century constituted a golden era of German history, and that the Reformation had caused an unnatural division in the unity of faith and people, one, moreover, that brought much destruction in its wake.[71] Pedantic, prudish, pro-

[69] See Onno Klopp, *Tilly, Gustav Adolf und die Zerstörung von Magdeburg* (Berlin, 1895); Paul Haffner, *Göthes Dichtung auf sittlichen Gehalt geprüft* (Frankfurt a.M., 1881); Ludwig Wattendorff, *Walter von der Vogelweide. Deutschlands größter Lyriker im Mittelalter* (Frankfurt a.M., 1894); Wilhelm Warnkönig, *Joseph von Görres. Ein Kampf für die Freiheit. Dem freien deutschen Volke geschildert* (Berlin, 1895); A. Zottmann, *Deutschlands größte Dichterin (Annette Freiin v. Droste-Hülshoff)* (Frankfurt a.M., 1897). For Catholic views on art, see August Reichensperger, *Vermischte Schriften über christliche Kunst* (Leipzig, 1856), and August Reichensperger, *Parlementarisches über Kunst und Kunsthandwerk* (Cologne, 1880), esp. 24 and 36. For a fascinating account of Reichensperger's carreer as an art critic, see Michael James Lewis, "August Reichensperger (1808–1895) and the Gothic Revival" (Ph.D. diss., University of Pennsylvania, 1989). On questions of great literature, Catholic critics often looked outside Germany. Shakespeare, for example, though Protestant, was deemed, after some discussion and a close reading of his moral positions, "spiritually Catholic." See M. Schuler, *Shakespeares Confession* (Berlin, 1899).

[70] Paul Majunke, Josef Galland, and Josef Krebs [Freunde der Wahrheit, pseud.], *Geschichtslügen. Eine Widerlegung landläufiger Entstellungen auf dem Gebiet der Geschichte*, rev. ed. (Paderborn, 1893), 222–23, 243–44.

[71] Johannes Janssen, *Geschichte des deutschen Volkes seit dem Ausgang des Mittelalters*, 8 vols. (Freiburg i. Br., 1879–94), esp. vol. 1, *Die allgemeinen Zustände des deutschen Volkes beim Ausgang des Mittelalters* (Freiburg, 1879). Like many Catholics who attempted to establish national traditions that were also Catholic, Janssen was not free from traditional German antagonisms toward other nations. See, for example, his pamphlet *Frankreichs Rheingelüste und deutschfeindliche Politik in früheren Jahrhunderten*, 2d ed. (Freiburg i. Br., 1883).

lific, Janssen was without peer in the Catholic milieu: all the Center party leaders read him; his multivolume *History of the German People since the End of the Middle Ages* was de rigueur for aspiring Catholic scholars; and, through historical pamphlets and the lessons and sermons of learned priests, he became common fare for countless Catholics of more modest station.[72] In his criticism of the prevailing Protestant views on German history, he was not alone. Onno Klopp, a Protestant from East Frisia who converted to Catholicism and wrote tracts for the Catholic cause, also attacked the "Prussian School" of historical writing: Klopp denounced Frederick II's invasion of Silesia as an act of naked power, and, in another work, he exonerated Tilly from the carnage of Magdeburg.[73]

It was in this spirit that Catholic intellectuals founded in 1876, on the occasion of the centennial of Joseph Görres' birth, the Görres Society for Educated Catholics. Originally intended as the Catholic counterpart to the Schiller centennial in 1859, the founding of the Görres Society must also be understood in the context of the Kulturkampf and the widespread denigration of Catholic learning.[74] Its initial purpose was to support Catholic legal, philosophical, and historical scholarship and to oppose the prevailing liberal and Protestant positions in the German world of learning with measured, reasoned, Catholic erudition. Under the leadership of Georg von Hertling, the Görres Society founded a number of academic journals and, starting in 1889, began to publish a Catholic encyclopedia, the *Staatslexikon*, which attempted to counter, concept for concept, the central tenets of the dominant culture.

The attempt to counter Protestant national traditions with Catholic erudition proved at best a limited success, however. In 1881, Hertling complained that "scholars of constitutional law who stand on Catholic ground can hardly be found in Germany."[75] To pen many of the legal articles for the first edition of the *Staatslexikon*, Hertling had to rely on Catholic priests. In the field of history, the initial attempts to bring a Catholic worldview to the interpretation of the past seemed equally inauspicious. In 1874, Klopp wrote Janssen that "we are lacking a his-

72 On Janssen, see Ludwig Freiherr von Pastor, *Aus dem Leben des Geschichtsschreibers Johannes Janssen* (Cologne, 1929).

73 Onno Klopp, *Der König Friedrich II. und die deutsche Nation* (Schaffhausen, 1860); Klopp, *Tilly, Gustav Adolph und die Zerstörung von Magdeburg.*

74 On the founding of the Görres Society (Görres Gesellschaft zur Pflege der Wissenschaft im Katholischen Deutschland), see Winfried Becker, *Georg von Hertling, 1843–1919,* vol. 1, *Jugend und Selbstfindung zwischen Romantik und Kulturkampf* (Mainz, 1981), 261–79.

75 Ibid., 274.

torical literature that is readable and imbued with the spirit of the Catholic worldview."[76] Twenty years later, the paucity of serious Catholic works on national history remained conspicuous—and this despite the founding, in 1880, of a Catholic historical journal, the *Historisches Jahrbuch*.[77] Still less successful was Peter Norrenberg's attempt to establish a canon of national literature that would reflect the concerns of Catholic culture. His *Universal History of Literature* was encyclopedic, multicultural, and wooden. In place of serious literary interpretation, he offered moral probity; for felicitous insight, he substituted Sunday school observation.[78] Part of the problem was talent. Regardless of his ambition, Norrenberg could not be counted as the Catholic equal of Rudolf Gottschall or Wilhelm Scherer, to name only two of the empire's leading Protestant historians of literature. Prejudice also played a part. Friedrich Meinecke's considered judgment, articulated in 1901, that "Catholic history professors are and remain a monstrosity" reflected not an extreme view but rather a professional consensus.[79] Neither Janssen nor Klopp ever received a university position—to say nothing of Norrenberg.

But beyond these formal obstacles to countering Protestant national traditions, a more serious problem presented itself. Here, of course, the historian can communicate only a subjective sense. But it would seem that in the late nineteenth century the Catholic confessional narration of the German past could not, like the Protestant, convincingly reflect recent German historical experience. So long as Catholics accepted the basic nationalist proposition that a politically unified Germany constituted a desirable achievement (and few questioned this as a matter of principle), and so long as they agreed on the great events

[76] Cited in Hans Schmidt, "Onno Klopp und die 'kleindeutschen Geschichtsbaumeister,'" in *Kirche, Staat und katholische Wissenschaft*, ed. A. Portmann-Tinguely (Paderborn, 1988), 390.

[77] It is perhaps indicative that Catholic historians wrote mainly about church and province, while the symbol that generated the most enthusiasm in the Catholic milieu was not a national hero but rather the pope. See Sperber, *Popular Catholicism*, 185–86, and Blessing, *Staat und Kirche*, 239–40. On the *Historisches Jahrbuch*, see "Programm der von der historischen Section der Görres-Gesellschaft zu gründenden Zeitschrift für Geschichte," appended to *Historisches Jahrbuch* 1, no. 1 (1880).

[78] On German literature, see Norrenberg, *Allgemeine Literaturgeschichte*, 174–455. For further attempts to construct a Catholic literary canon, see also Heinrich Keiter, *Theorie des Romans und der Erzählkunst* (Paderborn, 1876); Heinrich Keiter, *Katholische Erzähler der Neuzeit* (Paderborn, 1880); and Keiter, *Zeitgenössische Katholische Dichter Deutschlands*. Keiter also published a Catholic *Literaturkalender* because he believed that *Kürschners Literaturkalender* discriminated against Catholic literature.

[79] Cited in Ronald Ross, *Beleaguered Tower: The Dilemma of Political Catholicism in Wilhelmine Germany* (Notre Dame, 1976), 26.

in recent German history, and that in history it is great events that matter, they could not, in an age that made confession important, willfully disregard the Protestant faith of Schiller and Goethe, Frederick the Great and Wilhelm von Humboldt, Otto von Bismarck and Helmuth von Moltke. German Catholics could feel themselves both German and Catholic, but their Catholicism—despite the best efforts of Catholic polemicists—did not make them somehow more German.

Catholic historical and literary expression therefore manifested itself most strongly in regional cultures. It should not, for that reason, be underestimated. Surveying the literary field of Württemberg in 1887, the bibliographer Theodor Schott compared Catholic culture to the alternative culture of the socialists and considered that, together, they represented "the two most powerful movements affecting the inner life of the German people."[80] Like socialist culture, ultramontane culture was based on the partial rejection of German national culture. Schott observed: "It is well known how Catholic literature . . . increases and grows stronger from year to year. A new literary movement that opposes the essentially Protestant intellectual views that have thus far dominated in Germany is asserting itself more and more."[81]

Historians know very little about this movement, in part because it belongs to history's lost causes, in part because its power was regional. Moreover, it unfolded under clerical tutelage. In the Catholic part of Württemberg, 62 percent of all Catholic authors belonged to the clergy in 1887, and by 1914 priests still accounted for 49 percent.[82] There are few reliable guides to Catholic writing in this period. But by examining literary production, especially at the local and regional

[80] Theodor Schott, "Die Zeitungen und Zeitschriften Württembergs im Jahre 1886," in *Württembergische Jahrbücher für Statistik und Landeskunde*, vol. 3, ed. königliches statistisches Landesamt (Stuttgart, 1887), 27.

[81] Ibid.

[82] Even in Cologne, they made up 29% of Catholic authors in 1914. By authors I mean writers of books. In Württemberg in 1887, schoolteachers and university professors (23%) made up most of the rest of the authors. The remaining 15% included government officials, widows, and one journalist (total number = 79). In 1914, schoolteachers and professors constituted 28.8%, journalists 8.2%, free professionals 6.8%, civil servants 4.8%, and others 2% (total number = 146). In Cologne, the occupational structure of Catholic book writers in 1914 was as follows: teachers and professors 30%, clergy 29%, journalists 20%, free professionals 11%, civil servants 7%, and others 3% (total number = 158). The importance of secular professions in the Catholic culture of Cologne was, one may surmise, an important social factor putting Cologne in the vanguard of the "modernist heresy" in the Catholic literature debate that broke out before World War I. As we might expect, Württemberg was generally on the integralist side. For the statistical material on book writers, I have used Heinrich Keiter, ed., *Katholischer Literaturkalender* (Regensburg, 1891, 1914).

level, one can identify the concerns of this ultramontane culture. Figure 1 compares the subjects of published works of two separate cohorts of Catholic authors in Württemberg, one from 1887, the other from 1914. In both cohorts, the number of religious works produced outnumbered secular works. A measure of secularization in these years did set in, however. By 1914, historical works about the Catholic church no longer outnumbered books on secular history. Of greater importance, religious books, in the narrow sense, declined in num-

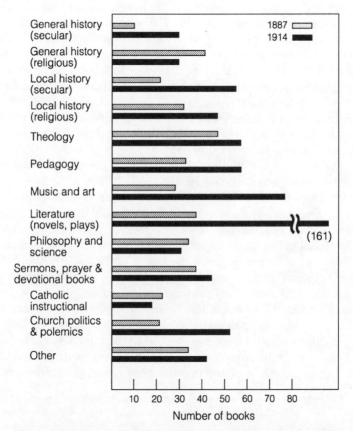

Book Production of Catholic Authors in Württemberg in 1887 (first bar) and 1914 (second bar)

Source: Katholischer Literaturkalender, ed. Heinrich Keiter (Regensburg, 1891 and 1914).

Note: To construct this chart from the entries of the Katholischer Literaturkalender, the names of the authors have been correlated with the Württemberg towns in which they lived (indexed in the back of the Literaturkalender) and the books they wrote.

ber. Catholic authors in 1914 produced proportionally fewer catechisms, prayer books, works of theology, and Catholic instructional
manuals than had Catholics in 1887. Conversely, the cohort of 1914
wrote more novels, plays, and literature. Most of this literature was
itself suffused by Catholic values so that one may suggest that, at
least in Württemberg, Catholicism was becoming more a matter of
culture and less purely a religious practice. Politics also became more
important to literary output. Despite the dismantling of the
Kulturkampf in Prussia, Catholics in Württemberg wrote more and
more about the uneasy relationship between church and state.

It is also useful to consider what Catholics in Württemberg did not
write. In the cohort of 1887, only one author wrote a book on the
national question, and that in 1848. No one wrote panegyrics to the
kaiser, to Germany's military heritage, or to the country's great cultural achievements. Among the books produced by the cohort of
1914, only a few such works are to be found. Even then, not one
pamphlet about Goethe was published. In general, Protestant poets
were shunned by both cohorts. Finally, national politics rarely served
as subject matter for polemical zeal.[83]

In the provinces, Catholic culture centered on regional themes: local saints, local religious custom, the land. Typically, Catholic authors
had local reputations. Thekla Schneider's poems of Lake Constance or
Max Hohnerlein's didactic plays for the Jesuit theater in Kempten
could hardly be considered serious literature outside the regional and
confessional milieu in which they were written. And yet such authors
were important to the regional identity of Catholics. It would be difficult to understand the peculiarities of Bavarian ultramontanism without reading the immensely popular but extremely coarse and acerbic
works of Konrad von Bolanden.[84] Similarly, Hessian Catholics knew
well the novels and polemical works of Phillip Lacius for their cunning disdain of liberal hypocrisy.[85] And in the Eifel, Georg Dasbach, a
"red chaplain" who controlled his own press imperium, worried censors, in part, because of the popularity of his often vitriolic pen.[86]

[83] The notable exception would, of course, have been Matthias Erzberger; but, because he lived in Berlin, he was not counted among the Württemberg authors.

[84] See for example, Konrad von Bolanden [Josef Bischoff], *Satan bei der Arbeit*
(Heiligenstadt, 1908); Konrad von Bolanden, *Die Sozialdemokraten und ihre Väter* (Mainz,
1894); and his novel, *Die Reichsfeinde* (Mainz, 1874).

[85] On Phillip Lacius [Philipp Wasserburg], see Stanley Zucker, "Philipp Wasserburg
and Political Catholicism in Nineteenth-Century Germany," *The Catholic Historical Review* 70, no. 1 (1984): 14–27.

[86] On Dasbach, see Hubert Thoma, *Georg Friedrich Dasbach: Priester, Publizist, Politiker*
(Trier, 1975); Ulrich Fohrmann, *Trierer Kulturkampfpublizistik im Bismarckreich. Leben und
Werk des Presskaplans Georg Friedrich Dasbach* (Trier, 1977).

Unlike Protestants, Catholics did not appeal to national identity or to the logic of German history in order to justify confessional polemics. This should not lead one to conclude that Catholics were somehow more tolerant than Protestants, or even that they were liberal in the sense of Gladstone.[87] The roots of Catholic intolerance lay elsewhere—not in the national organization of political Catholicism, nor in the national ideology of German Catholics, but rather in local life, in integralist pressure on piety, and in the periodic encyclicals that emanated from Rome.

At the local level, anti-Protestant sentiment could appeal to symbols and associations that made common sense to the regional population: in southern Württemberg, a predominantly agrarian area, Protestants were invariably portrayed as sly, urbane, and irreligious men from Stuttgart or Tübingen; in the Saarland, where the majority of the workers were Catholic, the preponderance of owners and managers Protestant, the prevailing image of the other confession suggested hardened, ill-spirited bosses consumed by their Protestant work ethic and indifferent to the plight of the Catholic poor.[88] Here, as Klaus Michael-Mallmann has shown, industrial disputes quickly became "a *Mixtum Compositum*" of religious, cultural, class, and political conflict.[89] Local factory owners understood this well enough. In Ottweiler, a confessionally mixed town northeast of Saarbrücken, the powerful Protestant employer, Freiherr von Stumm, forbade his Catholic workers to read the papers of the ultramontane Dasbach

[87] The latter view is presented in Winfried Becker, "Politischer Katholizismus und Liberalismus vom Kaiserreich zur Bundesrepublik," in Becker, ed., *Die Minderheit als Mitte. Die deutsche Zentrumspartei in der Innerpolitik des Reiches 1871–1933.* (Paderborn, 1986), 89–110. It is true that left-liberals and Center parliamentarians shared a common commitment to ensure certain negative freedoms, as Isaiah Berlin has defined them, against the encroachment of the state. But both sides started from radically different assumptions and had quite different ends in mind. On "negative freedom" see Isaiah Berlin, *Two Concepts of Liberty* (Oxford, 1959).

[88] On the antiurban, antiuniversity sentiment of Catholics in Württemberg, see David Blackbourn, *Class, Religion and Local Politics in Wilhelmine Germany: The Center Party in Württemberg before 1914* (Wiesbaden, 1980), 96, 99, 160–61. Blackbourn consciously plays down the confessional motives behind such sentiment. On this point, we are in disagreement. On the Saarland, see Klaus-Michael Mallmann, "Die neue Attraktivität des Himmels. Kirche, Religion und industrielle Modernisierung," in *Industriekultur an der Saar. Leben und Arbeit in einer Industrieregion, 1840–1914*, ed. Richard van Dülmen (Munich, 1989), 248. According to Mallmann, of the 70 managers who worked for the Saarbrücken Administration of Mines (*Bergwerkdirektion*) in 1903, all but 3 were Protestant. Conversely, among the miners, the ratio of Catholic to Protestant was roughly 3 to 1.

[89] Klaus-Michael Mallmann, "Ultramontanismus und Arbeiterbewegung im Kaiserreich. Überlegungen am Beispiel des Saarreviers," in *Deutscher Katholizismus im Umbruch zur Moderne*, ed. Wilfried Loth (Stuttgart, 1991), 80.

press because they "screamed rebellion against the other confession, against employers, against the officials and the government," and because "such papers are against everything that could be called authority, with the single exception of the authority of the priests and democracy."[90] The magistrate who filed the report added that the situation was similar in the Palatinate and in southern Germany.[91]

Indeed, it was. During the Reichstag election of 1903, the Stuttgart Catholic Sunday paper sent out a *"Wahlbrief"* spotted with bold-lettered terms that rendered further explanation to its readers superfluous: "Grassmann," "Hoensbroech," "Los von Rom." The list, quite long, went on.[92] To people outside the milieu, these terms may have meant little. But to even, or especially, the most ordinary and humble Catholic in southwest Germany, Robert Grassmann was well known as the author of a scurrilous pamphlet on Liguori's moral teaching, while Paul Hoensbroech, an ex-Jesuit, was vilified as the empire's most prolific antiultramontane publicist. For this Catholic audience, the words in bold print evoked a whole series of social, cultural, and political associations: all of them negative, all of them directed against Protestants.[93]

Anti-Protestant invective also poured forth from the Vatican. The Canisius Encyclical of 1897, in which Leo XIII compared Protestantism, the *"rebellio lutherania,"* to the plague, constituted only one of a series of papal affronts to the religious sensibilities of German Protestants.[94] Moreover, such slanders did not rest, dry and parched, in Latin encyclicals. Rather they made their way through both the Protestant and Catholic dailies in Germany and led, partly through the activity of the Protestant League, to mass antidefamation demonstrations.[95]

In Catholic apologetics, interconfessional dialogue was rarely carried on with great attention to the sensibilities of the other side. In Johannes Perronne's *Protestantism and the Rules of Faith*, a learned anti-

[90] LHAK 403/16008 District Magistrate Land to the president of the regency of Trier, 11.11.1906.

[91] Ibid.

[92] See 1903 *Wahlbrief vom Sonntagsblatt ans Katholische Volk*. The *Stuttgarter Katholisches Sonntagsblatt*, with a circulation of 72,000 in 1903, was easily the most popular Catholic weekly in southwest Germany.

[93] On confessional stereotypes in Württemberg, see Köhle-Hezinger, *Evangelisch-Katholisch*, 54–55. On the construction of confessional milieus, see more generally Urs Altermatt, *Katholizismus und Moderne. Zur Sozial- und Mentalitätsgeschichte der Schweizer Katholiken im 19. und 20. Jahrhundert* (Zürich, 1989).

[94] These pronouncements worried the Center as well. See StAK NL Bachem Nr. 37 Carl Bachem to state secretary of the Holy See, Cardinal Rampolla, 4.2.1900.

[95] Ibid.

Protestant treatise, the reader is informed that Protestantism in Germany is as a religion

> without faith, without a norm of faith, without unity, without a center, without leadership; it is marked by an obvious tendency to dissolution, to complete apostasy from faith, a forward progression toward death; we see before us a wild chaos, an absolute arbitrariness without any chance of aid, independence and servitude at once, an incomprehensible anomaly, a spiritual miscarriage.[96]

In Perrone's work, one discovers more about Martin Luther's alleged indecencies than about his theological propositions, more about the emergence of socialism and communism from Anabaptism than about sectarian differences. Perrone's chapter headings, far from subtle, revealed the flavor of his work: "Dissoluteness of Luther's Lifestyle after his apostasy:—his licentious being,—his sacrilegious marriage,—his shamelessness in speech,—his epicurean life.—His own admission that his teachings were nothing but deceit, lies and errors.—Premonition of his damnation."[97] To Protestants accustomed to a more discriminating theological palate, Perrone's philippics necessarily left a permanent bad taste.

While such polemics may strike us as extreme, they did, in fact, make their way into popular Catholic culture with considerably more ease than did complicated deliberations on doctrinal differences between the two religions.[98] In fact, scurrility played a significant role in popular aspersions cast across the confessional boundary. In cases of local, confessional conflict, the issue of Luther's private morality and specifically his marriage was often a subject of Catholic derision. Consider the case, one among many, of Anton Lerner, a Catholic peddler in Württemberg, who replied to the suggestion of the local Protestant pastor that the story of Saint Antonius is partly legend by saying: "Leave Saint Antonius in peace. He's different from your Luther, the greatest scoundrel [Lump], the biggest lecher [Hurenschlingel] that there ever was, who left the monastery with Käthe only to go whoring with her."[99]

---

[96] Johannes Perrone [Giovanni Perrone], Der Protestantismus und die Glaubensregel. Dritter oder geschichtlich-sittlicher Theil (Regensburg and Mainz, 1856), 298.

[97] Ibid., table of contents.

[98] Often, such criticisms entered popular culture through locally published catechisms. See, for example, Controvers-Katechismus oder wahrheitsgemäße und leicht verständliche Darstellung der Unterscheidungslehre (Kempten, 1899), which reproduces many of Perrone's moral criticisms of Luther.

[99] LKAS 26/417 Case Nr. 79. District attorney (Staatsanwaltschaft) of Rottweil, 30.4.1908.

In 1889, a group of conservative integral Catholics, who were primarily responsible for the contentious tone of Catholic tracts on confessional questions, attempted to establish an anti-Protestant mass organization. Led by Friedrich von Loë and Friedrich Carl von Fechenbach, the Catholic League would match, point by point, the polemics of its Protestant counterpart.[100] Ill-fated from the start, the organization would have been stillborn were it not for Bishop Korum of Trier, who supported the idea and pressed the Vatican for help. In a memorandum written in February 1890, Korum proposed that Catholic publicists in Germany collaborate with the Jesuits in order to counter the blasphemous claims of the Protestant League as well as the aspersions cast on Catholic historians by the Society for Reformation History. Since, as he was convinced, the German government "secretly encouraged" the anti-Catholic movement, Korum counseled the Holy See to desist from making further diplomatic concessions to the German empire, at least until the Protestant League ceased its agitation.[101] But Windthorst, the sensible and revered leader of the Center party, opposed the plan, in part because he disliked confessional polemics, in part because he mistrusted the integralist supporters of the Catholic League.[102] He also believed that existing Catholic organizations sufficed to defend the interests of Catholics. On 21 September 1889, he wrote Peter Reuß, his liaison to the church hierarchy: "I am *at this time* not yet for the establishment of a Catholic League."[103] In fact, he never warmed to the idea, choosing instead to outmaneuver his integralist opponents by influencing the founding, in 1890, of the People's Association for Catholic Germany, an organization more interested in solving the social problem than in engaging in *guerres des plumes* with Protestant pastors.[104] The integralists, however, did not let the matter rest. In 1890, they began to publish Catholic Pamphlets for Defense and Instruction (*Katholische Flugschriften zur Wehr und Lehr*), a series that did not inspire confidence by dint of its balanced approach to confessional problems. Alone the titles in this series—*The Boiling Blood* (on the Protestant League), *The Character of a Protestant Polemicist*—suggested that, if there were to be a war of pens, the resulting disputation would be anything but polite.[105]

---

[100] On the Catholic League, see Margaret Lavinia Anderson, *Windthorst*, 391–93.

[101] BAT NL Korum 108/383 Bishop Felix Korum, "Memoire sur les agissements de l'association évangélique, et la persecution sourde organisée contre les Catholiques en Allemagne," 3.2.1890.

[102] Margareet Lavinia Anderson, *Windthorst*, 391.

[103] BAT NL Reuss 105/1582 Ludwig Windthorst to Peter Alexander Reuß, 21.9.1889.

[104] Margaret Lavinia Anderson, *Windthorst*, 392–93.

[105] For a taste, see Lobgott Brodgut, *Das "wallende Blut" zur Wahrung der prote-*

If both Catholic and Protestant confessional ideology shored up internal differences within the respective religious communities, the impact of nationalism was not so self-evidently of one die. In Protestant Germany, national ideology, when supported with confessional logic, exacerbated differences between the two confessions. Among Catholics, however, confessional antipathy toward Protestants did not, in the period under consideration, manifest itself in a nationalist discourse. "German freedoms," as Ketteler had put it, were about the preservation of Christianity, not Catholicism itself. The German Catholic vision of a Christian state could be conceived as marginalizing Jews or Social Democrats but not Württemberg Pietists or Silesian Lutherans.[106] Catholic intolerance toward Protestants, quite prevalent at the local level, was never part of the Center party's positive program. Ludwig Windthorst, in the words of his biographer Margaret Anderson, felt "disgusted by this kind of confessional polemic."[107] His successors in the 1890s, men such as Adolf Gröber, Peter Spahn, Felix Porsch, Carl and Julius Bachem, Georg von Hertling, and Ernst Maria Lieber, expended considerable effort persuading Rome to exercise prudence in its anti-Protestant polemics. In February 1900, Carl Bachem implored the Vatican to avoid pronouncements, especially in the semiofficial *Osservatore Romano*, that could encourage "hate and prejudice" against Catholics and Jesuits in Germany.[108] He especially worried about the reaction of the Protestant League and about the possibility that the Vatican's uninterrupted invective would "incite a new Kulturkampf."[109] Intolerance, as Carl Bachem well realized, impeded Catholic integration into a national community with which he, and the generation of Center parliamentarians that emerged in the 1890s, increasingly came to identify.

The slow change in Catholic attitudes toward the collective aims of the German national state began in the 1880s with Catholic engagement in German colonialism. Partly through the antislavery campaign, partly through the missionary activity of German Jesuits, Catholic Germany became, for the first time, involved in the new national

---

stantischen Interessen. Zu Nutz und Frommen des Christenvolkes dargestellt, 2d ed. (Berlin, 1890); Charakterkopf eines protestantischen Polemikers (Berlin, 1892); Die Hexenangst des Evangelischen Bundes vor den katholischen Klosterfrauen (Berlin, 1898).

[106] On ideas of the Christian state, see Tal, *Christians and Jews in Germany*, esp. 121–59.

[107] Margaret Lavinia Anderson, *Windthorst*, 391.

[108] StAk NL Bachem Nr. 37 Carl Bachem to secretary of the Holy See, Cardinal Rampolla, 4.2.1900.

[109] Ibid.

state's "civilizing mission."[110] Although economic factors also played a role in Catholic involvement, it is of far greater significance to understand that German Catholics could now couple their religious sentiment with what they thought a positive, national contribution. In 1894, Ernst Lieber proclaimed before the Reichstag: "There are great German-national and great universal-cultural tasks to solve in our colonial policy."[111] And, looking back, Carl Bachem wrote "that from the very beginning the Center assumed the standpoint that (colonial policy) should be supported not so much for material reasons but far more for the goal of Christianizing and cultivating the African natives."[112]

As the relation between church and state altered, so too did the national and confessional position of German Catholics. The scene of conflict shifted from questions concerning the omnipotent state and its repressive measures against the Catholic church to questions concerning civil society and the relations between the two confessions. It is in this new context that a subtle but significant change in the national sentiment of German Catholics occurred. To the new generation of Catholic Center leaders, nationalism was no longer an ideology, like socialism or liberalism, to be countered point by point, but a feeling to be expressed, if with caution and with reserve. Unlike some conservative Catholics, whose national sentiment was wedded to dynastic fealty, this generation of Catholic parliamentarians appealed increasingly to specifically German, even Prussian traditions. In the 1892 edition of the *Staatslexikon*, the German-Catholic encyclopedia, Carl Bachem lauded Otto von Bismarck as the "greatest German statesman of the modern age," an evaluation telling enough when we consider the possible Catholic alternative—Metternich.[113] Moreover, the nationalist assumptions that pervaded the public life of Wilhelmi-

---

[110] On the antislavery movement, see Horst Gründer, "'Gott will es.' Eine Antisklavereibewegung am Ende des 19. Jahrhunderts," *Geschichte in Wissenschaft und Unterricht* 28 (1977): 210–24. For the centrality of this engagement for Catholic national consciousness, see Gründer, "Nation und Katholizismus im Kaiserreich," 75. For a succinct treatment of the Center's position, one may consult Hans Pehl, "Die deutsche Kolonialpolitik und das Zentrum (1884–1914)" (Ph.D. diss., Frankfurt, 1934). On Windthorst's skepticism about the Center's involvement, see Margaret Lavinia Anderson, *Windthorst*, 382–84.

[111] Cited in Pehl, "Die deutsche Kolonialpolitik und das Zentrum," 7.

[112] Cited in ibid., 8. For the actual engagement of Catholic missionaries in the colonies, see the important study of Horst Gründer, *Christliche Mission und deutscher Imperialismus. Eine politische Geschichte ihrer Beziehung während der deutschen Kolonialzeit (1884– 1914) unter besonderer Berücksichtigung Afrikas und Chinas* (Paderborn, 1982).

[113] Carl Bachem cited in Morsey, "Die deutschen Katholiken und der Nationalstaat," 60.

nian Germany increasingly influenced the Catholic subculture. In 1897, Karl Muth began his literary assault on Catholic writers by denouncing the sentimentality (*Gefühlswärme*) of Catholic novelists, the vast majority of whom, as he discerned, were women.[114] The founder of *Hochland*, a German Catholic literary magazine, Muth argued that only a more objective, bold, and masculine style of writing would allow Catholics, who had for so long been literary outsiders, to contribute to national literature.[115] In history, Martin Spahn wrote nationalist tracts virtually indistinguishable from those of his Borussian colleagues.[116] And in theology, Hermann Schell assumed, in a celebrated book entitled *Catholicism as the Principle of Progress*, the veracity of what had hitherto been a Protestant, or in any case a German nationalist, dichotomy between rising Germanic peoples and declining Latins.[117]

Carl Bachem, Ernst Lieber, Peter Spahn, and Windthorst's other successors continued to oppose "extreme nationalism" but rarely the fundamental assumptions of German nationalism itself. In nationality policy, they argued against harsh anti-Polish measures but affirmed the principle of Germanization. On the naval bills, they sometimes dragged their heels, but mainly because they feared that the resulting financial burden weighed too heavily on their constituents. Moreover, a number of leading Center parliamentarians, including Ernst Lieber and Adolf Gröber, supported the Kaiser's navy, not out of opportunism, but out of conviction.[118] Their nationalism was essentially conservative. Partly, this conservative nationalism reflected a history of ideological opposition to the homogenizing potential of the liberal national state; partly, it was a consequence of the nature of the inte-

[114] Karl Muth [pseud. Veremundus], *Steht die katholische Belletristik auf die Höhe der Zeit*, 2d ed. (Mainz, 1898), 1–2. Muth calculated the proportion of women to men among Catholic novelists to be 6 to 1.

[115] Ibid., 37.

[116] See especially Martin Spahn, *Deutsche Lebensfragen* (Kempten, 1914).

[117] Hermann Schell, *Der Katholizismus als Prinzip des Fortschritts*, 3d ed. (Würzburg, 1897). On the significance of this work, see Gründer, "Nation und Katholizismus im Kaiserreich," 72.

[118] Peter Winzen, *Bülows Weltmachtkonzept. Untersuchungen zur Frühphase seiner Außenpolitik 1897–1901* (Boppard am Rhein, 1977), 117–18. National issues, such as support for army and navy bills, threatened repeatedly to tear the seams that held the Center party together. But the details of the Center's policies toward Germany's military bills are well known and will not be recounted here. See (for the period until 1901) John K. Zeender, *The German Center Party, 1890–1906* (Philadelphia, 1976), and Herbert Gottwald, "Zentrum und Imperialismus" (Ph.D. diss., University of Jena, 1966). For the later period, see Stig Förster, *Der doppelte Militarismus. Die deutsche Heeresrüstungspolitik zwischen Status-quo-Sicherung und Aggression 1890–1913* (Stuttgart, 1985), and, in great detail, Wilfried Loth, *Katholiken im Kaiserreich* (Düsseldorf, 1984).

gration process itself. The "nationalization" of German Catholics proved an extremely uneven process, marked more by division and intra-Catholic discord than by general consensus on what could count as both national and legitimately Catholic. Moreover, Catholic integration brought forth an ideological reaction among Protestants who wondered about the consequences of this integration for the character of a national state whose glorious history had hitherto seemed an exclusive product of Protestant achievements. Integration, as Catholic Center leaders would learn, did not merely repress confessional conflict but rather brought it to the fore.

3

Religious Conflict and Social Life

WHAT did it matter? Of what consequence were the speculations, often sophomoric, of a wayward parish priest about the nature of his Germanness? Self-evidently, the relationship between religious and national identity was a subject of importance to pastors—but did it matter to the people? The simple answer to these questions must be yes, it did matter, and it mattered much more than German historians until recently have been willing to admit. For religion, like class, was a central, defining category for imperial German citizens, whether Protestant or Catholic. But there is also a complex answer to these questions: that religion mattered to some much more than it mattered to others, that confessional conflict possessed a complex geography of its own, that it was often reinforced by other tensions, by class, by gender, by urban-rural, by regional, by ethnic tensions. Moreover, confessional conflict took place within the context of profound historical change: irreversible population shifts that changed confessional landscapes, social and demographic mobility that brought Catholics and Protestants together in common space, and secularization.

Driven by industrialization, the reality of these transformations was marked less by the gradual unity of their sweep than by the swift, uneven nature of their strokes. Between the 1870s and 1900, in a span of less than a lifetime, a primarily agrarian state became a country in which the principal mode of production was industrial.[1] Conversely, integration—the creation of a community of meaning, a shared culture between Protestants and Catholics—proceeded slowly, staggeringly, hardly keeping apace of Germany's swift, if erratic, economic growth. The reemergence of confessional conflict in the late nineteenth century must be understood in the context of this unevenness—not as an atavism in an otherwise modernizing society, but rather as an integral part of the complexities of the jagged, irregular process by which German lands became a modern, secular, increasingly integrated, nationally cohesive polity.

---

[1] Wehler, *Das deutsche Kaiserreich*, 41.

The "Invisible Boundary"

What initially impresses is the persistence of confessional difference, the tenacity of the divide. The French historian Etienne François has aptly called the line separating Protestants from Catholics an "invisible boundary" dividing worlds similar on the surface, but beyond which lay foreign countries—people did things differently there.[2] Differences between Catholics and Protestants manifested themselves at many levels—in the choice of proper names, in dress, in folklore, in mobility, in rates of endogamy and of fertility, in educational levels, in what people heard, experienced, and, perhaps most impressively, what they read.

This was an old story, though one largely ignored by historians of German literature and culture. In the late eighteenth century, Friedrich Nicolai observed, upon his visit to the confessionally divided city of Augsburg, that "when a Protestant gets a look at one of these Augsburg Catholic publishing catalogues, he finds names of which he has never heard. When he reads these books, he must believe that he is in a different world."[3] A century thereafter, deep divisions between the "print cultures" of the two confessions endured, their contours perhaps less distinct, the worlds that they separated perhaps somewhat less strange. Nevertheless, they persisted.

They persisted, in part, as consequence of the circumscribed reach of German national literature. Although illiteracy had all but vanished in the imperial period and the reading public had become, by 1900, very wide, the vast majority of people continued to consume roughly hewn, popular literature.[4] In 1880, August Lammers, editor of the

---

[2] Etienne François, *Die unsichtbare Grenze. Protestanten und Katholiken in Augsburg 1648–1806* (Sigmaringen, 1991).

[3] Cited by François, *Die unsichtbare Grenze*, 132.

[4] By the 1870s, absolute illiteracy had already fallen to a very low rate in both Prussia and the empire. Official Prussian statistics put illiteracy, measured by the ability of army recruits to sign their names, at 4.6% in 1873, 2.3% in 1880, 0.8% in 1890. Catholics fared somewhat worse than Protestants, but this was probably due to counting Polish Catholics in the statistics without differentiating according to mother tongue. See Rudolf Engelsing, *Analphabetentum und Lektüre* (Stuttgart, 1973), 97–98. By the turn of the century, illiteracy had virtually vanished in the empire. In Württemberg, for example, 99.2% of the prison convicts could both read and write. See *Handbuch für die Statistik Württembergs* (Stuttgart, 1903), 164. The reading public was somewhat smaller, however. Rudolf Schenda estimates it to have been 25% of the population above 6 years of age in 1800; thereafter it rose to 40% in 1830, 75% in 1870, and 90% in 1900. See Rudolf Schenda, *Volk ohne Buch. Studien zur Sozialgeschichte der populären Lesestoff 1770–1910* (Frankfurt a.M., 1970), 444–45. See also Reinhard Wittmann, *Buchmarkt und Lektüre im 18. und 19. Jahrhundert* (Tübingen, 1982), 199–200. Even these statistics may be optimis-

literary journal *Nordwest*, estimated that of roughly 50 million reading Germans in both Austria and imperial Germany, 20 million, or 40 percent, read only prayer books, catechisms, breviaries, and almanacs. The rest could and did also read newspapers; of this group perhaps 10 million readers, or 20 percent of the total reading population, consumed more complex literature: journals, magazines, popular novels, and political pamphlets. Only 4 percent, he thought, read German national literature.[5] Although these last estimates were probably overly optimistic, the general impression offered by Lammers was accurate. Reading habits limited the reach of national literature. Even when such literature was transmitted through popular magazines, its audience, at the very best, could count for between 10 and 20 percent of the adult population in the 1870s and 1880s. The *Gartenlaube*, the most successful magazine of high culture in imperial Germany, sold 400,000 copies at its peak in 1874 and reached, according to one historian, 2 million readers.[6] Similarly, the realist novels of this period enjoyed a wide but still limited public to which they could appeal. Gustav Freytag's *Debit and Credit*, surely one of the most popular novels of German high literature, sold an estimated 186,000 copies between 1855 and 1915, placing it in a crowded field with the popular literature of both Protestantism and Catholicism.[7] Even national newspapers did not penetrate the barriers to a unified national culture erected by confessional, regional, and class divisions. Edged out of the market by a myriad of local, political, and confessional newspapers, the *Frankfurter Zeitung*, for example, only had 1,208 subscribers in the state of Württemberg in 1886.[8]

---

tic. In 1866 the *Deutsche Schriftstellerzeitung* considered "far more than half the population lost to literature." Cited in Wittmann, *Buchmarkt und Lektüre*, 200.

[5] Engelsing, *Analphabetentum und Lektüre*, 119–20.

[6] Ibid., 119. There is now a rich scholarship on popular literature. For recent introductions, see Reinhard Wittmann, *Geschichte des deutschen Buchhandels* (Munich, 1991), and Georg Jäger, "Medien," in *Handbuch der deutschen Bildungsgeschichte*, ed. Christa Berg (Munich, 1991), vol. 4, 473–99.

[7] For the popularity of *Soll und Haben* see T. E. Carter, "Freytag's Soll und Haben: A Liberal National Manifesto as a Best-Seller," *German Life and Letters* 21, no. 4 (1968): 328. Significantly, its popularity doubled during the Wilhelminian era. For a comparison with Christian literature, see Klaus Müller-Salget, *Erzählung für das Volk. Evangelische Pfarrer als Volksschriftsteller im Deutschland des 19. Jahrhunderts* (Berlin, 1984), 116–23. On the popularity of Catholic almanacs generally, see Ludwig Rohner, *Kalendergeschichte und Kalender* (Wiesbaden, 1978), 315–20; and on the *Regensburger Marienkalender* specifically, Engelsing, *Analphabetentum und Lektüre*, 118. On the confiscation of this almanac, see LHAK 403/7144 "Verzeichnis der im Gebiete des Preußischen Staates im Jahre 1893 auf Grund des Paragraph 56 Nummer 10 der Reichsgewerbeordnung vom Kolportagebetrieb ausgeschlossenen Druckschriften, anderen Schriften und Bildwerke."

[8] The *Frankfurter Zeitung* lost out not so much to other sophisticated newspapers

Beneath a common national culture, which was unified but thin, lay a denser cultural landscape marked less by unity than by class, confessional, and regional division. This divided culture became more apparent as one moved down the social ladder to artisans, shopkeepers, farmers, and to industrial workers. Let us, however, consider only the first three of these groups. Here, among the people as they were imagined by nationalist intellectuals, the division between the cultures of the two confessions was very basic and began with what Protestants and Catholics read.

In small cities, towns, and rural areas, confessional reading continued to predominate. Aside from local newspapers, which typically appealed to a distinct confessional or political audience, most farmers and townsmen read only what they possessed and what they could borrow from lending libraries. From a register of wills in Feldenbach, a small Protestant town in Württemberg, one may get a sense of the kinds of books passed on from generation to generation between 1650 and 1850. Of 4,539 books listed, 4,487 were religious works.[9] Until the end of the nineteenth century, religious works still formed the mainstay of the home libraries of townsmen. In 1894, the folklorist Elard Meyer surveyed books in the homes of Protestants and Catholics in rural areas of Baden. Aside from works of superstition, Meyer found, in Protestant households, Luther's homilies and prayer books from the Protestant revival movement of the 1840s. In Catholic homes, he discovered the almanacs of Alban Stolz and the novels of Christoph v. Schmidt as well as Counter-Reformation works on the life of Jesus and Mary, and, in almost every household, a book about the apparition of the Blessed Virgin at Lourdes.[10]

The most thorough regional survey of the reading habits of Protestants corroborates this general impression of a cultural landscape still dominated by confessional concerns. In 1889, the Baden State Society for Inner Mission distributed questionnaires to pastors in deaneries requesting reports on what Protestants in small towns and in the countryside read.[11] According to these reports, few people owned

---

with a national focus, such as the *Schwäbische Merkur*, as it did to the 128 other smaller newspapers, most of which had a circulation of between 1,000 and 4,000 copies. See Theodor Schott, "Die Zeitungen und Zeitschriften Württembergs im Jahre 1886," in *Württembergische Jahrbücher für Statistik und Landeskunde* (1887), pt. 3, 36, 55–58.

[9] Angelika Bischoff-Luithlen, "Alte Tröster im Bauernhaus," *Beiträge zur Volks- und Heimatkunde* (1971): 65–66.

[10] Elard Hugo Meyer, *Badisches Volksleben im 19. Jahrhundert* (Strasbourg, 1900), 351–57.

[11] *Gesetz und Verordnungsblatt der Evangelischen Kirche in Baden* (hereafter GVEKB), 1889, vol. 2, 14–15.

"secular" books.[12] Yet, "with very few exceptions, Protestant families possessed the Bible, a New Testament, a hymn book, and the trusty old devotional and prayer books."[13] They also read political newspapers, "even in the smallest communities." Political papers were often supplemented by such immensely popular Christian Sunday papers as the *Stuttgarter Evangelisches Sonntagsblatt*, which, with a circulation of 125,000 in 1886, easily ranked as the most popular single newspaper in southwest Germany.[14] Almanacs also found their way "into every house."[15] Like the Christian Sunday papers, many of these almanacs combined religious edification with practical suggestions for house and field as well as offering political advice. Because books continued to be expensive, lending libraries influenced the literature read by poorer people.[16] In small towns these lending libraries were usually set up by the local pastor, who ensured that reading material would have a religious bent.[17] They were, accordingly, replete with the works of W. O. Horn, Julius Hoffmann, Otto Glaubrecht, Oskar Höcker, Gustav Nieritz, and Emil Frommel— pastors who wrote popular works of religious orientation "for the people."[18] By contrast, national illustrated magazines (*Gartenlaube*, *Daheim*, *Über Land und Meer*) were reportedly read, "albeit infrequently."[19]

That the reading of the lower and middle strata of the rural and small-town Protestant population was heavily confessional does not

[12] *GVEKB*, 1890, vol. 5, 38–39.

[13] Ibid. The most common devotional books were Johann Arndt, *Wahres Christhentum*, Johann Friedrich Stark, *Tägliches Gebetbuch*, Immanuel Gottlob Brastberger, *Evangelische Zeugnisse der Wahrheit*, Ludwig Hofacker, *Erbauungs- und Gebetbuch für alle Tage*, Sixtus Carl Kapff, *Gebetbuch und Communionbuch*, Karl Gerok, *Palmblätter*, and a book by Christian Gottlieb Blumhardt that I could not identify.

[14] For circulation figures, see Schott, "Die Zeitungen und Zeitschriften Württembergs im Jahre 1886," 58.

[15] *GVEKB*, 1890, vol. 5, 38–39. Almanacs were inexpensive enough so that even poor peasants could buy them. See Müller-Salget, *Erzählung für das Volk*, 122. According to Wittmann, *Buchmarkt und Lektüre*, 202, almanacs were for years the only reading material of the agrarian lower classes.

[16] Wittmann, *Buchmarkt und Lektüre*, 142–43; and on this subject generally, see Georg Jäger, "Die deutsche Leihbibliothek im 19. Jahrhundert. Verbreitung—Organisation— Verfall," *Internationales Archiv für Sozialgeschichte der deutschen Literatur* 2 (1977): 96–133.

[17] In still more rural areas, "the pastor gets the books and lends them out." J. Lauterbacher, "Was die schwäbischen Bauern lesen," *Im Neuen Reich*, 10 (1880): 546. See also Rainer Marbach, *Säkularisierung und sozialer Wandel im 19. Jahrhundert. Die Stellung von Geistlichen zu Entkirchlichung und Entchristlichung in einem Bezirk der hannoverischen Landeskirche* (Göttingen, 1978), 161.

[18] *GVEKB*, 1890, vol. 5, 38–39.

[19] Ibid.

mean that it waxed anti-Catholic. On the contrary, Protestant popular literature, whether the novels of Otto Glaubrecht or old devotional books such as Arndt's *True Christianity,* emphasized practical Christianity shorn of dogmatic quarrel. Glaubrecht, for example, believed that good popular literature should be religious but not praise one confession over another.[20] Still, there remained in the popular reading material of Protestant Germany enough anti-Catholic material to reinforce centuries of mistrust. In almanacs such as the *Lahrer Hinkende Bote* and in Sunday Christian weeklies, anti-Catholic expositions mixed easily with a confessionally informed sense of national identity. Such anti-Catholicism tended, however, to be beholden to traditional stereotypes (anti-Jesuit sentiment), to be concentrated on specific "ultramontane transgressions" (especially with regard to mixed marriages), and, in the case of the Christian weeklies, to be confined to the Protestant retelling of Germany's confessional history. Thus while anti-Catholicism permeated this literature, it was not central to it.

Similar regional surveys of Catholic reading were never undertaken. But there is strong impressionistic evidence to suggest that the Catholic milieu mirrored the propensity to confessional reading demonstrably evident in Protestant areas. Here too priests attempted to control reading material, either by strongly discouraging villagers from reading liberal newspapers or by judging the suitability of works to be read.[21] In 1899, the clergy of Catholic Württemberg even conferred on the question of whether the Old Testament was fit reading for parishioners and decided that, except in special cases and then with guidance, it was not.[22] Although the educated laity may have read proscribed books anyway, the impact of clerical tutelage on the culture of the pious, especially on farmers and small-town artisans, should not be underestimated. Indeed, this self-censorship defined, in part, what it was to be Catholic. In *Juniper-Spirit against the Basic Evils of the World: Stupidity, Sin and Suffering*, the almanac writer Alban Stolz asserted: "When I come into a strange house and see lying on the table certain typical newspapers, journals, and heralds of the

---

[20] Müller-Salget, *Erzählung für das Volk*, 127.

[21] See, for example, Franz Hülskamp's speech, "Gegen die Farblose Presse," in *Generalversammlung der Katholiken Deutschlands. Stenographische Protokolle.* (Dortmund, 1896), 206–13. See also *Katechismus für den Wähler* (Freiburg, Switzerland, 1884) in GLA 236/14882, question number 84: "What is, then, one of the most important issues of our time? Answer: it is the propagation of the Catholic press and especially Catholic newspapers."

[22] *Pastoralblatt für die Diözese Rottenburg* 21 (November 1899): 1. See also *Das Bibellesen auf eigene Hand* in *Bonifacius-Broschüren* (Paderborn, 1890).

stripe of the old *Badische Landeszeitung*, or *Kladderadatsch*, then I know what to make of it; as I know the religion of a house with the Lahr almanac on the wall."[23] Catholic, this house was not.

Catholic popular literature functioned differently than Protestant popular literature. Though this must remain a subjective judgment, it seems that the popular literature of Catholicism more frequently and more aggressively denigrated the other confession than did Protestant popular literature. In this sense, it might be argued that it shared elements in common with the polemical literature of Protestant high culture: both consistently appealed to cultural values specific to the two confessions and, in doing so, opposed them. The graver cultural division was not, then, simply between Protestants and Catholics, though the two groups did not share the same print culture, but, more specifically, between Catholic popular culture, which assumed now particularistic, now universal hues, and Protestant high culture, which had become largely coterminous with German national culture.

Secularization

The persistence of this elementary division occurred in a society that, while by no means secular, was becoming increasingly secularized. Secularization refers to a historical process by which men and women come to abandon a worldview that orders material and spiritual life according to beliefs and practices of established religion.[24] In this definition, secularization is a matter of what people believe, how fervently they believe it, and how tightly they conform to established practice in order to express their belief. It is commonly assumed that in nineteenth-century Europe secularization followed an essentially linear path. An agrarian world ordered by religious ritual and practice gradually became a differentiated, industrial society emancipated from religious belief. This picture is not completely false: in the long

---

[23] Alban Stolz, *Wachhold Geist gegen die Grundübel der Welt: Dummheit, Sünde und Elend,"* in Stolz, *Gesammelte Werke*, vol. 12 (Freiburg, i. Br., 1886), 71–72. Stolz advocated Catholic newspapers but also pointed out to his readers that "actually a Christian family lives most peacefully without reading newspapers."

[24] In recent years the term "secularization" has come under criticism for two reasons: the first pertains to its use as a normative principle of modernity (see the critique in Hans Blumberg, *Säkularisierung und Selbstbehauptung* [Frankfurt a.M., 1974]); the second concerns its loose employment as a linear description of the plight of religion in the processes of modernization (see the astute comments in H. Lübbe, *Säkularisierung, Geschichte eines ideenpolitischen Begriffs* [Freiburg i.Br., 1965].)

run, religious observance declined over the course of the nineteenth century. But this image of the long, downward slope of religiosity, Max Weber's "disenchantment of the world," obscures as much as it illuminates. For it hides a history of periodic religious revival and religious conflict, which, if such matters may seem distant and alien to us now, were nevertheless central cultural events to the people who experienced them.

The place of theology in nineteenth-century German scholarship and literature provides a good example of the persistence of the religious imagination in a secularizing society. In terms of the numbers of titles published, theology was a relatively small field at the beginning of the nineteenth century. But by the middle of the century it had become the preeminent area of literary production in the German book market. It was followed by belles lettres, works on history and government, pedagogical books, and economic literature. Theology lost this position in 1871 and declined steadily thereafter.[25] Yet even this decline should not blind us to the continued significance of theology, and religious culture generally, for certain areas of Germany. As late as 1887, nearly a third of all books by Catholic writers in Württemberg were about theology, and more than half of all books written were concerned, in one or another way, with Catholicism.[26] Rather than as a steady, inexorable erosion of religious practice, secularization should perhaps be conceived as a historical process marked by important differences between confessions, epochs, regions, classes, and between the experiences of men and women.

It proceeded faster among Protestants than among Catholics. This cannot be a precise statement, in part because the statistics available to measure secularization—the percentage of people attending church and receiving Holy Communion—may reveal more about conformity to the pressures of a religious community than they do about the depth, or shallowness, of religious belief. These statistics are also incomplete. Whereas the Protestant churches in Germany counted annual communicants on an empire-wide basis as early as 1862, the Catholic church did so for the first time in 1915. In that year,

[25] These calculations are drawn from statistics on book production compiled by Il-sedore Rarisch, *Industrialisierung und Literatur. Buchproduktion, Verlagswesen und Buchhandel in Deutschland im 19. Jahrhundert in ihrem statistischen Zusammenhang* (Berlin, 1976), 98–105. In 1801, theology accounted for 7% of the total book market; in 1851, 16.2%; in 1871, 12.8%. In these three years, belles lettres accounted for 29.9%, 13.6%, and 12.5% respectively.

[26] These authors were Catholic by confession; they were not necessarily writing for the church as such. I have made these calculations from the lists of authors in Heinrich Keiter, ed., *Katholischer Literaturkalender* (Regensburg, 1887).

Catholic participation in Easter communion was higher than Protestant participation in annual communion in every state, save for the principality of Schaumburg-Lippe.[27] In Prussia, 57 percent of Catholics received communion whereas only 33 percent of Protestants did. In Baden, this ratio was 57:47; in Württemberg, 63:42; in Saxony, 53:36; in Hessen, 51:48, and in Bavaria (east of the Rhine), 63:61.[28] Of course, one cannot simply project these ratios backward in time. Yet, in 1884, the *Theological Yearbook* of the Protestant Consistory in Prussia reported that "even if we do not have the statistics from the Roman church before us, we must concede to Roman Catholicism a higher frequency of church attendance."[29]

The general movement in Protestant religiosity was toward less frequent observance of central religious rituals; but this movement varied considerably between men and women, between north and south Germany, across states (see figure 2), and, as other statistics reveal, within regions, particularly between city and country. Moreover, the general downward curve hides significant plateaus, years, even decades, in which religious observance, measured in Protestant communicants as a percentage of the population, held its ground. Despite the complexity of the data, it is possible to advance a number of generalizations.

The decline in Protestant observance in the second half of the nineteenth century, while continuous, was not steady, and, in a number of states and provinces, the twenty years between 1862 and 1883 represented a steeper decline than did the two decades following. To take a number of examples: communicants in the province of Saxony decreased from 58 percent in 1862 to 44 percent in 1883, but by 1903 to only 38 percent. In Bavaria, the percentage of communicants descended from 78 percent in 1862 to 67 percent in 1883, but then held steady with minor fluctuations for the next twenty years. And some states, such as Pomerania, even registered a slight increase in communion rates in the two decades between 1883 and 1903. But after the turn of the century, a more precipitous downward turn characterized religious observance in almost all states and provinces.[30] Thus, while

[27] Statistical material in Annemarie Burger, *Religionszugehörigkeit und soziales Verhalten* (Göttingen, 1964), 358–59. The percentage of people receiving communion in a given year is, however, a somewhat inflated measure because exceptionally pious Protestants received communion more than once a year.

[28] Ibid.

[29] *Theologisches Jahrbuch* 11 (1884): 141.

[30] For 1862 and 1913, see figure 2. For intervening years, see *Statistische Mitteilungen aus den deutschen Landeskirchen vom Jahre 1883 bis 1912.* For the relative stability of Protestant religiosity in the 1880s and 1890s, see also Manfred E. Welti, "Abendmahl,

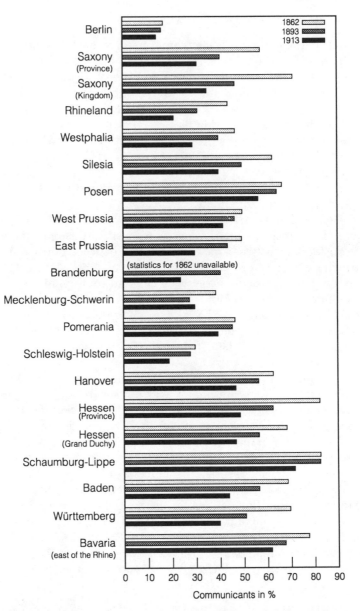

Berlin
Saxony (Province)
Saxony (Kingdom)
Rhineland
Westphalia
Silesia
Posen
West Prussia
East Prussia
Brandenburg (statistics for 1862 unavailable)
Mecklenburg-Schwerin
Pomerania
Schleswig-Holstein
Hanover
Hessen (Province)
Hessen (Grand Duchy)
Schaumburg-Lippe
Baden
Württemberg
Bavaria (east of the Rhine)

1862
1893
1913

0 10 20 30 40 50 60 70 80 90

Communicants in %

Protestant Religious Observance: Communicants as Percentage of
Protestant Population in 1862 (first bar), 1893 (second bar), and
1913 (third bar)

*Source: Statistische Mitteilungen aus den deutschen Landeskirchen vom Jahre
1883 bis 1913.* For 1862, Lucian Hölscher, *Weltgericht oder Revolution,* 143,
citing figures in Gerhard Zeller, *Zur kirchlichen Statistik des evangelischen
Deutschlands im Jahre 1862* (Stuttgart, 1865). For more precise detail, see
Hölscher's forthcoming atlas on religion and religiosity in nineteenth- and
twentieth-century Germany.

general trends suggest an overall decline in observance during the half century before World War I, closer scrutiny suggests that this decline was most marked at the beginning and end of this period.

As a group, women were more observant than men; in every state and province, they accounted for the majority of Protestant communicants. The disparity in observance was especially evident in the metropolitan cities. In Berlin, for example, women typically constituted over 60 percent of the communicants in the years 1884 to 1913; in Hamburg and Bremen, the same; in Frankfurt, they often made up 70 percent of all communicants.[31] Here, in the large cities, one may surmise that a certain "feminization" of Protestantism occurred.[32] In the provinces, the predominance of women in Protestant parishes was still noticeable, if also less pronounced. In 1913 in East Prussia, women made up 53.3 percent of all communicants; in Silesia, 53.8 percent; in Brandenburg, 56.4 percent; in Westphalia, 54.7 percent; and in the Rhineland, 55.2 percent.[33] Still, and the "feminization" of Protestantism notwithstanding, a decline in religious observance did occur among women. If female communicants are measured as a percentage of Protestant women, the resultant slope still curves downward, though less precipitously than it does for men.

There were also significant regional differences in Protestant observance. Protestants in the north tended to be less observant than those in the south—though to this rule there were important exceptions: Posen, a diaspora province in which Protestant Germans lived among Catholic Poles; the highlands of Hessen-Nassau, an economically backward area in which small-plot farming predominated; and Schaumburg-Lippe. In general, diaspora or mixed areas registered higher rates of communion than confessionally homogeneous areas.[34] The rates of

---

Zollpolitik und Sozialistengesetz in der Pfalz. Eine statisch-quantifizierende Untersuchung zur Verbreitung von liberal-aufklärerischem Gedankengut im 19. Jahrhundert," *Geschichte und Gesellschaft* 3 (1977), foldout chart entitled "Abendmahlfrequenz in der Pfalz des 19. Jahrhunderts."

[31] *Statistische Mitteilungen aus den deutschen Landeskirchen vom Jahre 1883 bis 1912.* In 1884, women counted for 62% of communicants in Berlin, 62% in Hamburg, 61% in Bremen, and 72% in Frankfurt (1885). In 1911, the picture was very much the same: Berlin, 61%; Hamburg, 65%; Bremen, 60%; Frankfurt, 69%. For similar figures, see Hugh McLeod, "Weibliche Frömmigkeit—männlicher Unglaube? Religion und Kirchen im bürgerlichen 19. Jahrhundert," in *Bürgerinnen und Bürger. Geschlechterverhältnisse im 19. Jahrhundert*, ed. Ute Frevert (Göttingen, 1988), 135.

[32] See Barbara Welter, "The Feminization of American Religion: 1800–1860," in *Clio's Consciousness Raised: New Perspectives on the History of Women*, ed. Mary Hartman and Lois W. Banner (New York, 1974), 137–57. For a comparative perspective, see McLeod, "Weibliche Frömmigkeit—männlicher Unglaube?" 135–37.

[33] *Statistisches Jahrbuch für den Preußischen Staat* (1913), 383.

[34] See also Nipperdey, *Religion im Umbruch*, 119–20.

communion in Silesia, a confessionally mixed area with a high degree of urbanization, were, for example, higher than those of East Prussia, a rural province made up almost exclusively of Protestants.[35] In the lowlands, where mobility was greater, large-scale farming more prevalent, and therefore the percentage of agricultural laborers higher, secularization seemed to advance more swiftly than in the less accessible highlands, especially where a history of partible inheritance and small-plot farming predominated.[36] Thus, Protestant communities in the gentle hills of northeastern Baden, in the wooded areas of Lower Franconia, in the Swabian Alps, and in the highlands along the Lahn and near Kassel counted among the most pious areas of Protestant Germany.[37] Conversely, the lowlands of Schleswig-Holstein, Mecklenburg, western Pomerania, and East Prussia became markedly less observant.

History and the deep imprint of physical geography also bequeathed sharp contours to the religious topography of German Protestantism. In areas scarred by the religious wars of the seventeenth century, Protestants continued in the nineteenth century to celebrate the Eucharist—as a ritual of confessional solidarity—more consistently than did their coreligionists with more peaceful pasts.[38] For theological reasons as well as for reasons of historical tradition, orthodox Lutherans in Saxony and Pietists in Württemberg were also more likely to emphasize such rituals than, for example, Calvinists in northwest Germany.[39] Often, natural landscape delineated changes

[35] On the exceptionally pious population of Upper Silesia, see Martin Schian, *Das kirchliche Leben der evangelischen Kirche der Provinz Schlesien* (Tübingen and Leipzig, 1903), 91.

[36] For the possible relationship between partible inheritance and religious observance, see the comments in C. Wagner, *Die geschlechtlich-sittlichen Verhältnisse der evangelischen Landbewohner im Deutschen Reiche*, 2 vols. (Leipzig, 1895–96), esp. vol. 2, 224, 274.

[37] For a regional breakdown of religiosity (measured by communicants as percentage of the Protestant population) in Baden, see *GVEKB*, 1872–1913. For Württemberg, see "Äußerungen des kirchlichen Lebens in der Evangelische Kirche," *Amtsblatt des Evangelischen Konsistoriums*, 1880–1913. In the district of Kassel, the principalities of Waldeck-Pyrmont and Schaumburg-Lippe had communicant rates in 1883 of 78%, 73%, and 75% respectively. By 1912 these had dropped in the principalities to 67% and 72%. Statistics were not available for Kassel for 1912. That even within single areas, rates of religiosity could markedly differ, see Clemens Zimmermann, "'Die Entwicklung hat uns nun einmal in das Erwerbsleben hineingeführt.' Lage, dörflicher Kontext und Mentalität nordbadischer Tabakarbeiter," *Zeitschrift für die Geschichte des Oberrheins* 135 (1987): 344.

[38] Lucian Hölscher, *Weltgericht oder Revolution. Protestantische und sozialistische Zukunftsvorstellungen im deutschen Kaiserreich* (Stuttgart, 1989), 147.

[39] Ibid.

in religious observance. In Pomerania, the Oder River seemed to mark a border between the "spiritual deadness" of the nearly de-Christianized west bank and the relatively pious east.[40] Along the great northern lowlands, secularization, as one pastor noted, advanced as one traveled westward.[41] In other areas—Schleswig-Holstein, Silesia, Thuringia—the south tended to be more observant than the north; and in Baden, the reverse was true.

Yet the deepest cuts were left by industrialization. One can observe this in the case of Saxony, where the contours marking differences in religious observance were especially distinct. The devotion of the Protestants in the Erzgebirge near Plauen and Marienberg contrasted conspicuously with the religious indifference of the workers of nearby Chemnitz and Leipzig, and even more markedly with the toilers of the smoke-rent, working-class suburbs of these industrial centers. Here, church attendance in the 1870s fell below 5 percent of the population, in some places below 1 percent.[42] Whatever else religion was, it was not the opiate of these people.

Urbanization also placed a great strain on the Protestant churches, with most metropolitan centers showing communion rates of less than 20 percent.[43] Already alarmingly low from the perspective of the Protestant churches, these statistics disguised a still more significant flight from the arms of the established religion. Lucian Hölscher, the historian who has studied this problem in most detail, offers the example of Hanover. In 1877, Hanover counted 17 percent of its Protestant population as communicants. A disproportionate number of these communicants belonged to special church establishments, such as those that cared for orphans, for widows, or for the poor; and many more were the families of boys and girls being confirmed and were not likely to return to church regularly. Of the rest (Hölscher estimates their number at not more than 8 percent), most were women, married men who came to church with their wives, and, in terms of class, people who belonged to the old *Mittelstand* (artisan

---

[40] Wagner, *Die geschlechtlich-sittlichen Verhältnisse*, vol. 1, 101–2.

[41] Ibid.

[42] Paul Drews, *Das kirchliche Leben der Evangelisch-Lutherischen Landeskirche des Königreichs Sachsen* (Tübingen and Leipzig, 1902), 86–90. On Saxony, see also Hölscher, *Weltgericht oder Revolution*, 142–48. And on the general phenomenon of de-Christianized industrial suburbs, Nipperdey, *Religion in Umbruch*, 120.

[43] The steep decline of religious practice, common to many German industrial cities, began much earlier, however. Lucian Hölscher estimates that the descent started in the middle of the eighteenth century, declined most precipitously in the early decades of the nineteenth, and thereafter continued its downward trend, albeit more gradually. See Hölscher, *Weltgericht oder Revolution*, 148.

masters, small merchants, store owners), as well as state and municipal officials and long-established Hanoverian families.[44] The majority of Hanover's citizens, and especially those of the working classes, were no longer within the reach, to say nothing of the grasp, of the Protestant church. Much the same held true in Dresden and Nuremberg, Breslau and Berlin.[45] Not only was the level of regular churchgoing in such cities shockingly low, but many of their denizens ceased to conform to the most fundamental church customs—baptism, church wedding, religious burial—even as these customs continued to mark out people's lives in smaller cities, towns, and villages throughout Protestant Germany.[46]

For Catholic Germany, the pace of secularization is more difficult to determine because statistics are more scattered and less reliable. Nevertheless, it is possible to suggest general trends. Unlike Protestantism, Catholicism does not present us with a picture of a religious culture eroding progressively throughout the century. In fact, the opposite is true. At the time of the Kulturkampf, Catholicism in Germany found itself at the crest of a religious revival.[47] The historian Thomas Nipperdey estimated that the proportion of practicing Catholics among adult males approached 90 percent during the Kulturkampf but that it declined to 60 percent by 1912. The general level of church attendance was probably somewhat higher, however, since women were decidedly more pious than men. Nipperdey based his estimate on the assumption that ties to the religious community (*Kirchenbindung*) can be roughly deduced from electoral support for the Catholic Center party. Thus, 83 percent of the Catholic electorate supported the Center party in 1874, but only 54.6 percent did so in 1912.[48]

Nipperdey was certainly correct to point out the great number of Catholics with close ties to the village parish or the local church. But there is evidence to suggest that a correlation of Center party votes to

[44] Lucian Hölscher, "Die Religion des Bürgers. Bürgerliche Frömmigkeit und protestantische Kirche im 19. Jahrhundert," *Historische Zeitschrift* 250 (1990): 609–11, and, for more detail still, Lucian Hölscher and Ursula Männich-Polenz, "Die Sozialstruktur der Kirchengemeinde Hannovers im 19. Jahrhundert. Eine statistische Analyse," *Jahrbuch der Gesellschaft für niedersächsische Kirchengeschichte* 88 (1990): 159–211.

[45] For statistics, see table 1 in Hölscher, "Die Religion des Bürgers," 628–29.

[46] For detailed statistics of adherence to church customs in cities in Saxony and Silesia, see Drews, *Das kirchliche Leben der Evangelisch-Lutherischen Landeskirche des Königreichs Sachsen*, 82–83; Schian, *Das kirchliche Leben der evangelischen Kirche der Provinz Schlesien*, 104–11.

[47] On this phenomenon, see especially Blessing, *Staat und Kirche*, and Sperber, *Popular Catholicism*.

[48] Nipperdey, *Religion im Umbruch*, 23.

churchgoing leads to an overestimation of Catholic observance in the empire. Consider the case of the bishopric of Trier. In 1909, 63.7 percent of the Catholic population received communion on Easter Sunday (the most popular day for church attendance in the Catholic calendar).[49] This figure includes women and children, so it should be adjusted downward if we wish to consider Catholic males. Let us, then, assume that 60 percent of adult males received Easter communion and then compare this figure with the Catholic vote for the Center party. In the Reichstag elections of 1907, 84 percent of the Catholic men in the bishopric of Trier voted for the Center.[50] Thus, it makes more sense to assume that Catholic religiosity (measured by communion attendance on Easter Sunday) was lower than support for the Center and that there existed among Catholics—as also among Protestants—a large group who identified with their confession but were no longer bound to the church.

Nevertheless, support for the Center party does suggest trends in religiosity and in the cohesiveness of Catholic culture. This culture was strongest in the countryside of confessionally unified areas. The eight administrative districts and provinces in which more than 75 percent of Catholic men voted for the Center were all confessionally enclosed and predominantly rural.[51] Conversely, in Germany's largest cities, the Center party fared poorly, even among Catholics. In Berlin, 19.7 percent of Catholic men supported the Center in 1907, and in the cosmopolitan city of Frankfurt, the Center party received only 9.3 percent of the Catholic vote. Support for the Center came predominantly from rural areas, and from small and medium-sized towns.[52] Here, Catholicism continued to flourish despite—or rather

[49] BAT 108/360 Note on communion statistics, bishopric of Trier, 1912.

[50] For the Reichstag elections in the bishopric of Trier, which encompasses the administrative district of Trier and Koblenz, see *Vierteljahreshefte zur Statistik des Deutschen Reichs* 16 (1907): Ergänzungsheft zu 1907, vol. 4, 58–59. For the confessional composition of the two districts, see H. A. Krose, *Konfessionsstatistik Deutschlands* (Freiburg, 1904), 179–80. The bishopric of Trier was 70% Catholic, and the Center party won 58.8% of the total vote.

[51] Johannes Schauff, *Das Wahlverhalten der deutschen Katholiken im Kaiserreich und in der Weimarer Republik*, ed. Rudolf Morsey (Mainz, 1975), 174–75. They included the administrative districts of Münster, Minden, Trier, Aachen, Sigmaringen, Upper Palatinate, and the states of Oldenburg and Württemburg. The Catholic populations of Minden, Oldenburg, and Württemberg were minorities but in large, confessionally enclosed areas. For confessional composition, see Krose, *Konfessionsstatistik Deutschlands*, 169–90. The situation of sparsely settled Catholics in diaspora areas is difficult to determine, because the voting law sometimes made it superfluous to vote for the Center when there was no chance of winning the election.

[52] The Center party received, in 1907, 24.1% of the valid votes cast by the German population living in villages (fewer than 2,000 inhabitants), 22.9% in small towns

because—of the impact of modernization on rural and small-town ways of life.

Catholicism, it seems, flourished especially among women. There is much impressionistic, and some statistical, evidence to suggest that women, more than men, filled the parish pews and populated the empire's many monasteries, and that in nineteenth-century Germany, as in nineteenth-century France, one can discern the outline of what Claude Langlois has called "le catholicisme au feminin."[53] The number of women taking religious vows might serve as an index. In 1866 (before the foundation of the empire and before the onslaught of antimonastic legislation, which was mainly directed at male orders), one Catholic statistician counted only 7,795 nuns in Germany as a whole (excluding Austria).[54] But by 1908, the number of women in religious vocations had increased, and dramatically. There were now nearly 50,000 nuns in the German empire; the likelihood of a woman entering a convent was four times higher in 1908 than in 1866; and indeed there had been something of an explosion of female piety in the intervening years.[55] Though still terra incognita to historians, the feminization of Catholic vocational life did not go unnoticed among contemporary critics of German Catholicism, most of whom were men. Rather, it provoked them; it aroused their confessional ire; it made them indignant as they imagined women to be enslaved by an imperious church; and it lent specious substance to their charge that Catholicism was a religion overdetermined by the spiritual delusions of dispossessed women.

Confessional Integration and Confessional Conflict

If religious belief and religious prejudice kept Protestants and Catholics apart, demographic pressures brought them together in common space. Once marked by a terrain in which confessional lines were

---

(2,000–10,000), 15.5% in medium-size cities (10,000–100,000), 11.5% in large cities (100,000–500,000), and 6.6% in metropolitan cities (over 500,000). Stanley Suval, *Electoral Politics in Wilhelmine Germany* (Chapel Hill, 1985), 81.

[53] Claude Langlois, *Le catholicisme au feminin: Les congrégations françaises à supérieure générale au XIX siécle* (Paris, 1984). For reflections and statistics on female vocations in the second third of the nineteenth century, see Eric John Yonke, "The Emergence of a Roman Catholic Middle Class in Nineteenth-century Germany: Catholic Associations in the Prussian Rhine Province, 1837–1876" (Ph.D. diss., University of North Carolina, Chapel Hill, 1990), 154–55.

[54] Paul Pollack, *Zur Entwicklung des katholischen Ordenswesens im Deutschen Reich* (Halle, 1909), 29.

[55] Calculations from statistics presented in ibid.

distinct, in which towns, with few exceptions, were either Protestant or Catholic, Germany, in the course of the nineteenth century, evolved into a more complex landscape, distinguished by confessional diasporas and shifting confessional compositions. Rapidly urbanizing and industrializing areas experienced the most marked changes. In Berlin, for example, the preponderance of Protestants living in the city fell from 95 percent in 1817 to 84 percent in 1900, while Berlin's Catholic population, coming mostly from Silesia, rose from 3 percent to 10 percent. By 1910, Berlin, with a Catholic population of 243,000, had become one of the largest diaspora cities in Europe.[56] Prussia also underwent important demographic changes in this period, especially at the provincial level. Its western provinces became demographically more Protestant while the east became more Catholic. In the Rhineland, the Protestant population rose from 23 percent in 1817 to 29 percent in 1900; in Westphalia, from 40 percent to 48 percent. The most significant change came about in Silesia, however. A province with a majority of Protestants (55 percent) in 1817 became, by 1900, a province with a Catholic majority (55 percent). Outside Prussia, the state of Baden manifested the most significant change. The percentage of Protestants in this predominantly Catholic state rose from 31 percent to 38 percent between 1817 and 1900, while its Catholic population declined from 67 percent to 61 percent. The confessional composition of the other states and provinces remained relatively stable.[57]

This statistical stability veiled important demographic developments at the local level. Most significantly, in all but the most rural hinterlands of Germany, confessionally enclosed areas ceased to exist. To cite a typical example: in an area around Konstanz known as the Seekreis, 85 percent of all towns and villages were exclusively

---

[56] Krose, *Konfessionsstatistik Deutschlands*, 60–67, 72–73. See also Hans-Georg Aschoff, "Berlin als katholische Diaspora," in Kasper Elm and Hans-Dietrich Look, eds., *Seelsorge und Diakonie in Berlin: Beiträge zum Verhältnis von Kirche und Großstadt im 19. und beginnenden 20. Jahrhundert* (Berlin and New York, 1990), 223–32; and Horst Matzerath, "Wachstum und Mobilität der Berliner Bevölkerung im 19. und frühen 20. Jahrhundert," in Elm and Look, eds., *Seelsorge und Diakone in Berlin*, 201–2. By 1910, 12% of Berlin's Catholic population was Polish.

[57] For an overview of demographic changes according to confession see Krose, *Konfessionsstatistik Deutschlands*, 60–97. Scholarly study of these long-term confessional migrations has hardly begun, yet their importance for regional life and politics was often decisive. For the impact of Catholic migrations into Protestant areas of the Saarland, see Mallmann, "Ultramontanismus und Arbeiterbewegung," 79. The example of the Saarland, where Catholic migrations in the wake of industrialization completely changed both the confessional composition and the nature of regional politics, suggests something of the complexities hidden by overarching statistics based on states and provinces.

Catholic in 1825. Fifty years later, only 19 percent remained without at least one Protestant inhabitant. By 1900, 14 percent of all communities contained Protestant minorities comprising at least 5 percent of the local population.[58] This was not an isolated phenomenon; the creation of diaspora communities in small market towns occurred throughout the empire. Typically, these communities erected modest, often incongruous steeples in the shadows of the towering spires of the dominant confession: bowed onion domes amidst austere, manly towers in the Protestant north, unpretentious chapels lodged in the sensuous, baroque skylines of the south. Yet the impact was more than aesthetic. By 1907, not one of Germany's national electoral districts was completely confessionally homogeneous (more than 99 percent). For many people, this integration brought with it the first confrontation with those on the other side of the confessional divide. Profound, the process of integration was, however, slow in some areas. Of the 397 electoral districts in the empire in 1907, 122 still contained populations with a confessional homogeneity of more than 95 percent. Of these districts, 96 were Protestant.[59] On the whole, Protestants were more likely than Catholics to live in areas of relative confessional homogeneity. This was especially true of the rural population of the north German flatland as well as the rural areas of Saxony and Thuringia. The confessionally homogeneous Catholic areas tended, on the other hand, to be concentrated on the periphery of the empire, especially in the south and west. But in the mixed areas along the Rhine, in middle Germany, and in some of the eastern provinces, Protestants and Catholics lived in close proximity, usually in the same city, often in the same village.

As a measure of confessional integration, the incidence of mixed marriages may be the most useful index. Unlike population shifts, mixed marriages can provide a measure of attitude. A high rate may suggest tolerance among religious groups, or, more likely, indifference toward religious values and culture. Between 1840 and 1900 mixed marriages in Prussia (measured as a percentage of all marriages) more than doubled, from 3.7 percent to 8.4 percent; in Bavaria,

[58] These statistics are calculated from data in *Religionszugehörigkeit in Baden in den letzten 100 Jahren*, ed. Badisches Statistisches Landesamt (Karlsruhe, 1927), 138–48. For other districts in Baden, see Martin Offenbacher, *Konfession und soziale Schichtung* (Tübingen, 1901), 71–75.

[59] Calculated from data in Alois Klöckner, *Die Konfession der sozialdemokratischen Wählerschaft 1907* (Mönchen-Gladbach, 1913), 34–35. For the confessional composition of electoral districts according to the census of 1900, see Krose, *Konfessionsstatistik Deutschlands*, 35–46. For a more detailed breakdown—according to the so-called small administrative units—see *Statistik des deutschen Reiches* 150 (1903): 108–15.

they trebled, going from 2.8 percent to 9.9 percent.[60] For the other states, statistics pertaining to the preunification period are incomplete. After 1870, it is possible to discern a steady increase until 1913, so that on the eve of the war 10.2 percent of all marriages in the empire were mixed.[61] This suggests a general trend toward greater confessional integration. In the cities of the Rhineland, Westphalia, Silesia, and of the Rhine-Main basin, the incidence of mixed marriages was especially high. In 1896, 34 percent of all marriages in Frankfurt were mixed; in Wiesbaden, 36.5 percent; in Breslau, 34 percent; in Düsseldorf, 22 percent; in Dortmund, 24.6 percent.[62] It seems probable that, given what we know about secularization, this integration occurred most rapidly among the working classes and was probably the result of indifference toward religious culture.[63] Mixed marriages also occurred in smaller cities and towns, a fact that local priests and pastors ceaselessly bemoaned, blaming military maneuvers, factory canteens, and profane dances as the source of the problem. In factory canteens, Protestants and Catholics ate together. And at dances, young ladies all too often neglected to query their suitors about their confession.[64] If members of the clergy were perhaps too sensitive to the evils of dance, they did nevertheless correctly perceive the impact of factory and city life on marriage patterns. In the period from 1867 to 1896, a city dweller in Prussia was three to five times more likely to enter into a mixed marriage than a farmer or villager.[65]

Demographic pressures pushing toward greater integration did not, however, ensure harmony and cooperation between the two religious communities—quite the opposite. In mixed communities, confessional competition and discord defined daily life. This was well

[60] Krose, *Konfessionsstatistik Deutschlands*, 137–38, 142. When Prussia acquired the new provinces in 1867, mixed marriages counted for 4.8% of all marriages.

[61] Burger, *Religionszugehörigkeit*, 138.

[62] *Statistisches Handbuch für den preußischen Staat* 3 (1898): vol. 2, 175–76.

[63] On the religious attitudes of workers, see Vernon Lidtke, "Social Class and Secularization in Imperial Germany—the Working Classes," *Leo Baeck Institute Yearbook* 25 (1980): 21–40; Hugh McLeod, "Protestantism and the Working Class in Imperial Germany," *European Studies Review* 12 (1982): 323–44.

[64] Wahl, *Confession und comportement*, vol. 2, 736–39.

[65] This discrepancy was greater for mixed marriages initiated by Catholic (rather than Protestant) men. On the whole, Catholic men were more likely to marry Protestant women than were Protestant men to marry Catholic women. But this fact is probably less indicative of the tolerance of Catholic men (assuming, as the Prussian Bureau of Statistics did, that men initiated courtship and marriage) than of two demographic factors: the percentage of Catholics living in diaspora areas, and the growth of industrial centers in the largely, though not exclusively, Catholic areas of the Rhineland, Westphalia, and Silesia. See P. Pieper, *Kirchliche Statistik Deutschlands* (Freiburg i. Br., 1889), 55–59.

understood by the Protestant Consistory of the Rhineland, which, in its annual report on confessional relations, remarked: "The modern transportation and economic systems draw the confessions into the same area, bringing forth more contact, but at the same time more causes for friction."[66] Clearly, geographical proximity did not necessarily diminish social conflict or social distance. Although Protestants and Catholics may have lived in the same towns and villages, their everyday life was marked by the tensions of segregated communities. Reports on confessional relations throughout Prussia typically spoke of "peaceful segregation."[67] Protestants often shopped at one set of bakers, butchers, and millers, Catholics at another.[68] In Ottweiler, a mining town in the Saarland, the local magistrate complained that Catholics "emphasized their confessional character at all opportunities, not just in church and school, but also in private and public life, in the selection of their employers or lords, in the stores and pubs they visit, in the company they keep, and even in the banks from which they take out loans."[69] To outsiders, this highly segregated local world often seemed strange, and sometimes disturbing. In 1896, the journal of the Association against Anti-Semitism (Verein zur Abwehr des Antisemitismus) complained that "the division of the confessions is progressing more and more"—"in confessionally mixed towns . . . everything has either a Catholic or a Protestant imprint: associations for the relief of the poor and for the support of the sick, reading clubs, public library support clubs, domiciles for factory girls, and so on and so on as if hunger were especially Catholic or Protestant, or consumption determined by a certificate of baptism."[70]

Local divisions were not easily overcome by organizations that claimed to be "above confessions." In imperial Germany, sociability centered primarily around religious and nationalist organizations. The former were naturally enough divided by confession; the latter, with the exception of the Veterans' League and in some cases the Navy League, typically failed to bridge local confessional division.[71]

[66] EZB 7/3693 Report of the Royal Consistory of the Protestant Church of the Rhineland, 30.3.1901.

[67] EZB 7/3691 Report of the Royal Consistory of the Protestant Church of the Rhineland, 1.4.1893.

[68] See, for example, EZB 7/3690 The report of Consistorial Assessor Altmann, "Planmäßige Zurückdrängung der Evangelischen in der Rheinprovinz," 4.2.1893.

[69] LHAK 403/16008 District Magistrate (Landrat) Land of Oberweiler to the president of the regency of Trier, 11.11.1906.

[70] Mitteilungen des Vereins zur Abwehr des Antisemitismus, 28 November 1896.

[71] On the Navy League, see chapter 5. On the Veterans' League as a factor of integration for Catholics and Protestants alike, see Thomas Rohkrämer, Der Militarismus der "kleinen Leute." Die Kriegervereine im deutschen Kaiserreich 1871–1914 (Munich, 1991), 43–

Moreover, there were many cases where "peaceful segregation" was not maintained by one or the other religious party. In diaspora communities, tacit confessional boycotts were not uncommon, and both Protestants and Catholics, in almost all mixed areas of the empire, complained of discrimination in the workplace. Thus, the president of the Protestant Consistory of Prussia, Friedrich Wilhelm Barkhausen, reported in January 1893 to the Prussian minister of culture, Robert Bosse, that "the overall picture in the . . . provinces may be characterized by the fact that in many cases Protestant workers and traders are set back because of their religion."[72]

The voluminous reports on confessional relations at the local and provincial levels suggest, with near unanimity, that relations between Protestants and Catholics, especially strained during the Kulturkampf of the 1870s, deteriorated once again in the 1890s. In a letter sent in February 1900 to Cardinal Rampolla, state secretary of the Holy See, Center party leader Carl Bachem complained that the pace of confessional integration "has produced an agitated and embittered mood among Protestants against Catholics that gets worse daily."[73] Similarly, the Protestant Consistory of the Rhineland reported to the Prussian Consistory in April 1893 that "it is unmistakable that the tension between ours and the Catholic church is becoming greater and that the relationship is becoming increasingly acrimonious."[74]

48, 203–13. That integration in the veterans' organizations did not always work without friction, see also Hans-Jürgen Kremer, "Die Krieger und Militärvereine in der Innenpolitik des Großherzogtums Baden (1870–1914,)" *Zeitschrift für die Geschichte des Oberrheins* 133 (1985): 301–36. Both works focus on Baden.

[72] EZB 7/3690 President of the Protestant Consistory of Prussia (Evangelischer Oberkirchenrat), Friedrich Wilhelm Barkhausen, to the Prussian minister of ecclesiastical affairs and public instruction (Kultusminister), Robert Bosse, 27.2.1893. The exception that he noted was Silesia.

[73] StAK NL Bachem Nr. 37 Carl Bachem to Cardinal Mariano Rampolla, 4.2.1900.

[74] This sentiment was universally shared among Protestants living in the mixed areas. In Westphalia, the Evangelical Consistory compared the situation to the problem of anti-Semitism in 1899. "Anti-Semitism in the last few years has much less often come to the fore. . . . Conversely, the opposition of the Roman church has unmistakably become sharper." EZB 7/3693 Report of the Royal Conistory of the Protestant church of Westphalia ("Geschäftsbericht 1897/98"), 6.3.1899. On the confessional tension in the kingdom of Saxony, see PAAA R8534 Graf Carl von Dönhoff to Bernhard von Bülow, 6.2.1900. For Württemberg, see LKAS A26/326 Dr. Julius Koestlin, "Jahresbericht über den Stand der Confessionellen Angelegenheiten," 22.1.1894. For Bavaria, see the manuscript "Zur Lage der Protestanten in Bayern," in the library of the Konfessionskundliches Institut des Evangelischen Bundes in Bensheim, Hessen. The ethnically mixed areas constitute an exception to this rule. In Posen, relationships between Protestants and German Catholics were allegedly "reasonably friendly," while the Polish Catholic clergy exhibited an "embittered aversion to whatever is German or Protestant." EZB 7/3696 Royal Consistory of the Protestant church of Posen ("Ge-

This tension, reported the consistory six years later, in 1899, "manifested itself here and there in open conflicts."[75]

These open conflicts were of many kinds, and often reflected long-standing local tensions. Boycotts and discrimination represented one sort of conflict, but the majority were symbolic in nature: they turned on the introduction of Corpus Christi Day processions into predominantly Protestant communities, on the defamation of women in mixed marriages, on the Catholic rebaptism of Protestant children, on funeral scandals in confessionally mixed cemeteries, on the refusal of local priests and pastors to ring church bells after the burial of a resident of the other confession. These conflicts, common to all the mixed areas of Germany, left their imprint on local confessional life; they shaped a sense of confessional community, defined against the "other," and they sharpened the symbolic sensibilities of the participants. In one town, Oberweiler in the Eifel, not far from Trier, the attempt to introduce Corpus Christi Day processions created "a deep disturbance among the Protestant population, especially of the educated classes, in which the Protestant element far outnumber the Catholic."[76] The case was quite typical. To the Catholics, the procession represented a ritual confirmation of their new community; but to the Protestants, these new processions symbolized the rebirth of confessional fanaticism in their hometown, the late nineteenth-century renaissance of Counter-Reformation Catholic intolerance in what had hitherto been a Protestant community. This tension, strung taught between confessional community and historical sensibility, and sometimes burdened by class conflict as well, lent to local controversies the air of epic confrontations, important precisely because they were so close to home, intractable because they concerned matters considered sacred.

Sources for the study of local conflicts can be found in many archives throughout Germany, but the most detailed accounts are in the files of the diocesan and consistory archives in Baden and Württemberg pertaining to "disturbances of the confessional peace" and "infringements on the rights" of one or the other church. These files

---

schäftsbericht für die Jahre 1908/9"), 19.3.1910. For a similar situation in West Prussia, see EZB 7/3693 Royal Consistory of the Protestant church of West Prussia ("Geschäftsbericht für 1898/9"), 24.4.1900. In Silesia, few conflicts were reported, supposedly because of the moderating influence of Cardinal Kopp. See EZB 7/3696 Royal Consistory of the Protestant church of Silesia ("Geschäftsbericht 1908/9").

[75] EZB 7/3691 Report of the Royal Consistory of the Protestant Church of the Rhineland, 1.4.1893.

[76] LHAK 403/16008 District Magistrate Land of Oberweiler to the President of the regency of Trier, 26.9.1906.

contain cases that could not be solved locally and were therefore referred to the central church administrators and, in some cases, to civil authorities. Between 1870 and 1914, 182 such cases were reported in the two states, 129 of which fell between 1890 and 1909.[77] The most common cause of conflict (57 cases) was intolerance, usually on the part of Catholic priests, in matters concerning mixed marriages. Their offenses included unreasonable proselytizing, improper behavior in the confessional, and rebaptizing children. Although these cases initially pertained to the relationship between a clergyman and a married couple, they were anything but private matters. More often, the "confessional theater of war" was a subject for small-town *guerres des plumes*.[78] The second most common offense was slander, usually directed against the Catholic church and its rituals (34 cases), though at times against the writings of Luther (6 cases). When directed against Catholicism, such charges included aspersions against the Jesuits or other religious orders, derogatory public remarks about the pope, the saints, or the clerical estate, and willful disturbances of processions. Personal libel was also prevalent (32 cases), and, as with mixed marriages, anything but a private affair. Indeed, libel cases often masked communal factions involved in political disagreements centering on confessional lines of division. There were also 18 cases of proselytizing, 11 cases of conflict over burial rites, and 8 cases of disruption of religious services.

Without the benefit of detailed local studies, it is difficult to discern the underlying causes of such local conflicts. Contemporary observers, whether Protestant or Catholic, pointed to a number of explanations. First, the pace of confessional integration accelerated in the 1890s, forcing confessionally isolated communities, for the first time, to confront the issue of assimilation. The most obvious manifestation of this problem was the increase in communal conflicts centered around mixed marriages.[79] Second, social and political life became increasingly organized after 1890, but, in most cases, organization ran at cross purposes with confessional integration.[80] Protestants worried that "Rome . . . is attempting to secure and ex-

[77] These cases are drawn from the following files: EAF B2/27–28; EAF B2/46.1; LKAK GA/4934; StAL E211/305–60; LKAS A26/413.

[78] See, for example, the articles on the rebaptizing of a child born into a mixed marriage in Mergentheim, Württemberg, entitled "Vom konfessionellen Kriegsschauplatz," in *Der Beobachter*, 27 February 1909, and in *Deutsches Volksblatt*, 9 March 1909. Clippings in LKAS A26/243, case 93, 21.2.1909.

[79] See, for example, EZB 7/3691 Report of the Royal Consistory of the Protestant church of the Rhineland, 1.4.1893

[80] On the phenomenon of confessional organization, see Nipperdey, *Religion im Umbruch*, 24–31, 79–84.

pand its power in all areas, specifically by founding journeymen's associations, women's and girls' clubs, and other associations."[81] But Protestantism, too, became better organized in this period. From an association of pastors and theology professors in 1887, the Protestant League became a mass organization with 100,000 members in 1897, 367,000 members in 1907, and 509,000 members on the eve of the war, in 1913.[82] The consequence of this rise in confessional organization was not only that sociability at the local level remained segregated but that Protestants and Catholics, especially those living in the mixed areas, became increasingly conscious of their confessional identity. Nearly all reports on the confessional problem commented on this phenomenon and considered it a determining factor in the revival of confessional conflict. Finally, these larger developments were subject to the peculiarities of local personalities and politics. As the Rhineland Consistory report stated in 1903: "The relationship of the Protestant to the Catholic church is very different according to individual town and parish, usually dependent on the influence that leading personalities, especially the clergy, exercise in such matters."[83]

The Social Bases of Confessional Conflict

In southwest Germany, confessional conflict was waged mainly among notables. In Baden and Württemberg, 54 percent of those accused of disturbing the confessional peace were Catholic priests. The rest were either Protestant pastors (15 percent), journalists (9 percent), town mayors or other high city officials (7 percent), teachers (3 percent) or businessmen (3 percent). Of those accused of disrupting the confessional peace, only 7 percent lacked an academic (gymnasium) education.[84] The paucity of detailed research in other parts of

[81] EZB 7/3693 Report of the Royal Consistory of the Protestant church of the Rhineland, 18.3.1899.

[82] The annual reports on the Protestant League, presented at the closed meetings of the general assembly, can be found in AKIEB S500.9.54–60. The statistics are drawn from these reports. See also Herbert Gottwald, "Evangelischer Bund zur Wahrung der deutsch-protestantischen Interessen (EB), 1886–1945," in Dieter Fricke et al., eds., *Lexikon zur Parteiengeschichte*, 4 vols. (Leipzig, 1984), vol. 2, 581. The Gustav-Adolf-Verein, an independent organization to support Protestants in the diaspora, did not count individual members. The Deutsche Protestantenverein, a left-liberal lay organization, counted only 25,000 members in 1904. See Herbert Gottwald and Heinz Herz, "Deutscher Protestantenverein (DPV), 1863–1945," in Fricke et al., eds., *Lexikon zur Parteiengeschichte*, vol. 2, 251.

[83] EZB 7/3694 Report of the Royal Consistory of the Protestant Church of the Rhineland, 3.4.1903.

[84] Statistics are drawn from the following files: EAF B2/27–28; EAF B2/46.1; LKAK GA/4934; StAL E211/305–60; LKAS A26/413.

Germany makes it difficult to generalize these findings. Yet as confessional conflict became increasingly organized, the participation of notables became even more apparent. On the Protestant side, the people who participated—both actively and passively—in anti-Catholic activities were usually well educated, socially established, and involved in civic life. Table 1 shows the social composition of people involved in "antiultramontane" activities by dividing their involvement into three levels of personal engagement: local leadership in the Protestant League throughout Germany in 1906, attendance of local citizens at three annual general assemblies of the Protestant League (1896, 1900, 1907), and the willingness of citizens in Heidelberg to sign a petition in 1902 against a proposal to allow monks to return to their monasteries in Baden.

TABLE 1
Social Composition of People Involved in "Antiultramontane" Activities

	Group 1	Group 2	Group 3
1. Clergy	49% (1622)	10.4% (56)	1.8% (25)
2. Academics and journalists	23.9% (790)	18% (97)	33.2% (467)
3. Managers and free professionals	6% (197)	15% (81)	5.6% (80)
4. High civil servants	2.3% (75)	9.6% (52)	3.5% (49)
5. White-collar workers and civil employees	7.6% (251)	8.9% (48)	26.4% (371)
6. Businessmen and merchants	5.4% (180)	13.2% (71)	17.9% (252)
7. Artisans	.8% (27)	6.1% (33)	7.1% (100)
8. Industrial workers	.06% (2)	.4% (2)	.07% (1)
9. Farmers and landowners	1.5% (50)	.18% (1)	0% (0)
10. No occupation	1.6% (54)	27.5% (148)	.6% (9)
11. Other	1.7% (57)	18% (97)*	.9% (13)
Total	3,305	686	1,404

*Eighty-two of the 97 in this category were women without an occupational designation.
Group 1 = Local leadership of the Protestant League, 1906.
Source: Verzeichnis der Haupt- und Zweigvereine des Evangelischen Bundes, 1906 (Leipzig, 1906), in AKIEB S500.9.37.
Group 2 = Attendance of local citizens at the national assemblies of the Protestant League in Darmstadt, 1896, Halberstadt, 1900, and Worms, 1907.
Source: Attendance lists in AKIEB S500.500.9, AKIEB S500.500.13, AKIEB S500.500.20.
Group 3 = Petition of Heidelberg citizens against the admittance of monks to the state of Baden, 1902.
Source: GLA 235/207

This table suggests that Protestant pastors had a powerful hold over the leadership of antiultramontane politics but that this hold was not a monopoly. By 1906, the clergy shared its leadership role with other members of the educated elite, primarily with academics, professional and managerial men, and high civil servants. Furthermore, the support base of antiultramontane activity seems to have consisted of social groups distinguished by their education and standing. Industrial workers and farmers were incidental to organized antiultramontanism, and artisans figured only as passive participants in political activities. Of the social groups without an academic education, only white-collar workers and civil employees made up an important anti-Catholic constituency. Yet because the majority of individuals in this group were public employees, their interest in anti-Catholic organizations can, to some degree, be traced to their material stakes in the outcome of a much publicized conflict between Protestants and Catholics over the issue of parity in government hiring and promotion practices. Yet for the vast majority of people involved, material interests seemed peripheral to their engagement in anti-Catholic activity.

Organized anti-Catholicism was, then, a middle-class phenomenon. It cannot be explained by reference to groups threatened materially by modernization. Neither aristocrats nor farmers nor petty merchants were important to it. Moreover, it was not an expression of cultural pessimism or the "doctrinaire besottedness" of intellectuals who should have known better.[85] Rather, anti-Catholicism represented a widespread sentiment among the most forward-looking of Protestant citizens. It is important to keep in mind that in Heidelberg, a predominantly Protestant city (63.9 percent in 1900) in which educated people were disproportionally represented, 1,404 of 4,393 registered voters signed the petition against the return of Catholic male orders.[86] Similar petitions with respect to the Jesuit question were

[85] Thus Gordon Craig, *Germany, 1866–1945* (New York, 1978), 77. For important reflections on the relationship between German liberalism and anti-Catholicism, see Dieter Langewiesche, *Liberalismus in Deutschland* (Frankfurt a.M., 1988), 180–87.

[86] It is difficult to avoid the impression that the signatures on the petition represented mainly National Liberal voters. In the Reichstag election of 1898, the last one before the petition drive, the voting in Heidelberg was as follows: 1,720 for the National Liberals, 644 for the Center party, 1,041 for the SPD, and 974 for the anti-Semites. It is safe to assume that few Center party supporters signed the petition, and, since there were virtually no workers who signed it, the involvement of the local SPD was probably also not very high. This would leave only anti-Semites and National Liberals to sign the petition, but in Heidelberg the anti-Semites drew their support from the lower middle class and directed their enmity against the local National Liberal politicians. As far as I could ascertain, public employees, especially railway and postal workers, constituted the only significant overlapping social group. For the election returns, see GLA

collected in many other cities, often with an equal measure of success.[87] Moreover, many of Germany's most distinguished intellectuals placed their signatures on such petitions. In Baden, the historians Dietrich Schäfer and Erich Marcks, the theologian Ernst Troeltsch, the philosopher Heinrich Rickert, and the sociologist Max Weber signed the petition against the monks.[88]

The social basis of Catholic antagonism toward Protestantism is more difficult to discern, partly because there were no popular anti-Protestant leagues in Catholic political life, partly because Catholic "intolerance" was a more complex phenomenon, rooted in an essentially defensive worldview. Catholic polemical literature portrayed German Catholicism as an embattled religious community, threatened by outsiders, whether Freemasons, Old Catholics, liberals, Social Democrats, Jews, or Protestants. Often, the outsider groups were interchangeable. Alban Stolz, the author of popular almanacs, wrote of "Protestant Jews," a term of opprobrium implying that neither group partook of true religion.[89] Defense of religious and cultural values frequently shaded into an aggressive posture. For this reason, a good deal of seemingly innocuous Catholic popular literature such as the *Regensburger Marienkalender* aroused the censors' ire.[90] The more local and rural the Catholic publication, the more likely it was to engage in confessional polemic. The district magistrate of Trier cited 245 articles in the rural Catholic press between 1891 and 1902 for their particularly aggressive confessional content. The articles singled out pertained primarily to national issues (Bismarck monuments, the army, naval buildup), to conflicts over public religious ritual, the Protestant League, anti-Catholic discrimination, and to confessional schools.[91] According to magistrate reports, this radical Catholic press

---

236/14926. For more detail, see Helmut Walser Smith, "Alltag und politischer Antisemitismus in Baden, 1890–1900," *Zeitschrift für die Geschichte des Oberrheins* 141 (1993): 294–98.

[87] Augsburg, for example, collected 4,455 signatures. In Bochum and its surrounding area, 65,828 signatures were gathered. For the list, see EZB 7/3690 Reichstag 8. Leg. Per. II Session, 1892/3. "Verzeichnis der bei dem Reichstag eingegangenen Petitionen. Beibehaltung des Jesuiten-Gesetzes."

[88] GLA 235/207 Petition to the grand duke of Baden, 4.8.1902. On the politics of the antimonastery movement in Baden, see Heinrich Röder von Diersberg, *Zur Klosterfrage in Baden* (Lahr, 1902).

[89] Cited by H. K. Lenz, *Alban Stolz und die Juden* (Münster, 1893), 29.

[90] LHAK 403/7144 "Verzeichniß der im Gebiete des preußischen Staates im Jahre 1891 auf Grund des Paragraph 56, Nr. 10 der Reichsgewerbeordnung vom Kolportagebetriebe ausgeschlossenen Druckschriften, anderen Schriften und Bildwerke."

[91] LHAK 442/6616 "Haltung der katholischen Presse gegen die evangelische Kirche und die staatlichen Schuleinrichtungen." The newspapers cited included the

had "the greatest influence, especially in the countryside" around Trier.[92] In general the audience for Catholic confessional polemics seems to have been concentrated in the rural and small-town population. In the Eifel, the rural population considered the *Kölnische Volkszeitung*, the cosmopolitan paper of the Rhineland's Catholic bourgeoisie, nominally Catholic.[93] Not surprisingly, that newspaper engaged in far fewer confessional polemics.

At the grass roots level, core and periphery of what counted as Catholic were still decisively influenced by the powerful, if not always respected, parish priest. This fact has sometimes been overlooked because at the national level clerical influence, though certainly important during the Kulturkampf, was thereafter on the wane. In 1903, the clergy counted for only 20 percent of the Center party's Reichstag deputies, and by 1912 its presence had fallen to 11 percent.[94] Moreover, with the notable exceptions of the chaplains Theodor Wacker in Baden and Georg Dasbach of Trier, members of the clergy rarely served as regional party bosses. Yet, for parish-pump politics, priests were crucial to Center party successes. As the Center politician Franz Bitter put it: "just once allow the clergy to remain neutral and the Center will be shattered."[95] In isolated towns and villages in which there were few competing local elites, the clergy controlled the flow of political information, organized election rallies, and distributed ballots. Liberal magistrates had few illusions about this influence. As late as 1907, they could complain about Trier that "it still lay completely under the influence of the clergy," whose members, according to one magistrate, "were less concerned with administering the parish than with serving as fanatical democratic agents of the ultramontane party."[96]

Not the Kulturkampf itself, but the conjuncture of the Kulturkampf

---

Saarzeitung, the *Paulinusblatt*, the *Trierische Landeszeitung*, the *Metzer Presse*, the *St. Johann Volkszeitung*, the *Neunkircher Volkszeitung*, the *Pastor Bonus*, and the *Mosella*.

[92] LHAK 403/8806 "Tätigkeit der Geistlichen und Beamten bei der Reichstagswahlbewegung," Trier, 24.2.1907.

[93] According to the *Bonner Zeitung*, 25.11.1904, one hears people say in the Eifel: "He is no longer Catholic; he reads the *Kölnische Volkszeitung*." Cited in Hartmann Bodewig, *Geistliche Wahlbeeinflussungen in ihrer Theorie und Praxis dargestellt* (Munich, 1909), 141.

[94] Suval, *Electoral Politics*, 69–70.

[95] Cited in Ross, *Beleaguered Tower*, 49. On the impact of the clergy, see Suval, *Electoral Politics*, 70–71.

[96] LHAK 403/8806 "Tätigkeit der Geistlichen und Beamten bei der Reichstagswahlbewegung," Trier, 24.2.1907. On the importance of the clergy as opinion leaders in Bavaria, see Werner K. Blessing, "Kirchenfromm—volksfromm—weltfromm: Religiosität im katholischen Bayern des späten 19. Jahrhunderts," in *Deutscher Katholizismus im Umbruch zur Moderne*, ed. Wilfried Loth (Stuttgart, 1991), 99.

with the introduction of universal manhood suffrage created the pre-condition for the formation of a politically active clergy.[97] Detailed reports on the activities of priests between 1860 and 1899 in the Catholic deanery of Überlingen in southeast Baden suggest that the clergy did not fully engage in ultramontane politics in the countryside until the 1870s, despite the fact that in Baden the Kulturkampf had begun ten years earlier.[98] And in Württemberg, a state without an officially directed Kulturkampf, the Catholic clergy was actively involved in politics twenty years before the Center party formed in 1895.[99] Depending on the state of clerical organization, the number of priests involved in politics often ran very high. A study of this problem ordered by Frederick II, the grand duke of Baden, revealed that during the Reichstag elections of 1893, "in about 800 parishes in the state, there were about 160 Catholic priests who initiated and maintained a well-organized agitation against the aims of the national government."[100]

The clergy considered itself to be an estate of notables charged with the political and religious task of leading a less-educated, easily pli-

[97] Sperber, *Popular Catholicism*, 190–91; Margaret Lavinia Anderson, "The Kulturkampf," 84.

[98] GLA 382/1924/56/2. This is a file of political reports on those priests who wished to change parishes, whether for a promotion or for other reasons. In the sixties, pro-government priests were still said to have the "spirit of Wessenberg," an enlightened Catholic bishop of the early nineteenth century whose influence was especially strong in Konstanz. From the seventies onward, very few priests were said to be of this spirit: they were either ultramontane *"Hetzkapläne"* (rabble-rousing chaplains) or politically uninvolved. For the political activity of Badenese clericals prior to 1870, see Lothar Gall, "Die partei- und sozialgeschichtliche Problematik des badischen Kulturkampfes," *Zeitschrift für die Geschichte des Oberrheins* 113 (1965): 151–96.

[99] On clerical agitation in Württemberg prior to the nineties, see the rich police reports in StAL E210/190–99. These reports raise the question of whether ultramontane political culture existed independently of the impact of specific Kulturkampf measures. I think the case of Württemberg demonstrates that it did. Despite the fact that there was no official Kulturkampf here and despite the fact that the Center party did not form at the state level until 1895, the Center won in Reichstag elections in Catholic electoral districts by a majority that mirrored the confessional makeup of the districts. District 16 (Biberach, Leutkirch, Waldsee, Wangen) was 91.5% Catholic, and the Center party typically won upward of 90% of the vote throughout the seventies and eighties. The same is true of district 17 (Ravensburg, Riedlingen, Saulgau, Tettnang). Fritz Specht, *Die Reichstagswahlen von 1867 bis 1897* (Berlin, 1898), 311–12. This is not to suggest, however, that ultramontane political culture developed independently of the Kulturkampf but only that one should construe the Kulturkampf in the widest sense. The persistence of this political culture may be gauged by the fact that in 1903 Erzberger won 79% of the communities in district 16 with at least a 95% majority. HStAS E150, 236–45 (Reichstagswahl 1903).

[100] PAAA R1431 Note by Friedrich Graf von Pourtalès on a discussion with the grand duke of Baden, Friedrich II, 29.7.1893.

able following. The appendix to the *Catechism for the Voter or 101 Questions and Answers on Voting*, published in 1884 by the St. Paulus Press of Einsiedeln, a Benedictine monastery in the canton of Schwyz and probably the most important source of German expatriate pamphleteering for the Catholic cause, defined "the rights and duties of the clergy to be active for good elections" as follows: "The priest should enlighten, guide, and direct the conscience of his flock. The priest has a particular responsibility with respect to issues more or less new to the people, especially where others consciously attempt to lead the people astray."[101] Unlike Protestant pastors, Catholic priests typically, and increasingly, came from the same rural milieu as their most dutiful flocks. In Baden, to take the best-researched example, 86.5 percent of all Catholic priests in the years 1870 to 1914 came from towns of fewer than 5,000 inhabitants.[102] To this rural-minded clergy, politics became, for good or ill, an inseparable part of the religious order they wished to preserve. Antiultramontane critics, not without reason, considered the politicization of Catholicism to be an important source of Catholic intolerance. Yet this politicization must also be seen as part of a larger reaction against social and political forces that threatened the Catholic community.[103]

It may, then, be suggested that two distinct social groups formed the front lines of Catholic-Protestant antagonism. On the Protestant side, the educated middle classes provided the most persistent and most vociferous advocates of anti-Catholic politics. But among Catholics, rural and small-town populations most readily gave confessional polemics a sympathetic hearing. Organized confessional antagonism was, therefore, grounded in social division: it drew its principal élan from tension between middle-class, typically urban Protestants, on the one side, and more rural and small-town Catholics, usually of a humbler station, on the other. The clergy played an important role in the mobilization of confessional antagonism on both sides, but, because of the Catholic clergy's overt involvement in politics and because of the relative absence of competing educated elites in rural

[101] *Katechismus für den Wähler oder 101 Fragen und Antworten über das Wählen* (Freiburg, Switzerland, 1884), in GLA 236/14882.

[102] Gerhard Merkel, "Studium zum Priesternachwuchs der Erzdiözese Freiburg, 1870–1914," *Freiburger Diözesan-Archiv* 94 (1974): 191. The percentage of Badenese priests from the archdiocese of Freiburg who came from rural backgrounds increased dramatically in the course of the nineteenth century. See the revealing statistical work of Irmtraud Götz von Olenhusen, "Die Ultramontanisierung des Klerus. Das Beispiel der Erzdiözese Freiburg," in *Deutscher Katholizismus im Umbruch zur Moderne*, ed. Wilfried Loth (Stuttgart, 1991), 50–51.

[103] For an analysis of this issue in the Swiss context, see Altermatt, *Katholizismus und Moderne*.

areas, the influence of the Catholic clergy on confessional antagonism was greater than that of the Protestant clergy.

Other constellations were possible, and did exist. In the Saarland, a different set of class tensions reinforced a religious conflict every bit as severe as in Baden, pitting unskilled Catholic laborers against Protestant factory managers and skilled workers. Partly economic, their conflict also concerned the symbolic order. As the historian Klaus-Michael Mallmann tersely puts it, "here miracles and ecstasy, there Kant with a cudgel."[104] In Düsseldorf, the tight confessional network of native Catholic workers daunted and alienated Protestant migrant factory hands coming from the Westphalian countryside.[105] And in Upper Silesia, class, confession, and ethnicity conspired to create a conflict of still greater complexity between skilled and unskilled, Protestant and Catholic, German and Polish workers. At the other end of the social scale, some members of the nobility, an estate otherwise underrepresented in organized confessional conflict, also engaged in confessional rancor. There were conservative Protestant nobles, such as Otto von Helldorff-Bedra, whose antiultramontane invective assumed disconcerting proportions, and Catholic aristocrats, like Friedrich von Loë, who wished to head an anti-Protestant mass organization.[106] Yet in the empire as a whole, the sociological groups who provided the foot soldiers for the organized confessional struggle were usually of a different stamp.

In the empire, the urban-rural split that reinforced confessional antagonism in the Kaiserreich manifested itself in the regional variations of confessional organization. The Protestant League found most favor in confessionally mixed areas close to the Rhine with an urbanization ratio of greater than 50 percent (see table 2).[107] Accordingly, its strongholds were in the western states of Alsace and Lorraine, Baden, Hessen, the Rhineland, and Westphalia. It was also a powerful force in Saxony and Württemberg, in part because of the importance of Protestantism to regional political traditions. Conversely, in areas of

---

[104] Mallmann, "Die neue Attraktivität des Himmels," 254–55.

[105] On the Catholic milieu in Düsseldorf, see Mary Nolan, *Social Democracy and Society: Working-class Radicalism in Düsseldorf, 1890–1920* (Cambridge, 1981), 112–18. For the import of the confessional division for voting behavior in the Ruhr, see Karl Rohe, "Konfession, Klasse und lokale Gesellschaft als Bestimmungsfaktoren des Wahlverhaltens—Überlegungen und Problematisierungen am Beispiel des historischen Ruhrgebiets," in *Politische Parteien auf dem Weg zur parlamentarischen Demokratie in Deutschland*, ed. Lothar Albertin and Werner Link (Düsseldorf, 1981), 109–26.

[106] See Otto von Helldorff-Bedra to Eulenburg, in John C. G. Röhl, ed., *Philipp Eulenburgs politische Korrespondenz* (Boppard am Rhein, 1979), vol. 2, 964–66.

[107] The exception to this rule seems to have been the large cosmopolitan cities along the Rhine and in middle Germany.

TABLE 2
Membership in the Protestant League and the People's Association for Catholic Germany in 1909 According to State and Degree of Urbanization.

Area	Urb.	PL	PA	1	2
East Prussia	33%	4,414	233	2	0
Posen	34%	4,020	11	7	0
West Prussia	40%	5,948	668	8	0
Bavaria	45%	7,347	24,796	5	6
Pomerania	45%	4,629	278	3	5
Hanover	46%	10,470	24,297	4	65
Württemberg	51%	24,178	30,100	15	43
Alsace-Lorraine	53%	5,100	32,526	13	24
Silesia	53%	29,438	25,816	14	9
Hessen (prov.)	54%	6,627	25,180	10	43
Saxony (prov.)	57%	24,128	4,028	9	17
Baden	57%	16,000	25,647	21	21
Schleswig-Holstein	59%	4,550	1,170	3	28
Hessen	61%	18,230	7,222	23	20
Brandenburg	68%	12,238	6,079	21	3
Saxony	73%	52,228	4,128	12	18
Oldenburg	78%	633	5,811	2	60
Rhineland	79%	54,947	77,217	29	39
Westphalia	80%	27,637	21,520	16	65
Hamburg	98%	2,597	1,173	3	29

Urb. = urbanization measured by the percentage of the population living in communities of more than 2,000 inhabitants in 1910.

1 = Protestant League members per 1,000 Protestant inhabitants.

2 = People's Association for Catholic Germany members per 1,000 Catholic inhabitants.

Source: Monats-Korrespondenz für die Mitglieder des Evangelischen Bundes 22, no. 2 (February 1908): 1. For the statistics on urbanization, see *Statistisches Jahrbuch für das deutsche Reich* 35 (1914): 4–5.

advanced secularization—Schleswig-Holstein, Brandenburg, Oldenburg, and large metropolitan centers—the Protestant League fared
poorly, regardless of urbanization. In Frankfurt, the league rarely
even held assemblies due, in the words of the league's annual report,
"to the general indifference and weak-willed raving for tolerance
among the Frankfurters."[108] Nevertheless, where it succeeded, the
Protestant League was essentially an urban phenomenon. Most of its
local chapters were in cities of more than five thousand inhabitants.
Moreover, it found considerably fewer adherents in predominantly
rural states and provinces, even when, as in the case of Bavaria and
West Prussia, Protestants lived in confessionally mixed areas.

　　The inability of the Protestant League to organize rural Protestants
in the north German flatland represents one of its greatest failings as
a mass organization. There were many reasons for this failure. Part of
the problem lay in the sphere of economics. Not only did the Protestant League not represent any recognizable agrarian interest, but anti-
Catholic politics often undermined strategies of agrarian advocacy.
"The growth of the league," according to the annual report for the
years 1908 to 1909, "is hindered in rural areas by the fact that the
agrarian representatives in the Landtag usually go hand in hand with
the Center."[109] The league's ability to recruit peasants and farmers
was further confounded by the underdeveloped public sphere in the
sparsely populated countryside. Consequently, the burden of the
league's organizational work rested on the shoulders of rural pastors.
Yet in the north of Germany, many pastors were politically conservative and confessionally Lutheran while the league was associated
with liberalism and the "Protestant Union" forged between Calvinists
and Lutherans in 1822. In Hanover, for example, the clergy refused to
organize for the Protestant League, because it perceived that "the
Protestant League works for the union, at the pinnacle of which
stands a vision of a national church; the league cannot therefore claim
to be Luther's work."[110] In contrast to the situation within Catholicism, particularism among Protestants militated against an anti-
Catholic position. Especially in the early years of Protestant organizing, this fact proved frustrating to such nationally minded leaders of
the Protestant League as Coelestin Leuschner, who decried "particularistic sentiments of all sorts, Guelf legitimists and ultraconserva-
tive tendencies" that "hid behind the name of the Protestant church"
and whose adherents "felt themselves closer to Rome than to us."[111]

[108] AKIEB S500.9.60 "Jahresbericht des Evangelische Bundes, 1901," 15.
[109] Ibid., 1908/9, 29.
[110] Ibid., 1907/08, 32, citing the *Hannoverische Pastoralkorrespondenz*, Nr. 9, 22.4.1908.
[111] Ibid., 1894, 13.

A second problem in the north German flatland was the sheer distance of the "ultramontane danger." Unless a Pomeranian lived in Stettin, there was little chance that he would come in contact with organized Catholicism. Finally, in the eastern provinces, the specifically Protestant interests were usually subordinated to "the larger concern with the preservation of German nationality."[112] Accordingly, in Posen, West Prussia, and Silesia "the great number of existing national associations and the necessity of supporting them makes it difficult for the Protestant League to gain ground."[113]

Catholic confessional organization suffered from few of these problems. In the Protestant League's annual report of 1900, league secretary Leopold Witte complained that in matters of organization, "we are being humiliated by the Catholic competition, namely the association that his Excellency Windthorst brought into being as an antidote to the Protestant League, the People's Association for Catholic Germany."[114] Though the People's Association was not, in fact, an anti-Protestant league (in theory antisocialist, it was in practice antiliberal as well), it does provide a useful comparison.[115] The People's Association maintained its organizational strength precisely where the Protestant League proved disappointing: in small towns in the countryside and in the large diaspora areas.[116] The unequivocal engagement of the Catholic clergy accounted for some of the People's Association's success, but of equal importance, the People's Association addressed the material interests of its members whereas the Protestant League generally separated economic and religious issues. Still, the People's Association for Catholic Germany was less effective in large industrial cities than in small towns. In Westphalia, People's Association membership comprised 30.6 percent of the Catholic males, but, as Stanley Suval pointed out, "only 7% in the smelting cities of Dortmund and Gelsenkirchen."[117] The People's Association also fared poorly in the

[112] Ibid., 1906, 27.

[113] Ibid., 1907/8, 38.

[114] Ibid., 1900, 5.

[115] On Catholic efforts to found an anti-Protestant league, and the reasons for their failure, see chapter 2. On the People's Association generally, see Horstwalter Heitzer, *Der Volksverein für das katholische Deutschland im Kaiserreich 1890–1918* (Mainz, 1979). For a thorough regional study of the People's Association, see Hans-Jürgen Kremer, "Der Volksverein für das Katholische Deutschland in Baden," *Freiburger Diözesan-Archiv* 104 (1984): 208–80.

[116] For the relative success of the People's Association in rural diaspora areas, see membership in Brandenburg, Hanover, the province of Hessen, Oldenburg, Schleswig-Holstein, and Württemberg. In the Protestant city of Hamburg, the People's Association also fared well.

[117] Suval, *Electoral Politics*, 74.

ethnically mixed areas of Posen, West Prussia, East Prussia, and Silesia, but for reasons quite different from those that handicapped the Protestant League in the western provinces. Specifically, the Catholic church attempted to organize across ethnic lines, and an organization devoted solely to German Catholics tended to defeat this purpose.

The two religious groups thus stood opposed, though the geography of their opposition was quite complex: in some areas conflict was strung taut by the pressures of integration, in others reinforced by social division and confessional organization. Moreover, to sketch the social geography of the sharpest antagonisms does not mean to cover the whole landscape. Peasants in Pomerania may have preferred to debate the price of rye to discussing the antiultramontane strategies of Protestant pastors; but that does not preclude them from having harbored anti-Catholic sentiments. Similarly, Catholic workers in the Krupp foundries of Essen, though perhaps more concerned with wages and working conditions than with confessional polemics, may have nevertheless eyed Protestants with deep suspicion. For in the German empire, religious distrust was pervasive, dividing Germans culturally, ideologically, and socially. Moreover, the persistence of religious distrust, indeed its modernization, carried far-reaching political implications as it undermined the attempt, central to the national project generally, to create a cohesive nation, to fashion a self-evident "we."[118] At the turn of the century, that "we" seemed at best incomplete, at worst threatening to break asunder. By appealing to the national consciousness of its citizens, the German state would attempt to stitch together a nation divided. But its leaders would soon discover the difficulty of constructing an imagined community of shared memory and sentiment across a torn confessional landscape.

---

[118] On the nationalist effort to create a common subject, see Geertz, "The Politics of Meaning" and "After the Revolution," in Geertz, *The Interpretation of Cultures*, 317 and 240.

Part Two

POLITICS

4

The Politics of Nationalism and Religious Conflict, 1897–1906

WELL AFTER the Kulturkampf, religious antagonism continued to be a prominent part of national life, leaving its mark on German culture, ideology, and society. At the turn of the century, it also left its imprint in the realm of national politics. As the German government devised strategies to mobilize the nationalist sentiment of both Protestants and Catholics, the constrictions that a long history of division and discord placed on the national state, far from diminishing, became increasingly evident.

Beginning in 1897, the imperial German government worked out a series of strategies to rally German national sentiment behind an imperialist program that would strengthen Germany's position abroad while cementing an antidemocratic status quo at home. Known as *Sammlungspolitik*, these strategies rested on four pillars: the harmonization of agricultural and industrial interests, the construction of a solid phalanx of political parties loyal to the state and opposed to both Social Democracy and to the demands for autonomy on the part of peripheral nationalities, the creation of a broad base of popular and parliamentary support for the buildup of a German navy, and, finally, the long-term independence of the military budget from parliamentary constraints.[1] Geoff Eley has described the common denominator of *Sammlungspolitik* as an "attempt to overcome a prevailing system of political and ideological fragmentation."[2] Here we shall consider this

---

[1] PAAA R4259 Meeting of the Royal Cabinet of Ministers, 22.11.1897. This must be considered the central document of Johannes Miquel's conception of *Sammlungspolitk*. See also John C. G. Röhl, *Germany without Bismarck: The Crisis of Government in the Second Reich, 1890–1900* (London, 1967), 246–50. On Tirpitz, see Volker R. Berghahn, *Der Tirpitz Plan* (Düsseldorf, 1971). Berghahn may well attribute too much political foresight to Tirpitz. See Geoff Eley's trenchant criticisms in "Sammlungspolitik, Social Imperialism and the Navy Law of 1898," in Eley, *From Unification to Nazism*, esp. 117–24. One may now consult the collection of documents in Volker R. Berghahn and Wilhelm Deist, eds., *Rüstung im Zeichen der wilhelminischen Weltpolitik. Grundlegende Dokumente, 1890–1914* (Düsseldorf, 1988). On Bülow, see Peter Winzen's excellent study, *Bülows Weltmachtkonzept*.

[2] Eley, "Sammlungspolitik," in Eley, *From Unification to Nazism*, 143.

unifying strategy as "official nationalism," the essence of which was a sleight of hand by which dynastic empires co-opted, and even advanced, popular, nationalist demands in order to protect the domestic status quo and ensure the power of the state in the international arena. A tool for the mobilization of popular support for conservative regimes, official nationalism attempted to divert attention away from social and sectional conflicts and, by appealing to common national goals, to overcome potentially destabilizing divisions, whether between classes, confessions, or regional identities.

Yet identities deeply rooted and antagonisms firmly set are not easily manipulated, now this way, now that. The leaders of the German empire would soon confront what must be seen as the central irony of Germany's long history of religious division and discord: that the national integration of Catholics, far from quieting confessional conflicts, quickened them. For nationalism does not just unify groups within a nation; it also gives diverse groups a vocabulary with which to articulate their differences. The subsequent political history of confessional relations was not therefore marked by a progressive march to ever more peaceful accord but instead by a deepening of conflict, a hardening of ideological opposition, and a mobilization not only of national consciousness but also of ideologies that expressed differences within the nation. At issue was not integration itself but the terms of integration, not the existence of a common nation but the way that nation was to be imagined.

Sammlungspolitik, Salutations, and the Jesuit Law: Symbolic Politics

The political integration of the Center party constituted the first prerequisite of successful *Sammlungspolitik*. This was true of Finance Minister Johannes Miquel's narrower strategy, which was simply to combine the interests of industry and agriculture in a national, antisocialist coalition, as well as of the more ambitious plans of Naval Secretary Admiral Alfred von Tirpitz and the secretary of the Foreign Office, Bernhard von Bülow. Tirpitz and Bülow pleaded for a wider and more permanent *Sammlungspolitik* based on the concentrated mobilization of national consciousness and its projection outward into foreign affairs. In either case, the support of the Center, and therefore the national integration of Catholics, was crucial. As Bülow had once put it: "only by gradually integrating the Center into the new empire of the Protestant Hohenzollerns" could confessional division, "the most dangerous wound in the body of the exalted mother Germania," be healed.[3]

Well-intentioned, the policy of integration was, however, ill-starred. It commenced concurrently with a number of highly charged symbolic issues that separated Catholics from Protestants: the Canisius Encyclical of 1897, in which Pope Leo XIII compared Protestantism to the Plague; Los von Rom, a movement in part organized by the Protestant League to convert German Catholics in Cisleithanian Austria to Protestantism; and, in 1898, the so-called Bülow affair, a storm in a water glass over the manner in which German Catholics in Rome toasted the kaiser on his birthday. The "Bülow affair" was especially revealing of the political and symbolic complexities of confessional integration. It began when, much to the consternation of the Protestant League, German Catholics gathered at the Vatican spoke the German kaiser's name in the same sentence in which they praised the pope, a scandal which to the Protestant League was made more serious still by their having excluded King Humbert of Italy from the salutation. Allegedly, the assembled also sang a hymn in praise of Pope Leo XIII—and this in the presence of the Prussian emissary.[4]

The League complained, first privately, then publicly, that such actions necessarily "increase the arrogance of anti-German ultramontanism."[5] But far from lending a sympathetic ear to Protestant cavil, Foreign Secretary Bernhard von Bülow replied that such toasts followed diplomatic custom and the rules of international courtesy. He then chastised the league for issuing public pronouncements in diplomatic affairs beyond its competence.[6] Harsher still, the kaiser charged Wintzingerode, the president of the Protestant League and the man in whose name the league's letters of protest were written, with "unbelievable presumptuousness" in a matter that did not concern him.[7]

---

[3] Bernhard von Bülow to Philipp zu Eulenburg, 8.2.1892. Cited in Winzen, *Bülows Weltmachtkonzept*, 40. On the importance of the Center to Bülow's *Sammlung*, see Winzen, *Bülows Weltmachtkonzept*, 108–19. On Tirpitz's views, see Berghahn, *Tirpitz Plan*, 151.

[4] On this controversy, see *Aktenstücke in Sachen: Evangelischer Bund gegen Bülow* (Leipzig, 1898).

[5] The national committee (Vorstand) of the Protestant League to Chancellor Hohenlohe, 17.2.1898. Reprinted in ibid., 12–14.

[6] Bernhard von Bülow to Count Wintzingerode-Bodenstein, 17.2.1898. Reprinted in ibid., 14–16. In private, Bernhard von Bülow allegedly accused Wintzingerode of "confessional fanaticism." This accusation, made in 1898, is referred to in PAAA R2564 Wintzingerode to Bülow, 22.2.1903.

[7] PAAA R2564 Marginalia of Kaiser Wilhelm II on a letter of Wintzingerode to Karl Heinrich von Bötticher, provincial governor of Saxony, 27.3.1898.

A man of deep monarchical sentiment, Wintzingerode drew the consequences of the kaiser's displeasure and gradually disengaged from public politics.[8] More important, the exchange revealed the enmity of official circles toward Protestant politics that worked against confessional integration. Graf Carl von Dönhoff, the Prussian emissary at the Saxon court in Dresden, expressed a widespread official sentiment when he disparagingly referred to Protestant League leaders as "the hot-blooded leaders of the clerical estate."[9]

The "Bülow affair" pointed up the deep tensions between an emerging popular Protestant politics, a phenomenon powerfully shaped by the reintegration of Catholics into the empire, and the interests, as opposed to the sentiments, of the Reich leadership. In anti-ultramontane sentiment, the Reich leadership fully indulged. Kaiser Wilhelm II, hardly a taciturn man, often took flight in antiultramontane rhetoric, a propensity all the more noticeable after he had read, and reread, Houston Stewart Chamberlain's *Foundations of the Nineteenth Century*.[10] Philipp zu Eulenburg, the kaiser's closest adviser at the turn of the century, was similarly obsessed with Vatican plots and visions of political counterreformation.[11] Yet it is difficult to discern how these ideas affected the political strategies of the government except in personnel practices. For despite the undeniable antipathy that Prussian throne and Protestant altar harbored toward the specter of ultramontanism, the logic of official nationalism, and especially of battleship-building, required that the Center be integrated. As Tirpitz laconically put it in a cabinet meeting of 6 October 1897: "What we want to achieve can only be achieved with the help of the Center."[12]

[8] PAAA R2564 Prussian Minister of the Interior Freiherr Eberhard von der Recke von dem Horst to Chancellor Hohenlohe, 16.4.1898. Wintzingerode, who served as provincial magistrate (Landeshauptmann), agreed that he would not seek reelection in two years time, when his period of office came to an end. Moreover, according to von der Recke, Wintzingerode agreed in the future "to distance himself from similar demonstrations." See also PAAA R2564 Bernhard von Bülow to Kaiser Wilhelm II, 22.4.1898.

[9] PAAA R2564 Prussian envy to Saxony, Carl von Dönhoff, to Bernhard von Bülow, 3.10.1904.

[10] In the spring of 1897, the kaiser caused a small crisis by calling Center party leaders "unpatriotic fellows" (vaterlandslose Gesellen). See StAK NL Bachem Nr. 81 Note of Carl Bachem, 8.5.1898. On the kaiser's affinity for the theories of Houston Stewart Chamberlain, see Geoffrey Field, *Evangelist of Race: The Germanic Vision of Houston Stewart Chamberlain* (New York, 1981), 248–55.

[11] On Eulenburg's ideas concerning Catholics, see John C. G. Röhl, *Kaiser, Hof und Staat. Wilhelm II. und die deutsche Politik* (Munich, 1987), 42, and Isabel Hull, *The Entourage of Kaiser Wilhelm II 1888–1918* (Cambridge, 1982), 94. For a document of his obsession, see Eulenburg to Leo Graf von Caprivi, 8.9.1892, in Röhl, ed. *Philipp Eulenburgs politische Korrespondenz*, vol.2, 931–36.

[12] "Auszug aus dem Protokoll der Sitzung des Preußischen Staatsministeriums vom

That help carried a price, and for many Protestants in the empire the price was too high. To make important concessions to the Catholics in the name of national unity changed not just the politics but more importantly the character of the German empire. "Where is the Germany," asked Friedrich Naumann, a pastor known more for his progressive ideas than for his confessional positions, "of which Treitschke spoke with pathos, the state that was nourished by Protestantism and philosophy, at whose gate stood the old *Aufklärer* of Sanssouci?" Like many Protestants, both inside and outside the Protestant League, Naumann envisioned Germany to be in "transition to a period defined by Rome," and blamed the appeasement policies of the government for "bringing us effortlessly, as if in a Venetian gondola, into a different empire."[13]

In a sense, Naumann was right. An empire based on parity and tolerance would indeed be of a different stamp than one based on Protestant predominance. Moreover, the shift was subtle, if far from effortless. Many Protestants assumed a direct correlation between critical concessions to the Center, such as the repeal of paragraph two of the Jesuit law, and the buildup of the German navy, the symbol of German prestige and power. And in fact, a relationship did exist, but it was not the crass horse trading that many Protestants imagined. The fate of the fleet did not depend on the grace of Rome, as Willibald Beyschlag for example supposed; neither did the government or the Catholic Center wish openly to swap Center votes for the navy in exchange for repeal of the Jesuit law.[14] Yet Center leaders assumed that parliamentary support for the kaiser's navy would bring Catholics recognition as equal conationals, and that the repeal of the Jesuit law, the most important exceptional law still directed against Catholics, would confirm their new status.[15] Conversely, Center party leaders feared that a candid exchange of the Jesuit law for the naval bill would have encouraged an anti-Catholic "odium" in "the eyes of the Protestant people."[16] Tirpitz, who strongly supported conces-

---

6. Oktober 1897. Berathung über den Entwurf eines Flottengesetzes." Reprinted in Berghahn and Deist, *Rüstung*, 136–46, esp. 139.

[13] Friedrich Naumann, *Demokratie und Kaisertum*, 4th ed. (Berlin, 1905), 144–45.

[14] For Beyschlag's analysis, see *DEB* 25 (1900): 69–71.

[15] See BAK NL Bülow, Nr. 22 Memorandum, February 1900. Winzen, *Bülows Weltmachtkonzept*, 114, fn. 68, cites the original document in StAK NL Bachem, Nr. 112, and dates it as 31.1.1900.

[16] Bachem to Kopp, 8.2.1900 and 25.2.1900. Cited in Winzen, *Bülows Weltmachtkonzept*, 114. See also StAK NL Bachem, Nr. 27 Bachem to Cardinal Kopp, 30.6.1900. "As your Excellency knows, on the accession of the navy bill we considered it undesirable to strive for a formal agreement with the government by which the Center would ac-

sions to the Center, agreed that the timing was not right.[17] But on 13 June 1900 he suggested to the Center representatives Carl Bachem and Adolf Gröber that "in the following winter the question of import tariffs will come up; then a better opportunity will present itself."[18]

After the Center supported the tariff bill of 1902, which allowed Germany to finance the Second Naval Bill through high grain tariffs, the government moved to repeal paragraph two of the Jesuit law (thus granting the Jesuits the right to return to Germany but not to repopulate their monasteries).[19] On 11 February 1903, Bülow and Posadowski argued in the Prussian Cabinet of Ministers that "for political reasons" it was necessary to support the repeal.[20] Not only had the Center backed the government on legislation crucial to *Sammlungspolitik*, but Center support was necessary for the government's antisocialist policy. "One cannot," Bülow explained, "carry on the struggle against Social Democracy effectively, especially in the upcoming elections, if at the same time one has the Center and the Catholic population as opponents."[21] Moreover, Cardinal Kopp, the politically influential archbishop of Breslau, gave his assurance to Konrad von Studt, the Prussian minister of culture, that the German Episcopate would prevent "Polish and other foreign Jesuits, from whom an anti-German propaganda is to be expected, from entering the country."[22]

It is not easy to recapture the full range of passion aroused by the Jesuit question—especially on the Protestant side. When Bülow announced the government's support for repeal, Protestants in the empire responded with indignation. Armed with the right to reject the repeal in the Bundesrat, the resistance of the Protestant courts in Germany's small states proved especially resolute. The Prussian emissary in Oldenburg even spoke of the "formation of a kind of Schmalkaldic League against any sort of concession to the Center."[23] Deeper in the

---

cept the naval bill if the government would repeal the Jesuit law. But during the deliberations on the bill, we did not neglect to point out, confidentially and decisively, that if the bill passes, we must surely expect the repeal of the whole Jesuit law."

[17] StAK NL Bachem, Nr. 27 Note of Carl Bachem, 13.6.1900.

[18] Ibid.

[19] On the politics of the tariff settlement, see Peter-Christian Witt, *Die Finanzpolitik des deutschen Reiches von 1903 bis 1913* (Lübeck, Hamburg, 1970), 63–74, and Kenneth Barkin, *The Controversy over German Industrialization, 1890–1902* (Chicago, 1970), 226–52.

[20] PAAA R9318 Meeting of the Royal Cabinet of Ministers, 11.2.1903.

[21] Ibid.

[22] Ibid. For a number of years, Kopp had worked to bring German Jesuits to Upper Silesia for help in the nationality struggle against the Poles. See StAK NL Bachem Nr. 23 Carl Bachem to Augustinus Lehmkuhl, 16.6.1896.

[23] PAAA R9319 Baron Viktor Henckel von Donnersmark, Prussian emissary in Oldenburg, to Bernhard von Bülow, 14.1.1904.

oppositional phalanx, if less strategically placed, stood the Protestant church of Prussia, and, deeper still, the Protestant League. Yet while the opposition of the church was severely circumscribed by its close ties to official circles, the Protestant League organized popular resistance to the government's new course with little heed to the polite precepts of throne and altar.[24] Indeed, it made little fuss of its principled rejection of the government's weak-willed policy toward the Catholic Center.

The fronts, stiffened from the Protestant side, hardened still further when, on 15 February 1903, the Catholic bishop of Trier, Felix Korum, declared that he would deny absolution to Catholic parents in his diocese who sent their daughters to confessionally mixed girls' schools. To Protestants in the empire, it was fuel to fire their vision of an intolerant Catholic church bent on dividing the German nation. The "Trier affair," according to Carl Bachem, "fell" into the existing disquiet "like a bomb."[25] And it rendered Bülow's position vis-à-vis the combined forces of German Protestantism, already difficult, nearly impossible.

The struggle over the Jesuit question deepened the antagonism between Protestants and Catholics and widened the rift between the government and the Protestant League. Angered by Chancellor Bülow's callousness toward Protestant interests, Count Wintzingerode wrote the chancellor a long, impassioned letter against the repeal of the Jesuit law. The German people would suffer most, he insisted, for the Catholics, led by the Jesuits, sought "to divide our people into two parts, as they did at the end of the sixteenth and at the beginning of the seventeenth centuries."[26] Now, at the dawn of the twentieth century, the signs of impending national division were once again omnipresent: they could be discerned in the growth of Catholic organizational life, in the popularity of Catholic vocations, in job discrimination, and in ultramontane support for the enemies of the empire, especially the Poles. His pen strained, Wintzingerode pleaded one last time that Bülow bar the Jesuits' return to Germany. "The German people and the future will thank you for it," he wrote.[27]

[24] For the opposition of the Protestant church of Prussia, see PAAA 9318 Friedrich Wilhelm Barkhausen, president of the High Consistory of the Protestant church of Prussia, to Kaiser Wilhelm II, 6.3.1903; and, for the government's response, Bernhard von Bülow to Barkhausen, 26.3.1903.

[25] StAK NL Bachem, Nr. 187 Note of Carl Bachem, 2.5.1903. Georg von Hertling considered Korum's actions "distasteful." See BAK NL Cardauns, Nr. 478–2 Hertling to Hermann Cardauns, 24.2.1903. The imperial government's attempt to get the Vatican to disavow Korum's actions were futile, however. See PAAA 9318 Baron Wolfram von Rotenhahn to the Foreign Ministry, 28.2.1903.

[26] PAAA R2564 Wintzingerode to Bernhard von Bülow, 22.2.1903.

[27] Ibid.

Unmoved, Bülow replied abruptly. He considered Wintzingerode's exposition trivial and naive, full of "unclear emotional outpourings" from which he "could not draw one single practical lesson."[28] For the league, the exchange "threw a glaring floodlight . . . on its unbearable predicament" as well as on the "indifferent and contemptuous manner in which our sacred and religious feelings are brushed aside by government leaders."[29] The league, affronted and irate, resolved "to give the chancellor an indelible impression . . . of Protestant bitterness."[30] On the eve of the Reichstag election of 1903, the league's central committee called on "fellow Protestants" to pressure candidates to resist further concessions to the Catholics. "We do not want a Protestant Center, but we demand that the interests of Protestants, who constitute two-thirds of the population of the German empire, not be sacrificed in order to satisfy the desires of ultramontanism."[31]

Yet satisfying ultramontane desires is exactly what Bülow had in mind. He informed the Protestant princes that if the Bundesrat did not concede the repeal of "paragraph two," then the Center would no longer support financial reform necessary to prevent an increase in *Matrikularbeiträge*—money that the states contributed to the central government.[32] The economic consequences, he reminded the princes, would be especially catastrophic for the states.[33] Moreover, Bülow feared that the Center might make the Jesuit question a campaign issue, a threat which, given the Center's tight organization, seemed considerably more menacing than the Protestant League's attempts at intimidation.[34] In general, Bülow hoped to avoid an election dominated by confessional agitation, which he thought "would only benefit the *extremists* [the Socialists and the Agrarian League]."[35] Bülow's fears of the Center proved exaggerated, however. Not only did the Center party not campaign on the Jesuit issue, but after the

[28] PAAA R2564 Bernhard von Bülow to Wintzingerode, 28.2.1903.

[29] AKIEB S500.9.125 Leopold Witte to the executive committees of the regional organizations of the Protestant League, 4.3.1903.

[30] Ibid.

[31] "An unsere evangelischen Volksgenossen," reprinted in *Württembergische Bundesblätter* 16, no. 4 (1903): 50–52.

[32] PAAA R9319 Bülow to Dönhoff, 30.4.1903. He argued this point after the election as well. See Bülow to the Prussian envoy in Baden, Karl von Eisendecher (top secret—Ultra Geheim!), 6.12.1903.

[33] Ibid

[34] PAAA R9318 Bülow to the Foreign Ministry, 3.4.1903.

[35] Ibid. The parenthetical qualification is in the original. See also PAAA R9318 Bülow to Dönhoff, 30.4.1903.

elections, when the Bundesrat continued to drag its heels, the Center continued to support Bülow.[36]

Few elections could have provided a less auspicious beginning for forceful Protestant politics. As a result of the Reichstag elections of 1903, the Center remained the largest political party in Germany while the Social Democrats nearly doubled their mandate. Alarmed more by the success of the Socialists than by the persistence of the Center, Prussian conservatives declared that "in the face of the Social Democratic danger the struggle between Wittenberg and Rome must cease."[37] Similarly, some National Liberals criticized the league for ignoring the social problem that prefigured Social Democratic success. As fear of Social Democracy increased, antagonism toward the Protestant League grew as well. The imperatives of *Sammlungspolitik*, with its tax and tariff policies, contributed to this climate of antagonism. The Agrarian League accused the Protestant League of "throwing sand in the people's eyes": not theological syllogisms, its leaders insisted, but butter logic and barley prices should govern the attitudes of Protestant peasants toward their Catholic conationals.[38]

A number of liberal Protestants close to Friedrich Naumann and the Christian Socialists also suspected that confessional rancor blinded Protestants to the more pressing dilemma confronting Wilhelminian society: the social question. Naumann, who saw in the working classes a potential support for a strong nation and a solid monarchy, put forward a series of progressive proposals to alleviate their misery. A pastor who possessed great appeal to the empire's Protestant intellectuals, he also urged closer contact with the Social Democrats as well as revision of Prussia's three-class suffrage system.[39] But if Naumann bravely faced the social question, the confessional issue was never far from his mind. The "watchword democracy and monarchy" would, he argued, save Germany from "Roman domination."[40] Yet by

---

[36] "I don't know who could replace him," wrote Cardinal Kopp to Peter Spahn, and added "even for paragraph two I would not be willing to give him up." StAK NL Bachem Nr. 218 Cardinal Kopp to Peter Spahn, 24.8.1903. Similarly Julius Bachem to Carl Bachem, 30.8.1903. Carl Bachem was also of this opinion, but his patience with Bülow now began to wear thin. Carl Bachem to Peter Spahn, 3.9.1903.

[37] Cited in *Württembergische Bundesblätter* 17, no. 1 (1904): 10–12.

[38] D.E.K. dispatch printed in *Württembergische Bundesblätter* 16, no. 6 (1903): 90–91.

[39] On Naumann, see Peter Theiner, *Sozialer Liberalismus und deutsche Weltpolitik. Friedrich Naumann im Wilhelminischen Deutschland (1860–1919)* (Baden-Baden, 1983). See also E. I. Kouri, *Der deutsche Protestantismus und die soziale Frage, 1870–1919* (Berlin, 1984), 129–46.

[40] Naumann, *Demokratie und Kaisertum*, 147.

1903, his National Social Association had failed miserably.[41] A political party that attempted to fuse working-class interest politics with deference to throne and altar, it captured roughly thirty thousand votes in the Reichstag election of 1903, and thereafter promptly disbanded.[42] Still, Naumann considered it counterproductive to confront ultramontanism head-on. Rather, it was necessary to turn Protestant attention elsewhere. For Naumann, that meant creating a bloc between liberals and socialists. "The Center will control German politics," he argued, "until there is a parliamentary majority to the left of the Center."[43]

The Protestant League responded to the range of its critics with an appeal to nationalism. "German people," exclaimed Friedrich Meyer at the league's 1903 general assembly in Ulm, "you have lost sight of the ideals of your past . . . amidst the economic worries of the present."[44] The German nation, brooded Kurt Schindowski, would no longer be of value if "the question of whether tariffs for wheat should be set at 50 cents rather than a mark were considered more important than . . . protecting spiritual, moral, and religious possessions against the sworn enemy."[45] The league also reiterated its position on Social Democracy, which it opposed, but considered less dangerous than ultramontanism because, while the one attacked the material foundation of the state, the other undermined its moral basis.[46] "We would not be worthy of the name of Luther," proclaimed one pastor, "if out of fear of the Red Sea we shut our eyes to the Roman danger."[47] To the league, the German nation still seemed awash in the rising floodwaters of the "Black Sea."

Though divided on almost every other question, Catholic Center leaders shared with their Protestant counterparts this vision of impending confessional struggle, symbolically centered on the Jesuit question. Ever sensitive to the potential of politically organized Protestantism, Carl Bachem warned Peter Spahn, the titular leader of the Center party, that "if the Center is pushed out of its position, then the religious peace is at an end for the Catholics, the agitation of the Protestant League will gain the upper hand, confessional division will

[41] For a concise account of this failure, see Dieter Düding, *Der Nationalsoziale Verein, 1896–1903* (Munich, 1972).

[42] According to Düding, *Der Nationalsoziale Verein,* 177, fn. 11, it received 30,500 votes; according to Theiner, *Sozialer Liberalismus,* 123, only 27,900 votes.

[43] Naumann, *Demokratie und Kaisertum,* 146.

[44] Cited in *Württembergische Bundesblätter* 16, no. 10 (1903): 146–50.

[45] D.E.K. dispatch, printed in *Württembergische Bundesblätter* 16, no. 6 (1903): 90–91.

[46] Wintzingerode, "Zur Verständigung über die Stellung des Evangelischen Bundes zum politischen Leben," *DEB* 29 (1904): 551ff.

become irreparable, and resistance against Social Democracy will thereby be paralyzed and diverted."[48] Yet no such calamity occurred. On 8 March 1904, the Bundesrat approved the repeal of "paragraph two" of the anti-Jesuit law by a margin of twenty-nine to twenty-five votes with four abstentions. It was an important victory, both for political Catholicism as well as for a policy of official nationalism that attempted, through conciliation, to integrate German Catholics into the national state. Bülow now considered it "imperative" that the Center support his nationalist policies. On 13 March he wrote Cardinal Kopp that "it is of decisive importance for the future that the Center party does not assume an overly critical or fault-finding position in its handling of defense questions and that it show understanding for serious financial reform."[49]

For the Protestant League, the repeal of "paragraph two" represented the Jena of the confessional war, a defeat not made any easier in 1904 by what seemed to be a series of setbacks, whether in the Trier school affair, in the question of a Catholic seminary at the University of Strasbourg, or through what the pastors perceived to be the infiltration of Prussian schools by Marian congregations.[50] To add insult to Protestant injuries, the Prussian government confiscated a series of Protestant League pamphlets for fear that their anti-Catholic invective would disrupt confessional peace.[51] In the Bavarian Landtag, deputies even discussed the proposition that the Protestant League, like the Catholic Center, should be treated as a political party.[52]

The Underground Politics of the Protestant League

Dismayed by these events, the Protestant League did, in fact, reconsider its political activity. At the Dresden general assembly in October

[47] *Württembergische Bundesblätter* 17, no. 1 (1904): 10–12.

[48] StAK NL Bachem Nr. 218 Carl Bachem to Peter Spahn, 3.9.1903

[49] StAK NL Bachem Nr. 218 Bülow to Kopp, 13.3.1904. See also BAK NL Bülow Nr. 107 Bülow to Franz von Ballestrem, 6.4.1904.

[50] AKIEB S500.9.60 "Jahresbericht der Generalversammlung des Evangelischen Bundes zu Dresden," 1904.

[51] LHAK 403/7145 Otto Everling to Theobald von Bethmann-Hollweg, 24.7.1905. The confiscated pamphlets included Friedrich Meyer, *Die evangelische Bewegung in Österreich;* J. L. Morin, *Evangelisches Erwachen im katholischen Kanada;* Otto Everling, *Los von Rom;* Dr. Warmuth, *Martin Luther im deutschen Lied;* Paul Bräunlich; *Die österreichische Los von Rom Bewegung;* Friedrich Meyer, *Der Protestantismus in Österreich;* W. Bauer, *Scheidbergers Sendbriefe. Die Unterscheidungslehre von einem Rheinischen Pfarrer;* J. Schoettler, *Was ist der Evangelische Bund, was soll er sein und bleiben;* E. Buchner, *Welche inneren Gefahren bringt der römische Missionsbetrieb unter die evangelische Mission?*

[52] AKIEB S500.9.60 "Jahresbericht des Evangelischen Bundes, Generalversammlung zu Dresden, 1904."

1904, pressure for more political intervention came from the right as well as from the left. The extremely conservative superintendent of the Protestant church of Schleswig, Theodore Kastan, urged the league to become a "political union" that would advance religious and moral goals. While warding off sharp attacks on the Protestant League by Protestants close to the Conservative party and to the Christian Socialist movement, Kastan pleaded for political involvement based on conservative principles of the state.[53] Richard Bärwinkel, a conservative of the league's founding generation, essentially concurred with Kastan, agreeing that Bülow's complaisance toward ultramontanism had forced the hand of the Protestant League.[54] Although the league should not support one or the other party, there was no longer an alternative to political engagement. While remaining loyal to the dynasty, the league should take on "political tasks . . . in a similar way as the Colonial League, the Navy League, and the German Society for the Eastern Marches."[55] If that did not help, it might be necessary to form a "Protestant Center."[56] Wintzingerode, though more circumspect about this possibility, considered "the old cartel idea best suited for all vital questions of state and Reich."[57] Yet for all their talk, the conservatives of the league were still beguiled by the idea of throne and altar; they therefore balked at a popular Protestant program based on the modern methods of political pressure groups. A younger generation of Protestant intellectuals, who appealed less to scripture than to culture, less to the monarchy than to the nation, had few such reservations.

Paul Hoensbroech, an ex-Jesuit whose innumerable tracts documenting Catholic abuses made him the best known antiultramontane publicist in Germany, belonged to this younger generation of Protestant League leaders. When Bülow announced his approval of the repeal of "paragraph two" of the Jesuit law, Hoensbroech responded by forming a political action committee to "combat ultramontanism during elections."[58] Though partly a creation of the Protestant League's

---

[53] These principles included true (not formal) parity, a popular rather then a territorial state church, and confessional schools under state aegis. See Theodore Kastan, "Welche Bedeutung hat der Evangelische Bund?" *Allgemeine Evangelische Kirchenzeitung*, 10 June 1904. See also the somewhat reserved comments of Erich Haupt of the Protestant Middle party in the *DEB* 29 (1904): 508–11.

[54] Richard Bärwinkel, *Hat der Evangelische Bund politische Aufgaben?* (Leipzig, 1904), 8.

[55] Ibid., 9.

[56] Ibid.

[57] Wintzingerode, "Zur Verständigung über die Stellung des Evangelischen Bundes zum politischen Leben," *DEB* 29 (1904): 552.

[58] AKIEB S500.9.106h "Vertrauliche Rundschreiben des Antiultramontanen Wahl-

Berlin branch, Hoensbroech's Antiultramontane Election Coalition (Antiultramontane Wahlvereinigung) operated independently of the league.[59] Under Hoensbroech's leadership, the coalition focused on the cultural and political peril that ultramontanism allegedly posed to the German nation.[60] "In politics and in art, in science and religion, everywhere ultramontanism hinders progress and the self-determination of the individual as well as the community."[61] Within the context of political Protestantism, this was a forward-looking view. A National Liberal who was also known for his strident anti-Polish positions, Hoensbroech waxed progressive on most counts: he advocated the abolition of class restrictions in suffrage questions, he expressed sympathy for the Social Democrats, he argued for lowering restrictive grain tariffs, and he believed in ministerial responsibility to the Reichstag.[62] Unlike conservatives in the Protestant League, Hoensbroech placed the will of the people before his loyalty to the monarch. In his monthly journal, *Deutschland*, he commented in 1902: "We are fighting solely against ultramontanism, which is hostile to religion and civilization. And in this struggle neither the chancellor nor the kaiser shall hinder us so long as we are true men; for above all is the good of the fatherland."[63] Hoensbroech expressed little faith in either throne or altar, for the struggle against "the most dangerous enemy of our people" was too serious to be left to monarchs and ministers. Rather, it had to be fought politically and with the people.

Hoensbroech envisioned the Antiultramontane Coalition as the cell

---

ausschusses," 1.1.1903; AKIEB S500.9.106 "Satzung der Antiultramontanen Wahlvereinigung." For a brief introduction to the Antiultramontane Coalition, see Herbert Gottwald, "Antiultramontaner Reichsverband," in Dieter Fricke et al., eds., *Lexikon zur Parteigeschichte*, vol. 1, 89–93.

[59] In addition to Hoensbroech, the coalition's provisional board of directors included Admiral von Knorr, Freiherr von Münchhausen, the director of the Protestant League's Berlin branch, Dr. Poensgen, a National Liberal lawyer, Heinrich Rippler, the editor of the *Tägliche Rundschau*, Wilhelm Schmidt, one of the Protestant League's experts on Polish policy, and finally Kurt Schindowski, the editor of the *Deutsch-Evangelische Korrespondenz*. Münchhausen, Rippler, Schmidt, and Schindowski held important positions in the Protestant League; the latter three also served on the league's secret political action committee.

[60] "The core of the ultramontane danger," he asserted, lies "in its antagonism toward culture, in its antinationalism." Paul Hoensbroech, "Streiflichter," *Deutschland* 2 (1903): 683.

[61] AKIEB S500.9.106 "Zur Abwehr des Ultramontanismus bei den politischen Wahlen."

[62] Hoensbroech, "Streiflichter," *Deutschland* 5 (1904/5): 798–903; Hoensbroech, "Eine Aufgabe der Volksvertretung," *Deutschland* 9 (1906/7): 255–62.

[63] Hoensbroech, "Streiflichter," *Deutschland* 1 (1902/3): 811–16.

of a popular political front.[64] But it was ill-fated from the start. By the outbreak of World War I, the Antiultramontane Coalition produced only a handful of pamphlets, and it seems doubtful that the coalition ever counted more than ten thousand members. In 1906, it merged with the Antiultramontane Union of Baden, led by Arthur Böthlingk, a vain and immoderate professor of history at the Technical University of Karlsruhe.[65] Despite Hoensbroech's best efforts however, the new union, the Antiultramontane Reichsverband, remained mired in organizational stagnation.

The importance of Hoensbroech's coalition lay elsewhere—in the pressure it exerted on the Protestant League to take up electoral politics. This pressure came most forcefully from National Liberals within the league, as well as from prominent nationalists, such as Hans Delbrück and Friedrich Lange, outside it.[66] As late as the summer of 1904, conservatives in the league could still resist this pressure. Leopold Witte, the league secretary, insisted that "the league should not divide, but unify. Party politics is not its task."[67] But the conservatives did not prevail. The league turned to direct political action despite their objections.

At the Dresden general assembly in October 1904, the league instated a "mediation committee" to influence elections and the political positions of parliamentary deputies.[68] The driving force behind the committee was Pastor Otto Everling, a member of the younger generation of league activists and a National Liberal Reichstag deputy covetous of power. Heinrich Rippler, the Pan-German editor of the

---

[64] AKIEB S500.9.106h "Vertrauliches Rundschreiben des Antiultramontanen Wahlausschusses," 1.1.1903.

[65] For a taste of his views, see Arthur Böthlingk, *Die römische Gefahr und die Reichstagswahl* (Lörrach, 1903); and Böthlingk, *Noch Einmal. Römisch oder Deutsch?* (Leipzig, 1904).

[66] AKIEB S500.9.125 "Streng vertrauliches Protokoll über die Gesamtvorstandssitzung des Evangelischen Bundes in Coburg, 24/25.5.1904." In 1903, Friedrich Lange, the founder and editor of the influential Pan-German *Deutsche Zeitung*, established a National League for Reich Elections, which attempted to unify the parties of order in "a great national party." He considered the Protestant League's base too narrow because the league retained its confessional statutes. National politics, he maintained, had to be pursued on the basis of national culture. On Lange, see also Eley, *Reshaping the German Right*, 186–87.

[67] AKIEB S500.9.125 "Streng vertrauliches Protokoll über die Gesamtvorstandssitzung des Evangelischen Bundes in Coburg, 24/25.5.1904."

[68] AKIEB S500.9.125 "Protokoll über die Verhandlung der Gesamtvorstandssitzung zu Dresden, 3/6.10.1904." The vote for this resolution, formulated by Wilhelm Thuemmel, was 101 to 15. For the wording of the resolution, see AKIEB S500.9.125 Leopold Witte to the directors of the regional organizations (Hauptvereine) of the Protestant League, 21.11.1904.

Tägliche Rundschau, and Kurt Schindowski assumed the role of official chairmen.[69] Schindowski resigned within a year, however, after having vexed his nationally minded colleagues by attending a celebration in Prague on behalf of the Czech Los von Rom movement.[70] A small group of active league leaders, mostly from the league's National Liberal wing, also sat on the committee. Among the most prominent were Johannes Hieber, the Pan-German director of the Protestant League in Württemberg, Albert Hackenberg, the chairman of the powerful Rhineland branch of the Protestant League, Rudolf von Campe, who was to become governor of the Rhineland in 1917, and Wilhelm Thuemmel, a firebrand pastor whose anti-Catholic tirades brought him a jail sentence in 1887.[71] Leopold Witte, the league secretary, exerted the only conservative influence on the committee.

The mediation committee operated clandestinely. Everling admonished his collaborators to avoid publicly associating the mediation committee with the league and, where possible, to avoid mentioning the committee at all.[72] In part, this secrecy stemmed from legal necessity: according to current laws governing combinations, open support for a political party meant that the league would be declared a political organization and that its assemblies would be subjected to police surveillance. The league wanted to avoid this at all costs. Moreover, Everling intended to create the "impression" that the waves of anti-ultramontane sentiment actually welled up from below, spontaneously.[73] The effectiveness of our political activity, he said, "depends on our preserving the impression that [our influence] comes directly from the voters."[74]

The committee's strategy, worked out between 1905 and 1908, was to influence voting at all levels of German political life, to shape not only the constellation of Reichstag deputies but also the composition of the Prussian Landtag, of the state and provincial diets, even of city councils.[75] Under its ambitious leader, Otto Everling, the secret medi-

[69] AKIEB S500.9.125 Otto Everling, "Vermittlungsausschuss: Bericht für die Gesamtvorstandssitzung," 9.10.1905; 9.10.1906.

[70] AKIEB S500.9.125 Otto Everling, "Vermittlungsausschuss: Bericht für die Gesamtvorstandssitzung," 9.10.1905.

[71] With the notable exception of Everling, all the members of the committee had supported the Antiultramontane Election Coalition.

[72] AKIEB S500.9.125 Otto Everling, "Vermittlungsausschuss: Bericht für die Gesamtvorstandssitzung," 9.10.1905.

[73] Ibid. Everling was also anxious to shield the league from the work of the mediation committee. Political action, as he well knew, inevitably divided the league along party lines.

[74] Ibid.

[75] AKIEB S500.9.125 "Streng vertrauliche Unterlagen zu einer Besprechung der Auf-

ation committee set out to purge German politics of ultramontane influence by felling Center candidates, one after the next. In some districts this meant raising the religious consciousness of Protestant
peasants who found the Center's position on grain taxes attractive; in
others it entailed convincing conservative Hanoverian particularists
to refrain from giving their Protestant votes to a Catholic party.[76] But
usually this tactic involved pressuring nonultramontane candidates to
refuse negotiations with the Center in run-off elections.[77] In this way,
it was hoped, the Center could be pushed out of confessionally mixed
electoral districts. The mediation committee also lobbied against Progressives, Conservatives, and National Liberals who could not be
trusted to take a hard line on Catholic grievances. In 1906, the committee identified forty-one such Reichstag deputies, most of them
Conservatives, and accordingly suffused their districts with pamphlets on the danger of ultramontanism to state and nation.[78] But this
was only a beginning, for in the long term such tactics condemned the
league to react to political events. Everling's goal, however, was to
create a stable Protestant front, to infiltrate the electoral committees of
the leading parties at all levels of political life with "clairvoyant men
from the league."[79] Only then, he argued, "could one speak of real
influence."[80]

For Everling, the mediation committee represented a first step toward the construction of a leaner, more effective and politically engaged Protestant League. "Our battle strategy needs to be fundamen-

---

gaben des Vermittlungsausschusses in der Sitzung zu Eisenach," 23.4.1908. The decision to infiltrate all levels of German politics became known in internal documents as
the "Eisenacher principle." For an earlier, less ambitious statement of strategy, see
AKIEB S500.9.125 Otto Everling, "Vermittlungsausschuss: Bericht für die Gesamtvorstandssitzung," 9.10.1905.

[76] AKIEB S500.9.125 Otto Everling, "Mitteilung an die Mitglieder des Ausschusses,"
16.12.1905; AKIEB S500.9.125 Otto Everling, "Vermittlungsausschuss: Bericht für die
Gesamtvorstandssitzung," 9.10.1905; AKIEB S500.9.125 "Kurzer Verhandlungsnachweis der Sitzung des Vermittlungsausschusses in Berlin," 23.1.1906.

[77] AKIEB S500.9.125 Otto Everling, "Vermittlungsausschuss: Bericht für die Gesamtvorstandssitzung," 9.10.1905.

[78] AKIEB S500.9.125 "Vermittlungsauschuss, Protokoll zur Sitzung in Berlin,"
23.1.1906. The number of Conservatives and National Liberals affected could not, for
1906, be discerned. In 1911, an internal document of the mediation committee reported
"close to 50 electoral districts" in which Conservative or Christian Socialists supported
the Center in the first ballot, but in only two districts was this the case with National
Liberals. See AKIEB S500.9.125 "Der Vorstand des Vermittlungsauschusses an die Vor-
stände der Vermittlungsausschüsse der Hauptvereine," 23.12.1911.

[79] AKIEB S500.9.125 "Streng vertauliche Unterlagen zu einer Besprechung der Aufgabe des Vermittlungsausschusses in der Sitzung zu Eisenach," 23.4.1908.

[80] Ibid.

tally reconsidered," he told the committee.[81] Political success, he thought, required organizational centralization. In 1905, he convinced the league to change its statutes so that the chairman (which he was soon to become), as opposed to the president (Wintzingerode), would have wider powers, and that a new presidium, rather than the central committee, which was now expanded to include twenty-one members, would preside over political activities.[82]

When, at the Hamburg assembly of 1905, Everling became chairman of the Protestant League, the young, predominantly liberal leaders of the League eclipsed the old, rather conservative generation. Progressive and politically active, the members of the younger generation were open to new ideas about Protestantism and the nation; they were willing to embrace the Germanic vision of Houston Stewart Chamberlain and likely to either belong to, or sympathize with, the Pan-German League. They saw in ultramontanism less a religious than a political threat; for their formative era was marked as much by the specter of a Catholic subculture as by the still greater danger of complete Catholic integration, so complete that the character of the Reich itself would necessarily be changed. Monarchists in their hearts, they found themselves increasingly in the national opposition. Loyal to the state, they could but appeal to the nation, sometimes in opposition to the state.

The Hamburg congress also marked the decline of conservative influence over the league. In a letter to Pastor Rhode, the host of the Hamburg congress, Count Wintzingerode complained that the new initiatives heralded the end of an era. "It would be a grave mistake," he wrote, "if we, who have for eighteen years been a religious organization, should suddenly reveal ourselves as a political league."[83] To engage in politics meant to give up a Protestant ethos against mixing politics with religion. The league, which had always been involved in "*nationale Politik*" (politics that supported and served the nation), would now devolve into a pressure group too closely tied to specific political parties. And as political parties divided the nation, they also severed the bonds that held Protestants in Germany together. Without these bonds, "the Protestant League would not be the Protestant League anymore" but only a narrow "political-religious party." And that, he warned, would encourage centrifugal tendencies, especially

[81] AKIEB S500.9.125 Otto Everling, "Vermittlungsausschuss: Bericht für die Gesamtvorstandssitzung," 9.10.1905.

[82] On the changes in the league's organizational structure, see Müller, "Der Evangelische Bund," 34–36.

[83] AKIEB S55.500.18c Wintzingerode to Pastor Rode, 21.9.1905.

on the right.[84] The first generation of league leaders perceived disunity to be the greatest weakness of Protestantism in post-Kulturkampf Germany. They had also worked hard, and with some success,
to bring diverse Protestant groups together. The ascendancy of the
young generation threatened to undo this work, for the new generation perceived not disunity but political paralysis to constitute the
central problem of the Protestant League.

The mediation committee revealed rather than remedied this paralysis. In the fall of 1905, Everling complained that "in the upcoming
legislative period economic problems will probably be in the center of
public attention" and worried that "as soon as they unleash a war of
interests the league will be in serious trouble."[85] More politically astute than most of his colleagues, Everling realized that conflicts
among Protestants would follow hard on the heels of differences over
taxes and tariffs. Moreover, foreign policy problems exerted a pressure to "suppress" polemics against the "threat of ultramontanism."
In October 1906, Everling reported: "International tension . . . makes
for an especially strong aversion toward domestic conflict and friction. Moreover the empire's tax laws are in the forefront of the political activities and concerns of the parties and tend to create a climate of
conciliation toward the Center so that the navy bills and the tax re-
forms can be passed. All of this is ill-suited to call forth a vigorous
policy for the promotion of German Protestant interests."[86] In the
province of Hessen, Hans Waitz observed a similar process but
warned against pessimism "because in the end the great idealist currents that come from the soul of the people can also have a great
penetrating power."[87]

The league fastened its hope on these idealist currents. In practice,
however, electoral geography and local conditions determined political fortune. In Baden, the league seemed politically superfluous, despite its great popularity. National Liberals in the grand duchy hardly
needed instruction in antiultramontane ideology, and, if anything,
Protestant agitation sometimes proved detrimental to an anti-Center
election campaign. Especially in Baden's liberal electoral districts with
Catholic majorities, the engagement of the Protestant League encouraged the wrath of the Catholic clergy and the political mobilization of

[84] Ibid.

[85] AKIEB S500.9.125 "Protokoll über die Gesamtvorstandssitzung in Hamburg,"
9.10.1905.

[86] AKIEB S500.9.125 Otto Everling, "Vermittlungsausschuss: Bericht für die Gesamtvorstandssitzung," 9.10.1906.

[87] AKIEB S500.9.125 "Verhandlungsnachweis über die Versammlung der Vermittlungsausschüsse der Hauptvereine," 13.4.1909.

the Catholic devout.[88] The same problem confronted the league in Bavaria and in Catholic districts in the Rhineland, causing the Catholic *Kölnische Volkszeitung* to mock the league as "the Society for the Propagation of the Center Party."[89] In Württemberg, the predominantly liberal thrust of the league's political engagement offended conservative Pietists.[90] And in Saxony, there were few deputies, liberal or conservative, whose antiultramontane credentials could possibly be questioned.[91]

Some critics, such as Paul Hoensbroech, saw the political liabilities of the league less in the circumstances of its agitation than in the facts of its organization and the shortcomings of its ideology. In an influential article written in 1906, Hoensbroech observed that despite twenty years of struggle against Rome, the Protestant League could not list one significant political success.[92] This failure, he thought, stemmed from the league's initial decision to adopt the statement of confession in the statutes of the Protestant League, thus alienating many secular minded anticlericals in the empire. Hoensbroech also argued against what he perceived to be the predominance of theologians and pastors in the Protestant League, a situation which assured that the league would be out of step with the demands of modern mass politics. The content of the Protestant League's propaganda, he argued, further contributed to its political problems. The league's pamphlets were certainly numerous, but for Hoensbroech's taste not popular enough; they neither addressed the people's material interests nor fully exploited their passions and anxieties. Most pamphlets, thought Hoensbroech, struck an unnecessarily academic tone. Finally, confessional differences between Lutherans and Calvinists, conservative and liberal Protestants, imparted to the league a tradition of unclear and contradictory political positions.[93] Hoensbroech hoped to rid the league of its paralyzing contradictions. Between 1902 and 1905 he attempted to win the Protestant League over to the idea of a popular front based on a critique of ultramontanism that was cultural rather than narrowly confessional. When by 1906 his program failed to con-

---

[88] AKIEB S500.9.125 Otto Everling, "Vermittlungsausschuss: Bericht für die Gesamtvorstandssitzung," 9.10.1905.

[89] Cited by Everling without specific references to date or edition in ibid.

[90] AKIEB S500.9.125 "Verhandlungsnachweis über die Versammlung der Vermittlungsausschüsse der Hauptvereine," 13.4.1909.

[91] AKIEB S500.9.125 Otto Everling, "Vermittlungsausschuss: Bericht für die Gesamtvorstandssitzung," 9.10.1905.

[92] Paul Hoensbroech, "Der Evangelische Bund. Eine Kritik," *Deutschland* 8 (1906/7): 631.

[93] Ibid.

vince league members, especially Otto Everling, who perceived it to be a threat to the league's specifically Protestant character, Hoensbroech broke openly with his anti-Catholic allies.[94]

Although the league did not follow the path that Hoensbroech marked out, it certainly marched in that general direction. In October 1906, Everling confidently asserted that, as a result of organizational changes as well as his own stewardship, the league could begin to take over the tasks originally assigned to the mediation committee.[95] Moreover, since 1905 the central committee, now expanded from ten to twenty-one members, counted three additional National Liberal Reichstag deputies: Rudolf von Campe, Johannes Hieber, and Albert Hackenberg.[96] The predominance of National Liberals within the league, as well as the league's increasing political activity, also brought more laymen into its leadership. Between 1887 and 1913, the percentage of pastors in the central committee dropped from 80 percent to 60 percent.[97] The league also became a true mass organization, not the least because of its political engagement in the empire and in the Los von Rom movement. Between 1902 and 1906, league membership more than doubled, growing from 156,000 to 328,0000.[98] Thus it became the fourth-largest noneconomic voluntary organization in Germany, trailing only the Veterans' Associations, the People's Association for Catholic Germany, and the Navy League, while utterly outstripping such smaller organizations as the Pan-German League, the Colonial League, the Imperial League against Social Democracy, and the Society for the Eastern Marches.[99]

The importance of a mass organization cannot be ascertained by

[94] Graf Paul von Hoensbroech, *Der Evangelische Bund und die Politik* (Leipzig, 1910); AKIEB S500.9.106s "Zur Kritik des Grafen Hoensbroech" (1906). See also AKIEB S500.9.106r Otto Everling to Paul von Hoensbroech, 20.9.1921.

[95] AKIEB S500.9.125 "Vermittlungsausschuss. Bericht für die Gesamtvorstandssitzung in Hamburg," 9.10.1905.

[96] Müller, "Der Evangelische Bund," 49.

[97] On the composition of the central committee, see ibid., 50.

[98] Membership figures are conveniently presented in Gottwald, "Evangelischer Bund zur Wahrung der deutsch-protestantischen Interessen (EB)," in Fricke et al., eds. *Lexikon zur Parteiengeschichte*, vol. 2, 581.

[99] For comparison, in 1910 the Pan-German League had c. 17,000–19,000 members; the Colonial Society, 39,025; the Society for Germandom Abroad, 45,272; the Society for the Eastern Marches, 53,000; the Navy League, 290,964. See Eley, *Reshaping the German Right*, 366. The Protestant League had 400,593; the People's Association for Catholic Germany, 652,645. The figure for the Protestant League, unlike that of the Navy League, includes members from organizations, such as the Evangelical Workers Union, who were corporately affiliated. In 1912, this amounted to about 120,000 members. See Müller, "Der Evangelische Bund," 43. For the "People's Association," see Heitzer, *Der Volksverein für das katholische Deutschland*, 315.

counting members alone, however. Despite its electoral setbacks, the
Protestant League significantly altered the German political landscape. In religious politics, it made forward movement toward passing the Bill of Toleration extremely difficult. This bill, which the Center first introduced in 1900 and then again in 1903 and 1905,
attempted to remove the remaining discriminatory laws against the
Catholic church in a number of Protestant states (Saxony, Mecklenburg, Brunswick), as well as to define a unified code regulating the
religious education of the children of mixed marriages.[100] Composed
by Adolf Gröber and Peter Spahn, the Bill of Toleration would have
given officially recognized religious communities complete equality
before the law.[101] In practice, however, it mainly benefited
Catholics—as the Protestant League did not fail to point out—by, for
example, eliminating the remaining restrictions on German Jesuits.[102]
In private, Carl Bachem agreed with this assessment but added, "the
Protestants have long had almost everywhere what we would also
like for ourselves."[103] In its first reading in the Reichstag, the Bill of
Toleration found a majority (163 to 60) but steadily lost popularity
thereafter.[104] As with the repeal of the Jesuit law, the Bill of Toleration
faced its most serious opposition in the Bundesrat, where the states
jealously guarded particularist rights to govern religious affairs.
Moreover, the Protestant League effectively lobbied against the bill.
In the fall of 1906, Everling could be "happy and grateful" for having
"created a climate of opinion opposed to it."[105] Indeed, the Bill of

[100] For a thorough, juridical treatment, see Hartwig Cremers, *Der Toleranzantrag der
Zentrumspartei* (Ph.D. diss., University of Tübingen, 1973).

[101] StAK NL Bachem, Nr. 27a Note of Carl Bachem, 3.12.1900. This, as Bachem explained to the influential Jesuit moral theologian Augustinus Lehmkuhl, was a "tactical" matter: "if we *only* demanded freedom for Catholics, we would surely be left alone
and would have failed miserably." StAK NL Bachem Nr. 185 Carl Bachem to Augustinus Lehmkuhl, 3.7.1901. For Catholic defenses of the Bill of Toleration, see Matthias Erzberger, *Der Toleranzantrag der Zentrumsfraktion des Reichstages* (Osnabrück,
1906); Hermann Roeren, *Der Toleranzantrag des Zentrums* (Hamm i. W., 1901).

[102] The most concise point by point position paper on the Protestant side is AKIEB
S500.9.103g Leopold Witte, *Zentrum und Toleranz. Im Auftrag des Zentralvorstandes des
Evangelischen Bundes zur Wahrung der deutsch-protestantischen Interessen* (1904). For a more
detailed, juridical treatment, see Wilhelm Kahl, *Die Bedeutung des Toleranzantrages für
Staat und evangelische Kirche* (Halle, 1902). Carl Mirbt, *Der Toleranz Antrag des Zentrums.*
(Leipzig, 1901), and Johannes Hieber, *Der Toleranzantrag des Centrums* (Berlin, 1901),
capture the combative spirit that marked the debate.

[103] StAK NL Bachem, Nr. 27a Bachem to August Lehmkuhl, 3.7.1901.

[104] Cremers, *Der Toleranzantrag der Zentrumspartei*, 23. By 1909 the Reichstag rejected
the bill as well, by 160 against 150 votes.

[105] AKIEB S500.9.125 Otto Everling, "Bericht des Vermittlungsausschusses,"
9.10.1906.

Toleration was not passed until 1919, when it became part of the Weimar Constitution.

The Reaction of the Catholic Center

More importantly, the popular anti-Catholicism mobilized by the league influenced the political strategy of the Center, a fact insufficiently appreciated by the vast scholarly literature on the party.[106] Center leaders understandably waxed anxious at the specter of mass demonstrations of anti-Catholic sentiment. "No doubt," thought Carl Bachem, this sentiment "had established itself among certain parts of the Protestant people in a threatening and alarming way."[107] A spate of anticlerical legislation in France as well as the advent, in 1905, of the grand coalition in Baden did little to allay such anxieties. Held together by common hostility to the Center, Baden's ruling coalition of Liberals and Socialists seemed especially ominous given that state's historical role as *Lehrmeister* to Bismarck's own Kulturkampf. Yet while Bismarck's Kulturkampf forced the Catholics to oppose the state, the popular Kulturkampf of the turn of the century bound Catholics ever more tightly to it. In 1905, Carl Bachem wrote Richard Müller, a Center deputy from Hessen: "The only thing that stops the new Kulturkampf, which the Protestant League and some other people are attempting to ignite, is the position of the imperial government and of the crown, in other words the kaiser and Bülow. If we make special trouble for the government now, it will have no reason to take us into consideration. Then perhaps a left block or a block of antiultramontanes will fall upon us."[108] Bachem insisted that it was not the Center that had changed but the conditions of Catholic politics. "A healthy opposition party" was perhaps desirable in Windthorst's time, but now "sharp opposition only encouraged this [new] Kulturkampf."[109]

Threatened by a Kulturkampf from the left, the Center moved to the right. At the Essen Catholic assembly (*Katholikentag*) of 1906, the prelates and the party called for "an alliance of all confessions faithful to God and Jesus Christ against the forces of atheism and revolution."[110]

---

[106] The exception is Ronald Ross, *Beleaguered Tower*, esp. 18–33.

[107] StAK NL Bachem, Nr. 28 Note Carl Bachem, 19.4.1904.

[108] StAK NL Bachem, Nr. 223. Carl Bachem to Richard Müller-Fulda, 22.1.1905.

[109] Ibid.

[110] Quoted in AKIEB S500.9.60 "Jahresbericht des Evangelischen Bundes, 1906/1907." The Protestant League rejected this call and countered by saying, "We feel ourselves at one with Christians of all churches and confessions who see in the Lord Christ the only source of grace."

To insiders, it was a thinly veiled appeal to cooperate with conservative Protestants. In an article entitled "We Must Come out of the Tower," Julius Bachem, the publisher of the *Kölnische Volkszeitung*, beseeched the Center to open its gates to Christians of other confessions. Until the Center shed its confessional exclusivity, he argued, it would not be accepted as the equal of other parties, regardless of its national engagement.[111] Like his cousin Carl, Julius believed that the terrain of confessional conflict had changed, that the danger to the church came less from the state than from popular movements against Catholicism. He realized that in church-state questions "not all of our wishes have been fulfilled," but thought that on balance "the Catholic church in Germany has by and large been restored to unrestricted sovereignty."[112] Now another danger ranged on the horizon. "The Center has recently been attacked more caustically than ever, with the exception of the worst years of the Kulturkampf," and "it was doubtless the Protestant League that had so poisoned the atmosphere."[113] Julius Bachem therefore proposed to counter the league's central criticism of the Center—confessionalism—by inviting moderate Protestants into the fold, foremost among them Christian Socialists. He even suggested surrendering a number of secure electoral districts to conservative Protestants who could be trusted to defend the interests of Catholics.[114] Although the position of Julius Bachem came to determine the party line (if not always party practice), it did not go uncontested. A younger group of Center politicians, including Matthias Erzberger, Hermann Roeren, and Franz Bitter, resolutely opposed it. They too registered the resurgence of anti-Catholic sentiment in the empire, but, unlike Bachem, they urged Catholics to fight back. In what came to be known as the *Zentrumsstreit*, Bachem's opponents argued for a return to the values of German Catholic culture: opposition to the centralizing state, solidarity with ethnic minorities, defense against liberal economics, and the right to confessional exclusivity in matters considered sacred. Less interested in Catholic integration into a national culture still saturated with Protestant values, they caustically attacked the excesses of German nationalism. Less timid in their own confessionalism, their anti-Protestant barbs cut considerably deeper.[115]

---

[111] Julius Bachem, "Wir müssen aus dem Turm heraus!" *Historisch-politische Blätter* 137 (March 1906): 376–86. Reprinted in Ludwig Bergsträsser, *Der politische Katholizismus* (Munich, 1923), 332–41. Citations follow Bergsträsser.

[112] Ibid., 334.

[113] Ibid., 337.

[114] Ibid., 340. The most thorough discussion of the "Turm" article can now be found in Noel Cary, "Political Catholicism and the Reform of the German Party System, 1900–1957," (Ph.D. diss., University of California, Berkeley, 1988), 93–105.

[115] For a provocative essay on the *Zentrumsstreit*, see Margaret Lavinia Anderson,

It is no accident, then, that in December 1906 Erzberger and Roeren should have spearheaded the Center's critique of the government's colonial scandals, including Germany's violent repression of the Herero uprising in Southwest Africa. Nor was it fortuitous that Carl Bachem as well as Peter Spahn and Adolf Gröber should have counseled Erzberger against it.[116] That Bülow would dissolve the Reichstag and direct the government's enmity against the Center seemed to the moderates and conservatives within the party to be the logical consequence of such sharp opposition. And, as the ensuing election campaign would demonstrate, their fears of renewed confessional antagonism were more than well founded.

"Interdenominationalism, Clericalism, Pluralism: The *Zentrumsstreit* and the Dilemma of Catholicism in Wilhelmine Germany," *Central European History* 21, no. 4 (August 1990): 350–78. For more detail, see Cary, "Political Catholicism," 66–177; Rolf Kiefer, *Karl Bachem 1845–1945* (Mainz, 1989), 129–55; and, for a sympathetic account of the "Bachemites" position, Ross, *Beleaguered Tower*, 49–78.

[116] StAK NL Bachem, Nr. 259 Note Carl Bachem, 15.12.1906; StAK NL Bachem, Nr. 268b Carl Bachem to Felix Porsch, 5.10.1907. Hertling also opposed Erzberger's sharp criticism of Bülow. BAK NL Hertling 36,43 Hertling to Friedrich Althoff, 20.12.1906. Despite the predisposition of prominent Center leaders to oppose Erzberger's strategy, Bachem realized that Erzberger had "the majority of the party behind him."

5

The Politics of Nationalism and
Religious Conflict, 1907–14

ON 11 DECEMBER 1906, Chancellor Bernhard von Bülow dissolved the Reichstag and publicly summoned nationally minded men to an electoral "struggle against ultramontanes, Guelfs, socialists, and Poles."[1] Throughout the empire, German nationalists reacted to Bülow's battle call with swift pens, producing a profusion of placards and penny pamphlets maligning Catholic patriotism, vilifying the Center party.[2] "Roman ultramontanism is not national," asserted one broadside in particularly bold print. Rather, it is "the greatest enemy of our people and fatherland."[3] Pundits, liberal and conservative alike, praised Bernhard von Bülow for pointing the German people in the direction of its national destiny while, with one stroke, freeing the empire of its Roman fetters. If this was the hour of integral nationalism, it was also a moment of great satisfaction to the Protestant League. "We have experienced . . . something joyful and exciting," proclaimed Otto Everling.[4] For so many years the imperial government had ignored the premonitions of the Protestant League; now the heads of state seemed to take these premonitions to heart.

In Catholic Germany, the Reichstag election of 1907 was viewed with apprehensive eyes. Although the Center managed to maintain its stable bloc of Reichstag representatives, it found itself along with the Social Democrats and the national minorities pitted against a much larger, almost exclusively Protestant, coalition of Conservatives, National Liberals, and left-liberals. And the problem was not just parliamentary. Pointing to ominous signs—the Los von Rom movement, the proliferation of evangelical societies, the growth of

[1] A concise description of the confessional politics behind the dissolution of the Reichstag can be found in Witt, *Die Finanzpolitik*, 152–57.

[2] For the atmosphere of the elections, compare Paul Bräunlich, *Zentrum und Regierung im Kampf* (Leipzig, 1907), with Matthias Erzberger, *Bilder aus dem Reichstagswahlkampf. Die Agitation der Zentrumsgegner, beleuchtet nach deren Wahlschriften* (Berlin, 1907).

[3] AKIEB S500.9.112a. This campaign poster was presumably, though not certainly, put out by the Protestant League.

[4] AKIEB S500.500.20f Otto Everling, speech at the 20th general assembly of the Protestant League, 30.9.1907.

the Protestant League, and the noticeably shriller, anti-Catholic tone in liberal circles—parish priests, Catholic village schoolmasters, and local Center politicians warned the faithful of the coming of a second Kulturkampf.[5] More than mere demagogy, their foreboding reflected fears shared by the party leadership. In his private notes, Carl Bachem pondered the "real reason" for the dissolution of the Reichstag: not the "maladroit and excessive . . . if more or less correct criticisms of Erzberger," but rather "the agitation of the Protestant League and the *Tägliche Rundschau* as well as the bloc politics of all the liberal parties." This agitation, he thought, "has reached a stage where they believe they can wage a new, united struggle against the Center."[6]

German Nationalism and the Catholic Center in the Bülow Bloc

The threat of a second Kulturkampf, its emotional élan drawn from integral nationalist visions of a German national state purged of Catholic influence, exercised the anxieties, the imagination, and the politics of Center leaders in the two and one-half years of the Bülow bloc. Within the Center itself, two responses to this threat emerged. Matthias Erzberger and Hermann Roeren argued for unrelenting criticism of the new nationalism, especially its anti-Catholic edge, as well as an uncompromising stance toward the government. Georg von Hertling, the influential Bavarian Center representative, eloquently pleaded for the opposite position: patience and conciliation. He feared that Erzberger's brash confrontation with the government had ruined years of work toward Catholic integration, "putting an end to a decade of efforts aimed at allaying passions and overcoming the confessional division by emphasizing national unity."[7] The populist wing of the Center tended to support Erzberger's position, while the curia and the episcopate leaned toward Hertling's stance, though not necessarily for the reasons he advanced.[8] In the late summer of 1907,

[5] See, for examples, GLA 69/NL Partei, 87 "Obacht Wähler" and LHAK 403/8806 "Tätigkeit der Geistlichen und Beamten bei der Reichstagswahlbewegung," Trier, 24.2.1907.

[6] StAK NL Bachem, Nr. 259 Note of Carl Bachem, 20.12.1906.

[7] BAK NL Hertling, 43 Georg von Hertling to Friedrich Althoff, 20.12.1906.

[8] Loth, *Katholiken im Kaiserreich*, 122. Pope Pius X "strongly regretted" the Center's position on the colonial question. PAAA/R1431 Wolfram von Rotenhahn to Bülow, 21.3.1907. He also instructed the German bishops to "preach restraint in German and Polish matters." PAAA/R1431 Rotenhahn to Bülow, 18.3.1907.

Center leaders worked out a common line: no compromise with Bülow, a tempered tone toward the bloc, discipline and reserve on questions of taxes and financial reform, and cautious movement toward compromise with the Conservative party.[9]

Carl Bachem—especially eager to allow the bloc parties to manage Bülow's unpopular tax reform by themselves—assented to all these points.[10] Yet it would be incorrect to reduce the Center's position in the first year of the Bülow bloc to that of an opportunistic party waiting on the banks until economic contradiction wrecked the coalition. The logic of religious conflict also played a role, pushing the Center slowly toward the Conservative party, with which it shared dynastic sentiment, a common outlook on the question of confessional schools, and, at least with some Conservatives, antipathy toward integral, as opposed to official, nationalism.[11] Fear of popular anti-Catholicism from the left also dictated a cautious policy toward Bernhard von Bülow, whom Bachem considered neither inveterately anti-Catholic nor bent on beginning a Kulturkampf "if he did not have to."[12] If the Center tried to break up the bloc now, argued Bachem, Catholics would face the wrath of the Protestant majority, and if Bülow fell, the Center could not be sure who would succeed him. Conceivably, a new chancellor "would attempt a new Kulturkampf in order to hold the opponents of the Center together," and that Kulturkampf would be greeted by the National Liberals "with shouts of hurrah," while the Conservatives, "already shaken up by the Protestant League, would only offer very weak resistance." Thus Bachem concluded in the fall of 1907, "I think we will do best to allow Bülow and the bloc to rest for a while."[13]

National and confessional issues also threatened to undo the cultural fabric of the Center party from within the Catholic fold. On 10 January Graf Wilhelm von und zu Hoensbroech, the brother of the ex-Jesuit Paul von Hoensbroech, called together nationally minded Cath-

[9] BAK NL 36 NL Hertling, 36. "Streng vertrauliches Protokoll einer Konferenz von Zentrumsparlamentariern und Vertretern der Zentrumspresse, Mönchen-Gladbach," 22/23.7.1907.

[10] StAK NL Bachem, Nr. 268b Note Carl Bachem, 17.9.1907. For the continuity of this thinking, see StAK NL Bachem, Nr. 280a Note of Carl Bachem on a discussion with Julius Bachem, 30.9.1908. In this context it is also interesting to consider that in both memorandums Bachem justified his reluctance to play a decisive role in the new tax reform by his fear that the Protestant parties would once again turn their enmity against the Catholics should the reform fail.

[11] On confessional schools, and the negotiations surrounding the Prussian school law of 28 July 1906, see Lamberti, *State, Society, and the Elementary School*, 154–210.

[12] StAK NL Bachem, Nr. 268b. Note of Carl Bachem, 29.10.1907.

[13] Ibid.

olics "whose patriotic and monarchical sensibilities were offended" by the Center's refusal to approve funds to suppress the Herero uprising in Southwest Africa.[14] Armed with the slogan "We shall stand behind the government in all national, army, navy, and colonial questions," the National Catholics—as they called themselves—ran seven candidates in the Reichstag election, all of them in the Rhineland, all of them without success.[15] Dismayed by their defeat in grass-roots politics, the National Catholics created an organization "above politics." On 27 November 1907, Wilhelm Hoensbroech established the German Union (Deutsche Vereinigung), an organization of nationally minded Catholics that drew its membership primarily from the well-off, elevated classes of the Catholic Rhineland.[16] Though predominantly Catholic, it also included a small number of prominent conservative Protestants.

Herein lay the union's novelty. It proposed that German Catholics bind together with German Protestants to support patriotic interests and assure the Christian and national foundation of the state.[17] "Confessional division," proclaimed the union's first public statement, "threatens to poison the life of our nation."[18] In a pamphlet entitled *What Does the German Union Want?* Graf Hoensbroech outlined the union's three programmatic points: confessional peace, dynastic loyalty, and economic harmony. The first point was directed against the Center, a confessional party in the worst sense, but also against the Protestant League, an organization that seemed to make it impossible for Catholics, of whatever ilk, to be accepted fully as Germans; the second point expressed the union's conservative sentiment; the third advanced a corporatist vision of the economic order designed to protect the interests of artisans and farmers, as well as the interests of

[14] Horst Gründer, "Rechtskatholizismus im Kaiserreich und in der Weimarer Republik unter besonderer Berücksichtigung der Rheinlande und Westfalens," *Westfälische Zeitschrift* 134 (1984): 127.

[15] Ibid., 128–29. The National Catholics received a meager total of 18,000 votes in the Reichstag election of 1907, and in only one electoral district—Wittlich-Bernkastel, a wine-growing area northeast of Trier—did they receive more than 20% of the vote.

[16] Ibid., 133–34. The founding petition is reprinted in *Deutsche Wacht* 1 (1908): 2–5. Of the 826 men who signed the union's founding petition, 7.4% were manorial lords while a further 18.8% consisted of nonnoble farmers, most of whom owned their own manors. Thus the agrarian influence, especially of the landed nobility, was especially weighty, but that influence was shared with representatives of high civil service (9%), with merchants and businessmen (19.2%), with academics (9.4%), and with the legal professions (5.6%). Among artisans, workers, and small farmers, the German Union fared poorly.

[17] Proclamation of the "Deutsche Vereinigung," in *Deutsche Wacht* 1 (1908): 2.

[18] Ibid.

civil servants. The union also opposed Social Democracy and believed confessional peace to be a prerequisite for stemming it.

Historians have tended to perceive the union's ideology of confessional reconciliation as a mask hiding its true identity as an antisocialist organization.[19] But while fear of working-class radicalism animated the Catholic notables of the German Union, it was not their central concern. Rather, the purpose of the German Union was to challenge the Center's monopoly on the political loyalties of Catholics in post-Kulturkampf Germany. Often former Center activists themselves, the leaders of the German Union conceded that Bismarck's repressive measures required, at the time, a Catholic political response. But now they objected to the Center's democratic politic style, its spurious confessionalism, and its conspicuous lack of patriotism. These issues, and not antisocialism, motivated the Catholic notables to pursue politics independently of the Center.

If the union never achieved great popularity, it was, however, symptomatic of a shift in political sentiment, most pronounced among well-educated, upper-class Catholics, toward a less narrowly confessional view of the world and toward more deeply felt national values. A gradual electoral drift away from the Center and to the national parties reflected this change. The historian Horst Gründer estimates that by 1907 "nearly one-sixth of voting Catholics voted for parties to the 'right' of the Center" and concludes that in the Kaiserreich "Catholics wandered into the 'conservative' camp in far greater measure than to Social Democracy."[20] Although such statements remain to be proved by detailed studies of Catholic voting behavior, it does seem likely that Catholic support for national parties was increasing, was regionally concentrated (the Rhineland, Silesia, the cities of south Germany), was more predominant among the young than the old and among those who had not been engaged in the struggles of the Kulturkampf.[21]

[19] Gründer, "Rechtskatholizismus," 118. For similar interpretations of the Deutsche Vereinigung as primarily an antisocialist organization, see Dirk Stegmann, *Die Erben Bismarcks. Parteien und Verbände in der Spätphase des Wilhelminischen Deutschlands, Sammlungspolitik 1897–1918* (Cologne and Berlin, 1970), 48–50, and Herbert Gottwald, "Deutsche Vereinigung (DV) 1908–1933," in Fricke et al., eds., *Lexikon zur Parteiengeschichte*, vol. 2, 403–12.

[20] Gründer, "Rechtskatholizismus," 129. For an argument for the stability of the milieu, based not on the percentage of Catholics that gave their support to the Center but rather on the relative percentage of voters held by the combined parties of the Catholic milieu (including the national minorities), see Rohe, *Wahlen*, 99.

[21] For a sense of popular Catholic attitudes toward the navy bills, see Carl Bachem's memorandum of 31.1.1900. BAK NL Bülow, 22. See also Winzen, *Bülows Weltmachtkonzept*, 111–12.

But voting represented only one index of the national sentiment of German Catholics and was not necessarily the most revealing. Quite conceivably, many Catholics expressed national feeling without severing traditional political loyalties. As Bethmann-Hollweg's adviser Kurt Riezler observed, the Center had itself "converted to the national idea."[22] With Erzberger's criticism of the colonial administration constituting the notable exception, the Center offered ever weaker resistance to the forward march of the empire's military demands.[23] Even in the period of the Bülow bloc, when the Center was cast into the opposition, the party remained restrained. "In committee meetings on the military budget," the Bavarian military attaché in Berlin reported on 15 February 1908, "the speakers of the Center, especially Erzberger and Gröber, were so reserved, indeed they spoke so favorably, that it attracted attention."[24] After the Second Naval Bill of 1900, Tirpitz's naval plans confronted an equally small measure of resistance from the Catholic Center in the German Reichstag. More important, the Center no longer opposed the vast array of patriotic propaganda—festivals, monument building—that saturated the German landscape. Even in Bavaria, ultramontane culture came to coexist with increasing ease with Hohenzollern dynastic ritual and the symbolism of the German national state.[25]

The Organization of the Nation: Religious Conflict inside the Nationalist Pressure Groups

It is often thought that Catholics gradually integrated into the national state, and that this integration brought with it recognition as equal conationals. Though not completely false, this view obscures the precariousness of the "integration process" and ignores the Protestant and integral national reaction to it.[26] Furthermore, the simple integration thesis presupposes a unified national ideology to which Catholics one-sidedly, if gradually, assented. In fact, German nationalism was neither a unified nor always a unifying ideology. Rather, it divided over many issues, including the terms, even the desirability, of Catholic integration.

[22] Cited by Deuerlein, "Die Bekehrung des Zentrums zur nationalen Idee," 434.
[23] Förster, Der doppelte Militarismus, 108.
[24] BHStA Mkr/42,440 "Bericht über die Verhandlung im Reichstag über den Militäretat," 15.2.1908.
[25] Blessing, Staat und Kirche, 248–50.
[26] Morsey, "Die deutschen Katholiken und der Nationalstaat," remains the best treatment, but here as well, integration is conceived as a one-sided affair.

The experience of Catholics in Germany's nationalist pressure groups revealed the precariousness of this integration process. In membership predominantly Protestant, the national pressure groups were, according to their statutes, confessionally neutral. In practice, however, confessional conflict affected the life of all the nationalist organizations, though its impact varied considerably, depending on the organization's ideological orientation, method of agitation, and size.

The Pan-German League, the most important integral nationalist organization in Germany, professed to be confessionally neutral. Whether Protestant or Catholic, Germans could be ardent patriots if they subordinated their religious adherence to their national involvement. Moreover, the Pan-Germans advocated redrawing the map of central Europe in such a way that, as an unintended consequence, the confessional balance, which had hitherto favored Protestants, would be fundamentally altered to the advantage of Catholics. Yet the Pan-German League's radical profile, its association with the Protestant League, and its connections with the Los von Rom movement all conspired to render spurious its claim to confessional neutrality. Consequently, few Catholics joined the Pan-German League, and those who did were themselves anticlerical.[27] Thus, for example, the local branch of the Pan-German League in Düsseldorf, which presumably included a number of Catholics, requested in 1906 that the Pan-German League change its statutes to "recognize its main opponent, which it must fight with the greatest vigor, to be anti-German ultramontanism."[28] The league's national presidium voted against this resolution, however, claiming instead that antiultramontanism should be the domain of "völkisch Catholics."[29] But of such völkisch Catholics who populated the Pan-German imagination, few actually found their way to the Pan-German League. As Roger Chickering, the historian who has written the most scholarly account of the Pan-German League, writes: "In its ideology as well as in its composition, the Pan-German League was, protests to the contrary notwithstanding, a distinctly Protestant phenomenon."[30]

The Imperial League against Social Democracy, a second, though considerably less influential, integral nationalist organization, was also closed to Catholics. Founded in 1903 in response to Social Demo-

---

[27] Roger Chickering, We Men Who Feel Most German: A Cultural Study of the Pan-German League, 1886–1914 (Boston, 1984), 140. See also Otto Bonhard, Geschichte des Alldeutschen Verbandes (Leipzig, 1920), 89.

[28] See Bonhard, Geschichte des Alldeutschen Verbandes, 92–93.

[29] Ibid.

[30] Chickering, We Men Who Feel Most German, 138.

cratic electoral success, the league set out to break Social Democracy's hold over the German working class. Yet the violent antisocialism of the league's chairman, Eduard von Liebert, was nearly matched by the vehemence of his anti-Catholic attitudes. In an address to the Protestant League entitled "Germandom or Cosmopolitanism," he marshaled Houston Stewart Chamberlain's racial arguments against ultramontanes, who, he believed, sapped the strength of the German nation.[31] In Liebert's imagination, Social Democrats and Center politicians colluded in an unholy alliance against the German nation. To combat one meant to weaken the other. A decline in Social Democratic strength, he once argued, would also "break the power and influence of ultramontanism."[32]

The German Society for the Eastern Marches fared considerably better among Catholics, but only among those in Upper Silesia whose politics were marked by the peculiar conditions of ethnic borderlands.[33] The same may be said of the General German School Society, which in 1908 became the Society for Germandom Abroad (Verein für das Deutschtum im Ausland). It also recruited mainly among the educated Protestant middle classes, except in Silesia, where it enjoyed considerable Catholic and even Center support.[34] But even here it is telling that Catholics in the Silesian branch resisted the society's transition from a school association to an organization offering wide cultural support for conationals outside the empire's borders.[35] Mainly, the Silesian Catholics feared the possible implications of political activity too akin to Pan-German work and ideology. But under Otto von Hentig, who became chairman in 1906, the society remained faithful to official nationalist positions—support for government policies, distance from Pan-German agitation, reserve on Los von Rom—and consequently remained acceptable to nationally minded German Catho-

[31] General Eduard von Liebert, "Deutschtum oder Weltbürgertum," in *Reden und Vorträge bei der 25. Generalversammlung des Evangelischen Bundes* (1912).

[32] Cited by Klaus Saul, *Staat, Industrie, Arbeiterbewegung im Kaiserreich. Zur Innen- und Außenpolitik des Wilhelminischen Deutschland 1903–1914* (Düsseldorf, 1974), 119. Saul's discussion of the Imperial League against Social Democracy remains the most incisive. See also Dieter Fricke, "Reichsverband gegen die Sozialdemokratie (RgS) 1904–1918," in Fricke et al., eds., *Lexikon zur Parteiengeschichte*, vol. 3., 63–77; and Fricke, "Der Reichsverband gegen die Sozialdemokratie von seiner Gründung bis zu den Reichstagswahlen von 1907," *Zeitschrift für die Geschichtswissenschaft* 7 (1959): 237–80.

[33] This "special case" will be treated in chapter 6.

[34] Gerhard Weidenfeller, *VDA. Verein für das Deutschtum im Ausland. Allgemeiner Deutscher Schulverein (1881–1918)* (Frankfurt a.M., 1976), 301–5. Cardinal Kopp sent a welcoming telegram to the society's general assembly in Breslau in 1906.

[35] Ibid.

lics. Toward the Colonial Society, Catholics tended to show more sympathy, in part because of Catholic involvement in colonial missions. A number of prominent Center leaders, including Ernst Lieber, even belonged to the Colonial Society.[36] Nevertheless, the Colonial Society remained an organization of notables interested in technical aspects of Germany's colonial mission. It seems not to have organized Catholics on a broader scale.[37]

Of the nationalist organizations with mass followings, only the Navy League, which set out to educate Germans of all classes and confessions on the necessity of a strong fleet, counted significant numbers of Catholics among its members. This followed from the circumstances of the Navy League's founding. Through the patriotic propaganda of the Navy League, Admiral Tirpitz hoped to create a lasting Reichstag majority for his long-term plan to build up the kaiser's navy and stabilize domestic conflicts in the service of the dynastic status quo. The Center, however, held the key to that majority; and Catholics in western Germany, but especially in the south, showed little enthusiasm for the fleet. For Tirpitz and the Naval Office, Catholics who still resisted naval buildup therefore counted among the most important groups to be targeted by the Navy League.

Yet the Navy League's organizational success among Catholics proved modest: it fared best in areas where Catholic liberalism flourished—South Baden, the cities of the Rhineland, Munich—as well as in ethnically mixed areas—Silesia, Alsace—and it appealed more to Catholics in cities and towns than in the countryside. In liberal South Baden, for example, such Catholic towns as Donaueschingen boasted significant local branches; while in deeply Catholic areas of Württemberg, the Navy League barely existed unless propped up by a government official.[38] In the Rhineland, the league

---

[36] On Lieber's membership, see PLB NL Lieber/A36 Franz Ludwig Prinz von Arenberg to Ernst Lieber, 19.9.1899. On the Center and the empire's colonial ambitions, see Horst Gründer, "Nation und Katholizismus im Kaiserreich," 74–78; for more detail, Pehl, "Die deutsche Kolonialpolitik und das Zentrum."

[37] On the composition of the Colonial Society, see Eley, *Reshaping the German Right*, 119–22.

[38] For membership in Baden by locality, see GLA 69P/Seeverein Karlsruhe, yearly membership lists from 1898 to 1911; for Württemberg, HStAS E14/1345 "Württembergischer Landesverband des deutschen Flottenvereins, Rechenschaftsbericht für das Jahr 1909". See also Marilyn Shevin Coetzee, *The German Army League: Popular Nationalism in Wilhelmine Germany* (New York, 1990), 73. To the Navy League's lack of popularity in Württemberg's Catholic towns, there were but two exceptions—Ravensburg, an old parity city with a significant Protestant population, and Friedrichshafen, a port city on Lake Constance.

successfully recruited in Trier, Koblenz, and Bonn, but not, for example, in rural parts of the Eifel.[39] The hold of the Navy League on the
small towns of Bavaria was similarly tenuous, except in those cases
where clerics and Center leaders headed local branches.[40] Nevertheless, the league enjoyed nearly as much popularity in Catholic as in
Protestant parts of Bavaria.[41] Information about Catholic participation
in Silesia's Navy League is less clear, but impressionistic evidence
suggests that it made significant inroads, not only into the German
Catholic population that had turned away from the Center in favor of
the national parties, but also into Catholic groups that remained in
the Center's fold.[42] The value of the Catholic contribution to the national cause did not go uncontested, however. Despite its confessionally neutral statutes, the Navy League energetically contributed to the
antiultramontane agitation of the 1907 Reichstag election. "Navy
League people who voted Center, Poles, Guelfs are worthless to our
national task" declared August Keim, a volatile and vociferous na-

[39] For the partial success of the league in Catholic cities, see statistics in GLA
69P/Seeverein Karlsruhe/F8 "Wie viele Einzelmitglieder besitzt der Deutsche Flotten-
Verein in den deutschen Städten, die mehr als 20,000 Einwohner zählen," November
1902. The local at Aachen had 641 members, Trier 332, Bonn 500. Such figures are
comparable to Protestant cities of similar size. On the other hand, Karlsruhe with 3,154
members was the only predominantly Catholic city in Germany with an especially large
local branch, a result, one suspects, of the strength of National Liberalism there. In
places like Trier and Aachen, it was probably more decisive that important local
officials—such as the city mayor—assumed the leadership of the organization. See
Eley, *Reshaping the German Right*, 125–26.

[40] In Bavarian Swabia, according to one report, "many Catholic priests and Center
party members were active with great success." See GLA 69P/Seeverein Karlsruhe/F8
Rundschreiben von Braun, Vorsitzender des Kreisausschusses für Schwaben und Neuburg, 7.3.1907. Similarly, Baron von Würtzburg pointed out that in Bavaria as a whole
"many parish priests of both confessions are members and also chairmen of local organizations" of the Navy League. BA/MA RM/3v 9914 Denkschrift Würtzburg, April/May
1906.

[41] Membership in the five predominantly Catholic areas of Bavaria was, in January
1907, as follows: Upper Bavaria 3,686, Upper Palatinate 890, Lower Bavaria 1,713,
Swabia and Neuburg 7,866, Lower Franconia 2,526. The two predominantly Protestant
areas of Upper Franconia and Middle Franconia had 2,591 and 3,983 members respectively. The Palatinate, which had 4,453 members, was too confessionally mixed to draw
convincing conclusions. As the low turnout in the Upper Palatinate and Lower Bavaria
suggests, the success of the Navy League in Catholic areas depended on energetic
organization and probably the support of Catholic notables. The popularity of the Navy
League in Swabia and Neuburg gives a hint of what could be achieved. For membership statistics, see GLA 69P/Seeverein Karlsruhe/F19 Mitteilung des deutschen Flottenvereins, "Zu- und Abgang im Deutschen Flottenverein," 2.5.1907.

[42] GLA 69P/Seeverein Karlsruhe/F1 "Vortrag Dr. Georg Michaelis gehalten in der
Hauptversammlung der Schlesischen Vertreter des deutschen Flottenvereins, Breslau,"
7.2.1908.

tionalist and a member of the Navy League's executive council.[43] To this renewed "*furor protestanticus*," Catholics responded with indignation; *Germania*, the leading Catholic newspaper in Germany, adjured its readers to lay down their membership cards immediately.[44] But when a number of Catholics did exactly that, integral nationalists found their suspicions confirmed: Catholics, whatever their rhetoric, were nationally unreliable.

The subsequent crisis revealed nationalism's ability to divide more than to unify a nation. The Navy League's integral nationalists who sided with Keim insisted on ideological purity and total commitment to the national cause: they had no place for Catholics whose loyalties were multiple and whose conception of the nation, and its history, did not conform to integral nationalist visions. The conservative, official nationalists in the Navy League—men such as Baron von Würtzburg, the leader of the Bavarian branch of the Navy League—saw the problem of the German national state not so much in its ideological but rather in its formal disunity. Germany, official nationalists argued, was severed by regional and confessional differences that, if they could not be erased, could at least be ameliorated. If not unison, then consonance could be achieved. Catholics, if they were patriotic, could be admitted to the national community even if they continued to vote for the Center, even if they clung to their peculiar Catholic habits. Questions of naval policy also divided integral from official nationalists. Arguing for a fleet equal to the British navy, the first group lobbied to push naval buildup beyond the will of the government. Content to serve the government's will, official nationalists defended the necessity of a German navy large enough to deter but not necessarily to defeat the British. Tirpitz thought the matter crucial: the Reichstag would support the one proposal but not the other.[45] The Navy League crisis of 1907–8 concerned points of ideology but also, as Geoff Eley has shown, political style. While official nationalists clung to the politics of traditional notables, integral nationalists pursued

[43] BHStA GS/1158 August Keim to the district committee (Kreisausschuß) of the German Navy League of Schwaben and Neuburg, 3.1.1906. On Keim's anticlericalism, see Eley, *Reshaping the German Right*, 180–83, 271–72. It should be pointed out that Keim, who was not religious, was born a Catholic.

[44] *Germania*, 10 February 1907. On Erzberger's role in disclosing Keim's letter, see Klaus Epstein, "Erzberger and the German Colonial Scandals, 1905–1910," *The English Historical Review* 74 (1959): 637–63.

[45] "Entwurf der Denkschrift des Staatssekretärs des Reichsmarineamts, Admiral v. Tirpitz, für den Reichskanzler, Fürst v. Bülow, Mitte November 1905 zur politischen Begründung der Flottennovelle 1906." Reprinted in Berghahn and Deist, *Rüstung*, 180–86.

politics in a new key. Not imperial decrees from above but grass-roots engagement from below marked their new style. Not servility but ideological commitment determined their politics. For not just the well-being of the state but more importantly the survival of the nation seemed at stake.[46]

The problem of the Center party in national politics constituted a central axis around which the debate within the Navy League turned. Würtzburg and the official nationalists believed it possible to "win the Center over to our side."[47] With tact, they thought, Catholics could be coaxed onto "solid national ground."[48] Unbridled anti-Catholic agitation, by contrast, only "blew wind in the sails of the Center extremists."[49] But to Keim and the integral nationalists, true German sentiment, *echtes Deutschtum*, was a siren song that ultramontane Catholics could only faintly hear; the attempt to lure them was therefore misguided, a quest quixotic from the start.

Between the spring of 1907 and the winter of 1908, the conflict between these two positions precipitated a serious crisis in the Navy League, a crisis that made manifest the ideological balance of forces among German nationalists and laid bare the continuing impact of confessional antagonism on the politics of the radical right. The crisis passed through three stages. The first stage represented Keim's ascendancy—and therefore the preeminence of the integral nationalist position. Würtzburg attempted to condemn Keim's electoral activity, particularly his attacks on the Center. But, at the Navy League's general assembly in Cologne in March 1907, Würtzburg's resolution failed by a wide margin. Only fourteen of the fifty-three provincial organizations supported it. The second stage—between late November 1907 and January 1908—represented the integral nationalists' bid for institutional control over the Navy League. But the bid was unsuccessful, for the presidium's appointment of August Keim to the position of executive chairman failed to hold, not for want of popularity, but because of ministerial intervention.[50] In the third and final stage, between February and November 1908, the official nationalists reas-

---

[46] Eley offers an incisive discussion of these differences, albeit with a slightly different vocabulary, in *Reshaping the German Right*, 160–235.

[47] BHStA GS/1158 Baron von Würtzburg to Graf von Lerchenfeld, 21.2.1907; Würtzburg to Lerchenfeld, 22.5.1907.

[48] Ibid.

[49] BHStA GS/1158 Würtzburg to Lerchenfeld, 21.2.1907.

[50] See Wilhelm Deist, *Flottenpolitik und Flottenpropaganda. Das Nachrichtenbureau des Reichsmarineamtes 1897–1914* (Stuttgart, 1976), 224–25. Eley, *Reshaping the German Right*, 275, emphasizes the popular opposition within the Navy League to ministerial intervention and underplays the actual outcome of the struggle.

serted their control over the Navy League. Through his mediator, Captain Boy-Ed, Tirpitz pressured the league to instate leading moderates in key executive positions in place of Keim and Fürst Otto von Salm, who, as president of the Navy League, supported the integral nationalist stance. At the Danzig conference in June 1908, Salm was replaced by Admiral Hans von Koester, a man who was not close to Tirpitz but who distanced himself from the populist, antigovernmental, and anti-Catholic agitation of Keim and who, because of his own naval career, enjoyed the confidence of the Imperial Naval Office.[51] Koester insisted on the independence of the league (the position of the integral nationalists), but he also resisted detailed intervention in naval planning (to the relief of Tirpitz). His position on party politics and confessional agitation also pleased the confessionally sensitive Bavarians, who considered it "the best declaration that the Navy League has yet to deliver."[52] Yet his references to "national politics" sufficiently placated the integral nationalists to dissuade them from mass defection to an independent *Flottenliga*.[53] By December, Koester could in good faith proclaim "that complete harmony" had returned to the Navy League.[54]

Geoff Eley has argued that the victory of the moderates at Danzig was only superficial and that at a deeper level a shift in the terrain of nationalist politics had occurred. Even traditional notables now explicated their nationalism in a discourse defined by their more radical opponents. But was the moderate victory only superficial? Certainly, the Naval Office did not think so, nor for that matter did Keim, who shifted his allegiances to the Pan-German League.[55] Moreover, it seems reasonable, given the volatility of the league in 1908, to assume that Koester's rhetorical overtures to the integral nationalists represented little more than rhetoric in the service of organizational unity. In fact, in the period after the Danzig conference, the Navy League never again participated in parliamentary politics in anything even

---

[51] Deist, *Flottenpolitik und Flottenpropaganda*, 235–40.

[52] BA/MA RM/3v 9918 Captain Boy-Ed to Admiral Tirpitz, 17.11.1908

[53] BA/MA RM3/v 9918 Boy-Ed to Tirpitz, 23.9.1908. See especially Deist, *Flottenpolitik und Flottenpropaganda*, 245.

[54] Deist, *Flottenpolitik und Flottenpropaganda*, 246. The Ministry of the Interior was, at this point, also satisfied that the league would now refrain from engaging in party politics. PAAA R2297 Note of the Ministry of the Interior to the Foreign Ministry, 19.10.1908.

[55] On the Naval Office and the resolution of the crisis, see Deist, *Flottenpolitik und Flottenpropaganda*, 239–47. For criticism of Eley's interpretation of the Danzig conference, see Deist, *Flottenpolitik und Flottenpropaganda*, 237, fn. 327, and Richard J. Evans, *Rethinking German History* (London, 1987), 76. On Keim's move to the Pan-German League, see Heinrich Class, *Wider den Strom* (Leipzig, 1932), 84.

approaching the same measure as in the previous period.[56] Nor did it oppose the Catholic Center on national questions.[57] Certainly, integral nationalists remained in control of some of the Navy League's provincial branches, but that is a far cry from claiming that the radicals emerged victorious in 1908. Really, the opposite is true: official nationalists reasserted institutional control of the largest nationalist organization in the Kaiserreich.

The Collapse of the Bülow Bloc and the Eclipse of Integral Nationalist Politics

The failure of integral nationalists to put forth their grand program in the Navy League did not represent an isolated setback. By 1909, such setbacks were the common fate of a series of ideological attempts to create a unified polity based on an exclusive idea of what it meant to be German. The anti-Semites, who proposed to restrict the citizenship rights of Germany's Jews, fell into parliamentary disarray after 1907—a fact that did not, however, hinder their flight into ever more extreme racist rhetoric, or stop their ideas from becoming ever more presentable in good society.[58] Similarly, the Society for the Eastern Marches fell into increasingly acrimonious relations with the considerably more influential Agrarian League and Conservative party.[59] Unable to overcome economic contradictions among the Germans of the Prussian East, the society suffered, as one scholar has put it, from "a spirit of indifference and organizational ennui."[60] Especially after 1908, the society's proposals for a more aggressive Germanization program found ever fewer adherents in official circles. The Imperial

---

[56] PAAA R2279 Note of the Ministry of the Interior, 19.10.1908.

[57] During the debates for financial reform in 1909, the Naval Office instructed the Navy League to support the government in this eminently "national question," which meant "politics and polemics against the Center are to be avoided." BA/MA RM3/v 9918 Captain Boy-Ed to Würtzburg, 17.9.1908, on a confidential discussion between Boy-Ed and Hans von Koester. See also "Notiz des Kontreadmirals Capelle für Korvettenkapitän Boy-Ed vom 10.10.1908 über die Einschaltung des Flottenvereins in eine Propaganda zugunsten der Reichsfinanzreform." Reprinted in Berghahn and Deist, *Rüstung*, 230.

[58] On the politics of anti-Semitism, see Richard S. Levy, *The Downfall of the Anti-Semitic Political Parties in Imperial Germany* (New Haven and London, 1975). On the currency of racial anti-Semitism on the eve of the war, see Peter Pulzer, *The Rise of Political Anti-Semitism in Germany and Austria*, rev. ed. (London, 1988), 185–285.

[59] William W. Hagen, *Germans, Poles and Jews: The Nationality Conflict in the Prussian East, 1772–1914* (Chicago, 1980), 278–85.

[60] Ibid, 285.

League against Social Democracy hardly fared better. Although its membership steadily increased, its influence, despite the anxiety caused by the Social Democrats' electoral success, remained slight. It not only failed to attract many workers, but it received no significant financial support from leading industrialists.[61] The national euphoria of the Bülow bloc, depicted in integral nationalist poetry as the springtime of the German nation, spawned a series of national projects—such as Friedrich Lange's attempt to unite all the truly nationalist organizations. But such projects inevitably ended in failure.[62]

The experience of the Pan-German League seems to suggest an exception to the rule of general stagnation among Germany's integral nationalist organizations. In 1908–9, its membership slightly expanded, partly as the result of defections from the Navy League, though primarily as a consequence of the *Daily Telegraph* crisis, which cast a dark shadow of doubt over the kaiser's foreign policy competence.[63] Still, with fewer than twenty thousand members, the Pan-German League remained a small organization. Under Heinrich Class, who became chairman in 1908, the league cultivated an image of itself as an elite, nationalist avant-garde. In the years that followed, the Pan-German League advanced radical positions on national questions, worked to disseminate racist ideology (particularly anti-Semitism), and advocated repressive measures against groups that Class considered *volksfremd* (alien to the nation): Jews, Poles, Danes, French, and foreign workers.[64] Although the league continued to harbor anticlericals, antagonism toward the Center fell from its program, as did support for Los von Rom. Class himself insisted that "the Jews are the worst enemy, followed by the Social Democrats, who without Jewish leadership and financial support would never have become nearly so powerful."[65] The Center he thought "less dangerous than Social Democracy," for not only was the Center a conservative party that supported authority, but as a confessional party it was "safe from Jewish infiltration."[66] He therefore warned against efforts, particularly from politically organized Protestants, to destroy the Center.[67]

---

[61] Saul, *Staat, Industrie, Arbeiterbewegung im Kaiserreich*, 124.

[62] On the unsuccessful attempt to create a "Verband der Verbände," see Eley, *Reshaping the German Right*, 282–83.

[63] Chickering, *We Men Who Feel Most German*, 261.

[64] On the ideology of the Pan-German League, see ibid., 74–101. For the views of Class, see especially Heinrich Class [Daniel Frymann], *Wenn ich der Kaiser wär*, 4th ed. (Leipzig, 1913).

[65] Class, *Wenn ich der Kaiser wäre*, 193.

[66] Ibid., 197–98.

[67] Ibid., 199–200.

In the years before the war, the political influence of the Pan-German League increased considerably, but that influence derived less from the ideological content of Class's program than from the general shift in public sentiment that followed in the wake of a series of foreign policy crises (Morocco in 1911 and the Balkan wars of 1912–13), as well as from the agitation to expand the size of the German army and from the widespread feeling that Germany was encircled and war inevitable. The resulting nationalist surge, which reached well into the Center, seems to have fed upon fear of external enemies and, especially after the Reichstag election of 1912, upon middle-class anxieties concerning the mounting strength of the Social Democratic Party. Traditional antagonisms toward other groups considered by integral nationalists to be internal enemies (Jews, ethnic minorities) still remained present in German national consciousness; some evidence even suggests that so-called scientific racism—to take one kind of antagonism—even became more widely accepted in this period.[68] But such antagonisms did not bring great political advantage to those who made them the centerpiece of their political program.

It is in this context that we must evaluate the paradoxical situation of the Protestant League between 1909, when the Bülow bloc collapsed, and 1914, when war broke out. As an organization the league reached the zenith of its popularity, but as a political rallying point for Protestants it fell to its nadir. Like a number of other nationalist organizations, the Protestant League paid for its exclusive visions and radical politics with political isolation. For two years the Bülow bloc had provided the league with a measure of what could count as Protestant politics on the national level. But in June 1909, the Conservative party found common cause with the Catholic Center and the Polish party on the issues of inheritance tax and financial reform, causing the Bülow bloc, like a dried-out castle of sand, to crumble. To league leaders, the Conservative-Center coalition that followed signaled an ominous turn in German politics. The league appealed to Protestant solidarity against what would now become the "renewed predominance of the ultramontane powers."[69] But it was an isolated voice, a call in the wind. To the Conservative party, the inheritance taxes were evidently of greater moment. The league aired its frustration, vented its anger, but more it could not do. "Further measures," Everling told the central committee, "were hardly possible."[70]

[68] See Pulzer, *The Rise of Political Anti-Semitism*, 230–39.

[69] AKIEB S500.9.125 "Eine Kundgebung des Evangelischen Bundes," 16.4.1909.

[70] AKIEB S500.9.125 "Verhandlungsnachweis über die Sitzung des Zentralvorstandes des Evangelischen Bundes," 9/10.6.1909.

The rub was on the right, with conservatives who allegedly placed their material interests and long-standing privileges before their national principles and their Protestant ideals. Vexed, the league was tempted to publicly denounce the Conservative party. It desisted, however, mainly because league leaders feared the consequences of a conservative rebellion within its own ranks. Nevertheless, the league's private disapproval of the Conservative party's cooperation with the Center disaffected, more than ever, the league's conservative critics. The *Kreuzzeitung*, the national newspaper most closely tied to the Conservative party, inveighed against the league's increasingly overt liberal affinities, while, in East Prussia, the *Ostpreußische Zeitung* warned "fellow conservatives" to "keep their eyes open" for "liberal agitators" carrying the banner of the Protestant League.[71] Indeed, over the league's manifest partisanship, few conservatives failed to communicate their ire.

The fissure left by the breakup of the Bülow bloc was primarily political, but its reasons were religious as well. Especially after a series of conflicts involving the Protestant church's dismissal of liberal theologians—in Prussia and in Württemberg—conservative publicists began to extol the virtues of a Christian state based on cooperation between conservative Catholics and like-minded Protestants.[72] Despite the gravity of the conflict between the two confessions, it was necessary, they argued, to recall what Catholics and conservative Protestants shared: a theistic world view opposed to materialism and religious indifference, a common striving to ensure the strength of the nation's moral fabric against the pressure of "destructive forces," a commitment to social and charitable work in order to maintain the cohesion of the Christian community, and monarchical sentiment.[73]

Such were not secluded sentiments after the fall of the Bülow bloc. The *Deutsche Adelsblatt*, the weekly forum of the German nobility, began to run articles on Catholic life that seemed—to the irritation of the Protestant League—to shed more warmth than light.[74] Christian Socialists, who now benefited from generous Center support in run-off elections, also found it opportune to praise German Catholicism

---

[71] AKIEB S500.9.112 Article from the *Kreuzzeitung* reprinted in *Preußische Kirchenzeitung*, 19 February 1911.

[72] AKIEB S500.9.125 "Verhandlungsnachweis über die Sitzung des Zentralvorstandes," 17/18.11.1910. Here the central committee deliberated over a response to H. von Berger's *Conservatismus und die Parteien*, a popular pamphlet arguing for "a Christian community between the Center and the Conservatives."

[73] See, for example, *Evangelische Kirchenzeitung*, 19 December 1909.

[74] AKIEB 500.9.133t "Material über die bedauerliche Unterstützung des Ultramontanismus."

and, while doing so, to take the Protestant League to task for its intolerance. In October 1909, in a public ceremony commemorating the Reformation, Georg Oertel, a conservative Christian Socialist, a previous Reichstag representative, and the editor of the *Deutsche Tageszeitung*, asked rhetorically: "Why should we not pay our respects to the Corpus Christi Day processions of devout Catholics?"[75] A simple question, it set off an acrimonious debate with the Protestant League. Even the anti-Semites criticized the league for encouraging religious discord—though, in truth, they were more troubled by the Protestant League's manifest affinity for National Liberal politics than by the dearth of confessional harmony in the German empire.[76]

The Protestant League's most tenacious and dangerous opponent was, however, the Agrarian League. Predominantly Protestant in its composition, the Agrarian League nevertheless observed strict neutrality in confessional questions, cooperated with the Center on tariff issues, and warned Protestant peasants against the divisive polemics of the Protestant League.[77] Chagrined, Hermann Kremers, the leader of the Protestant League's organization in the Rhineland, advocated "a ruthless course of action against the Agrarian League."[78] But nothing came of it. Everling considered it too "difficult and dangerous to attack such organizations."[79] Already adrift from its conservative moorings, the Protestant League could scarcely afford to alienate still more supporters.

Other efforts to cooperate with potentially antiultramontane groups proved equally futile. Everling considered making contact with industrial and commercial circles opposed to the Center's position on financial issues. But the attempt to harness "their rich financial resources in the service of our cause" seems to have come to naught.[80] Similarly, the Protestant League failed to build bridges to Catholic groups opposed to the political power of the Center party. The German Union, for example, might have been an organization that shared common assump-

[75] See appendix to ibid., "Briefwechsel zwischen Dr. Oertel und Pfarrer Proebsting-Lüdenscheid."

[76] See the comments of the anti-Semitic Reichstag representative Liebermann von Sonnenberg, cited in *Vorstandsblatt des Evangelischen Bundes* 2 (1910): 54–57.

[77] Agrarian admonitions against the Protestant League hindered the latter's ability to organize in the countryside. See AKIEB S500.9.60 "Jahresbericht des Evangelischen Bundes, 1908/9," 29.

[78] AKIEB S500.9.125 "Verhandlungsnachweis über die Sitzung des Zentralvorstandes des Evangelischen Bundes," 8/9.1.1911.

[79] Ibid.

[80] AKIEB S500.9.125 Otto Everling (central committee) to the central committees of the regional organizations of the Protestant League, 12.6.1909. One may surmise that Everling had the Hansa Bund in mind.

tions with the Protestant League: both groups, after all, fought the Center in the name of a higher German nationalism. Yet the league assumed that the German Union, presumably because it remained Catholic, actually weakened Protestant defenses.[81] The Protestant League's position on Catholic modernists—Catholic intellectuals who tried to bring the church out of its subcultural exclusion and into stride with modern developments—seemed more stubborn still. Hermann Kremers thought the movement "a hindrance to our organization," even though Catholic modernists urged a rationalization of Catholic religious practice as well as Catholic assimilation into German national culture.[82] But the league, by now a hostage to its exclusive religious and national visions, would have none of it.

The consequent isolation of the league became manifest in the Reichstag elections of 1912. For the first time in many years, the league abstained from publishing an election statement for the general public, though secretly the mediation committee continued the league's political work.[83] The results of the election did little to change the Protestant League's predicament. Along with Center and Conservative losses came a massive Socialist electoral victory that seemed, to some, nearly as ominous.

But only to some. On the Social Democrats, the Protestant League, to the consternation of most of its conservative and some of its National Liberal members, equivocated: it did not issue a public denunciation of the SPD; it did not consider the SPD, now the largest party in the Reichstag, more dangerous than the Center.[84] Instead, the league meekly urged its members to oppose materialism and Social Democratic historical views.[85] The problem of Social Democracy,

[81] *Vorstandsblatt des Evangelischen Bundes* 1 (1910): 113. The tension between the two organizations antedated the fall of the Bülow bloc, however. See AKIEB S500.9.125 "Bericht über die Tätigkeit des Zentralvorstandes," 24.3.1909.

[82] AKIEB S500.9.124 "Verhandlungsnachweis über die Gesamtvorstandssitzung des Evangelischen Bundes," 30/31.3.1910.

[83] AKIEB S500.9.125 "Nachweis über die Sitzung des Zentralvorstandes des Evangelischen Bundes," 8/9.2.1912. On the work of the mediation committee, see AKIEB S500.9.125 Executive committee of the mediation committee to the executive committees of the regional mediation committees, 2.11.1911. For a sample of an election poster that is presumably the work of the mediation committee, see AKIEB S500.9.113r "Deutscher Protestantismus und Reichstagswahl." Here it is interesting to note that the committee felt the necessity to warn fellow Protestants against the slogan of a "common Christian worldview."

[84] AKIEB S500.9.125 "Verhandlungsnachweis über die Sitzung des Zentralvorstandes," 8.2.1912. See also AKIEB S500.9.125 "Protokoll über die Sitzung des Zentralvorstandes," 5/6.3.1913. In Bavaria, where the Center still dominated, the league continued to cooperate with the Socialists against the dominant Center.

[85] AKIEB S500.9.125 "Verhandlungsnachweis über die Sitzung des Zentralvorstandes," 9.2.1912.

according to one Protestant League position paper, could be understood only in the wider context of the Christian and spiritual life of the nation—"for the spiritual and moral development of all of Germany, including that of the German Catholics, rests upon Christianity, the German Christianity of the Bible and the Reformation."[86] To critical observers, the rhetoric was old, a saw without teeth. And it alienated league members—National Liberals who came to see the Social Democratic riptide as portending an imminent flood that would engulf Germany in revolution, Conservatives who worried that the Protestant League preferred a "Germany better red than black."[87]

Again, the right proved more menacing. Politically, it perceived the league's reticence to be the product of a new and threatening liberal-socialist political alignment "from Bassermann to Bebel."[88] In religious issues, conservatives criticized the league for its silence on the so-called Jatho affair, the case of an extremely liberal pastor who lost his post in 1911 after repeatedly asserting that nothing objective could be known about Christ. The league, in the words of the *Kreuzzeitung*, the leading conservative paper in Germany, was "hypnotized by the Roman danger" while liberal pastors threatened to transform Protestantism into a religion "acceptable to Jews and pagans."[89] Similarly, in the pages of *Der alte Glaube* (The Old Faith), a paper of the religious right, an anonymous author denounced the league's ties to the "Jewish press" and, affronted by the league's liberalism, sarcastically suggested that "any Jew or Turk should now be able to join."[90] Conservative discontent with the Protestant League, perhaps in part a result of genuine fellow feeling toward Catholic conationals, resulted in greater measure from a volatile mixture of traditional religiosity, some Christian anti-Semitism (though the ability of anti-Semitism to bring Protestants and Catholics together should not be overrated), and obsessive fear of socialism. The Protestant League might wave the bloody shirt of ultramontanism, but for Conservatives the real battles were elsewhere. After the Socialist victory in the 1912 elections, the *Kreuzzeitung* declared the political position of the Protestant League

[86] AKIEB S500.9.125 "Verhandlungsnachweis über die Sitzung des Zentralvorstandes des Evangelischen Bundes in Berlin," 5/6.3.1913.

[87] For the Conservative critique, see AKIEB S500.9.112b "In Sachen des Evangelischen Bundes" (1912).

[88] *Vorstandsblatt des Evangelischen Bundes* 3, no. 5 (May 1912): 160. Citing D. Möller in the *Allgemeine evangelisch-lutherische Kirchenzeitung*, 19 January 1912.

[89] *Neue preussische Zeitung (Kreuz-zeitung)*, 23 July 1911.

[90] AKIEB s500.9.112 "Evangelische Kirche und Evangelischer Bund. Gedanken eines Sorgenvollen," *Der alte Glaube. Evangelisch-Lutherisches Gemeindeblatt*, 5 August 1910.

"suicidal" in view of the revolutionary threat at hand, and "unjust" considering that, by 1912, the Center had more than demonstrated its adherence to throne and altar.[91] The same—in the opinion of conservative critics of the Protestant League—could not be said of Jews, socialists, and liberals.[92]

The conservative polemic did not remain dry ink in the yellowing papers of the right-wing press. In the fall of 1912, a group of conservatives seceded from the Protestant League and founded a rival organization: the German-Evangelical People's Association (Deutsch-Evangelischer Volksbund). In the history of the Protestant League, marked throughout by tension between liberals and conservatives, this constituted the first open break. The new organization, which consisted mainly of pastors from Mecklenburg and East Prussia, particularists from Hanover and Brunswick, and Lutherans from Saxony and Bavaria, represented, far more than the Protestant League, conservative piety in the north German flatlands, the views of rural against urban Protestants and of orthodox against modern, liberal, suspiciously secular theologians. The People's Association charged the league with indifference toward the "grave diggers" within the ranks of German Protestantism as well as benighted tolerance of "atheists, enemies of Christ."[93] If the People's Association's polemics against liberal Protestants attained a pitch nearly shrill, its tone on Catholic questions rang noticeably softer. The association argued that differences between Wittenberg and Rome neither precluded peaceful coexistence with Catholics nor a common Christian front, based on shared Christian truths, against "the enemies of Christian faith and Christian morality."[94]

The association seems not to have been a popular success, and it is difficult to imagine rural farmers in Oldenburg or East Prussia mobilizing against liberal pastors over tactical questions of how best to oppose ultramontane influence. Nevertheless, the secession revealed both the fault lines within the Protestant League and the ideological divisions within Protestant Germany. For parallel to the intransigence of the religious right, the theologians of the left pursued intra-Protestant polemics with increasing stridency. The complex history of the long conflict between liberal and conservative Protestants cannot

---

[91] *Neue preussische Zeitung (Kreuz-zeitung)*, 29 October 1912, supplement 508, "Evangelischer Bund und Deutscher Evangelischer Volksbund."

[92] Ibid.

[93] AKIEB S500.9.112b "In Sachen des Evangelischen Bundes" (1912). For the league's polemic with the German Evangelical People's Association, see *Vorstandsblatt des Evangelischen Bundes* 3 (1912): 154–76, 226–31, 435–41, 463–79.

[94] AKIEB S500.9.112b "In Sachen des Evangelischen Bundes," 1912.

be pursued here. Yet in the decade before World War I, relations between these two camps had become especially strained. The relationship of the gospel to the dogma, and the degree to which the latter
should be seen as a historical accretion, constituted the main theological issue that separated liberal theologians such as Adolf Harnack and
Ernst Troeltsch from their conservative counterparts. In religious politics, the question of academic freedom—whether pastors and professors could pursue biblical research without church intervention—
created further conflict. Arguing for a historical understanding of
Christianity and for the widest academic freedoms, Harnack and
Troeltsch defined their position in sharpest opposition to their conservative opponents.

Yet they also did not warm to the Manichaean visions of the Protestant League. In an address entitled "Protestantism and Catholicism in
Germany" given on the occasion of the birthday of Kaiser Wilhelm II,
on 27 January 1907, Harnack argued that confessional division was
one of the gravest fault lines dividing the German nation, but that to
overcome division meant to explore what Protestants and Catholics
held in common. Dialogue, not diatribe, would ease confessional antagonism. And dialogue was not always aided by "settling accounts"
of the past.[95] Similarly, Ernst Troeltsch, whose subtle analyses of contemporary Catholicism rose far above the common din of confessional
clamor, turned against the thesis, almost self-evident in Protestant
circles, that Protestantism represented the principle of modernity, Catholicism, by contrast, tradition and decline.[96] Modern scholarship,
Troeltsch maintained, was unthinkable without "Galileo, Pascal,
Machiavelli, Bodin, Descartes," men who were "Catholics, not Protestants."[97] Conversely, the crisis of religion in the modern period affected both Catholicism and Protestantism. Indeed, both Troeltsch
and Harnack saw in the Catholic modernists legitimate and powerful
interlocutors, theologians not to be dismissed as insufficiently Protestant but to be respected as Catholics from whom Protestants could
also learn.[98]

The positions of Harnack and Troeltsch, sensible and sophisticated,

[95] Adolf Harnack, "Protestantismus und Katholizismus in Deutschland," *Preußische
Jahrbücher* 127 (1907): 310.

[96] The most important statement is Troeltsch, "Die Bedeutung des Protestantismus
für die Entstehung der modernen Welt," *Historische Zeitschrift* 97 (1906): 1–66.

[97] Cited by Karl Ernst Apfelbacher, *Frömmigkeit und Wissenschaft. Ernst Troeltsch und
sein theologisches Programm* (Munich, 1978), 246.

[98] Ibid., 249. On Catholic modernists, see Ernst Troeltsch, "Der Modernismus," in
Troeltsch, *Gesammelte Schriften*, vol. 2, *Zur religiösen Lage, Religionsphilosophie und Ethik*
(Tübingen, 1913), 45–67.

did not however pass uncriticized. Harnack's address was met, in the words of the educator and philosopher Friedrich Paulsen, with "head-shaking, as if too many concessions had been made to the enemy confession."[99] Troeltsch, for his part, would later be suspected of Catholic sympathies.[100] But in the years before the war, their implicit irenicism imperiled the work of the Protestant League, while their modernism further widened the rift between liberal and conservative Protestants. One should not overestimate this threat. Harnack and Troeltsch wrote for a learned audience, not a mass base. The real menace to the league was still on the right. Ever sensitive to the political dangers confronting the league, Otto Everling increasingly worried about the necessity of suppressing a new and "fateful" cleft—"conservative-orthodox Protestantism and ultramontanism as a 'Christian Party'" on one side of the divide, "liberal Protestantism, liberalism, socialism as an 'anti-Christian party'" on the other.[101] Where the Protestant League would then fall was difficult to say—probably to the left, but most likely it would be torn in two.

German politics had not yet reached that point, however. Indeed, political Catholicism continued to be beset by the same kind of conflict that now confronted the Protestant League. There was, however, one important difference: in the Catholic Center, it was the dominant group within the party that longed for confessional integration, for acceptance in the national community, for a peace between Protestants and Catholics that would be centered on dynastic loyalty and a common Christian front against what was perceived to be working-class radicalism. In 1906, Julius Bachem had argued that Catholics should come out of their isolation—part self-willed, part imposed—in order to demonstrate that Catholics, too, could be counted as equal conationals, that Catholics, long marginalized, could contribute to German national culture.

But the "integralists" within the Center remained resistant. On Easter Tuesday, 1909, shortly before the Bülow bloc would unravel, they rekindled the Zentrumsstreit—the question of the exclusively confessional nature of the Catholic Center party. Edmund Schopen, the host of a conference of integralists, now criticized the Center, and particularly the "Bachemite" position, for attempting "to resolve the national problem through the mutual lessening of orthodoxy . . . and

[99] Cited by Kouri, Der deutsche Protestantismus, 166. For the range of reactions, see Oskar Hermens, Professor Harnacks Kaisersgeburtstagsrede 1907 erwogen von einem Mitgliede des Evangelischen Bundes (Leipzig, 1908).

[100] Apfelbacher, Frömmigkeit und Wissenschaft, 250.

[101] AKIEB S500.9.115 Otto Everling, "Denkschrift über die Verlegung des Geschäftssitzes von Halle nach Berlin," 1912.

by confessional mixing."[102] Similarly, in a letter to the episcopate, the integralists Hermann Roeren and Franz Bitter denounced the "striving for a so-called interconfessional cultural community with the goal of limiting religion to the inside of church buildings in order to bring about a reconciliation of the confessions on a patriotic foundation."[103] This attack paralleled but was not ideologically congruent with an episcopal assault on the interconfessional nature of the Christian trade unions. For while the conflict over trade unions pitted the Catholic church establishment against the political sensibilities of Catholic union organizers, the integralists' attack on the Bachemites was in many senses radical. The integralists not only repudiated confessional integration, but they also denounced the nationalist sentiment that went along with it. As they decried the secular state and the corrosive effects of modern culture, they condemned the increasing ease with which the Center seemed to make its peace with the status quo. Bound to the rural Catholic subculture, the integralists insisted that Catholics continue to cultivate their own particularities, their own literature, their own culture and habits. In the same breath, they damned as unchristian those across the confessional divide.[104]

Within the Center, Bachem's position prevailed, not by dint of democratic process, but by ideological policing: Erzberger converted to the party line; Bitter and Roeren were censored and silenced.[105] Loyal but not uncritical toward the state, cautious about its confessionalism, the Center continued to court the Conservative party. In 1912, the two parties entered into a temporary alliance, in part because a certain affinity existed between their political and confessional outlook, in part because they held economic interests in common, in part because both parties feared Social Democracy. Of equal moment, the Center's nationalist discourse became increasingly strident, increasingly difficult to differentiate from the common clamor of conservative nationalism. This was particularly evident in the Center's pronouncements on foreign policy. Concerning the Moroccan crisis of 1911, Bachem's *Kölnische Volkszeitung* insisted that Germany should be strong and steadfast, and that "if war must come, then our bells will ring with merriment."[106] Other Catholic papers struck a similar tone. Still, and

---

[102] Cited by Cary, "Political Catholicism," 109, and, for more detail, 93–178. See also Margaret Lavinia Anderson, "Interdenominationalism," 359–64.

[103] Quoted in Cary, "Political Catholicism," 108.

[104] For a portrait of the integralists, see Margaret Lavinia Anderson, "Interdenominationalism," 359–64.

[105] Ibid., 354.

[106] Cited in Klaus Wernecke, *Der Wille zur Weltgeltung. Außenpolitik und Öffentlichkeit im Kaiserreich am Vorabend des 1. Weltkrieges.* (Düsseldorf, 1970), 84.

the occasional aggressive statement notwithstanding, one could detect reticence. The *Kölnische Volkszeitung* insisted on a strong hand in foreign policy, but it also added, "we don't exactly wish war," and warned against superpatriots who attempted to whip up anti-English sentiment.[107]

When war broke out in August 1914, Catholics responded as Protestants: with relief, with enthusiasm, with a call to arms.[108] Kaiser Wilhelm II proclaimed that he no longer recognized parties, only Germans. There would, he said, be peace in fortress *Germania*. It was a moment—fleeting as it would turn out—of respite from the many antagonisms that divided Germans: from class conflict, from religious division, from political tension. Even the Protestant League ceased its nettling. The central committee quickly communicated to the local and regional branches that "in these weeks, heavy with the weight of destiny, all confessional conflict must be quelled."[109] Alas, however, habits of mind conditioned by a long history persisted. The central committee still questioned the wisdom of allowing Jesuits to administer the sacrament to Catholics fighting on the front.[110] And in Württemberg, one Protestant League member interpreted the war as a "European Kulturkampf"—a Kulturkampf, moreover, before which the struggle of the 1870s must appear as "child's play."[111] A sad comment, one might think, on the endurance of an illusion.

---

[107] Ibid.

[108] Even in deeply Catholic areas of Bavaria, this seems to have been true. See the query of the Bavarian army concerning antimilitary activity in the countryside in BHStA MKr. 955/22188 Report of the Generalkommando I. Armeekorps, 1.8.1914. This impression is further corroborated by the Catholic press in Bavaria. See *Fränkisches Volksblatt*, 8 August 1914; *Bamburger Volksblatt*, 1 August 1914; *Bayerischer Kurier*, 2 August 1914. Only *Das Bayerische Vaterland* (the newspaper of the Bavarian Peasant League) seems to have adopted a more modest tone. "We in the countryside do not have the loud patriotic euphoria of the city folk," 11 August 1914.

[109] *Vorstandsblatt des Evangelischen Bundes* 5 (September 1914): 1.

[110] Ibid.

[111] *Württembergische Bundesblätter*, 27 September 1914, 123.

Part Three

RELIGIOUS AND NATIONALITY
CONFLICT IN THE BORDERLANDS
OF THE IMAGINED COMMUNITY

6

Protestants, Catholics, and Poles: Religious and Nationality Conflicts in the Empire's Ethnically Mixed Areas, 1897–1914

THROUGHOUT MOST of Germany, religious conflict occurred in ethnically homogeneous areas. The main issue of contention between Protestants and Catholics was not who belonged to the nation but how the nation, to which both groups belonged, was to be imagined—who was to determine its history, who was to define its culture and politics, and who was to guard its memory. In the areas of mixed religion and ethnicity—in Alsace and Lorraine and in the lands of Prussian Poland—conflicts between the confessions assumed added layers of complexity.[1] Here populations were more fluid, the sense of who counted as German, who as Polish or French, less assured. Moreover, the situation of the national minorities in the ethnic borderlands was precarious—both in the German empire and elsewhere throughout central and eastern Europe. For by the turn of the century, state-directed repression of national minorities had become a ubiquitous phenomenon of European empires in which ethnic and political boundaries were not congruent. Though not as ethnically fractured as the Russian, Ottoman, or Habsburg empires, Germany's national minorities comprised close to 8% of its total population. And while the nationalities problem did not tear at Germany with the same tenacity as it did the great multinational empires, the Reich, and especially Prussia, struck at the nationalities on its periphery, particularly the Poles, with peculiar ferocity.

In Germany, especially between 1897 and 1914, political persecution of Polish nationals in Prussia proceeded as part of a larger strategy to mobilize popular nationalism.[2] At a meeting of the Prussian

[1] On the relationship between religion and nationality in Alsace and Lorraine, see Christian Baechler, *Le parti catholique alsacien 1890–1939* (Paris, 1982); Hermann Hiery, *Reichstagswahlen im Reichsland. Ein Beitrag zur Landesgeschichte von Elsaß-Lothringen und zur Wahlgeschichte des deutschen Reiches 1871–1918.* (Düsseldorf, 1986); and Brigitte Favrot, *Le gouvernment allemand et le clergé catholique lorrain de 1890 à 1914* (Metz, 1980).

[2] On Prussia's Polish policy, see Martin Broszat, *Zweihundert Jahre deutsche Polen-*

Cabinet of Ministers on 22 November, Finance Minister Johannes Miquel, one of the principal architects of *Sammlungspolitik*, outlined his political grand strategy, of which repression of the Poles was to be a part. "Political conflicts," he argued, "must be placed in the background and a basis for agreement found in the economic sphere. At the next election, national questions should be stressed. In addition, national feeling should be strengthened by a stern policy toward the Poles, *even* against the Center."[3] An "official nationalist," Miquel attempted to unify the principal nation of the state in order to preserve monarchical legitimacy and consolidate dynastic strength. The nationalism thus harnessed was not to be self-contained but rather directed against outsider groups: Poles and, in other imperial utterances, Social Democrats. Moreover, the marginalization of these groups depended, in part, on bridging differences between German Catholics and German Protestants. For the dynastic national state did not simply find a nation, conveniently culturally unified. Rather, to some extent, the state created the nation by involving its constituent parts (German Protestants and German Catholics) in the repression of national minorities, most conspicuously the Poles.

The Geography of National and Religious Conflict in the Ethnic Borderlands of the Prussian East

If the nation was made by directing antagonism across the ethnic frontier, its creation was subject to the peculiarities of Prussia's eastern territories: Posen, East and West Prussia, and Upper Silesia. The ethnically mixed areas of these provinces constituted a strange, delicate world, now lost, in which Protestant and Catholic Germans lived among Polish Catholics, Protestant Masures, Catholic Cassubans, and German Jews. Sometimes national and religious groups struck a balance; more often they existed in conflict. The terrain of conflict

---

politik, 2d ed. (Frankfurt a.M., 1972), esp. 152–72, and Hans-Ulrich Wehler, "Von den 'Reichsfeinden' zur 'Reichskristallnacht': Polenpolitik im Deutschen Kaiserreich," in Wehler, *Krisenherde des Kaiserreichs 1871–1918* (Göttingen, 1970), 181–99. The most comprehensive treatment is Hagen, *Germans, Poles, and Jews*. See also Richard Blanke, *Prussian Poland in the German Empire (1871–1900)* (Boulder, Colo., 1981), and, for a stimulating review of the scholarship, Geoff Eley, "German Politics and Polish Nationality: The Dialectic of Nation Forming in the East of Prussia," in Eley, *From Unification to Nazism*, 200–228.

[3] PAAA R4259 Meeting of the Prussian Cabinet of Ministers, 22.11.1897. As I intend to demonstrate, Miquel's "even" proved unnecessary in many aspects of Prussia's Polish policy.

was, moreover, complex, shifting as the religious and national land-scapes changed. It is necessary, therefore, to survey this terrain more closely.

In the Ermland, a sparsely populated agricultural region adminis-tratively encompassed by the district of Allenstein in East Prussia, three nationalities—Germans, Poles, and Masures—coexisted. Both Germans and Poles were confessionally divided (though the latter were mostly Catholic); the Masures, a people who spoke a Polish dia-lect heavily influenced by Luther's German, were Protestant and loyal to the state of Prussia.[4] In the Ermland, national tension did not usu-ally involve religious conflict: Protestant Masures, concentrated in the north, lived in areas populated by German Protestants, while Ger-man Catholics, more often to be found in the southern parts of the Ermland, usually shared borders with their Polish coreligionists. Cleavage patterns were therefore crosscutting, nationality conflicts not as severe.[5]

To the south and to the west, the same could not be said. In the provinces of Posen and West Prussia, ethnic tension proved more profound and less likely to be mitigated by common religion. In most areas of Posen and West Prussia, German Protestants lived among Catholic Poles; nationality conflicts, already severe, were typically ex-acerbated by religious division and, often enough, by class antago-nism as well. In the mixed areas (see table 3), German Protestants were disproportionately represented among the free professions and in the commercial sector; they paid most of the income tax and held most of the important positions in state and municipal bureaucracies. By contrast, the Polish population, almost exclusively Catholic, made up most of the agricultural wage-labor force, the vast majority of the nascent industrial working class, and only a small percentage of the free professions.[6] National antagonism was, then, overdetermined, with religion and class tending to reinforce antipathies already in existence.[7]

There were, however, some areas with significant German Catholic populations: in West Prussia, Catholics accounted for nearly one-

[4] On the Masures in East Prussia, see Walther Hubatsch, *Masuren und Preußisch-Litthauen* (Marburg, 1960); Hans-Ulrich Wehler, "Zur neueren Geschichte der Ma-suren," *Zeitschrift für Ostforschung* 11 (1962): 147–72.

[5] On nationality and religious conflicts in East Prussia, see PAAA R4063 Ernst Eilsberger, "Die polnische Frage in der Provinz Ostpreußen," May 1902.

[6] On class and the nationality conflict, see Hagen, *Germans, Poles, and Jews*, 208–24.

[7] A parallel, if less severe, situation existed between German Protestants and Cas-subans, a Slavic people of the Catholic faith, who constituted a significant minority in the part of West Prussia to the north and west of Danzig.

TABLE 3
Ethnic and Confessional Composition of the Six Regencies in Prussia in
Which Ethnic Fractionalization Exceeded 10%.*

Regency	G	GP	GC	P	O
Allenstein (534,469)	50.4	66.2	32	15.6	33.6
Bromberg (763,947)	49.7	83.6	13	50.2	—
Danzig (532,620)	71	68	29	15	14
Marienwerder (960,855)	59	75	23	41	—
Oppeln (2,207,981)	40	17	81	57	3
Posen (1,335,884)	32	75	21	68	—
Total (6,545,759)	47	57	40	48	5

G = % of German population.
GP = % of Protestants among Germans.
GC = % of Catholics among Germans.
P = Poles.
O = other nationalities: In Allenstein O = Masures; in Danzig O = Cassubans; in
Oppeln O = Moravian Czechs.
Source: Computed from statistics in *Statistisches Jahrbuch für den preußischen Staat, 1912*
(Berlin, 1913), 24.
*According to the Prussian census of 1910, the first that counted both confession and
mother tongue.

quarter of the German population; in Posen, roughly 15 percent, with
especially strong concentrations in the western and northern counties. According to the census of 1910, the first to count both confession and mother tongue, roughly 400,000 German-speaking Catholics
lived in West Prussia and Posen.[8] And while the census may overestimate the number of Germans in the ethnically mixed regions, it nevertheless suggests that there were many areas in Posen and West
Prussia where German and Polish Catholics coexisted.[9] One might
imagine that common religion eased nationality conflicts in these

[8] *Statistisches Jahrbuch für den Preußischen Staat, 1912* (Berlin, 1913), 24.
[9] Volker Hentschel, "Wirtschaftliche Entwicklung, soziale Mobilität und nationale

areas; in reality, it proved a weaker vessel for ethnic understanding than historians often suppose. In Upper Silesia and, after the Polish migrations, in the Ruhr, German and Polish Catholics also lived in the same towns and cities, worked in the same factories, toiled before the same blast furnaces, and drew their breath from the same sulfur-dioxide-suffused air. Here religion now sharpened, now softened national antagonism: as time progressed, more the former than the latter.

German Protestants and Catholic Poles

Religion, then, left its imprint on the nationality conflict between Germans and Poles. Though sometimes an ameliorating force, religion in the ethnic borderlands more typically exacerbated conflict. This was especially true of the antagonism between German Protestants and Catholic Poles. It is difficult to reconstruct fully the range and profundity of the antipathy that marked German Protestant attitudes toward Catholic Poles. That antipathy saturated daily life; it seeped into personal relations; it poisoned popular attitudes; it even permeated the literature of the east. To borrow from Ezra Pound, verse gave this antagonism "an image of its accelerated grimace." That image was partly based on confessional antipathy, but even more profoundly on ethnic hatred. Arthur Jonetz's "To the Germans in the Eastern Marches," written in 1905, began:

> Von Osten her weht scharf die Luft
> Und Kampfesrufe tönen
> Die Völker trennt der Zwietracht Kluft
> Sie finden kein Versöhnen

> A sharp wind blows from the east
> And calls to battle sound
> The nations are in strife
> And no reconciliation is to be found

Jonetz, like many other German nationalists, stressed the implacability of the Poles, the fundamental differences between the two nations, and the fatal inevitability of the struggle between them. Imaginary dikes and barricades were constructed against the Poles outside, who were "mischievous," "deceitful," "wild," and, in the lyrics of the nationalist poet Felix Dahn, "like wolves."

Bewegung in Oberschlesien 1871–1914," in *Modernisierung und nationale Gesellschaft im ausgehenden 18. und im 19. Jahrhundert*, ed. Werner Conze et al. (Berlin, 1979), 244, 255.

As the bards of the borderland conflicts envisioned the "other," they also shaped the identities of Germans living in the ethnic frontier. In broad strokes, songs and ballads offered two self-portraits: one of hard workers tilling the soil, the other of steady sentinels guarding against Slavic intrigue. In the first, plowmen scraped at the infertile earth, making it fecund, thus making it German. Work, blood, love, and genealogy bound Germans to the land east of the Oder. "Mother Earth" was "Father's native soil"—sacrosanct because "much soaked with German blood."[10] Conversely, the image of the sentinel "holding guard day and night" betrayed the frailty of German national consciousness at the frontier.[11] Grub Street poets wrote paeans to the land in the context of Germans leaving it, heralds to German work against the background of Polish economic ascendancy. Divided by class, confession, and geographic provenance, Germans imagined themselves fraternally united behind safe walls.

> Und in den Höfen, germanischer Art, wohnt deutsches
> Fühlen und Denken, die deutsche Treue mit Liebe gepaart, frei von den
>   slawischen Ränken.

> And in the courtyards of Germanic kind, lives German
> Feeling and thought, German loyalty paired with love, free from Slavic
>   plots.[12]

Characteristically, frontier verse suffused life's objects with national epithets: seeds and sperm, blood and trees and virtue, even death received a name. German, they became tropes around which to structure identity, ideology, around which to imagine oneself, as well as those across the ethnic frontier.

In the German-Protestant imagination, a steep cultural precipice existed between the two nationalities. If Germans were steadfast, Poles roamed; where Germans loved, Poles fell to passion; and when Germans received the word of God in serious silence (*Innerlichkeit*), Poles pursued their piety ostentatiously, irrationally, and with an inclination to superstition.[13] Religious prejudice further reinforced cul-

---

[10] See "Ostmarken-Lied" (Karl Pröll, 1905), in Otto Münzer, ed., *Des Landwirths Liederbuch. Ostmarkenausgabe* (Lissa, 1906), 138; and "Deutsche Erde" (Robert Bickenbach, 1905), ibid., 134–35.

[11] See, for example, "Die Wacht in des Reiches Osten" (Georg von Rohrscheidt, 1906), ibid., 139–40.

[12] "Die Ostmark deutsch" (Wilhelm Schindler, 1906), ibid., 140–41.

[13] Gustav Freytag's *Soll und Haben* was the literary source of many such stereotypes. See Helga B. Whiton, *Der Wandel des Polenbildes in der deutschen Literatur des 19. Jahrhunderts* (Ann Arbor, 1980), 179–86. On anti-Polish sentiment in the novels of the eastern marches, see also Richard W. Tims, *Germanizing Prussian Poland: The H-K-T-Society and*

tural contempt and ethnic aversion. If Polish backwardness flourished in the soil of a piety adequate for peasants but not for the higher attainments of Kultur, then Polish nationalism seemed to be an evil weed cultivated by a fanatical Catholic clergy. In Clara Viebig's *The Dormant Army*, a popular novel of life in the eastern marches, the Polish clergy are portrayed as manipulative and cunning, their parishioners as stupid sheep obediently and diffidently following their unprincipled shepherds. Polish priests did not serve true religion but rather sacrificed their piety on the altar of Polish nationalism—a fact well evidenced by their role in mixed marriages. In Viebig's novel, the "fanatical" Polish priest Gorka tells Ruda, a Polish girl who covets the German Catholic settler Valentin Bauer, "Either you are a good Christian and a faithful son of Poland, or——."[14] Viebig's readers could well fill in the blanks. In the novels of the eastern marches, Polish priests typically cast webs of intrigue to rob German settlers, through mixed marriages, of both their religion and their nationality. In literature, and one may surmise in life, such anti-Catholic and anti-Polish stereotypes flourished. German Protestants typically equated Polish with ultramontane and disdained both alike. But Protestantism, too, represented an important force in this conflict. In 1903, the conservative Protestant *Reichsbote* asserted that "the question of the Germanization of the east can only be seen in its correct light when we place it in the wide horizon of the German cultural mission."[15] In its essence Protestant, this cultural mission constituted Prussia's manifest destiny.

In this nationality conflict, the Protestant church in the ethnic borderlands was to represent a bastion of German ethnicity, a haven where Germans could consolidate national strength.[16] The West Prussian Synod, for example, declared a strong church "the most basic means of binding the deeply pious population to German nationality and ethnicity."[17] Prussian officials generally concurred in this view. The provincial governor of West Prussia, Gustav von Gossler, be-

---

the *Struggle for the Eastern Marches in the German Empire, 1894–1919* (New York, 1941), 256–60.

[14] Clara Viebig, *Ausgewählte Werke*, vol. 5, *Das schlafende Heer* (Berlin, 1905), 204.

[15] EZB 7/1847 *Der Reichsbote*, Nr. 45, 22.1.1903.

[16] Little has been written on the Protestant church and Prussia's Germanization program. See the brief comments in Adam Galos et al., *Die Hakatisten. Der Deutsche Ostmarkenverein (1894–1934)* (Berlin(O), 1966), 179–80, as well as the uncritical remarks of Arthur Rhode, *Geschichte der evangelischen Kirche im Posener Lande* (Würzburg, 1956), 173–94.

[17] EZB 7/1846 Provincial Synod of West Prussia, Request to Kaiser Wilhelm II, 23.12.1899.

lieved "every Protestant church, every Protestant vicar to be a mainstay and a meeting place, often more for German than for Protestant interests."[18]

Yet the image of a vigorous Protestant church in the vanguard of the struggle against Polish ultramontanism must be qualified. Protestantism may have informed prejudice, it may have been central to German national identity in the east, but the Protestant churches of Posen and West Prussia suffered from too many problems to emerge as the center of nationalist organization. Typically, the churches in the east suffered from a dearth of pastors, from dispersed settlements that made pastoral care difficult, and from poverty. Surveying his own province, the superintendent of the Protestant church of West Prussia compared the "miserable situation" to "the American wilderness."[19]

Bismarck attempted to ameliorate this sorry state. The settlement law of 1886 included provisions to rebuild churches and parsonages, to divide parishes into smaller units, to grant pastors extra subsidies, and to build new churches.[20] In the settlement law of 1902, Prussia further augmented state support of the Protestant church by adding an extra annual fund of RM 500,000 for church construction.[21] When combined with money from the discretionary fund, this meant that Prussia allotted roughly RM 600,000 annually between 1902 and 1914 "to raise German churches in the provinces of Posen and West Prussia in places where the support of German ethnicity may be expected."[22] By 1909, seventy-three new parishes were founded in Posen alone and nearly as many churches, parsonages, and chapels built.[23] The Protestant church also received funds to alleviate local tax burdens, to supplement the income of pastors, and to build Protestant hospitals

[18] PAAA R4063 Memorandum of the provincial governor of West Prussia, Gustav von Gossler, on Polish policy, 6.9.1896.

[19] EZB 7/1845 Royal Consistory of West Prussia, 7.6.1889. "Protokoll zur Conferenz über die Neubegründung evangelischer Kirchensysteme." On the general problems of the Protestant churches in the east, see Superintendent Johannes Hesekiel's long memorandum, written in 1886, on religious life and the condition of the clergy in Posen in ADW CA 2188/32.

[20] EZB 7/1843 Minister of culture, Gustav von Gossler, to the Royal Consistory in Posen, 21.4.1886.

[21] EZB 7/1846 Minister of culture, Konrad von Studt, to Wilhelm Barkhausen, 12.2.1902.

[22] EZB 7/1847 "Komissarische Berathung über die Stärkung und bessere Ausgestaltung des deutschen Kirchenwesens in den ehemals polnischen Landestheilen," 26.5.1902.

[23] EZB 7/1850 Der Reichsbote Nr. 84, 9.4.1909.

and orphanages as well as confirmation boarding schools.[24] When taken together, the total annual state support of the Protestant church for the purpose of strengthening German national consciousness in the years 1902 to 1914 may well have approached RM 1 million.[25]

More important, the Royal Settlement Commission peopled the eastern provinces with new Protestant parishioners. This was part of the German government's grand strategy to redress the demographic predominance of Poles over Germans in the east. Between 1887 and 1909, the Settlement Commission parceled out land to 15,916 Protestant families (but to only 613 Catholic households).[26] In an internal memorandum on the settlement issue, the governor of West Prussia argued that "from the political standpoint the Protestant Germans of West Prussia are the only citizens on whom the state can truly count in any conceivable situation."[27] But other factors also contributed to the disproportionate number of Protestant settlers. Between 1887 and 1909, there were nearly thirteen times more Protestant applicants for settlement land than Catholic.[28] Partly the result of the more enthusiastic nationalist engagement of German Protestants, this disparity was also the consequence of geographic factors. The vast majority of applicants came from the eastern marches themselves and from the predominantly Protestant, contiguous states and provinces of Pomerania, Saxony, and Brandenburg.[29] Furthermore, the Settlement Commission redistributed land in areas that were, at least in their German composition, already Protestant. To send Catholics into these areas would entail placing them into a national as well as a religious diaspora. Few Catholics in the Rhineland or in Silesia could be at-

[24] PAAA R4067 Prussian minister of ecclesiastical affairs and public instruction, Robert Bosse, to Bernhard von Bülow, 4.7.1898.

[25] The total sum of money that went to the Protestant church is difficult to estimate mainly because money that went to the church was put in the same bookkeeping column as money for schools. Also, the Catholic church received some of this money. Nevertheless, the total expenditures of the Royal Settlement Commission between 1886 and 1911 came to RM 483,198,258. Of this, RM 6,905,772 went to "the establishment of new positions and the regulation of communities, churches, and schools," while a further RM 14,102,005 went to "church, school, and communal contributions [Patronats-Beiträge]" See EZB 7/1852 "Anlage XIV zu der Denkschrift über die Ausführung des Gesetzes, betreffend die Beförderung deutscher Ansiedlung in den Provinzen West Preußen und Posen, vom 26.4.1886 und seiner Nachträge."

[26] Johannes Altkemper, Deutschtum und Polentum in politisch-konfessioneller Bedeutung (Leipzig, 1910), 124.

[27] PAAA R4063 Memorandum of the provincial governor of West Prussia, 6.9.1896.

[28] Altkemper, Deutschtum und Polentum, 124.

[29] Ibid., 128–29. In 1909, there were 625 settlers from the eastern provinces, 286 from the western provinces.

tracted by such prospects. But even when these considerations are taken into account, official preference for Protestant settlers remained painfully conspicuous.

In part, this preference was based on the perception, shared by leaders of the Center party, that German Catholics were more likely than Protestants to enter mixed marriages with Poles and, along with their offspring, to learn Polish.[30] In the opinion of Prussian leaders, such marriages undermined the demographic cohesion of the German population.[31] This was especially true since the settlement of Protestant Germans in Posen and West Prussia served to ensure German majorities in elections for Kreistag, Landtag, and Reichstag. Although officially a Catholic's adherence to the Center party did not disadvantage his application for a land grant, in practice there were only a few settlement areas where the government trusted such people. And in the western electoral districts of Posen, where German electoral majorities were marginal, the Settlement Commission refused to settle German Catholics for fear "of turning weak majorities into minorities."[32]

Poland a wilderness

The Protestant League and the Limits of Protestant Organization in the Ethnic Borderlands

The confessional aspect of the Germanization program was not lost on the Protestant League, which counted among the largest nationalist groups in the east (see table 4). Confessional to its marrow, well versed in the antipathies that marked and marred life in the east, the league focused its polemical fire on the Polish ultramontane clergy. To break the resistance of the Poles, one had to break the power of the church. Distrusted for religious as well as racial reasons, the Poles were perceived to be dull-minded reactionaries resisting the refining influence of German culture and civilization. In *Our Position on the*

[30] On the Center's private assent to this position, see StAK NL Bachem, Nr. 162 "Protokoll über die Außerordentliche Generalversammlung des Augustinus-Vereins," 3.2.1901.

[31] The government distrusted Jews as well. See PAAA R4070 Meeting of the Royal Cabinet of Ministers, 9.10.1900. Studt complained: "The Germans, amongst whom the Catholics create some difficulties and the Jews are for the most part not dependable, are no match for the politically unified Poles, whose organization and patronage is superior."

[32] PAAA R4099 "Protokoll über die 23ste Sitzung der königlichen Ansiedlungskommission für die Provinz West Preußen und Posen am 21. Januar 1902." See also PAAA R4099 Memorandum of the provincial governor of Posen, Wilhelm von Waldow, 31.5.1907.

TABLE 4

Membership in Leading German Nationalist Organizations in the Eastern Provinces of Prussia

	East Prussia	West Prussia	Posen	Silesia
Navy League	5,042	11,738	7,185	16,177
Pan-Germans	150	11	127	571
Protestant League	11,118	8,241	10,500	42,738
Society for the Eastern Marches	4,637	9,528	12,102	11,172

Source: Richard W. Tims, *Germanizing Prussian Poland: The H-K-T-1 Society and the Struggle for the Eastern Marches in the German Empire, 1894–1919* (New York, 1941), 287 (Appendix A: The Membership of the German Eastern Marches Association in the year 1913); Evangelischer Bund, *Verzeichnis der Haupt-und Zweigvereine und ihrer Vorstandsmitglieder* (Halle, 1912); GLA Seeverein Karlsruhe/19 "Mitteilung des deutschen Flottenvereins," 2.5.1907; Lothar Werner, *Der Alldeutsche Verband 1890–1918* (Berlin, 1935), 65. The Pan-German statistics are for 1901.

Polish Question, Wilhelm Schmidt asserted that "as Protestants we absolutely recognize on principle the right of the state to stand up for and spread German language and culture, especially against the onslaught of inferior, alien, national groups."[33] At its general assembly in Hagen in 1902, the league declared its "enthusiastic approval of measures by the Prussian government to protect the imperiled German ethnic community in the east."[34] The Protestant League, which had from its inception advocated a more active cultural role for the state, now supported Prussia's settlement plans, anti–Polish language decrees, and exceptional laws.[35]

But Protestants in the east did more than follow well-meaning directives from the state. A number of Protestants, both inside and outside the league, proposed a more radical and permanent solution to the nationality problem: the conversion of all Catholics, German and Polish, to Protestantism. In 1908, for instance, Pastor Joseph Rosenberg of Kempen, a man obsessed by secret Vatican plots to Slavicize German Catholics, founded the Evangelical Society for Catholic Poland.[36] The purpose of this society was to settle small cells of pious

[33] Wilhelm Schmidt, *Unsre Stellung zur Polenfrage* (Leipzig, 1902), 14.

[34] AKIEB S500.500.15 "Kundgebung der XV. Generalversammlung des Evangelischen Bundes," 1902.

[35] See ibid. See also EZB 7/3893 "Verhandlungsnachweis über die Konferenz der in den Ostmarken arbeitenden Vereinigungen am 16.12.1907."

[36] ADW NL Johannes Hesekiel CA 2188/33. The initial declaration for the Evangelical Society for Catholic Poland was signed on 11.6.1908 by Rosenberg, Arthur Rhode,

German-Protestant peasants in the midst of Polish ultramontane villages. Model farmers by day, these peasants would be exemplary missionaries by night; they would, in Rosenberg's words, "work on their Catholic neighbors and win them over to the *Evangelium*."[37] An eccentric idea, the Protestant church of Posen "decisively rejected" it, as did all but the most radical members of the Protestant League.[38] More serious, but hardly more successful, was Friedrich Meyer's attempt to bring Los von Rom to the Kaiserreich. Los von Rom, which we will address in the following chapter, was a movement to convert nationally minded German Catholics in the Austrian lands to Protestantism, to create, as it were, a "Protestant Pan-Germany." Meyer, who had always thought Los von Rom in Austria to be "a rehearsal for our work in the empire," believed the moment for the mass conversion of German Catholics in the east to be especially propitious.[39] In 1901, he attempted this with the German Evangelical Society in Barmen, then, in 1905, by creating a special Committee for the Enlightenment of German Catholics.[40] Short of converting all Catholics in Germany, there was, he thought, "no other way to get around the Center."[41] But his plans miscarried. The dynastic-conservative Protestant church of Prussia "could not reconcile itself" with the potentially disruptive, messianic visions of the Evangelical Society. And the Enlightenment Committee, despite Meyer's zeal, suffered from organizational diffi-

---

and Berthold Harhausen. These three pastors also organized the Deutsche Klein-siedlungsgenossenschaft (German Small Settlements Cooperative) in Posen. For a taste of Rosenberg's nationalism, see his *Endlich Gelöst!* (Leipzig, 1905) and *Der polnische Klerus, das deutsche Zentrum und das evangelische Deutschtum* (Lissa, 1908).

[37] ADW NL Johannes Hesekiel CA 2188/33 Joseph Rosenberg, "Vorschläge zur praktischen Ausführung der Evangelisation der Polen," 1908.

[38] EZB 7/3939 General Superintendent Johannes Hesekiel to Pastor Joseph Rosenberg, 12.9.1908. Everling thought it would be "grist for the mills of the Poles and the Center." See EZB 7/3893 "Verhandlungsnachweis über die Konferenz der in den Ostmarken arbeitenden Vereinigungen," 16.12.1907.

[39] AKIEB PL "Mitteilungen vom Ausschuss zur Förderung der evangelischen Kirche in Österreich," Nr. 29, 18.4.1906.

[40] On his support of the German Evangelical Society, see AKIEB S185.810.29 "Protokoll über die Sitzung des österreichischen Ausschusses," 11.3.1901; AKIEB S185.810.25 "Protokoll über die Sitzung des Ausschusses zur Förderung der evangelische Kirche in Österreich," 5.6.1905. The Committee for the Evangelical Enlightenment of German Catholics consisted of Friedrich Meyer, Paul Bräunlich, Carl Braun, Pastor Eckardt, Carl Fey, Theodor Geiger, Dr. Kietz, Hermann Kremers, Max Lehmann, Prof. Lander-Wittemberg, Prof. D. Scholz-Berlin, Pastor Schneitzer-Strasbourg, Factory owner Simon, Pastor Weichelt, Dr. Weitbrecht. See AKIEB S500.9.122t "Protokoll der Sitzung des Ausschusses unter den deutschen Katholiken," 17.4.1906.

[41] AKIEB PL "Mitteilungen vom Ausschuss zur Förderung der evangelischen Kirche in Österreich" Nr. 29, 18.4.1906.

culties and the resistance of league members who cautioned against making the nationality struggle into a religious conflict.[42]

This resistance proved considerable. Oskar Hermens of the league's executive committee considered Meyer's effort problematic "because it would unleash a wild confessional war in which we would predictably come out on the short end against the tightly organized Catholic church."[43] Similarly, some league members, particularly those from the east, argued that "it would be a serious tactical error for the Protestant League to confront the Polish movement directly."[44] Not only would the Germans lose a confessional war, but their own ranks would, as a result, fall divided. Even Otto Everling, ever eager to pursue nationalist projects, realized that the complex confessional and national composition of the east necessitated that "our relationship to German Catholics be so ordered that they have no reasonable grounds to complain."[45]

Here was the rub. The league could wave the bloody shirt, but it could not itself go to battle. For all its ideological posturing, the success of the Protestant League's engagement in the Germanization of the eastern marches was modest. This engagement started very late. Although the league discussed work in the eastern marches as early as 1897 and even diverted some resources toward this end, it was not until the Worms general assembly in 1907 that the league finally agreed to constitute a Committee for the Eastern Marches.[46] The delay, far from resulting from the ideological reticence of league leaders, rather came as a consequence of the resistance of Protestant circles from Posen and West Prussia who feared that "the emphasis on confessional difference would drive a dividing wedge into the solid phalanx of German unity."[47] But even at this late date, the committee was

[42] On the Evangelical Society and the Protestant Church's attitude toward it, see EZB 7/3939 Royal Consistory of the Rhineland, 19.6.1901. The official church pleaded, instead, for coexistence with Catholics. On the debate over the Evangelical Society within the Protestant League, see AKIEB S500.9.125 "Protokoll über die Gesamtvorstandssitzung des Evangelischen Bundes in Erfurt," 16/17.5.1900.

[43] AKIEB S185.810.29 "Protokoll über die Sitzung des Österreichischen Ausschusses," 11.3.1901.

[44] H. Braune, Der Evangelische Bund in der Ostmark (Leipzig, 1906), 14. According to Everling, "not all circles were satisfied" with Braune's speech. See EZB 7/3893 "Verhandlungsnachweis über die Konferenz der in den Ostmarken arbeitenden Vereinigungen am 16.12.1907."

[45] EZB 7/3893 "Verhandlungsnachweis über die Konferenz der in den Ostmarken arbeitenden Vereinigungen am 16.12.1907."

[46] AKIEB S500.9.122y "Verhandlungsnachweis über die Sitzung des Ostmarkenausschusses des Evangelischen Bundes am 14.3.1908."

[47] AKIEB S500.9.60 "Jahresbericht über die Generalversammlung des Evangelischen Bundes in Hamburg, 1905."

a failure. The Protestant League gave it RM 10,000 annually in order to disseminate propaganda, hire traveling orators, and maintain an orphanage.[48] Founded in 1897, this orphanage cared for "ethnically and confessionally endangered children" until they could be passed along to good German Protestant families. In some ways well-meaning, its ultimate purpose was to strengthen the racial-confessional stock of Germans in the eastern marches—bearing, therefore, a disturbing, if distant, resemblance to later projects to populate the east with racially pure Aryans.[49] But by 1913 the orphanage was near bankruptcy, an orator had yet to be hired, and the league had published only three pamphlets on Germanization.[50] The league also organized the Conference of Organizations Working in the Eastern Marches. This conference, which met annually from 1897 on, coordinated the activities of leading German national groups working in the east: the Society for the Eastern Marches, the Pan-German League, the Inner Mission, the Protestant League, and various smaller organizations.[51] But it met too infrequently to be effective and could do little more than express satisfaction with Germanization projects already in progress.[52]

Nevertheless, the Protestant League incurred the ire of numerous German national groups—in the first order the Society for the Eastern Marches (Ostmarkenverein), the most influential national organization in Posen and West Prussia. In some ways the eastern agendas of the two pressure groups ran parallel. An integral nationalist organization dedicated to the repression of the Polish language in Prussia, the

[48] AKIEB S500.9.122y "Verhandlungsnachweis über die Sitzung des Ost-markenausschusses," 14.3.1908; 30.1.1909.

[49] The Pan-German League founded the first such orphanage in 1896. One year later the Protestant League followed the Pan-German example and bought a *"Rest-Gut"* (the manor of a parceled-out estate) in Groß-Tilliz in West Prussia. See Everling, "Unsere Ostmarkenarbeit," *Vorstandsblatt des Evangelischen Bundes* 3 (1910): 113–18.; Johannes Burchard, "Fürsorge für die evangelischen Deutschen in unseren Ostmarken," *Vorstandsblatt des Evangelischen Bundes* 11 (1913): 455–70. For a general picture of this work with orphanages, see EZB 7/3893 "Verhandlungsnachweis über die Konferenz der in den Ostmarken arbeitenden Vereinigungen am 16.12.1907"; AKIEB S500.9.125 "Verhandlungsnachweis über die Konferenz der in den Ostmarken arbeitenden Vereinigungen, 11.12.1909.

[50] AKIEB S500.9.125 "Verhandlungsnachweis über die Sitzung des Ost-markenausschusses," 11.2.1911. AKIEB S500.9.125 "Verhandlungsnachweis über die Sitzung des Ostmarkenausschusses," 23.4.1913.

[51] On the origins of the conference, see Everling, "Unsere Ostmarkenarbeit," 115. According to Everling, the "main purpose of the society . . . was mutual support." EZB 7/3893 "Verhandlungsnachweis über die Konferenz der in den Ostmarken arbeitenden Vereinigungen," 16.12.1907.

[52] In 1908, at the height of tension between Germans and Poles, the conference failed to meet. EZB 7/3893 Otto Everling to the board members of the organizations working in the Eastern Marches, 22.11.1909.

Society for the Eastern Marches aggressively asserted German claims to the land as well as the absolute superiority of German national culture.[53] Like the Protestant League, it also placed its trust in the coercive potential of the state. "Protecting German ethnicity in the east is primarily the task and obligation of the government and the authorities," announced the society in a programmatic statement in 1897.[54] Moreover, the society's membership, which consisted mainly of landowners, bureaucrats, artisans, schoolteachers, and some clergymen, was mostly Protestant.[55]

But here the similarities ceased. The influence of the Protestant clergy on the Society for the Eastern Marches, unlike its influence on the Protestant League, was slight: there were but eight pastors in the society's general committee (358 members), and they made up only 4 percent of local chairmen.[56] More importantly, the reticence of the Protestant clergy—far from reflecting resistance to the government's Germanization measures—was actually a reaction to the interconfessional character of the Society for the Eastern Marches.[57] For despite the private anti-Catholicism of many of its Protestant members, the society publicly advocated settling German Catholics so that "finally the absurd idea that posits the equivalence of Protestant and German as well as Polish and Catholic can be destroyed."[58] The Protestant League, protests to the contrary notwithstanding, fueled and fanned this "absurd idea."

[53] On the Society for the Eastern Marches, the best study remains Tims, *Germanizing Prussian Poland*; it ought to be supplemented by Galos et al., *Die Hakatisten*, which in some points is more comprehensive but not always more insightful. See also Hagen, *Germans, Poles and Jews*, 267–87, especially on the society's relationship to the government and to the Agrarian League.

[54] *Die Ostmark* 2 (February 1897): 9

[55] Galos et al., *Die Hakatisten*, 77. See also Eley, *Reshaping the German Right*, 63; Tims, *Germanizing Prussian Poland*, 219. PAAA R4063 Memorandum of the provincial governor of West Prussia, Gustav von Gossler, 6.9.1896.

[56] Beilage zur *Ostmark* 2 (July 1897). Moreover, there were no pastors in the central committee (Vorstand). See also Tims, *Germanizing Prussian Poland*, 224–27.

[57] The superintendent of Posen, Johannes Hesekiel, complained of the government's "preference for interconfessional organizations (in particular the Society for the Eastern Marches) all the more because . . . the most important and truly propitious way of strengthening Germandom is to strengthen Protestant consciousness." EZB 7/1848 "Auszug von der Abschrift des Berichts des Generalsuperintendenten der Provinz Posen, Johannes Hesekiel, betreffend die Superintendenten Konferenz am 15. und 16. Februar 1904," 17.3.1904.

[58] *Die Ostmark* 3 (April 1898): 38. See also Erich Liesegang, "Protestantisierung oder Germanisierung," *Die Ostmark* 3 (November 1898): 124–25. The society also supported the Union of German Catholics (the nationalist organization of German Catholics in Posen and West Prussia). See "Verein deutscher Katholiken," *Die Ostmark* 10 (March 1905): 19–20. *Die Ostmark* carried many articles on German Catholics in the east. Although the Society for the Eastern Marches criticized the Center party, especially for its

Fearful that further confessional rancor would weaken ethnic solidarity, many German nationalists emphasized the Catholic contribution to the ethnic struggle. In 1907, Robert Höniger of the Society for
the Eastern Marches asserted "precisely the Catholic church has done
much for the Germanization of the east."[59] Some went even further.
Christian Rade, editor of *Die Christliche Welt*, the journal of liberal
Protestantism in Germany, argued that not Protestantism but Catholicism should play the decisive role in the nationality struggle. In 1902,
he listed his "theses on the Polish danger":

1. The only effective means of doing away with the Polish danger is to
   separate German Catholicism from its alliance with Polonism.
2. This task is in German Catholicism's own vital interest.
3. Protestantism is not in a position to overcome the Polish danger. It
   lacks all religious and other means to achieve this.[60]

Rade, a peculiarly perspicacious Protestant intellectual, understood
that the agitation of the Protestant League, far from supporting the
German national cause, may have hindered it. Even the government
warned the Protestant League against pursuing confessional polemics in the eastern marches with too much vigor. The governor of
West Prussia, Ernst von Jagow, implored the league "to see in our
brothers of the other confession what we have in common and what
binds us together."[61]

Rather than reinforce the widespread view that Germanization

---

opposition to Prussia's Polish policy, it did so with optimism as early as 1898 that the
party "would undergo a transformation." The society's reserved attitude toward anti-
Catholicism stemmed, in part, from its reliance on the Agrarian League in organizing
Protestant peasants; the Agrarian League, in turn, depended on the Center to pass
high grain tariffs. Also, in Silesia, roughly half of the society's members were themselves Catholic. See Tims, *Germanizing Prussian Poland*, 253, fn. 45.

[59] Robert Höniger, *Ansprache gehalten auf dem Deutschen Tag des Ostmarkenvereins zu
Bromberg am 18. August 1907* (n.p., 1907). For the league's reaction to Höniger's speech,
see AKIEB S500.393.111 "Der Hauptverein des Evangelischen Bundes in der Provinz
Posen, Betr: Interkonfessionalität des Ostmarkenvereins," 3.9.1907. Note the league's
appropriation of the historical arguments of Houston Stewart Chamberlain. On Everling's views, see EZB 7/3893 "Verhandlungsnachweis über die Konferenz der in den
Ostmarken arbeitenden Vereinigungen," 16.12.1907. The Agrarian League also criticized the Protestant League for not recognizing the positive contribution of German
Catholics to national solidarity (see AKIEB S500.9.125 "Verhandlungsnachweis über die
Sitzung des Ostmarkenausschusses," 10/11.12.1909) while the Union of German Catholics condemned the Protestant League's ideological conflux of Protestantism and German national identity (see *Katholische Rundschau*, 15 October 1905).

[60] See Christian Rade, "Thesen zur Polengefahr," *Die Christliche Welt*, Nr. 7, 13 February 1902, 159–60.

[61] AKIEB S500.500.19a "Bericht über die neunzehnte Generalversammlung des
evangelischen Bundes," 1906.

equaled Protestantization, Prussian leaders attempted to enlist German Catholics in the nationality struggle against Catholic Poles. "Instead of aggravating national differences with confessional conflicts," argued the provincial governor of Posen, Freiherr von Wilamowitz-Möllendorff, "it would be more advantageous to encourage the emigration of German Catholics into Polish areas, and by introducing the German language [into religious affairs] and by bringing in German Catholic priests with true national consciousness, break the solid phalanx of the Polish Catholic clergy."[62] To this end, it was imperative that Prussia "maintain confessional parity as far as possible" and "never give the appearance . . . of hostility toward the Catholic church or the Catholic faith."[63]

German Catholics and Polish Catholics:
The Making of an Antagonism

German Catholicism played an altogether different but in some ways more profound role in the nationality struggle. It was different because Germanizing Catholic priests hid their Germanization efforts behind pro-Polish rhetoric and appeals to interethnic harmony. And it was more profound because the Catholic church's attempt to make Polish religious life ring German affected Polish national culture in matters considered sacred.

The clash between German and Polish Catholics, although profound, was limited geographically to Upper Silesia, to the industrial areas of the Ruhr, to pockets of German Catholic settlements in West Prussia and Posen, and to the sparsely populated Ermland of East Prussia. In these areas German and Polish Catholics lived in the same town, prayed the prayers of the same bishop, and often went to the same church. But their coexistence was also marked by discord—class, religious, and national.

In Upper Silesia, for instance, class stratification severely strained

[62] LHAK 403/7046 Frhr. von Wilamowitz-Möllendorff, "Denkschrift betreffend die Grundsätze für das Verhalten der Staatsregierung gegenüber den Staatsangehörigen polnischer Muttersprache in der Provinz Posen," 23.11.1895. This memorandum became the basis for Prussian Polish policy in the post-Caprivi era. Bismarck himself had seen the strategic advantage to be gained by decoupling Germanization from the anti-Catholic measures of the Kulturkampf. After repealing the May laws, he wrote Kurd von Schlözer, his ambassador in the Vatican, in April 1887: "I have always had the desire to deal with church affairs in the Polish-speaking parts of the country *separately*." PAAA 4125 Bismarck to von Schlözer, 29.4.1887.

[63] LHAK 403/7046 Frhr. von Wilamowitz-Möllendorff, "Denkschrift betreffend die Grundsätze für das Verhalten der Staatsregierung gegenüber den Staatsangehörigen polnischer Muttersprache in der Provinz Posen," 23.11.1895.

relations between German and Polish Catholics. Especially in counties east of the Oder, German Catholics lived in greater proportions in the cities, and were more likely to work in light industry, commerce, or in the tertiary sector than Polish Catholics, who, concentrated in industrial suburbs and in agrarian areas, worked mainly in brown coal mines, iron foundries, or on small farms.[64] In Upper Silesian industry, social inequality was particularly crass. In 1907, 93.4 percent of the Polish population employed in industry were workers, whereas among the Germans only 65 percent belonged to the working class. The rest were either salaried employees or independent entrepreneurs.[65] Class tensions therefore created the preconditions for ethnic as well as for intra-Catholic religious conflict. The same may be said of Polish areas in the Ruhr. By 1910, Polish immigration into the mining and smelting districts of Germany's largest industrial basin had created a national diaspora of close to 300,000 Poles. Here too Polish workers settled primarily in areas populated by German Catholics, and, as in Upper Silesia, national differences left their imprint on religion, often depriving it of its capacity to mediate between competing national claims.

There is an impressive body of scholarship devoted to understanding the influence of the Polish clergy on the Polish national movement.[66] Conversely, the efforts of German Catholics, particularly the German episcopate, to Germanize their Polish coreligionists remain largely terra incognita to historians.[67] Yet these efforts were considerable. In Upper Silesia, Georg von Kopp, prince-bishop of Breslau, dedicated himself to the Germanization of his Polish parishioners with considerable engagement. In 1888, soon after he became prince-bishop, he censured clergy members "suspected of secretly or openly resisting Germanization efforts."[68] In the following year, he assembled the archdeacons of his diocese and instructed them to "strictly monitor" the clergy so that Germanization could proceed in confes-

---

[64] Hentschel, "Wirtschaftliche Entwicklung," 243–50.

[65] Ibid., 260. See also Lawrence Schofer, *The Formation of a Modern Labor Force: Upper Silesia, 1865–1914* (Berkeley, 1975).

[66] On the clergy and Polish nationalism during the Kulturkampf, see Lech Trzeciakowski, *The Kulturkampf in Prussian Poland, 1870–1890* (New York, 1990), esp. 141–83. See also the many works of scholarship on the Polish school strikes. Among them, the best works in western languages are John Kulczynski (Kulczycki), *School Strikes and Prussian Poland, 1901–1907* (New York, 1981), and Rudolf Korth, *Die preußische Schulpolitik und die polnischen Schulstreiks* (Würzburg, 1963).

[67] The exception, Lech Trzeciakowski, "The Prussian State and the Catholic Church in Prussian Poland, 1871–1914," *Slavic Review* 26 (1967): 618–37, is mostly concerned with the archbishopric of Gnesen-Posen.

[68] PAAA R3948 Cardinal Georg von Kopp to Gustav von Gossler, 30.10.1888.

sion and communion class.[69] In 1890, he admonished against the use of the Polish catechism—presumably because of its national hues. And, in the same year, he gave "secret instructions to the bishop's commissaries" to discourage the pious from making pilgrimages to Cracow, a center of the Polish national movement.[70]

In his furtiveness, Prince-Bishop Kopp, who had been named cardinal in 1893, was not alone. The German-Catholic clergy, similarly eager to serve the cause of Germanization, also did not shy from clandestine initiative. In 1902, the Benedictine monks of Maria Laach and Beuron on the Danube conspired with Chancellor Bernhard von Bülow and Kaiser Wilhelm II to establish a monastery in Posen that would "give spiritual aid to German nationals" in "those parts of the country oppressed by the Poles."[71] Kopp himself advised the state of Prussia on measures to reorganize the bishopric of Culm so that the Polish danger could be countered.[72]

Resolute in religious matters, Kopp consistently sided against Polish national aspirations in the political field as well. In the Reichstag election of 1903, he issued a pastoral letter that warned against nationalist agitators from Warsaw who "present themselves as defenders of religion" but are in fact the "grave diggers" of Catholicism.[73] In 1905, he prevailed upon the archbishop of Gnesen-Posen to take measures to purge Polish liturgical books in his archdiocese of their nationalist tones.[74] And in the Polish school strike of 1906, in which Polish children refused to attend religious instruction taught in German, Cardinal Kopp proved instrumental in preventing the Vatican from taking a position against the state of Prussia.[75] For his activ-

[69] PAAA R3948 Kopp to von Gossler, 7.1.1899. Kopp insisted that these classes "*at all times* and without exception be given in two sections and all children who understand German be placed in the German section." Thus he hoped to achieve Germanization gradually, but decisively.

[70] On Kopp's effort, see PAAA R4060 Gustav von Gossler to Leo von Caprivi, 25.11.1890. On the cardinal's influence on Vatican politics in this matter, see PAAA R3943 Kurd von Schlözer to Caprivi, 15.11.1890.

[71] The quote is from Bülow in PAAA R4124 Bernhard von Bülow to Studt, 3.8.1902. For negotiations, see Placidus Wolter (abbot of Beuron) to Kaiser Wilhelm II, 8.7.1902; Bülow to Kaiser Wilhelm II, 14.7.1902 (with enthusiastic marginalia from the kaiser); Bülow to Freiherr Fidelis von Slotzinger (abbot of Maria-Laach), 3.8.1902

[72] Studt to Bülow, 9.3.1905. Reprinted in E. Gatz, ed., *Akten zur preußischen Kirchenpolitik in den Bistümern Gnesen-Posen, Kulm und Ermland, 1885–1914* (Mainz, 1977), 207–8.

[73] The pastoral letter was issued on 3 June and was reprinted in *Germania*, 9 June 1903. See Ilse Schwidetzky, *Die polnische Wahlbewegung in Oberschlesien* (Breslau, 1934), 62.

[74] PAAA R4087 Note of the Ministry of Culture to Bernhard von Bülow, 2.6.1905

[75] PAAA/R4095 Bülow to Kopp, 18.12.1906. On Kopp's anti-Polish stance, see also Trzeciakowski, "The Prussian State and the Catholic Church in Prussian Poland, 1871–1914," 630.

ities, the Polish press regularly singled Kopp out as "the worst of all Germanizers."[76] Though hyperbolic, this was not far from the mark.

The extent of German Catholicism's complicity in Prussia's Germanization program was, however, most evident in the Ruhr. Here German Catholic priests combated Polish national consciousness in Catholic social organizations, in the church, and in the rituals that mark out the life of the pious: baptisms, pilgrimages, marriage ceremonies, and funerals. In the Ruhr, Polish social and national life flourished in an array of clubs and societies. But, at the beginning of the mass migration from the east, Polish sociability was concentrated in Catholic organizations dedicated to raising religious and moral consciousness and protecting Polish workers from the temptation of socialism. These clubs, whose names—St. Vincent, St. Barbara—betrayed their religious intent, were directed by German Catholic priests who, as club chairmen, saw their principal task in keeping Polish nationalist agitation at bay.[77] But as Polish national consciousness in Ruhr settlement areas waxed, the influence of German Catholic priests on the religious sociability of Poles waned. And as the German Catholic priests lost influence, they also lost power and respect: the members of Polish Catholic clubs, in the words of one internal Prussian report, "scoff . . . at the priests, whom they universally consider, and call, a Germanizer."[78]

The axis around which German and Polish Catholic conflict turned was language. The Poles in the Ruhr wanted priests who could speak to them in their mother tongue, who could hear confession in Polish; they wanted Sunday sermons in Polish, and they wanted their children to read the Polish catechism and to receive holy communion in Polish. But the German clergy would have none of it. In March 1904, the bishops of Mainz and Paderborn, and the archbishop of Cologne, convened to discuss the concessions they could possibly make to the Poles. These concessions proved niggardly. In principle, the bishops wanted "to make only as many concessions as the requirements of church life absolutely demanded."[79] In practice, that included Polish

[76] For the tone of the Polish press, see Leonhard Müller, *Nationalpolnische Presse, Katholizismus und Katholischer Klerus* (Breslau, 1931), 205–11.

[77] On German Catholic priests and Polish clubs in the Ruhr, see Christoph Klessmann, *Polnische Bergarbeiter im Ruhrgebiet, 1870–1945* (Göttingen, 1978), esp. 137–41; Krystyna Murzynowska, *Der polnische Erwerbsauswanderer im Ruhrgebiet während der Jahre 1880–1914* (Dortmund, 1979), 124–30. For a short, general introduction to the situation of Poles in the Ruhr, see Hans-Ulrich Wehler, "Die Polen im Ruhrgebiet bis 1918," in Wehler, *Krisenherde des Kaiserreichs 1871–1918*, 219–36.

[78] LHAK 403/7051 The regency president of Düsseldorf, Schreiber, to the provincial governor of the Rhineland, 29.6.1904.

[79] LHAK 403/7051 Report of the provincial governor of Westphalia, Eberhard Freiherr von der Recke von dem Horst, 18.3.1904.

Sunday services with Polish sermons and hymns on alternate Sundays in communities with significant Polish populations. But the bishops also emphasized that "confession and communion class be given in *German* without exception."[80] In the following month, members of the Catholic clergy secretly convened to discuss the matter further. To the bishops' resolution, they appended a distinction, which would henceforth govern the religious relationship between the German clergy and the Catholic Poles: "The Poles must be granted what religious requirements make necessary: confession, Polish devotion with sermons on afternoons. The Poles must be denied everything that serves political-Polish agitation: communion and confession class, baptism, wedding ceremonies, funerals in the Polish language, Sunday mass with Polish hymns; . . ."[81]

After the results of the meeting were leaked to the press, the Poles responded with a litany of counterproposals, which, when taken together, amounted to the demand that their religiosity remain Polish.[82]

A schism threatened Catholic life in the Ruhr. The breach was, of course, national, but even more deeply religious and cultural. In the clergy's zealousness to Germanize Polish Catholics, the silent denouement of political Catholicism's commitment to cultural diversity in the national state became evident. For what they proposed to take away from the Poles was not Catholicism but Catholicism's rootedness in local culture, and this at the elementary level of language.

The relationship of national and religious identity to life was also germane to this conflict. Both nationalism and religiosity are deeply concerned with birth and morality, and with the symbolic representation of stages of life. In nationalist imaginings, one is born Polish and baptized Catholic. Marriages are mixed across confession or nationality. At death, the vernacular dirge sung would be recognizable to the deceased. And even if, as an unknown soldier, one dies without a name, it will be clear that the cenotaph, without needing to state it, shall stand in, and for, the nation. As Benedict Anderson asks of such tombs, "what else could they be but Germans, Americans, Argentinians?"[83] In some religiously divided countries, they would also be Catholics, Protestants, Jews. In many parts of Germany even Christian cemeteries remained confessionally divided until the late nineteenth century. It is this close relationship between national identity

---

[80] Ibid.

[81] LHAK 403/7051 Father Walter to Wilhelm Schneider, bishop of Paderborn.

[82] LHAK 403/7054 Police commissioner of Essen, Hansch, to the regency president of Düsseldorf, 28.11.1906.

[83] Benedict Anderson, *Imagined Communities*, 10.

and religious ritual that was at issue, and that, to some extent, the German Catholic clergy proposed to erase from the consciousness of Poles in the Ruhr.

Nationalism and religion also have in common iconographic richness. In the case of the Polish national movement, symbolically centered on Catholicism, national and religious iconography were deeply intertwined. But the German priests attempted to undo this as well. Together with Prussian officials, they forbade Poles from making pilgrimages to the sanctuary of Werl (a smelting town in the Ruhr Valley, east of Dortmund), from wearing Polish national caps or carrying with them flags and banners belonging to Polish clubs, from singing the interdicted Polish-Catholic song "Serdeczna Matka" (Our Dear Virgin Mother), and from consecrating crucifixes with Polish inscriptions.[84] Thus the archbishop of Cologne, Cardinal Fischer, could assure the Prussian government that the German clergy "is strictly instructed to . . . warn against Polish national aspirations whenever possible," while confidently adding, "I believe that in this matter the clergy is beyond reproach."[85] Indeed, from the perspective of the government, it was.

But the Polish national movement was not a soft clay to be easily molded. It too had a considerable history of organization, of ideological commitment, of tenacious defense of minority rights (if also, at the same time, of startling intolerance). Rather than acquiescing to the demands of the German Catholic clergy, the Polish nationalists raised their demands for Polish clergymen, though now the demand was not for Germans who could speak Polish but for Polish national priests "who could see into the soul of the people."[86] Concurrently, Polish nationalists urged Polish-Catholic organizations to stop heeding the advice of German clerical leaders. In 1913, the Polish Congress, which met in Wynkerswyk in Holland, resolved that Germans "may not be accepted as members of Polish clubs" and emphasized

[84] On pilgrimages and their relationship to Polish national identity, see LHAK 403/7052 Report of the Dortmund police commissioner Göhrke, "Die nationalpolnische Bewegung, ihre Überwachung und Bekämpfung," 3.12.1904; LHAK 403/16008 Prussian Minister of the Interior Theobald von Bethmann-Hollweg to the provincial governor of Westphalia, 18.5.1907; LHAK 403/16008 Report of the mayor of Neviges, von Hardenberg, 28.3.1907; LHAK 403/16008 Regency president of Düsseldorf to the provincial governor of the Rhineland, 27.61908. On the efforts of the Catholic church, see LHAK 403/16008 Bishop Schneider of Paderborn to the provincial governor of Westphalia, 28.12.1906.

[85] LHAK 403/13538 Cardinal Fischer, archbishop of Cologne, to the provincial governor of the Rhineland, 30.1.1911.

[86] LHAK 403/13539 Police Commissioner Gerstein to the regency president of Arnsberg, 22.4.1912.

"that the clergy . . . is not to be exempted from this rule."[87] Though it did not effect a complete collapse of religious relations, such a proclamation indicated something of the enmity in the air. Similarly, extremist voices in the Polish community called for a mass conversion to the Armenian rites so that the Poles could "evade the power of German bishops and put themselves under the patronage of Archbishop Teodorowicz in Lemberg."[88] Finally, some Poles demanded a boycott of pilgrimages. "No," exclaimed a member of the St. Joseph parish in Bochum, "under such conditions it is better that Polish pilgrims do not take part in the German pilgrimage but instead stay home and pray to the queen of the Polish crown that we homeless may receive a better lot."[89]

The Catholic Center and the Nationality Conflict

With the deterioration of religious relations, ties between the German Center party and the political spokesmen of the Poles loosened as well. This process began with the end of the official Kulturkampf and accelerated during the 1890s. Its immediate background must be seen in the rise of Polish nationalism in areas previously dominated by the Center party and in the concurrent integration of the Center into a political system oriented toward the status-quo stabilization of the Prussian-German state.

The first Polish challenge to Center hegemony came in Upper Silesia in 1893, and it characteristically mixed religious with social and national motives. Julius Szmulza, a Pole who ran as a competing Center candidate in the heavily industrialized, predominantly Polish lignite mining district of Beuthen-Tarnowitz, addressed "Polish voters who love the faith and the Catholic church, who treasure their mother tongue, who hold dear the forgotten and oppressed Upper Silesian people, and who value the honor of their nation."[90] He won his district with two-thirds of the vote. Polish candidates also usurped Center strongholds in Pless-Rybnik, another highly industrialized electoral district in Upper Silesia, and in Allenstein-Rössel, a reli-

[87] LHAK 403/13539 "Bericht über den Verlauf des Polenkongresses in Wynkerswyk," 1/2.11.1913.

[88] LHAK 403/13539 Police Commissioner Gerstein to the regency president of Arnsberg, 25.5.1912. See also "Kann man in der Diöcese Paderborn zugleich Katholik und Pole sein?" Wiarus Polski, 10 May 1912.

[89] Cited in LHAK 403/13538 Police Commissioner Gerstein to the regency president of Arnsberg, 1.4.1911.

[90] Cited in Schwidetzky, Die polnische Wahlbewegung, 39.

giously and ethnically mixed district in East Prussia.[91] Yet, through a series of clever concessions, the Center parried the first Polish thrust and, in 1898, regained its "Polish" mandates in Upper Silesia. But thereafter the Center, to cite Yeats, could not hold.

It is difficult to pinpoint exactly when the alliance collapsed, or whether the alliance, burdened by the weight of growing national antagonism, would well have come crashing down anyway. Yet a decisive moment seems to have been the Center's ineffective resistance to the so-called Studt language decrees of 1900. These decrees, implemented mainly in the towns and cities of Posen, forbade the use of Polish in primary school religious instruction and, for this reason, constituted an affront to both the religious and the national sensibilities of the Poles.[92] In response to these decrees, school strikes of Polish children broke out in Wreschen in the province of Posen. These strikes, enthusiastically supported within Polish society, also inaugurated the ascendancy of the populist National Democrats, whose primary focus was not parliamentary politics but rather the national organization of Polish society. Hardly interested in the politesse of parliamentary negotiations with Center leaders, the National Democrats preferred polemics, often acerbic, against the Center.[93] Even old Polish loyalists, who had hitherto attempted to work together with the Center in defending Polish rights, now found themselves increasingly in retreat.[94]

The rise of the National Democrats in Polish society also encouraged a reorientation of Center party policy toward the Poles. Under Carl Bachem's leadership, the Center attempted to isolate the National Democrats from Polish loyalists. Bachem considered the former "pure chauvinistic nationalists," the latter "ardent Catholics."[95] The Center could work with the one but not with the other.

Within the Center, positions toward the Poles ranged from a principled stance against Germanization measures to a desire to support all Germanization measures short of those that infringed on the rights of

---

[91] On these electoral battles, see ibid., 38–42.

[92] On the language decrees, see Lamberti, *State, Society, and the Elementary School*, 139–40.

[93] See Blanke, *Prussian Poland*, 221–22; and, for a taste of the integral nationalist rhetoric of the Polish National Democrats, see the compendium, admittedly biased, in Müller, *Nationalpolnische Presse*.

[94] Hagen, *Germans, Poles and Jews*, 230. On the ideology of the National Democrats, see Andrej Walicki, *Philosophy and Romantic Nationalism: The Case of Poland* (Oxford, 1982), 337–57. See also Peter Brock, "Polish Nationalism," in *Nationalism in Eastern Europe*, ed. Peter Sugar and Ivo Lederer (Seattle, 1969), 310–72.

[95] StAK NL Bachem, Nr. 170 Carl Bachem to Richard Müller, 20.8.1901.

the Catholic church.[96] The first position, represented by Hermann Roeren and Matthias Erzberger, and typically shared by the Catholic integralists within the party, asserted the rights of the Poles to full ethnic expression within the German national community.[97] Roeren argued that "the natural right that every nation has is the right to preserve its nationality, its mother tongue, and its national essence."[98] Comparing Germans in the Habsburg monarchy to Poles in the German empire, he believed that both groups could cultivate their national feeling without compromising their status as citizens. Erzberger concurred with this view. A caustic critic of Prussian policy in the east, he considered the battery of anti-Polish language decrees and exceptional laws "beyond what one could imagine in a civilized state."[99]

But some German Catholics could well imagine the imperatives of a harsh policy directed against the Poles. Graf Franz von Ballestrem, esteemed Center leader, then president of the Reichstag, gained notoriety among Poles and German Catholics alike when, at the Silesian *Katholikentag* of 1891, he suggested that "the Polish nationalist agitators need a smack in the mouth."[100] Graf Friedrich von Praschma, a powerful landlord and Center party notable, also vented his disdain for Polish nationalists—hypocrites and radical agitators who made a mockery of religion. "Catholicism, class hatred, and undermining authority do not go together," he argued, concluding that the Center must collaborate with conservative Protestants to repress Polish radicalism, which "undermines all authority."[101] Still more extreme were the German Catholics who belonged to the German Union, the Deutsche Vereinigung. Graf Wilhelm zu Hoensbroech, its leader, insisted that "Prussian Polish policy can have only one goal: to suffi-

[96] A competent summary of the Center's position on Polish questions can be found in Brigitte Balzer, *Die preußische Polenpolitik 1894–1908 und die Haltung der deutschen konservativen und liberalen Parteien* (Franfurt a.M., 1990), esp. 44–47, 116–27, 201–15, 278–83. Unfortunately, Balzer does not exploit unpublished sources of Center party leaders.

[97] See Hermann Roeren, *Zur Polenfrage* (Hamm i.W., 1903); Matthias Erzberger, *Der Kampf gegen den Katholizismus in der Ostmark* (Berlin, 1908). For the position of the Bavarians, see PAAA R318 Anton Graf von Monts de Mazin to Bülow, 7.6.1902. The connection between integralists and support for the Poles is suggested in Margaret Lavinia Anderson, "Interdenominationalism," 363.

[98] Roeren, *Zur Polenfrage*, 47.

[99] Erzberger, *Der Kampf gegen den Katholizismus*, 5.

[100] Cited in *Die Ostmark* 2 (July 1897): 51.

[101] His speech, delivered in 1895, was approvingly reprinted in *Katholische Rundschau*, 1 December 1905. This way of looking at the Polish issue was endemic to what the authorities called "good Catholic circles in the Lower Rhine." See LHAK 403/7049 The regency president of Düsseldorf to the provincial governor of the Rhineland, 4.9.1901.

ciently strengthen German ethnicity in the east so that it is capable of building a lasting barricade against the Slavic flood."[102]

The Center had for a long time found it necessary to navigate between these two positions. Under Windthorst, a principled defense of ethnic minorities predominated. But by the turn of the century, anti-Polish voices within the Center had gained in influence so that, by 1902, the Center's support for the Poles seemed increasingly equivocal. In parliament, the Center still defended the civil rights of individual Prussian citizens whose mother tongue was Polish as well as the right of Prussian Poles to "maintain their national customs and folkways, especially their mother tongue."[103] But it made these rights contingent on "the duty, and not just the legal but also the moral duty [of the Poles] to be faithful subjects of the Prussian state."[104] In practice, the Center even supported government censorship of the National Democratic press and incarceration of disloyal polemicists.[105] The official position of the Center on German colonization was similarly ambivalent; the party no longer criticized the principle of German colonization, only its execution. Publicly, it faulted the colonization program for not maintaining religious parity.[106] In closed committee, it advocated "settling Catholic farmers on a large scale wherever they can maintain their Germanness."[107] Moreover, the Center's critique of the "Hakatists" (slang for the extreme nationalists in the Society for the Eastern Marches) focused increasingly on the confessional aspect of their agitation. In a letter to the Center deputy Richard Müller, Carl Bachem insisted that the "Hakatists hate the Poles mainly because they are Catholics; that is my deep conviction, and therefore we must fight the Hakatists to the end."[108]

[102] See the foreword by Graf Wilhelm zu Hoensbroech in Johannes Altkemper, *Deutschtum und Polentum*, i–v. For a similar view, see Martin Spahn, "Polenpolitik," *Hochland* 5, no. 2 (1908): 83–103.

[103] See Alois Fritzen's speech concerning "our principled position on the Polish question" in Stenographische Berichte über die Verhandlungen des Preußischen Hauses der Abgeordneten (Hereafter Stenographische Berichte), 13.1.1902, 94–95.

[104] Ibid.

[105] Ibid. To the applause of the Conservatives and the National Liberals, Fritzen urged the government "to pursue such excesses of high treason with the sharpest legal means."

[106] See the speech of Carl Bachem, Stenographische Berichte, 4.3.1901. Moreover, the Center party's critique of the "Ostmarkenzulagen" for Prussian officials was not so much directed against the principle of granting such officials extra subsidies as it was that Catholic officials would be disadvantaged. See, for example, Heinrich Krückemeyer, "Ostmarkenzulagen," *Historisch-politische Blätter* 133, no. 3 (1904): 167–84.

[107] See PAAA R4075 "Bericht des XXII. Kommission zur Vorberathung des Gesetzentwurfes betreffend Maßnahmen zur Stärkung des Deutschtums," 2.6.1902.

[108] StAK NL Bachem Nr. 170 Carl Bachem to Richard Müller (Fulda), 16.9.1901. The

Even had it wanted to, the ability of the Center to wage a successful campaign against Prussia's Germanization policy was limited. Polish policy was conducted in the Prussian Landtag, and there, thanks to the three-class suffrage system, the Cartel parties (Conservatives and National Liberals) enjoyed safe majorities. The Center could block legislation only by working behind the scenes to prevent it from reaching the floor or by threatening the Conservative party in the Reichstag with withdrawal of Center party support for protective tariffs. The Center's attempted resistance to the settlement law of 1902, which envisioned an extra RM 200 million for colonization purposes, revealed the party's weakness. Even before the bill was publicly announced, the archbishop of Gnesen-Posen, Florian Stablewski, a man closer to the Polish than to the German cause, implored Carl Bachem to make clear to Chancellor Bülow that if this bill came to pass, the "Center would no longer support the government's measures in the Reichstag."[109] Bachem threatened exactly that, first to Prussia's minister of the interior, Count Posadowsky, then to Bülow "to the limits of cordiality."[110] But neither Posadowsky nor Bülow budged. Frustrated, Bachem replied to Stablewski: "When Bülow points out that the Center must in any case support (tariff) legislation, he is unfortunately in a certain way right . . . because in all these unfortunate economic questions we are pressured by our constituents."[111] Bachem added that "these economic questions make it impossible to steer a consistent oppositional course."[112] Structurally implicated in the economic imperatives of *Sammlungspolitik*, the Center's resistance to Prussia's settlement laws proved ineffective. At best the Center influenced the timing of such legislation.

For its part, the Polish party charged the Center with contributing to the government's Germanization efforts.[113] In an anonymously published pamphlet entitled *Away with the Center* (Precz z Centrum), the leader of the Upper Silesian National Democrats, Wojciech Korfanty, accused "Center priests" of removing Polish hymns from the

---

Center also opposed the Hakatists because their agitation "contributed to the sharpening of [national] differences" and "necessarily provoked an exaggerated counterreaction." See Fritzen, Stenographische Berichte, 3.1.1902.

[109] StAK NL Bachem, Nr. 161. Archbishop Florian Stablewski to Carl Bachem, 2.5.1902.

[110] On negotiations between Bachem and Bülow, Bachem and Posadowski, see StAK NL Bachem, Nr. 161 Note Carl Bachem 4.5.1902.

[111] StAK NL Bachem Nr. 161 Carl Bachem to Archbishop Florian Stablewski, 4.5.1902.

[112] Ibid.

[113] For an impassioned critique of "Catholic Hakatists," see LHAK 403/7050 *Wiarus Polski*, 5 September 1903.

churches of Upper Silesia, of Germanizing children, of cooperating with the Hakatists, and of denying Polish pastoral care to Polish workers in Berlin and Westphalia.[114] Similarly, the Westphalian *Wiarus Polski* declared that "the worst and most dangerous Germanizers are the Germanizing priests."[115]

The two parties broke on the eve of the Reichstag election in 1903. The Polish Central Election Committee demanded that the Center desist from running candidates in the Ermland, West Prussia, East Pomerania, Posen, and Upper Silesia. German Catholics in these areas were to support Polish candidates, in return for which Poles in the Ruhr would support the Center. The Polish election committee further demanded that German Catholic priests cease their Germanization efforts, especially in religious newspapers and in Catholic organizational life, and that the Center bring about the repeal of exceptional laws directed against Polish assemblies in mining districts in the Ruhr. Finally, the Polish party called upon the Center to force German bishops to guarantee Polish sermons, hymns, prayers, religious instruction, confession, and communion in areas with Polish minorities.[116] Infuriated by the extent of Polish demands, the Center refused to negotiate and instead put up candidates in opposition to the Poles in all Polish areas in which there were significant numbers of German Catholics. That proved a mistake, for the Center lost three seats in Upper Silesia and was prevented from reaching runoff elections in three more districts in the Ruhr.[117] More alarming than mandates lost were statistics on the percentage of Poles who supported Polish candidates in opposition to the German Center. In the heavily industrialized districts east of the Oder, close to 40 percent of the Polish population followed national rather than exclusively religious affiliation (this figure would increase still further in 1907).[118] More precisely, the elections of 1903 demonstrated that political Catholicism had itself divided along national lines.

---

[114] German-language excerpts of this pamphlet can be found in LHAK 403/7048 under the title "Fort mit dem Zentrum." On its authorship, see Schwidetzky, *Die polnische Wahlbewegung*, 55.

[115] LHAK 403/7049 *Wiarus Polski*, 28 June 1902.

[116] StAK NL Bachem, Nr. 195 Circular of Lambert Lensing (Center Party representative in Westphalia), 30.3.1903.

[117] In Upper Silesia, Korfanty won in the runoff election with the help of Social Democratic votes in the district of Kattowitz-Zabrze. The other two victorious Polish candidates ("Major" Julius Szmula in Oppeln and Theophil Krolik in Beuthen-Tarnowitz) ran as competing Center candidates during the election but joined the Polish party soon afterward. See Schwidetzky, *Die polnische Wahlbewegung*, 57–69. In the Ruhr, separate Polish candidates kept the Center party from reaching the runoff elections in the districts of Duisburg-Mülheim, Bochum-Gelsenkirchen-Hattingen, and Dortmund-Hörde. See Altkemper, *Deutschtum und Polentum*, 210–11.

On the morrow of the elections, the Center party reconsidered its relationship to the Polish party. Bachem's policy of placating the Poles had long irritated the leaders of the Silesian Center, who advocated a harder line. Felix Porsch, the most influential among them, argued against Carl and Julius Bachem that attempts to mollify the Poles only threatened to unleash a mass exodus of German Catholics from the Silesian Center.[119] The ensuing conflict over Polish policy attained such proportions that it threatened to create an internal east-west split within the Center party.[120] But in the winter of 1903, Carl Bachem came around to Porsch's position despite his distaste for the Silesian Center's *"Hakatismus moderatus."*[121] Bachem realized that "the Upper Silesian Poles are lost to us, and we must now at least do what we can so that we do not completely split apart from the German Catholics in Upper Silesia."[122] Moreover, Lambert Lensing, the Westphalian Center leader in charge of negotiations with the Poles in the Ruhr, a man who had previously advocated a conciliatory policy toward the Poles, now came to the conclusion that they were impossible to please.[123] As a result, the Center changed its Polish policy. On 7 March 1904, it resolved to follow the course advocated by the Silesian wing in matters concerning Upper Silesia and to adopt a "cool reserved posture" toward Polish politicians.[124]

In this anti-Polish turn, the Center enjoyed the support of the Vatican. On 23 February 1905, the Congregation for Extraordinary Church Affairs debated the Polish question in eastern Prussia and resolved to instruct Cardinal Secretary Merry del Val to write the apostolic nuncio in Munich, Monsignor Caputo, that: "he ought to be careful and cautious in entering into and maintaining relations with the Poles of the kingdom of Prussia as well as in listening to their protests and complaints; in such conflicts he ought to enter into contact with Cardinal Kopp and ask for his counsel."[125] This decision, sanctioned by Pope Pius X, put the Vatican on the side of the German bishop most active

---

[118] Schwidetzky, *Die polnische Wahlbewegung*, appendix: Das Verhältnis der Parteien bei den Reichstagswahlen 1871–1912.

[119] See StAK NL Bachem Nr. 251a Carl Bachem to Franz Xavier Bachem, 14.12.1903; Felix Porsch to Nienkemper, 14.12.1903.

[120] See StAK NL Bachem Nr. 251a Carl Bachem to Franz Xavier Bachem, 14.12.1903.

[121] StAK NL Bachem, Nr. 251a Carl Bachem to Franz Xavier Bachem, 28.12.1903.

[122] StAK NL Bachem, Nr. 251a Carl Bachem to Franz Xavier Bachem, 14.12.1903.

[123] StAK NL Bachem, Nr. 251a Note of Carl Bachem, 7.3.1904.

[124] Ibid.

[125] PAAA R4087 "Die polnische Frage im östlichen Preußen." The author of this document, excerpts in German translation of a report given to a meeting of the Congregation for Extraordinary Church Affairs on 27 February 1905, is, according to Wolfram von Rotenhahn (imperial envoy to the Vatican), probably Secretary Monsignor Goszarri. See PAAA R4087 Rotenhahn to Bülow, 30.3.1905.

in Prussia's Germanization policy.[126] A bitter opponent of Polish nationalism, Kopp entreated Poles to abandon it.[127] By 1905, this had also become the position of the Vatican. On more than one occasion, Pope Pius X had reportedly vented his frustration that the Poles did not follow his advice "to go hand in hand with the Center"— "they are first Poles," he was supposed to have said, "and then Catholics."[128]

The enmity between the Polish party and the Center did not thereafter abate. Even when the Center joined the Poles in the parliamentary opposition, the antagonism between them continued.[129] On 2 September 1907, the general assembly of the Polish League (*Polenbund*) of Rhineland and Westphalia passed a resolution stating that "compromise [with the Center] is not to the advantage but rather the disadvantage of the Polish party."[130] Similarly, the Silesian Center leader Felix Porsch adjured his party to abstain from entering into negotiations with the Poles for the purpose of defending Catholic interests against the Bülow bloc. Porsch argued that a compromise between the Center and the Catholic circle in the Polish party was neither necessary, "if the Catholic Center declared itself to be an *exclusively* political party," nor feasible, since "at the moment the Poles are a closed phalanx." Moreover, a compromise might "ignite a new Kulturkampf," which, although directed primarily against the Poles, would be difficult to localize. At the very least, a compromise with the Poles would make the Center party's negotiations with the government difficult and would provide the Protestants of the Bülow bloc with a "national bond." Porsch also thought that it would make life for Catholic officials in the east "vexatious" and that in any case many German Catholics in the east would not follow such a compromise. This eventuality, in turn, would encourage German Catholic splinter groups to "put up [nationally] dependable German Catholics who would cooperate with us only in church matters." A compromise with the Poles would mean to "risk losing a large number of our voters in Upper Silesia, if not the majority," and, he added, it is better "to go down with honor than to go down with derision."[131]

---

[126] On Pope Pius X's support for this policy, see PAAA R4087 "Die polnische Frage im östlichen Preußen."

[127] For Kopp's position on the nationality question, see his pastoral letter, reprinted in *Germania*, 9 June 1903.

[128] PAAA R4087 Rotenhahn to Bülow, 27.5.1905; 23.11.1905. On Pope Pius X's view of Polish nationalism, see also PAAA R4096 Rotenhahn to Bülow, 11.1.1907.

[129] Schwidetzky, *Die polnische Wahlbewegung*, 77–82.

[130] LHAK 403/7054 Police Commissioner Fabian of Essen, "Bericht über die am 29.9.1907 stattgehabte Generalversammlung des Polenbundes von Rheinland, Westfalen und angrenzenden Provinzen," 30.9.1907.

[131] BAK NL 176 Carl Herold, Nr. 2 Memorandum of Felix Porsch, 17.7.1907.

Porsch's memorandum, though it did not ultimately determine party strategy, nevertheless revealed a deep rift between the Silesian Center and the Polish party, and underscored the Center's precarious relationship to the German national sentiment of its borderland constituents.[132] In the exclusively Catholic but predominantly Polish areas east of the Oder, the German national parties and not the German Center emerged in 1907 as the second-strongest force in local politics. In the heavily industrialized and densely populated districts of Beuthen-Tarnowitz and Kattowitz-Zabrze, Center support cascaded from 64.6 percent in 1893 to 10.4 percent in 1907, while support for the German national parties increased from 2.3 percent to 15.4 percent and for the Polish party from zero to 38.4 percent.[133] Similarly, in agricultural districts east of the Oder, Center support dropped from 37.3 percent to 13.9 percent.[134] As Porsch feared, the Center was losing the support of its nationally minded middle classes, a fact rendered painfully evident by the alarming conversion rate of Silesian Catholics to Protestantism. Between 1880 and 1897, one-third of all converts in the empire came from Silesia.[135]

This general process was even more advanced among German Catholics in Posen and West Prussia. Especially in the regencies of Marienwerder and Posen, German Catholics constituted a significant minority. Settled in scattered diasporas, they usually lived in towns populated by their Protestant conationalists and their Polish coreligionists. The first group suspected them of being nationally unreliable; the second denounced them as Germanizers.[136] Their loyalties split, some German Catholics sided with German Protestants, others with Polish Catholics. The two main protagonists in Clara Viebig's *Dormant Army*, a novel about life in the east, are both Catholic settlers: one becomes an engaged "Hakatist" but is never quite accepted into his Protestant surroundings; the other falls into a mixed marriage with a Polish woman. It is difficult to determine the number of Catholics

---

[132] On Felix Porsch and the negotiations with the Polish party, see August Hermann Leugers-Scherzberg, *Felix Porsch, 1853–1930* (Mainz, 1990), esp. 130–39. On the urging of Julius Bachem, a temporary accord with the Poles in Upper Silesia was attained, but the old spirit of cooperation had long since withered.

[133] Hentschel, "Wirtschaftliche Entwicklung," 266.

[134] Ibid. Here too the Center party was surpassed by both the Poles (0% to 38.3%) and the Conservatives (13% to 21.2%).

[135] *DEB* 24 (1900): 216. Between 1895 and 1899, the average annual conversion rate was 1,197. See Krose, *Konfessionsstatistik Deutschlands*, 128–29.

[136] On the confessional and national composition of towns in Posen with a population of more than 1,000 in 1910, see *Statistisches Jahrbuch für den preußischen Staat*, 1913 (Berlin, 1914), vol. 2, 22–25. The vast majority of the population (88%) lived in smaller villages, however. On the attitude of the Polish press toward German Catholics, see Müller, *Nationalpolnische Presse*, and Altkemper, *Deutschtum und Polentum*.

who by dint of time, mixed marriages, and the influence of the Polish clergy became culturally Polish. But in 1907 the Prussian Ministry of Culture estimated their number at 200,000.[137] Perhaps high, this figure nevertheless dramatized the tension and fluidity of German-Catholic ethnicity in the borderlands.

In the absence of local studies and of reliable statistics on ethnicity, one may at best surmise the political loyalties of the borderland Catholics. Yet it would seem that as German Catholics were torn between their national and religious affiliation, they were divided in their political loyalties as well. In national elections a significant percentage (though less than 50 percent) probably supported German national parties over the Center in the first ballot. In run-off elections, German Catholics who had supported the Center divided over the question of whether to back national parties or, as the Center party directives usually demanded, the Polish party. In Posen, German Catholics tended to give their weight to the Germans in runoff elections; in West Prussia, especially in Konitz-Tuchel and Schlochau-Flotow, Catholic support appears to have gone more typically to the Poles.[138] Moreover, the conversion rate of German Catholics in these two provinces was also high, and, if not as portentous as in Silesia, it nevertheless caused considerable debate.[139]

In contrast to the situation in Silesia, the national identity of German Catholics in Posen and West Prussia found institutional support. The Union of German Catholics, first established in Posen in 1900,

---

[137] PAAA R4101 Note from Ministry of Culture (Nells) to von Bülow, 14.11.1907. On the fate of one German Catholic settlement, see, see Max Bär, *Die Bamberger bei Posen. Zugleich ein Beitrag zur Geschichte der Polonisierungsbestrebungen in der Provinz Posen* (Posen, 1882). For a scholarly account of German Catholics in the interwar years, see Wojciech Kotowski, "Die Lage der deutschen Katholiken in Polen in den Jahren 1919–1939," *Zeitschrift für Ostforschung* 39, no. 1 (1990): 39–67.

[138] For the difficulties of getting German Catholics to vote for the Poles in runoff elections in Posen, see StAK NL Bachem, Nr. 251a F. Grisard to Julius Bachem, 4.10.1903. My observations on electoral behavior are estimates arrived at by comparing ethnicity and religion (from the census of 1910) to voting, assuming that Poles, if they can, vote Polish and Protestants, unless forced to, will not vote for a Center party candidate or a Pole. Election returns are in *Vierteljahreshefte zur Statistik des deutschen Reiches*, 12, no. 1 (1903): vol. 3, 42–53; *Statistik des deutschen Reiches*, vol. 250 (Berlin, 1912), 4–16.

[139] This problem was particularly acute among Catholic state officials. See EZB 7/3694 Royal Consistory of the province of Posen, 29.4.1904. "Geschäftsbericht für das Jahr 1902/3"; Justizrath Halbe [Bromberg], "Deutsche Katholiken in der Provinz Posen," *Deutsches Wochenblatt* 12, no. 3 (January 1899): 102–9. Between 1895 and 1899, average annual conversions in Posen amounted to 216; in West Prussia, 309. For comparison, the conversions from Protestantism to Catholicism numbered 25 and 40 respectively. See Krose, *Konfessionsstatistik Deutschlands*, 128–30.

defended the idea that one could be both "a good German and a good Catholic," that between these two identities there need not be conflict.[140] Its motto—"true to our faith until death, raise our banner black-white-red"—has led historians to see in the union little more than a Catholic organization "in the service of the Hakatists."[141] But the union was more complex than that, for while it supported Germanization policy, it shied away from the integral nationalism of the Society for the Eastern Marches. Rather, the union stood in a nineteenth-century tradition of enlightened Catholicism that appealed not to confessional particularity but rather to the unity of German national culture. "We should not think what divides us, but only what unifies us," urged the editor of the *Katholische Rundschau*, the organization's newspaper.[142] Christianity, a common history, and a common statehood created a cultural bond among Germans of both confessions and set them apart from Catholic Poles, whose cultural level German Catholics typically considered inferior. Loyal citizens of Prussia, the German Catholics in the union embraced its cultural mission. The state, the text of one union broadside maintained, "has brought [the Poles] to a cultural and economic level that previously they could only have dreamed about."[143] Polish criticism of the state, the German Catholics therefore considered "unjust."[144]

The union was organized and led by the German-Catholic middle class, although it was financially supported by Prussia's discretionary fund for the Germanization of the east.[145] In regency capitals such as Bromberg and Marienwerder, union membership consisted chiefly of schoolteachers, middle-level bureaucrats, and artisans.[146] In smaller towns, it reached deeper into the population. But even here there were class limits to the nationalist organization of Catholics. This can be observed in the case of Czarnikau, a small town in Posen for which membership lists of the Union of German Catholics have survived as well as a petition signed by German and Polish Catholics defending a Polish vicar "unjustly accused of slander by certain Catholics of Ger-

---

[140] Although 5 local branches existed as early as 1895, it was not until 1900 that the union organized at the provincial level. See *Katholische Rundschau*, 1 April 1905.

[141] Adam Galos et al., *Die Hakatisten*, 177–79. Aside from the few comments of Galos, there have been no scholarly studies written on the Union of German Catholics.

[142] *Katholische Rundschau*, 1 April 1905.

[143] *Katholische Rundschau*, 1 January 1907.

[144] Ibid.

[145] PAAA R4080 Memorandum of the provincial governor of Posen, Wilhelm von Waldow, 12.8.1903.

[146] In 1904, for example, the Bromberg branch of the Union of German Catholics counted 188 members including 30 schoolteachers and 40 bureaucrats. GStAPK 30,841 district magistrate (Landrat) of Bromberg, 15.1.1904.

man tongue, namely members of the Union of German Catholics." A comparison of the two lists suggests that the educated and propertied classes more typically supported the union, while less-educated, financially and occupationally dependent German Catholics were more closely allied with the parish and the Polish vicar.[147] Shopkeepers also tended to keep their distance from the union, supposedly out of fear of Polish boycotts, as did the clergy members, who were forbidden by Archbishop Stablewski to join.[148] Finally, there were relatively few farmers among the union's ranks (see table 5).[149]

Among German Catholics, nationalist organizations were town phenomena. Particularly in towns where the Polish clergy was reluctant to speak German with German parishioners, the union offered alternative religious sociability: German choruses to sing patriotic songs, local libraries for national literature, and family nights in which Catholic schoolteachers delivered lectures on the great events of German history.[150] But the union saw its principal cultural task in encouraging the use of German in church life. It pressured the archbishop to provide German Catholic communities with German priests who could deliver sermons and take confession in "pure German."[151] The union also pursued political goals. It lobbied the state to settle Catholic administrators in the eastern marches and, during elections, called on its members to support German national candidates, even against the Center.[152]

From the day of its founding, the Union of German Catholics drew strong, often contradictory criticism. The archbishop of Gnesen-Posen, Florian Stablewski, denounced it for "staging attacks against priests," while the Polish party newspaper *Orendownik* (The Advocate) decried it as "Hakatistic."[153] Conversely, the Protestant League

---

[147] On the case of the Polish vicar Graszyinski, see *Katholische Rundschau*, 1 November 1905.

[148] On shopkeepers and boycotts see GStAPK 30,841 Provincial Governor of Posen, von Waldow, to the regency president of Bromberg, 29.12.1903. On Stablewski's injunction, *Posener Tageblatt*, 21 March 1906.

[149] *Katholische Rundschau*, 1 April 1905. This is noteworthy only because Posen remained an essentially agrarian province. As late as 1910, urbanization hovered at 34%.

[150] GStAPK 30,841 District magistrate of Inowrazlow (Hohensalza), 14.4.1904; StAK NL Bachem, Nr. 162 Verein deutscher Katholiken Thorns to Carl Bachem, 18.3.1901.

[151] GStAPK 30,841 District magistrate of Inowrazlow (Hohensalza), 14.4.1904. See also *Katholische Rundschau*, 1 June 1905.

[152] GStAPK Provincial governor of Posen, von Waldow, to the regency president of Bromberg, 29.12.1903. For the union's position on the Hottentot election of 1907, *Katholische Rundschau*, 1 January 1907. See also PAAA R4099 Report of von Waldow, 31.5.1907: "Until now and especially at the last election Catholic settlers have fulfilled their national duties."

[153] GStAPK 30,841 Archbishop Florian Stablewski to Provincial Governor von Waldow, 20.11.1905. The *Orendownik* is cited in *Katholische Rundschau*, 15 May 1905.

TABLE 5
Social Composition of the Union of German Catholics

Occupation	1	2	3	4
Merchant	7	2	—	—
Professional	2	—	—	—
Civic official	3	6	1	6
Property owner	9	13	—	5
Teacher	29	6	—	—
Artisan master	15	4	2	3
Artisan	34	5	5	15
Artisan appr.	1	2	5	6
Innkeeper	4	—	—	—
Worker	26	—	5	12
Farmer	13	—	1	1
Other	5	2	4	—

1 = Membership in the Union of German Catholics in four small towns. Source: GStAPK 30,841 Mitgliederverzeichnis des Vereins deutscher Katholiken (VDK) von Somatschin und Umgegend; Mitgliederverzeichnis des VDK zu Filehne, 9.1.1906; Mitgliederverzeichnis des VDK von Losens und Umgegend, 26.2.1906; GStAPK 30, 842 Mitgliederverzeichnis des VDK Friedheim und Umgegend, 4.7.1907.

2 = Membership in the Union of German Catholics in Czarnikau. Source: GStAPK 30,694 Mitgliederverzeichnis des Vereins deutscher Katholiken zu Czarnikau, 20.7.1903.

3 = German Catholics in Czarnikau who signed a petition to keep a Polish vicar accused of slandering Germans. Source: GStAPK 30,841 Nachweisung der Unterschriften der Eingabe deutscher Katholiken an den Herrn Erzbischof von 3.10.1905. (The petition was signed by 28 Germans, 41 Poles, and 2 people whose nationality was not known. It was also signed by 30 women. But I have ordered them according to class (either their occupation or the occupation of their husband).

4 = Polish Catholics who signed the petition to keep the Polish vicar. Source: ibid.

questioned the union's national credibility, and at least one Protestant official reported that it seemed "ethnically suspicious."[154] The sharp-

[154] On the Protestant League and the union, see EZB 7/3893 Verhandlungsnachweis über die Konferenz der in den Ostmarken arbeitenden Vereinigungen, 16.12.1907; *Katholische Rundschau*, 15 October 1905. For the idea that the union might have been "ethnically suspicious," GStAPK 30,842 District magistrate of Czarnikau, 22.9.1909.

est vitriol came from the Center, however. The party denounced the union's collusion with the Hakatists as un-Catholic, considered its interest group politics for Catholic bureaucrats to be narrow-minded, and charged the union with indifference toward the legacy of the Kulturkampf.[155] But the Center did not actively attempt to subvert the union until 1907, when, to the Center's ire, the union gave its full support to the parties of the Bülow Bloc.[156] Thereafter the Center arranged for the People's Association for Catholic Germany to organize in Posen in order "to keep the working class away from Social Democracy and . . . to fight against the advance of the Polish nation."[157] But as one German Catholic put it: "the People's Association is absolutely unnecessary in Posen and West Prussia. Whoever wants to be a German man and a Catholic can do this well enough in the Union of German Catholics."[158] This, coupled with the intimation that the organizers of the People's Association for Catholic Germany were pro-Polish, ruined its chances from the start.[159]

By the first decade of the twentieth century, German Catholics in the eastern marches had become sufficiently engaged in the common nationality struggle against Catholic Poles so that, by comparison, confessional differences with Protestant Germans seemed slight. Even the Protestant Consistory in Posen recognized this and, in 1910, characterized the relationship between German Catholics and German Protestants as "reasonably friendly."[160] In this sense, the nation was made in the province. Prussia's repressive measures against the Poles failed utterly, for they called up the Polish nationalist spirits they were to silence. Yet by drawing German Catholics and German Protestants into a common destiny, based on a common cultural mission to combat Polish nationalism, these measures contributed to the creation of a common national culture. Poles were not Germanized;

---

[155] Criticism came especially from the Center party in south and west Germany. See, for example, *Kölnische Volkszeitung* Nr. 248, 25 March 1905, and, for a Bavarian view, *Bayerische Zeitung*, 7 May 1904. The union's views were closer to the Silesian wing of the party, and the *Katholische Rundschau* often printed the text of speeches delivered by Silesian Center leaders. See, for example, *Katholische Rundschau*, 1 December 1905.

[156] GStAPK 30,842 Veterinary (Veterinärrat) Peters in Bromberg to the regency president of Bromberg, June 1907.

[157] GStAPK 30,842 The lord mayor of Bromberg to the regency president of Bromberg, 12.12.1908. See also the Bromberg police report of 29.10.1908. The struggle against the Poles was written into the statutes of the People's Association for Catholic Germany in Posen.

[158] GStAPK 30,842 Bromberg police report, 18.12.1908.

[159] GStAPK 30,842 Report of the lord mayor of Bromberg, 25.10.1910.

[160] EZB 7, 3696 Royal Consistory of the province of Posen. "Geschäftsbericht für das Jahr 1908/09."

but German Catholics in the border areas became increasingly conscious of their nationality, not just in the objective, but also in the subjective, sense. As one Catholic polemicist put it, "as Germans we are just as good as our countrymen of the other confession, and we do not just want to feel German but to actively support our German national community."[161]

Partly a product of Prussia's nationality policy, this newly constructed sense of German identity was also a result of a long history of conflict at the local level. In the religious and ethnic borderlands, German Catholics faced not only the pressures of an increasingly militant Prussian Polish policy, not only the battery of Protestant prejudice, but also the ever increasing antagonism of an ascending Polish nationalism. At once agents and victims of ethnic antagonism, Polish nationalists could, it must be said, also be intolerant, exclusive, and aggressive—even if, or precisely because, the Poles of Prussia were defamed, discriminated against, and denied their basic rights. Polish nationalism therefore exerted a profound impact on German Catholics living in the ethnic borderland. For in the vortex of these complicated lines of conflict, religious and ethnic, German Catholics constructed their own national identity, an identity informed by German nationalism, by German Catholicism, by confessional conflict, and by the experience of ethnic antagonism in the borderlands of the imagined community.

[161] Rector Matchewsky, chairman of the Union of German Catholics, in *Katholische Rundschau*, 1 April 1905.

7

Los Von Rom: Religious Conflict and the Quest for a Spiritual Pan-Germany

FOR INTEGRAL nationalists who reified the nation above the more pro-saic concept of state, the imagined community did not cease to exist at the empire's political borders. From the Pan-German perspective, Germans who lived in Upper Austria or in the western parts of Bo-hemia constituted an extension of a national community of shared language, culture, and destiny. Conversely, irredentist Germans from Tirol to Triest looked to imperial Germany as the locus of their politcal aspirations.[1]

Yet one issue continued to disturb the family romance between Ger-man irredentists in Austria-Hungary and their Pan-German patrons in the German empire: religion. If imperial Germany was predomi-nantly Protestant, the German areas of the Habsburg monarchy were almost exclusively Catholic. The creation of a Pan-German empire would have meant replacing Protestant predominance with rough re-ligious parity. But to some Pan-Germans the two religions could never be equal. Whereas one imparted vigor, strength, and spiritual suste-nance to a nation embattled, the other weakened and crippled it. The only way to cut the Gordian knot, some Pan-Germans supposed, was to convert Catholics to Protestantism on a mass scale. From this con-viction arose Los von Rom, a turn-of-the-century movement to bring a Germanic-inspired *Evangelium* to the German Catholics of Cisleitha-nian Austria. A radical movement with potentially profound conse-quencs, Los von Rom also represented the logical conclusion of a long tradition of German nationalism that narrated German history and Protestant history as one.

The proximate origins of the Los von Rom movement were more mundane, however. On 6 April 1897, the Austrian prime minister Count Kasimir Badeni issued a decree assigning equal juridical status to Czech and German in the crown lands of Bohemia and Moravia.[2]

---

[1] For important reflections on the effects of the historiographical separation of Ger-man and Austrian history in this period, see James Sheehan, "What is German History? Reflections on the Role of Nation in German History and Historigraphy," *Journal of Modern History* 53, no. 1 (1981): 17–23.

[2] For a detailed account of the Badeni decrees, see Berthold Sutter, *Die Badenischen*

German officials, who as a rule did not speak Czech, were given four years to learn it. And German peasants, many of whom could barely read ordinances written in their mother tongue, now faced the possibility of needing to decipher a Slavic language, especially if they had a legal grievance against a Czech. Although in some ways a just act, the Badeni language decrees of 1897 provoked, in the words of Oscar Jaszi, "a paroxysm of indignation among the Germans."[3] Replete with anti-Slavic rage, the resulting German national awakening of 1897 brought demonstrations to the streets of Vienna and disorder to the Austrian Parliament. Fueled by ethnic hatred, fanned by bourgois contempt of lower-class Czechs, Pan-German ideology then spread throughout the national border areas like a fire in a dry field.[4]

In the wake of this agitation, Austrian Pan-Germans called forth a new cultural struggle to emancipate German Catholics from the clutches of a seemingly Slavophile church. The call "Los von Rom" found its first echo among fraternity students, but then achieved more permanent resonance among Germans in Bohemia, especially in the national borderlands where most of the Catholic clergy was, in fact, Czech.[5] Here mass conversions took place, which were then emulated in other parts of the Austrian empire.[6]

Although initially an Austrian affair, Los von Rom attracted wide attention among German nationalists in the Kaiserreich. Theodor Mommsen, the otherwise circumspect historian of the Roman Empire, counseled "be tough—the Czech skull is not receptive to reason, but it understands blows."[7] Similarly, Pan-Germans of all shades saw

---

Sprachenverordnungen von 1897, 2 vols. (Graz, Cologne, 1960–65). For its impact on Pan-German politics in the Dual Monarchy, see Lothar Höbelt, *Kornblume und Kaiseradler. Die deutschfreiheitlichen Parteien Altösterreichs 1882–1918* (Vienna, 1993), 150–65.

[3] Jaszi, *The Dissolution of the Habsburg Monarchy*, 290.

[4] See Adam Wandruszka and Peter Urbantisch, eds., *Die Habsburgermonarchie*, vol. 3, *Die Völker des Reiches* (Vienna, 1980), 224. See also Jaszi, *The Dissolution of the Habsburg Monarchy*, 290.

[5] Barbara Schmid-Egger, *Klerus und Politik in Böhmen um 1900* (Munich, 1974), 223–24. Western Bohemia was also the locus of Pan-German strength. See Höbelt, *Kornblume und Kaiseradler*, 188.

[6] On Los von Rom generally, see Lothar Albertin, "Nationalismus und Protestantismus in der österreichischen Los-von-Rom Bewegungum 1900" (Ph.D. diss., University of Cologne, 1953). Albertin emphasizes the movement's theological and intellectual roots and details its connections to political groups in Austria but does not fully explore the movement's ideology, its relationship to official nationalism, or the reasons for the movement's success and failure. Andrew Whiteside, *Socialism of Fools: Georg Ritter von Schönerer and Austrian Pan-Germanism* (Berkeley, 1975) is useful for the Pan-German aspect, but with respect to the Protestant League he draws primarily on Albertin.

[7] Cited in Wandruszka and Urbantisch, eds., *Die Habsburgermonarchie*, vol. 3, pt. 1, 226.

in the movement a spiritual awakening, the raising of German national consciousness in the Habsburg empire to religious heights. Initially as important as its nationalist resonance, the movement's religious inflection immediately brought it within the purview of the Protestant League. In the fall of 1897, soon after Badeni promulgated his language decrees, the league discussed whether to lend its considerable organizational support to anticlerical groups in Austria. In the following year, at the Magdeburg general assembly in October 1898, the league then created a Committee to Support the Evangelical Movement in Austria. Led by two pastors, Friedrich Meyer and Paul Bräunlich, the committee consisted of eleven members, seven of whom also sat on the Protestant League's central committee and one of whom, Ernst Hasse, was chairman of the Pan-German League.[8] Convinced that the historical moment for Los von Rom had arrived, the Protestant League assumed its leadership—and pursued it with messianic zeal.

It is difficult to recapture fully the idealism that Los von Rom ignited in the breasts of imperial German pastors. Bräunlich believed that a new Reformation would dawn, that the movement would "unite our entire people for eternity in the faith of Luther and Bismarck."[9] Like his collaborators in Bohemia, Bräunlich aspired to create "a spiritual Pan-Germany," a new and better, because religiously cohesive, Germany, a Germany of one confesssion, one culture, and, ultimately, one state—a Protestant, Pan-German state.[10]

In an anonymously published contraband pamphlet entitled *Germanic Faith*, Bräunlich argued for his "Protestant Pan-Germany" by appealing to the hand of God and the logic of social Darwinism. History, he wrote, had demonstrated that "the races that have adopted Protestantism stand at the pinnacle."[11] Following Houston Stewart Chamberlain, Bräunlich reasoned that "Protestantism is the religion of master nations [*Herrennationen*]" whereas Roman Catholicism is "the religion of peoples in decline." A "robust, masculine, and therefore essentially German Christianity," Protestantism strengthened the nation; effeminate, irrational, and Latin, Catholicism weakened it.[12] In the coming life-and-death struggle of nations, "Germany," he

---

[8] On the prehistory of the "Committee to Support the Evangelical Movement in Austria," see Albertin, "Nationalismus und Protestantismus," 13–24.

[9] AKIEB S185.810.60 Paul Bräunlich, "Streng vertraulicher Reisebericht 'Zur Evangelisierung in Böhmen,'" 6.11.1898.

[10] Ibid.

[11] AKIEB S185.810.100 "Deutsches Glaubenstum. Ein Gruß an die Ostmarkendeutschen von einem reichsdeutschen Pfarrer (= Paul Bräunlich)." This pamphlet was published by Carl Braun in Leipzig, n.d., probably December 1898.

[12] Ibid.

prophesied, "could only survive if it became completely Protestant."[13] Fate therefore demanded that Germany be guided by one faith, one church—"a church of the German nation," a church that would steel Germans spiritually and undergird them with a hard-wrought structure of common religious belief. To this end, he called upon ethnic Germans in the Habsburg empire to break from Rome and "come home to German Protestantism."[14]

Bräunlich's ideas were widely shared among the active organizers of Los von Rom, especially in Austria, where he wielded considerable influence.[15] In the German empire itself, Friedrich Meyer served as the movement's spiritual director. Like Bräunlich, Meyer drew from Chamberlain's ideas and was especially influenced by *The Foundations of the Nineteenth Century*, a book from which he believed "one could learn something about the importance of race, especially the Germanic race, for history."[16]

At the turn of the century, the German word *Rasse* meant both nationality, in the sense of a community bound by a coherent culture, and race, a people with similar physical features and purity of blood. Strictly speaking, racists adhered to the second definition; they insisted not only on the purity and superiority of their own nationality but also on the proposition that national differences were caused by immutable genetic factors beyond the influence of culture and historical circumstance.[17] Jews, for example, could not be counted as conationals, because no matter how much they assimilated culturally, they could never become part of a community defined by blood.

Ideologically, integral nationalists were of a slightly different hue. They insisted not on the deleterious effects of ethnic mixing but rather on the radical assimilation of national minorities: to make Germans out of Poles, it was necessary to eradicate their Polish habits, culture, and language; to make German Catholics acceptable as equals in the national community, they must be divested of their ties to their ("foreign") church and its specific values. Marrying across national or confessional lines may have been disdained by integral nationalists, even

[13] Ibid.

[14] Ibid.

[15] See the statements of Bräunlich's coconspirators in Bohemia, in AKIEB S185.810.60 Paul Bräunlich, "Streng vertraulicher Reisebericht, 'Zur Evangelisierung in Böhmen.'" 6.11.1898.

[16] AKIEB PL Friedrich Meyer, "Mitteilungen vom Ausschuss zur Förderung der evangelischen Kirche in Österreich" (hereafter "Mitteilungen vom Ausschuss") 17 (1902): 3. For the Protestant reception of Chamberlain, see Field, *Evangelist of Race*, 235–44.

[17] For this carefully circumscribed definition of racism in another context, see George M. Fredrickson, *White Supremacy: A Comparative Study in American and South African History* (New York, 1981), xii.

considered traitorous; but it did not carry with it the odium of an eternal contamination.[18] This was the crucial difference. To racists, Jews polluted the nations in whose midst they lived. Late nineteenth-century racism envisioned a series of "loathsome copulations" leading to the contamination of peoples.[19] Integral nationalists wished— only—to annihilate differences within the national state.

Meyer and Bräunlich were somewhere between the two poles. In "Christianity and the Germans," Meyer argued: "experience demonstrates that bastard peoples, who cannot be considered valuable creations [Gebilde], come from unsuitable miscegenation [Blutmischung]."[20] But when Meyer imagined German racial characteristics, he thought specifically about Germanic Christianity. The "Semitic race," for example, did not adopt Christianity, because the religion of Christ did not "correspond to the national character of the Jews."[21] More specifically, he conceived the fate of the German race to be indissolubly tied to Protestantism. From Chamberlain, he learned that "the greatest and most dangerous enemy of the Germanic race is the Roman church."[22] But Rome was not just a foreign power; rather its danger lay in its ability to corrupt and spoil German national character at home, not the least through mixed marriages. Thus it was necessary to root out ultramontanism, which weakened the German nation. "Only when ultramontanism is broken," Meyer thought, "is a strong German policy possible."[23]

Protestant League engagement beyond the political borders of the German empire followed from these propositions. "Wherever our nationality [Volkstum] tries to defend itself against Rome and hold on to Protestantism, the league must be there to support it," Meyer asserted.[24] But he had more in mind than simply sending spiritual sentinels to the faraway posts of the imagined community. Rather, he envisioned the league as pursuing the "world-historical mission" of

[18] On the relationship of racism to ideas of pollution, see Mary Douglas, "Pollution," in Douglas, Implicit Meanings (London and Boston, 1975), 47–59.

[19] Benedict Anderson, Imagined Communities, 149. For an analysis of the tension between concepts of race and nationality in fin-de-siècle Cisleithania, see Pieter M. Judson, "'Whether Race or Conviction Should Be the Standard': National Identity and Liberal Politics in Nineteenth-century Austria," Austrian History Yearbook 22 (1991): 76–95.

[20] Friedrich Meyer, "Christentum und Germanen," in Beiträge zur Weiterentwicklung der christlichen Religion, ed. D. A. Deissmann et al. (Munich, 1905), 207.

[21] Ibid.

[22] AKIEB PL Meyer, "Mitteilungen vom Ausschuss," 17 (1902): 3.

[23] Friedrich Meyer, "Bismarck in der Walhalla (1908)," in Meyer, Heroldsrufe und Hammerschläge, 41–47.

[24] AKIEB PL Meyer, "Mitteilungen vom Ausschuss," 12 (1901): 4.

the Germans—to complete the work of the Reformation. Through Los von Rom, the league would create a national religion and a common national culture among all Germans by converting Catholics—first outside, then inside the empire—to Protestantism.

The Allure of Nationalism: The Appeal of Los von Rom

The success of this messianic vision depended on the willingness of Catholics in Austria, many of whom saw no necessary tension between their religion and their nationality, to convert. Here was the sticking point. As a nationalist movement, Los von Rom sought the support of Germans of all classes and stations; in fact, however, it succeeded only in specific areas among discrete groups. Beyond its initial successes in Vienna, Los von Rom fared best in predominantly German yet nationally mixed areas that had been under Protestant influence for a brief time during the sixteenth century but had been under Catholic rule ever since: north and west Bohemia, Styria and Carinthia, and, though here its fortunes were more modest, Moravia and Silesia.[25] In these areas, in which two nationality groups often stood opposed, conversions sharpened conflicts that had previously been tempered by common religious identification. Cleavage patterns, once crosscutting, now coincided, making nationality conflicts increasingly intractable. In areas of more complex national and religious composition, the possibilities for the success of Los von Rom proved less propitious. This was, for example, the case in Bukovina, where Uniate Ruthenians and Eastern Orthodox Rumanians lived in the same area as Yiddish-speaking Jews and confessionally mixed Germans. In Bukovina, there were very few conversions, and even these were concentrated in Czernowitz. As one pastor wryly observed: "Here nationality stands in the forefront of all efforts, behind which religious affiliation must recede."[26] In many central European mixed areas with complex national and religious compositions,

[25] Between 1899 and 1911, the regional division of conversions to Lutheranism (according to superintendents and crownlands) was as follows: Vienna (Lower Austria, Styria, Carinthia, South Austria) 26,035; Upper Austria (Upper Austria, Salzburg, Tirol, Vorarlberg) 2,360; German West and North Bohemia 19,777; Czech. Bohemia 906; Moravia and Silesia 5,396; Asch 675; Galicia and Bukovina 1308. Source: Georg Leusche, "Los von Rom," in *Realencyclopaedie für protestantische Theologie und Kirche* (Leipzig, 1913), vol. 29, 33.

[26] AKIEB S185.810.25 "Bericht des Pfarrer Buller in Hermsdorf über seine Reise nach der Bukowina und Mähren zum Besuch der evangelischen Gemeinden vom 5.8.1906 bis 18.8.1906."

religious differences were purposely, if not always successfully, repressed.

In areas where it enjoyed popularity, the evangelical movement could recruit its local leadership from the lower and upper middle class, from the city as well as the countryside. Bräunlich's contact men included professionals, low-level civil servants, merchants and businessmen, artisans and farmers, and, less prominently, lay church officers.[27] Academics and high civil servants shied away from the movement because of official antagonism toward it, not because they considered Pan-German proselytizing beneath them. The relatively high proportion of professionals among Bräunlich's contact men (*Vertrauensmänner*) suggests that Los von Rom was quite acceptable to the Austrian upper middle class. The clergy was, however, underrepresented. Few pastors from the Protestant churches in Austria (whether Calvinist or Lutheran) became actively involved in Los von Rom.[28] As a consequence, a strong secular impulse prevailed in local organization. Contact men called Los von Rom gatherings, organized family nights in which spouses and children of converts could participate, and encouraged readings of anticlerical and integral nationalist literature. They also supervised the activity of the young vicars from Germany and reported to Bräunlich on the success of the movement. This often led to tension between the predominantly lay contact men, all of whom were committed Pan-Germans, and the vicars sent by the Protestant League, the former typically complaining that the latter insufficiently appreciated the gravity of national conflict in the border areas.[29]

Social and demographic factors influenced not only the composition of the local leadership of Los von Rom but also the propensity of

[27] One list of his contact men included 9 clergymen (only 2 of whom were pastors), 18 professionals, 16 civil servants, 15 merchants and businessmen, 12 artisans, and 19 farmers, but only 2 high civil servants and 2 workers. AKIEB S185.810.63b "Namensverzeichnis von Vertrauensmänner für die oesterreichische L.v.R. Bewegung," 21.3.1901.

[28] AKIEB PL Meyer, "Mitteilungen vom Ausschuss," 5 (1900). Schmid-Egger, *Klerus und Politik*, 145, 225.

[29] AKIEB S185.810.63d Franz Stepan to Paul Bräunlich, 23.5.1901. See also AKIEB S185.810.25 "Bericht über die Sitzung des Vertrauensmännerausschusses des Deutsch-Evangelischen Bundes für die Ostmark," 2.2.1905. In this limited sense, it is correct to argue that the Protestant League had a moderating influence on integral nationalism in the nationally mixed areas. See here especially Schmid-Egger, *Klerus und Politik*, 238. On the other hand, this was less the consequence of Bräunlich's leadership than of the fact that the league was forced to send young, inexperienced vicars to Austria. Bräunlich himself complained of the difficulty of finding vicars who were sufficiently committed to the national struggle. See AKIEB S185.810.70 Paul Bräunlich to Ludwig Jahne (Klagenfurt), 13.5.1910.

Catholics to convert to Protestantism. From fragmentary statistical evidence found in Bräunlich's papers, as well the impressions of his contact men, it seems that Los von Rom enjoyed more success in the cities than in the countryside and proved more attractive to men than to women.[30] Records from the Styrian city of Graz make it possible to discern more exact information, at least for one city, on the occupational status, age, gender, and geographical origins of converts. Between 1898 and 1901, there were 1,201 converts in Graz, of whom 613 were men, 318 women, and 207 children.[31] Thus, Bräunlich's idea that Protestantism represented a man's religion corresponded to a demographic trend.[32] It was, moreover, a young man's religion: roughly 40 percent of all converts were in their twenties, and nearly 70 percent were newcomers to the city.[33] Like the quintessential central European integral nationalist, the typical convert to Protestantism in Graz was probably a young man not especially tied to established structures of communal life.

The influence of social class is more difficult to determine. Although it certainly affected one's predisposition to strong anticlerical sentiment, it revealed less about one's proclivity to convert than either age, gender, or place of origin. Converts to Protestantism came from nearly every class in Graz, but among the established professions the predilection to convert was less pronounced than among the less-educated middle classes (see table 6). Academics made up only 4 percent of converts, and most of these came from the ranks of free-lance writers, journalists, and artists. The number of conversions among the professional and managerial class also remained modest. The educated elite of Graz did not disdain the movement, but neither did Los von Rom enjoy the active and unequivocal support of educated notables characteristic of anticlerical politics in imperial Ger-

[30] AKIEB S185.810.63b Adolf Schmidt to Paul Bräunlich, 17.5.1900. See also the statistics for Bohemia in PAAA R8537 von Seckendorff (Prussian envoy in Prague) to Bernhard von Bülow, 24.3.1903.

[31] AKIEB S185.810.51 "Zahltafel über die Übertritte in Graz nach Alter, Herkunft und Stand." For the local background of nationalist agitation in Graz, see William H. Hubbard, *Auf dem Weg zur Großstadt. Eine Sozialgeschichte der Stadt Graz 1850–1914* (Munich, 1984), 171–74.

[32] On the inability of the movement to recruit women, see PAAA R8531 Prince Karl Max von Lichnowski to Chancellor Hohenlohe, 9.7.1899

[33] Only 31.7% were born in Graz. The rest came from Steiermark (26.5%), Austrian lands outside Steiermark (33.7%), and foreign states (8.1%), including Hungary, the German empire, Russia, Italy, and Turkey. AKIEB S185.810.51 "Zahltafel über die Übertritte in Graz." It should be pointed out, however, that Graz in this period was a rapidly growing city with a large nonnative population. See Hubbard, *Auf dem Weg zur Großstadt*, 23.

TABLE 6
Age and Occupation of Catholic Converts to Protestantism in Graz
between 1898 and 1901

Age	Number	%	Occupation	Number	%
1–10	164	15.5	Clergy	2	0.2
11–20	82	7.7	Academics	40	4
21–30	433	40.8	Students	118	11.6
31–40	217	20.5	Professional and managerial	38	3.7
41–50	93	8.8	Civil servants	47	4.6
51–60	35	3.3	White collar	83	8.1
61–70	25	2.4	Businessmen and merchants	41	4
71–80	9	0.8	Artisans	103	10
81–90	2	0.2	Workers	112	11
Total	1,060		None given	140	13.7
			Other*	198	19.4
			Total	1,020	

Source: AKIEB S185.810.51 Zahltafel über die Übertritte in Graz nach Alter, Herkunft
und Stand.
*Includes 155 women without occupation or 15.1% of the total.

many. Nevertheless, the movement reached deeper into the population. Unlike the Protestant League in German cities, Los von Rom in Graz penetrated part, though only a small part, of the industrial working class.[34]

The movement's structural antecedents (class, nationality, age, gender) shed light on the reasons for its success. In its appeal to national feeling, Los von Rom also evoked emotion and elicited sacrifice; for some, it even effected authentic experiences of religious conversion. To understand how the movement tapped profoundly felt na-

[34] Those few workers who did convert were typically members of so-called National Socialist Workers' Organizations. And when they converted, they tended to become Old Catholics rather than Protestants, since in many parts of the Austrian empire, and especially in Bohemia and Moravia, Protestantism was considered the religion of "factory owners." AKIEB S185.810.25 "Bericht von Rechnungsrat Stade über eine Reise nach Salzburg, Wien, durch die Steiermark nach Goerz und Abbazi," April 1911; "Bericht des Pfarrer Buller in Hermsdorf über seine Reise nach der Bukowina und Mähren zum Besuch der evangelischen Gemeinden vom 5.8.1906 bis 18.8.1906"; and AKIEB S185.810.63m Richard Schmidt (Groß Ullersdorf in Moravia) to Paul Bräunlich, 13.8.1900.

tionalist sentiment, and how it brought about conversion from Catholicism to Protestantism, it is necessary to scrutinize its cultural products, its figurative language, its images—to ask what it meant and how it constructed meaning.

The movement's ideological literature was coarse, crude, and effective. A sense of it, and therefore of what people read, can be culled from the orders of pamphlets and poetry sent to Bräunlich by his contact men in the Dual Monarchy.[35] These order lists, which Bräunlich then sent on to his publishers, were based on his contact men's perception of local demand and typically included the following works (in rough order of popularity):

> Robert Grassmann's *Excerpts from the Moral Theology of Dr. Alphonsus Maria de Liguori and the Terrible Consequences of This Moral Theology for the Morality of Peoples*
>
> Paul Bräunlich, *Leo Taxil's Satanic Swindle*
>
> [Paul Bräunlich], *Germanic Faith*
>
> *Twelve Questions of Conscience*
>
> *Onward with Enlightenment!*
>
> Los von Rom poems (in several editions as well as booklets with songs and scores)
>
> *How Bohemia Became Catholic Again* (there were variations on this theme for Salzburg, Tyrol, and Carinthia)
>
> *Dr. Martin Luther*[36]

The most popular works aimed to desacralize the church. The *Excerpts from the Moral Theology of Dr. Alphonsus Maria de Liguori,* or the "Grassmann pamphlet" as it was known to police spies in both empires, sought to demonstrate that ex cathedra sanctioned practice allowed Catholic priests to entice lurid details from the connubial life of women parishioners who came to confess. According to this tract, which claimed to offer authentic translations from the writings of Liguori, priests were allowed to seduce married parish women without coming into conflict with canon law. Though wholly spurious, this pamphlet went through at least ninety-three printings between 1898 and March 1901 (when it was censored by the state court of Nurem-

---

[35] For requests of pamphlets, see the order lists in AKIEB S185.810.63a; AKIEB S185.810.55; AKIEB S185.810.52 H.

[36] The German titles are Robert Grassmann, *Auszüge aus der Moraltheologie des Heiligen Dr. Alphonsus Maria de Liguori und die furchtbare Gefahr dieser Moraltheologie für die Sittlichkeit der Völker* (Stettin, 1898); Paul Bräunlich, *Leo Taxils Teufelsschwindel* (Munich, 1910); [Paul Bräunlich], *Deutsches Glaubensthum* (prob. 1898); and the following anonymous works: *Zwölf Gewissensfragen, Aufklärung Vor!,* and *Wie Böhmen wieder Katholisch wurde.*

berg), making it one of the most widely distributed underground pamphlets in central Europe at the turn of the century.[37] A bit less popular, but no less damaging to the reputation of the Catholic church, was the story of Leo Taxil. A French anticleric who operated undercover as an ultramontane publicist for twelve years, Taxil wrote long disquisitions on the worship of Satan in Masonic lodges, making him an ultramontane literary hero. Then, one day in 1897, he announced that his writings had been a hoax and that the infallible Leo XIII, who had decorated him with honors, had been fooled. Los von Rom thrived on such confessional scandals. More than learned theological tracts, confessional scandal was necessary to convince nationally minded men, partly secularized, to break not with a set of ideas, or even a series of rituals, but with part of their identity.

The relationship of popular profanity to nationalism is complex. "The national," one pastor from the Moravian city of Brunn reported, "is the foundation and the ground." He then asserted: "But to it is added a large measure of another specific anticlerical sentiment. Especially confessorial practices and the avarice of the priests is looked upon with disgust. Grassmann's tract on Liguori, which many people read, has been very effective."[38] In the honest accounts of conversion experience, most people admitted their outrage at the clergy to be as important to their decision as their national consciousness. As one Bohemian convert laconically put it, "I just cannot get myself to trust those priests [*Pfaffen*] with my children."[39] But why turn to Protestantism? This same nationalist gave one answer: "A nation [*Volk*] without religion is not a nation anymore, but rather a horde." The theoretical proposition that nation and religion should be one, and that religion, as part of culture, should have a civilizing influence on nationalities, swayed people in a society that was becoming secular but still considered its deepest experiences sacred.

Another answer lies in the way national identity is constructed. This may be conceived as a story people tell about themselves, as a

---

[37] On this pamphlet, see PAAA R8534 Eulenburg to Bülow. For the debate about it in the Austrian Parliament, see *Die Liguori-Moral und die geheime Sitzung des österreichischen Abgeordnetenhauses vom 23. Februar 1901*, 3d. ed. (Vienna, 1901). This pamphlet also brought forth a flood of Catholic counterpropaganda. See, for example, Heinrich Brück (bishop of Mainz), *Die systematische Verunglimpfung der Sittenlehre des Hl. Alphons von Liguori* (Mainz, 1901); Hermann Roeren, *Der internationale Kulturkampf insbesondere die Grassmann'sche Schmähschrift* (Trier, 1901); *Guano und Superphosphat aus der Los von Rom Fabrik oder Die Firma Grassmann & Co.* (Dieburg, 1901).

[38] AKIEB S185.810.63a "Bericht über die von Pastor O. Hoffmann und von P. Lic. Dr. Schian ausgeführte Evangelisationsreise in Nordmähren (10.12.1899–16.12.1899)."

[39] Recorded in AKIEB S185.810.60 Paul Bräunlich, "Streng vertraulicher Reisebericht, 'Zur Evangelisierung in Böhmen,'" 6.11.1898.

people. While not usually false, and only partly invented, the details of the story must always be molded to fit an imagined narrative; and if they do not fit, the details—points of one's identity—must be ignored, reshaped, or cast away. For many Germans who conceived of their national identity in the context of a struggle among nations, Catholicism was a run-down house full of corrupt caretakers. In its traditionalism, it oppressed an awakening German nation; in its language policy, it suppressed German. Antagonistic toward vernacular language and secular culture, progress and freedom, Catholicism, unlike Protestantism, could hardly find a place in the imaginary narrative of modern German nationalists.

That narrative, revealed in the poetry of Los von Rom, provides a key to the emotional élan of both anticlericalism and integral nationalism. In an anonymous poem entitled "Los von Rom" and written to the music of "Deutschland, Deutschland über alles," the reader is admonished:

> Greift zum Schwerte, zu den Waffen
> Schlagt den Feind am deutschen Strom;
> Ringt für Freiheit todesmutig
> Mit dem Kampfruf Los von Rom![40]

> Seize the sword, take up arms
> bring down the enemy on the German stream
> Defy death in the struggle for freedom
> With the battle cry Los von Rom.

Analyses of nationalist language typically proceed from the centrality of aggression in its rhetoric. And, without doubt, the poetry of Los von Rom betrays fantasies of aggression. Yet imagined violence against the Catholic clergy, while apparent, was, on balance, atypical of the movement's verse. More important, and even evident in this stanza, is not so much the necessity to kill as to die for the cause. The deeper language of such nationalism is less the language of aggression than the language of sacrifice, though the two are related.[41] This is partly because the relationship of nationalism, religion, and death is strung taut with ambiguity. Only through readiness to die can one seize life. The central movement of "In der Ostmark" (In the Eastern March) is from death and "fatal silence" to "a new life all at once" because of Los von Rom. This turn to life was often cast in the imag-

---

[40] The Los von Rom poetry cited here and in the following paragraphs can be found in AKIEB S185.810.80. This was Bräunlich's personal collection. See also the rich treasure of Los von Rom poetry in the volumes of *Die Wartburg*.

[41] See Benedict Anderson, *Imagined Communities*, 141–42.

ery of spring. In "Zehn Jahre evangelische Bewegung in Österreich" (Ten Years of the Evangelical Movement in Austria), a new spring, a new awakening, is envisioned: "Ten years we march through the field, / and it still remains springtime." The theme of liberation also pervaded the movement's poetry. This is often overlooked by historians of German nationalism combing its cultural products for fantasies of domination.[42] In fact, the idea of liberating the German nation from its fetters is the most common theme of German integral nationalist poetry. The poets of Los von Rom, integral nationalists of a peculiar kind, imagined the Catholic church to lay chains on the souls of an awakening nation. National revival could take place only if the constraints that Catholicism placed on the conscience of men were broken. "Yes, just break your chains," urged a Los von Rom balladeer.[43]

The idea of coming of age was closely related to these themes. In the poetry of Los von Rom, breaking away from clerical tutelage seemed akin to a national rite of passage. Sons could now become compatriots of their fathers. But the fathers were distant, imagined fathers of the sixteenth century. "The spirit of Luther sounds through history like a continuous complaint / To us from the days of our fathers." In the poetry as well as the prose of the movement, history represented less a search for the causes of the present than a standard by which to judge the present wanting. That standard was neither mythical nor purely an "invented tradition." The claim, in "Hutten's Spirit," that "What our fathers once believed, we are no longer allowed to have as our faith" was not completely false. The brutality of the Counter-Reformation could be denied only by the most inveterate apologists. Yet as with nationalist history generally, Los von Rom's version of history portrayed truth out of context. Repression in the sixteenth century had little, if anything, to do with issues concerning nationality. Yet, as an ideology, nationalism must construct a credible past that can make, if not the present, than at least the future seem predestined, preordained.

Finally, the movement appealed to gender-specific values. The "New Jesuit Song" called on "the German man to steal back his bride" from the clutches of the clergy. A "Los von Rom" poem confiscated in Eger claimed that the sexual inquisitiveness of Catholic priests in confessionals robbed women of honor. And in a broadside written in

[42] This is the method of Klaus Theweleit, *Männerphantasien*, 2 vols. (Hamburg, 1977, 1980). If it has a certain validity for fascism, its use for understanding the emotional pull of integral nationalism is, I think, one-sided and therefore limited.

[43] AKIEB S185.810.80 Bräunlich's personal collection of Los von Rom poetry.

1900, Bräunlich encouraged Bohemians to join the movement by goading "now we will see if German Bohemians are men or not." He then signed his broadside "Heil und Sieg."[44] Although Los von Rom also convinced women to convert, the movement's language was clearly the language of men.

Throne, Altar, and National Religion

The language of Los von Rom and the messianic vision behind it pushed a certain tradition of thinking about the confluence of religious and national identity perilously close to the edge of an ideological precipice. The demand for one nation, one Reich, one religion not only foreshadowed more ominous appeals in the not too distant future, but it also posed a direct, and present, challenge to the house of Hohenzollern and the house of Habsburg, both of which (especially the latter) ultimately based their legitimacy on traditions of dynastic aquisition. As official nationalists, statesmen in both empires exploited nationalism; but they did not assume the interests of the dynasty to be somehow subordinate to the requirements of the *Volk*. Yet the leaders of Los von Rom, integral rather than official nationalists, asserted precisely this: the primacy of national over state, ethnic over dynasic interests. And they pursued their radical ends with ardor, at times against the state, at times in defiance of the dynasty.

Not surprisingly, then, the Los von Rom movement provoked the ire of the imperial government in Berlin and the consternation of court circles in Vienna. On 13 December 1898, Philipp von Eulenburg, the German ambassador in Vienna, wrote to Chancellor Hohenlohe that Los von Rom "posed serious difficulties to the prosperous continuation of our alliance with Austria."[45] He also worried that Los von Rom, which he considered "a political not a religious matter," would "further divide the Germans" in the Austro-Hungarian Empire.[46] Kaiser Wilhelm II agreed, adding "they could easily turn out to be Hussites."[47]

The movement's initial success (1898/99: about eight thousand conversions) convinced the two governments to repress Los von Rom.[48]

---

[44] AKIEB S185.810.63b Paul Bräunlich, "Werte Volks- und Glaubensgenossen," n. d., probably written between 8.7.1900 and 13.7.1900.

[45] PAAA R8530 Philipp Eulenburg to Chancellor Hohenlohe, 9.2.1899.

[46] Ibid.

[47] Marginal comment of Kaiser Wilhelm II to ibid.

[48] For statistics on conversions see Fritz von der Heydt, *Die evangelische Bewegung in Österreich*, 2d ed. (Berlin, 1938), 12. For 1898/99 he gives the figure 7,953, but this does

Tellingly, the initiative to repress the movement came from the Protestant Consistory in Vienna. On 19 January 1899, the consistory declared the movement nationalistic, antimonarchical, and bereft of "religious motivation."[49] Moreover, in many ways Los von Rom posed a greater danger to the Protestant than to the Catholic church of the Dual Monarchy. The movement's association with Pan-German politics could only exacerbate tensions, already taut, between Czech Calvinists and German Lutherans.[50] And even if many thousands of Catholics converted, Protestants would remain a small minority vulnerable to state repression. This was especially true if the Catholic church reacted by reasserting its political power.[51]

The presence of the imperial German Protestant League in the Los von Rom movement further aggravated these problems, for it fueled popular suspicion that Austrian Protestants harbored irredentist sympathies.[52] In March 1899, Eulenburg therefore suggested to Hohenlohe that Germany should "as far as possible prevent an overly conspicuous involvement of imperial German Protestants, but especially the rabble-rousing activity of the Protestant League, in this delicate matter."[53] The kaiser concurred—"by all means"[54]—and ordered Bülow, then foreign secretary, to inform Wilhelm Barkhausen, the president of the Protestant Consistory in Berlin, of the imperial government's disapproval of the Los von Rom movement.[55] Barkhausen essentially agreed with the official position.[56] On 18 February, he wrote Wintzingerode, the president of the Protestant League: "In the interests of the Protestant church I can only advise with utmost ur-

---

not include conversions from South Tirol, Carinthia, Steiermark, and Galicia. For conversion statistics from 1899 to 1911, see Georg Leusche, "Los von Rom," 20–34.

[49] See PAAA R8530 Eulenburg to Hohenlohe, 9.2.1899.

[50] Ibid. On Calvinists and Lutherans, see also AKIEB S185.810.29 "Protokoll über die Sitzung des Ausschusses für die protestantische Bewegung in Österreich," 22.3.1899. For a critical polemic against Los von Rom from the standpoint of a Calvinist in Moravia, see Ferdinand Cisar, *Chauvinismus, eine Gefahr für den Österreichischen Protestantismus* (Erlangen, 1909), 11.

[51] PAAA R8530 Eulenburg to Hohenlohe, 9.2.1899.

[52] Ibid.

[53] Ibid. See also PAAA R8530 Eulenburg to Hohenlohe, 9.3.1899.

[54] Marginal note of Kaiser Wilhelm II to ibid.

[55] Barkhausen's résumé of the negotiations in EZB 7/423 Wilhelm Barkhausen to Kaiser Wilhelm II, 19.4.1899.

[56] He also feared that if the Protestant League organized the Los von Rom movement, the Austrian church would pull out of the Eisenach Conference, the only organized association of German, Protestant church governments, encouraging, in turn, separatist movements among Protestant state churches in the German empire. EZB 7/423 Barkhausen to Wintzingerode, 18.2.1899. With the exception of Saxony, the Protestant state churches supported Barkhausen's position.

gency against any involvement, and especially any agitation, of the Protestant League in this matter."[57]

Initially, the Protestant League resisted the intervention of the imperial government. Although Wintzingerode conceded that the "Los von Rom movement owes its inception mainly to Pan-German [völkisch] inspiration," he countered that "the movement is in its essence directed against Roman clerical domination" and therefore "goes much deeper."[58] As a burgeoning popular movement, Los von Rom was, moreover, difficult to control. "Even if we wanted to stop it, if I wanted to or the executive committee wanted to, if the league wanted to, we could not bring a halt to it."[59] Unsatisfied, Barkhausen also met with Leopold Witte, the secretary of the league, and Friedrich Meyer. According to Barkhausen, Witte and Meyer responded to official injunctions against the involvement of the Protestant League in Los von Rom by pointing out that "not the Protestant League as such, but an independent committee handles the matter so that there will be little danger of the Protestant League appearing in the foreground and its organization being put in the service of the movement."[60] To conciliate the imperial government, the leaders of the Protestant League agreed to proceed in cooperation with the Protestant Consistory in Vienna. Barkhausen, now convinced that the league would at least exercise circumspection, informed the kaiser at the end of March 1899 that Witte and Meyer "fully agree with our position."[61] Although Eulenburg still considered Los von Rom "best suited to tarnish relations with our allies," the kaiser believed the matter settled.[62]

But it was not settled. The claim that the Committee to Support the Evangelical Movement in Austria operated independently from the Protestant League was not true; the promise that the league would henceforth cooperate with the Viennese Consistory proved hollow; and Barkhausen's belief that he and the leaders of the Protestant League were of one mind was ill-founded. Barkhausen's admonitions notwithstanding, the Protestant League continued to dominate and direct the evangelical movement in Austria. Of the members of the

---

[57] EZB 7/423 Barkhausen to Wintzingerode, 18.2.1899.

[58] Ibid. Wintzingerode to Barkhausen, 20.2.1899.

[59] Ibid.

[60] EZB 7/423 Barkhausen to Kaiser Wilhelm II, 19.4.1899. This fiction saved the league from more stringent police surveillance. See EZB 7/424 Bernhard von Bülow to Konrad von Studt, 15.3.1901.

[61] Ibid.

[62] PAAA R8530 Eulenburg to Hohenlohe, 31.3.1899. To this, the Kaiser commented in the margins, "this is true, but cannot be changed." To Barkhausen's report, the kaiser wrote "in agreement." See EZB 7/423 Bülow to Barkhausen, 7.5.1899.

Los von Rom committee, only Ernst Hasse, the leader of the Pan-German League, was not a prominent Protestant League leader. Between 1899 and 1907, the Protestant League poured RM 1,700,000 into the Los von Rom movement, an investment that nearly bankrupted the league.[63] Far from retreating to the background, the Protestant League asserted its leading role in the movement against other Protestant organizations. The Gustav Adolf Verein, for example, agreed in 1898 to allow "the Protestant League the initiative," especially in agitation for Los von Rom, while the Gustav Adolf Verein restricted its activity to collecting money for church construction.[64] Negotiations between the Protestant League and the Protestant Consistory in Vienna also made little headway. The consistory accepted a limited number of imperial German vicars (but not pastors) in Austrian parishes, while the Protestant League agreed to strike "evangelical movement" from the name of its committee and replace it with Committee to Support the Protestant Church in Austria.[65] The name change was cosmetic. By 1901, it became clear to Meyer that further negotiations with Vienna would be "useless" and that the league could not bring the consistory to shed "its quivering, anxiety-ridden wisdom."[66] Nor were Barkhausen and the Protestant League leadership of one mind concerning imperial German agitation for Los von

[63] Friedrich Meyer, "Über die Dezentralization in der Arbeit für die evangelische Bewegung in Österreich. Ansprache in der Versammlung von Vorstandsmitgliedern der Hauptvereine am 8.2.1908 in Halle." This document can be found in a box with the call number B42.428 in the library of the Evangelische Bund zur Wahrung deutsch-protestantischer Interessen in Bensheim, Hessen.

[64] AKIEB S185.810.29 "Sitzung des Ausschusses für die evangelische Bewegung in Böhmen," 28.12.1898. At the general assembly of the Protestant League in Gotha on 18 April 1906, Meyer characterized the relationship between the Protestant League and the Gustav Adolf Verein with regard to the Los von Rom movement in the following way. "If the Gustav Adolf Verein and the Inner Mission have promoted the primarily feminine virtues of Christianity, it has been the task of the Protestant League to promote primarily masculine virtues." Meyer, "Mitteilungen vom Ausschuß," 29 (1906): 4.

[65] For negotiations on the admission of imperial German pastors, see AKIEB S185.810.29 "Protokoll über die Sitzung des Ausschusses für die protestantische Bewegung in Österreich," 22.3.1899, and EZB 7/423 Barkhausen to Kaiser Wilhelm II, 19.4.1899. Negotiations to force the Protestant League to change the name of its committee were conducted principally between Saxony and the Dual Monarchy. The immediate conflict between the two states arose when Saxony, on 16 December 1900, lifted its ban on public proclamations in favor of Los von Rom. On the ensuing negotiations see PAAA R8534 Eulenburg to Bülow, 24.1.1901; Eulenburg to Bülow, 30.1.1901; Prussian emissary to Saxony, Carl von Dönhoff to Bülow, 6.2.1901; Dönhoff to Bülow, 14.2.1901; Eulenburg to Bülow, 19.2.1901; Dönhoff to Bülow, 22.2.1901.

[66] AKIEB S185.810.29 "Bericht Friedrich Meyer über eine Reise durch die Steiermark und Kärnten," 4.8.1901.

Rom. While Meyer assured Barkhausen that the league would not become publicly involved, he explained to the executive committee on 12 April 1899 that "if the movement fails, it would be a death sentence for German Protestantism."[67] When, in later years, dissenting voices within the Protestant League argued that the league had invested too much energy and money outside Germany's borders, Meyer replied, quite correctly, that it was precisely the league's nationalist engagement that made it popular in the empire.[68] Even Wintzingerode, who for personal reasons wished to conciliate the imperial government, believed that as the Los von Rom movement waxed, the Protestant League would expand as well.[69]

In part a matter of practical politics, the tension between throne and altar on the one side, the Protestant League on the other, was in even greater measure an issue of ideological principle. For Friedrich Meyer and the integral nationalists of the Protestant League, nation clearly came before state. "The German empire," Meyer argued, "only stands in the foreground for us because it is the noblest concentration of national strength."[70] In his "visionary" political theory, the state constituted the first servant of the nation; its task was to "protect . . . its nationality from foreign influences that are alien to [the nation], indeed that can bring it down and spoil it."[71] But by this measure, Barkhausen's fainthearted policies and Bernhard von Bülow's official nationalism proved wanting, for they both rested on the mistaken assumption that Catholicism could be checked by prudent concessions, or co-opted by polite diplomacy. Yet appeasement served neither state nor nation; instead, it represented "a denial of the historically revealed spirit of the German people."[72] History would side with the people. "The essence of a nation," Meyer wrote, "cannot be changed and redirected by a single statesman whose

[67] AKIEB S500.9.124–25 "Protokoll der Gesamtvorstandssitzung des Evangelischen Bundes in Eisenach," 12.4.1899.

[68] AKIEB PL Meyer, "Mitteilungen vom Ausschuss," 18.4.1906.

[69] EZB 7/423 Wintzingerode to Barkhausen, 19.4.1899. As with respect to the secret political action committee of the Protestant League, Wintzingerode found himself on the side of those urging less political involvement. He, for example, urged the Protestant League to "admonish the Protestant converts in the Reichsrat to calm and loyal action." AKIEB S185.810.29 "Protokoll über die Sitzung des Österreichischen Ausschusses," 11.3.1901.

[70] AKIEB PL Meyer, "Mitteilungen vom Ausschuss," 12 (1901): 3.

[71] Meyer, "Christentum und Germanen," 206.

[72] Friedrich Meyer, "Einiges über die Bedeutung der evangelischen Bewegung," *Die Wartburg* 1, no. 1 (1902): 1. See also AKIEB PL Meyer, "Mitteilungen vom Ausschuss," 17 (1902): 3, and Meyer, "Mitteilungen vom Ausschuss," 19 (1903): 4, as well as Meyer, "Der zornige Kanzler," in *Heroldsrufe und Hammerschläge*, 102–5.

thinking is not in harmony with it."[73] The "world-historical mission" of the Germans to complete the work of the Reformation would have to be pursued against Chancellor Bernhard von Bülow, and against the state. "We no longer expect the state of its own accord to repress ultramontanism," he declared: "only from the people, only from below can help come."[74]

Thus, the Protestant League did not, as the guardians of throne and altar wished, withdraw its public support for Los von Rom. It had, however, been forced to operate underground, especially after the Habsburg police stepped up censorship and expelled prominent Protestant League organizers from Austro-Hungarian territory: Everling in May 1899 and Bräunlich (for life) one year later.[75] Despite the appeals of the Protestant League and the Pan-German League to rescind these expulsions, the imperial German government did not intervene on the Protestants' behalf.[76] To avert further government repression of the movement, the Protestant League insisted that under its guidance Los von Rom would take a "religious turn" and cease to be a political movement.[77] Doubtless, many of the league's members

[73] Meyer, "Einiges über die Bedeutung der evangelischen Bewegung," 1.

[74] AKIEB PL Meyer, "Mitteilungen vom Ausschuss," 19 (1903): 4, 13. See also Meyer, "Heil dem deutschen Geist!," *Die Wartburg* (1907): 2–3.

[75] On the confiscation of Los von Rom literature, see PAAA R8534 Eulenburg to Bülow, 25.2.1901. See also AKIEB S185.810.55 R. Holzapfel (Vienna) to Paul Bräunlich, n.d., probably between 26.5.1900 and 30.5.1900. On Everling's expulsion, see PAAA R8531 Konrad von Romberg (imperial envoy in Vienna) to Hohenlohe, 12.5.1899. On Bräunlich's expulsion, EZB 7/424 von Romberg to Bülow, 5.11.1900. For Bräunlich's own account, Paul Bräunlich, *Meine Ausweisung aus Österreich. Bilder aus den Tagen der Zentrumsherrschaft in Deutschland und Österreich*, 5th ed. (Munich, 1910). On the reaction of the press to Bräunlich's expulsion, AKIEB S185.810.39 clippings.

[76] Both Everling and Bräunlich attempted to have these expulsions rescinded, most conspicuously through the lobby of the Pan-German League. See AKIEB S185.810.39 Ernst Hasse to Bräunlich, 11.2.1901: Hasse convened a meeting of the 34 Reichstag representatives who belonged to the Pan-German League at that time, but they decided to quietly try to influence Bülow rather than bring the matter to public attention on the Reichstag floor.

[77] As early as May 1899, the league decided to follow Everling's suggestion "to emphasize the religious turn of the movement" in its public proclamations. AKIEB S185.810.29 "Protokoll über die Sitzung des Ausschusses zur Förderung der evangelischen Kirche in Österreich," 4.5.1899. In negotiations with state and church officials, Protestant League leaders always emphasized the nonpolitical aspect of the movement. When, for example, the president of the Protestant Consistory in Vienna told Leopold Witte that "he considers it unfortunate that the movement began with Schönerer and his comrades," Witte emphasized that the movement "is no longer a matter of political parties, but rather an independent religious experience that also has a hold on circles besides the radical nationals." AKIEB S185.810.29 "Protokoll über die Sitzung des Ausschusses für die protestantische Bewegung in Österreich," 22.3.1899. Like the Navy League, the Protestant League was able to evade the police surveillance

believed that under the league's tutelage the Los von Rom movement would emancipate itself from the more radical implications of its involvement in Pan-German politics. This view has even persisted in the best scholarship on Los von Rom.[78] Yet it is belied by the facts.

Pan-German Politics and the Demise of Los von Rom

From beginning to end, the Los von Rom movement and the Protestant League's support of it were influenced by the shifting sands of Pan-German politics in the Dual Monarchy. At the hour of the movement's inception, on 15 January 1899, Meyer and Witte participated in the Vienna conference of Pan-Germans organized by Georg Ritter von Schönerer, the Austrian anti-Semite best known for a petition he submitted to the Reichsrat in 1887 that claimed that "our anti-Semitism is not directed against the religion but against the racial characteristics of the Jews."[79] A convinced racist and a zealous Pan-German, Schönerer was also the most important secular leader of the Los von Rom movement.[80] At the Vienna meeting, he along with other Pan-German and Protestant League leaders decided to cooperate in the organization of Los von Rom.[81] No evidence exists to suggest that the Protestant League ever reneged on its commitment to cooperate with, indeed support, the Austrian Pan-Germans.[82] Nor does it seem that the Protestant League publically objected to Schönerer's overt racism. Indeed, neither in Bräunlich's voluminous correspondence nor in Meyer's prolific writing could I find any trace of an attempt on the part of Protestant League leaders to censure the racism of their Pan-German comrades. Quite evidently they tolerated it. Yet, for tactical reasons,

---

that would have occurred had it declared itself to be in favor of a political party. In public, the league denied such connections. See EZB 7/424 Bernhard von Bülow to Studt, 15.3.1901.

[78] Albertin, "Nationalismus und Protestantismus," 45.

[79] Cited in F. L. Carsten, *Faschismus in Österreich* (Munich, 1978), 14.

[80] On the role of Schönerer in the Los von Rom movement, see the more detailed analysis in Whiteside, *The Socialism of Fools*, 243–62.

[81] AKIEB S185.810.29 "Protokoll über die Sitzung des Ausschusses für die evangelische Bewegung in Böhmen," 2.2.1899 (incorrectly dated as 1898). See also Albertin, "Nationalismus und Protestantismus," 22–24.

[82] Whiteside, *Socialism of Fools*, 251, suggests that the paucity of the Protestant League's financial support for various Pan-German newspapers meant a turning away from Pan-German sympathy. In reality, the league's parsimony resulted from its difficult financial circumstances. See AKIEB S185.810.63h Bräunlich to Heinrich Schicht, 22.4.1907. For Bräunlich's support of Schönerer's *Alldeutsches Tageblatt*, see AKIEB S185.810.63h Paul Bräunlich to Ferdinand Heidler (Chodau), 23.2.1909.

Protestant League leaders feared the consequences of making Los von Rom "the appendage of one political party."[83] The Protestant League therefore supported, often simultaneously, a wide variety of Pan-German voluntary organizations and political parties: the German National Workers' Unions (Deutsch-völkische Arbeitervereine),[84] the radically anticlerical and anti-Semitic Schererbund,[85] the secular minded, anticlerical Huttenbund,[86] and, most important, the two major Pan-German political parties: the Pan-German party headed by Schönerer and the Radical Germans (later the Free Pan-Germans) under the leadership of Karl Hermann Wolf.

The Protestant League backed Pan-German parties according to the measure of their success and the degree of their engagement in anti-Catholic activity. Between 1898 and 1907, the league's closest ties were to Schönerer: in 1901 one of Bräunlich's Austrian colleagues even believed that "the Los von Rom movement made (Schönerer's) Pan-Germans popular."[87] But after Schönerer's party declined and Karl Hermann Wolf's rival "Free Pan-German party" scored a moderate success at the 1907 Reichsrat elections, the Protestant League shifted its support. On 2 September 1907, Meyer wrote Bräunlich, "I consider it desirable that you cultivate relations with the Radical Germans."[88] Bräunlich also hoped that the Radical Germans would become Los von Rom's principal political protagonists. On 10 June 1908, he wrote his contact man in Triest: "If the Radical Germans adopt a resolute anticlerical position, then in my opinion they could become the party around which the truly progressive [freiheitlichen] and nationalist elements could rally."[89] Even as the fortunes of Los von Rom and Pan-Germany waned in the years before the war, Bräunlich continued to support more vigorous Pan-German activity. On 23 February 1909, he wrote Franz Stepan in Bohemia, "I too am worried about the development of the national movement in Austria and desire a strengthening

---

[83] Meyer, "Mitteilungen vom Ausschuss," Nr. 21, 1.10.1903

[84] On support for the German National Workers Unions, see AKIEB S185.810.25 Memorandum Friedrich Meyer, 30.6.1907; AKIEB S185.810.63h Paul Bräunlich to "deutsche Volksgenossen" [deutsch-völkischer Arbeiterverein], 12.7.1907. This circular was leaked and reprinted in Germania, 22 August 1907.

[85] AKIEB S185.810.29 "Protokoll über die Sitzung des Ausschusses," 11.3.1901.

[86] AKIEB PL Meyer, "Mitteilungen vom Ausschuss," 5 (1900): 5.

[87] AKIEB S185.810.55 R. Holzapfel to Paul Bräunlich, 4.4.1901.

[88] AKIEB S185.810.38 Friedrich Meyer to Paul Bräunlich, 2.9.1907. The initiative came, however, from Paul Pogatschnigg, Bräunlich's contact man in Triest. See AKIEB S185.810.38 Paul Bräunlich to Friedrich Meyer, 30.8.1907.

[89] AKIEB S185.810.38 Paul Bräunlich to Paul Pogatschnigg, 10.6.1908. On the tensions between Pan-German groups in the Dual Monarchy, see Höbelt, Kornblume und Kaiseradler, 187–99.

of the Pan-German party in the interests of our movement."⁹⁰ Without one or the other Pan-German party, Los von Rom, Bräunlich realized, would quietly pine away.

But, alas, pine away it did. Despite its rhetoric, the Los von Rom
movement failed to inspire a second Reformation. By 1913, seventy
thousand Catholics had converted to Protestantism. To some it was
an impressive number; to others it meant only that the rate of conversion had failed to keep pace with Catholic population growth.⁹¹ More
important, conversions had already slowed by 1902, and thereafter
the movement never again fully recaptured its initial élan—until it
returned with a vengeance as part of the "Heim ins Reich" movement
of the thirties.⁹² But in the period before World War I, Los von Rom
neither significantly changed the structure of German national politics in Austria nor succeeded in gripping the mass of the Catholic
pious; instead, it sapped the strength of the Protestant League.

The league assumed that the Catholic church, like an old tree gone
rotten inside, would fall when pushed. In fact, the church proved
more resilient. Both the Catholic hierarchy and the lower clergy "mobilized" against the Los von Rom movement.⁹³ On Easter 1899, the
Austrian bishops issued a pastoral letter on the nationality problem
and the Los von Rom movement. They emphasized that "differences
of language were a consequence of sin" and therefore "a work of
God." Nationalist and anticlerical, Los von Rom was a movement of
renegades, and, as the pastoral letter made clear, "there is no salvation outside the church."⁹⁴ In the following month, a Catholic Action
Committee was founded in order to combat Los von Rom in the field.

⁹⁰ AKIEB S185.810.63h Paul Bräunlich to Franz Stepan in Reichenberg, 23.2.1909.

⁹¹ Paul Samassa, *Der Völkerstreit im Habsburgerstaat* (Leipzig, 1910), 67; Wandruszka
and Urbantisch, eds., *Die Habsburgermonarchie*, vol. 3, pt. 1, 276, give the figure of
76,192. If, however, the number of people who converted from Protestantism to Catholicism are subtracted, the net gain for Protestantism was significantly less. According to Leusche, "Los von Rom," 32, the net gain for Protestantism in Austria between
1899 and 1911 was only 49,115 converts.

⁹² This was particularly true in Bohemia. In Lower Austria, Styria, Carinthia, and
southern Austria they continued unabated. See Leusche, "Los von Rom," 33; Whiteside, *Socialism of Fools*, 255; Heydt, *Die evangelische Bewegung in Österreich*, 12.

⁹³ On the initial reaction of the Catholic church to Los von Rom, see PAAA R8530
Eulenburg to Hohenlohe, 16.3.1899. See also Schmid-Egger, *Klerus und Politik*, 241–44.
Friedrich Engel-Janosi, *Österreich und der Vatikan 1846–1918*, 2 vols. (Graz, Vienna, Cologne, 1958, 1960), does not, unfortunately, address this issue. For a general overview
of the relationship of the church to national movements, see Friedrich Engel-Janosi,
"The Church and the Nationalities in the Habsburg Monarchy," *Austrian History Yearbook* 3 (1967): 67–82.

⁹⁴ *Hirtenbrief 1899* (Pastoral Letter) of Archbishop Theodor Kohn of Olmütz (Olmütz,
1899).

In its public summons of 15 April 1899, it appealed to "Catholics and patriots" with the slogan "With God, for Our Faith—for Our Kaiser—for Our Fatherland."[95] Under the leadership of Father Alban Schachleiter, a Benedictine monk of the Emanus Monastery in Prague, the Action Committee produced a flurry of anti-Protestant propaganda in the form of almanacs and pocket books, newspaper editorials, catechisms and theological tracts for the layman, gratis flyers, broadsides, and pamphlets.[96] Typically Los von Rom organizers were portrayed as deceitful pagans, as foreigners, and as betrayers of the Austrian fatherland.[97]

The results of the Austrian Reichsrat elections of 1901, in which the Pan-Germans won twenty-one seats and the divided Catholic parties (Christian Socialists and the German Clerical party) made only modest gains, convinced both throne and altar in Vienna and Rome to redouble their efforts to put an end to the evangelical movement.[98] In April 1902, Archduke Ferdinand took the unusual measure of assuming the protectorate of the obviously partisan Catholic School Association because, as he publicly stated, the Los von Rom movement was "also a Los von Austria movement."[99] Shortly beforehand, the archbishop of Olmütz published a letter in which Pope Leo XIII addressed the language question. The papacy, the letter made explicit, would uphold the requirements of European dynasties to rule with a language of state against the rights of national minorities to express themselves in their mother tongues at public gatherings.[100] Implicitly,

---

[95] Summons in *Vaterland*, 15 April 1899. See also PAAA R8531 Konrad von Romberg to Hohenlohe, 18.4.1899

[96] Schmid-Egger, *Klerus und Politik*, 242–43.

[97] See, for example, "Wie der Seppl protestantisch wurde," in *Papstkalender* 1 (1903): 84–102, and the anonymous *Katholiken Wachet auf!*, (n.p., n.d.).

[98] On the deterioration of confessional relations in Austria after the election, see PAAA R8535 Eulenburg to Bülow, 12.6.1901. For the election results, see "Die Ergebnisse der Reichsrathswahlen in den im Reichsrathe vertretenen Königreichen und Ländern für das Jahr 1900/1901," *Österreichische Statistik* 59/3 (Vienna, 1902). In terms of Reichsrath seats, the relative strength of the German parties, after the runoff elections, was as follows: German People's party 48, German Liberals (Deutsche Fortschrittspartei) 31, Constitutional Manorial Lords (Verfassungstreue Großgrundbesitzer) 30, German Clericals 29, Christian Socialists 25, Pan-Germans 21, Social Democrats 10, German Farmers party 4.

[99] Cited in Wandruszka and Urbantisch, eds., *Die Habsburgermonarchie*, vol. 3, pt. 1, 277–78.

[100] This letter, originally dated 20.8.1901 and addressed to the Bishops of Bohemia and Moravia, was published at Archbishop Kohn's request in *Vaterland* on 2.4.1902 and in *Germania* on 4.1.1902. Eulenburg was correct to see the import of the letter as saying that "within certain limits the mother tongue has a certain justification, but the common good of the state may not, as a consequence, be disadvantaged." PAAA R8536 Eulenburg to Bülow, 4.1.1902. In the margins, Kaiser Wilhelm commented "very important for us in the struggle against the Poles." That the kaiser's interpretation was

the Vatican sided with the Germans against the Czechs and the Poles. Three years later, in 1905, Pope Pius X reaffirmed this position.[101] The national turn of German Catholicism in Austria that followed, and was supported by the church hierarchy, redounded to the political benefit of the burgeoning Christian Socialist party led by Karl Lueger. German nationalist and German Catholic, anti-Protestant and anti-Semitic, socialist and loyalist all at once, the Austrian Christian Socialists were, when it came to demagoguery, more than a match for Bräunlich and the Protestant League.[102]

If Protestant League leaders underestimated the Catholic church, they overestimated the appeal of Los von Rom to potential political allies, especially to Austrian liberals. Although Austrian liberals shared the movement's anticlericalism, they disdained its uncompromising irredentism, distrusted its antidynastic tendencies, and found the movement's collusion with vulgar anti-Semites distasteful. To them the multinational empire was a symphony best conducted by Germans to a score written together with the monarchy.[103] Close cooperation with irredentist Pan-Germans only encouraged discord.

The inability of the evangelical movement to win broad support for its solution to the national question led, in turn, to organizational stagnation. In 1907, Pastor Buller, one of Bräunlich's few perspicacious colleagues, reported from Moravia that the new emphasis that both Catholic priests and liberal German notables now began to place on their nationality had caused Los von Rom agitation to cease. Short of there being another clerical scandal, the movement, he thought, was condemned to remain at a standstill.[104] The case of Moravia proved typical, and in the Reichsrat elections of 1907 the full extent of this stagnation became evident. In Austria's first general election based on universal manhood suffrage, the Christian Socialists emerged as the largest party (11.7 percent) among the Germans, who, together, accounted for 38.4 percent of all Reichsrat votes. The Chris-

---

consistent with Vatican intentions can be seen from PAAA R8539 Wolfram von Rotenhan (imperial envoy to the Vatican) to Bülow, 11.1.1902; and Rotenhan to Bülow, 17.1.1902.

[101] PAAA R8539 Carl von Wedel to Bülow, 6.4.1905; Rotenhan to Bülow , 14.4.1905.

[102] On the early period of the Christian Socialists, the definitive work is John Boyer, *Political Radicalism in Late Imperial Vienna: Origins of the Christian Social Movement, 1848–1897* (Chicago and London, 1981). See also Reinhard Knoll, *Zur Tradition der christsozialen Partei. Ihre Früh- und Entwicklungsgeschichte bis zu den Reichsratswahlen 1907*, (Vienna, 1973).

[103] On Austrian liberals and nationalism, see Wandruszka and Urbantisch, eds., *Die Habsburgermonarchie*, vol. 3, pt. 1, 302–4.

[104] AKIEB S185.810.25 Pf. Buller, "Bericht über eine Reise nach Mähren," 27.7.–3.8.1907.

tian Socialists were followed by the Social Democrats (11.1 percent), the Conservative party (4.2 percent), the moderate German People's party (2.9 percent), the Agrarians (2.8 percent), and the Liberals (2.2 percent).[105] Among the major political groups, the Pan-Germans fared the worst: Karl Hermann Wolf's Free Pan-Germans received 1.5 percent, and Schönerer's Pan-Germans, who had previously sent twenty-one delegates to the Reichsrat and had been the most avid political supporters of Los von Rom, finished with only 20,693 votes (0.5 percent) and sent only three delegates to Parliament.[106]

The Reichsrat elections of 1907 sealed the political fate of Los von Rom. Not only had political Catholicism emerged as the most powerful force in Austro-German politics, but the Pan-Germans who had supported Los von Rom had been reduced to political marginality. The relative success of Wolf's Free Pan-Germans could not make up for this loss, since he himself broke away from Schönerer in 1902 because the latter refused to cooperate with German Catholics in tactical matters.[107] Moreover, despite Bräunlich's efforts to maintain contact with Wolf, the Free Pan-Germans increasingly distanced themselves from Los von Rom. In May 1909, Friedrich Meyer lamented: "The Wolfianer do not consider it to be an opportune time for [Los von Rom]. They would sacrifice the movement for the blue eyes of the Christian Socialists."[108] To make matters worse, Meyer perceived that the Pan-German League "seemed to be moving to Wolf's side."[109] The initiative to decouple the Los von Rom movement from Pan-German politics came from the Pan-Germans themselves, not from Protestant League leaders. Its importance lay not in the religious turn that this signaled but rather in the evangelical movement's subsequent descent into political obscurity.

The political decline of Los von Rom was accompanied by Pan-German criticism of its detrimental influence on the fate of the Ger-

[105] Wandruszka and Urbantisch, eds., *Die Habsburgermonarchie*, vol. 3, pt. 1, 294, table 17.

[106] Ibid. After the runoff elections in May 1907, the relative strength in terms of Reichsrat seats of the German parties was as follows: Christian Socialists (together with the Conservatives) 96, Social Democrats 86, German People's party 31, German Agrarians 21, Liberals (Deutsche Fortschrittspartei) 17, Free Pan-Germans 12, Schönerer's Pan-Germans 3. See Eduard Pichl, *Georg Schönerer und die Entwicklung des Alldeutschtums in der Ostmark*, 6 vols. (Oldenburg, 1938), vol. 5, 234.

[107] On the dispute between Wolf and Schönerer, see Pichl, *Georg Schönerer*, vol. 5, 358–72.

[108] AKIEB S185.810.45. See Friedrich Meyer's request, at the beginning of May 1909, that the Deutsch-Evangelische Wehrschatz donate money to the *Alldeutsche Tageblatt*, the newspaper of the Pan-Germans.

[109] Ibid. Meyer added, "the movement also has fallen into the background for Hasse; the same is true of Samassa."

man nation. In 1910, Paul Samassa, a prominent member of the Pan-German League in Germany and perhaps the most important link between Pan-Germans in the empire and in the Dual Monarchy, argued in *The Nationality Conflict of the Habsburg State* that Los von Rom should have been abandoned as soon as it became evident that the movement could not win over the lower classes. Instead, it had created yet another division among an already torn German nation.[110] Samassa's criticism reflected a growing disenchantment among Pan-German League leaders with the Los von Rom movement. In October 1898, the Pan-German League of imperial Germany had agreed to make support for Los von Rom a matter to be decided by individual members; but as an organization it would not support the movement publicly or financially. Tactical considerations dictated this official distance: the Pan-German League did not wish to alienate Catholics in the German empire.[111] Nevertheless, in the early years a strong personal union between prominent members of the Pan-German League and the Los von Rom movement existed. Ernst Hasse, the chairman of the Pan-German League, supported the movement as did J. F. Lehmann, Friedrich Hopf, Joachim Petzold, Paul Samassa, and Graf du Moulin-Eckart.[112] But this faction lost power with the ascendancy of Heinrich Class, who became chairman in 1908. An uncompromising racist, he considered antiultramontanism a disorder of a nationalist ideology grown old. Youth, he maintained, recognized the Jews to be the real enemy of the German people.[113] This idea was shared by a number of integral nationalists in Austria initially sympathetic to Los von Rom, among them Adolf Hitler. In *Mein Kampf*, Hitler would later criticize the movement for its inability to address the lower classes, for its halfhearted attempt to bring about historical change through the parliamentary system, and for its directing national attention away from the group that he too believed to be the true enemy of the German people.[114] But even before the outbreak of World War I, these criticisms had become commonplace among Pan-Germans in both empires.

Finally, financial problems also contributed to the demise of Los von Rom. Most of the Protestant league's annual investment in Los von Rom (between RM 200,000 and 300,000) covered the salaries of vicars from the German empire. Since the movement did not enjoy

[110] Samassa, *Der Völkerstreit im Habsburgerstaat*, 67–69.

[111] On the Pan-German League and the Los von Rom movement, see Class, *Wider den Strom*, 49, 77–78.

[112] Ibid. See also Albertin, *Nationalismus und Protestantismus*, 105–7, and, for Hasse's position, 101–5. On Hopf, see Eley, *Reshaping the German Right*, 245.

[113] Class, *Wider den Strom*, 88, 130.

[114] Adolf Hitler, *Mein Kampf* (Munich, 1940), 118–28 (chapter on Los von Rom).

official support, it could not draw on tax revenues and was therefore forced to solicit contributions. But when the movement began to stagnate, contributions slowed as well. Between 1903 and 1906, stopgap measures kept the movement above water, but in 1907 the league found itself in the midst of a financial crisis.[115] On 4 March 1907, Meyer considered the financial crisis so serious that the question had to be put "whether the league wants to continue its work in Austria or not."[116] In the following month, the league agreed to continue bankrolling Los von Rom and resolved to raise RM 300,000 by the end of the year. But by August, barely half of that amount had been raised.[117] Faced "with a declaration of bankruptcy in front of all Germany," Meyer threatened repeatedly to resign.[118] Although it did not come to that, the Protestant League was forced to decentralize its financing of the movement. Henceforth the league's provincial organizations shouldered the financial burden.[119] That, however, meant the end of the ideological unity of Los von Rom, the decline in Meyer's and Bräunlich's influence, and, consequently, the movement's political collapse. Less interested in Pan-German projects, the provincial organizations of the Protestant League confined themselves to paying the salaries of pastors.[120] Ironically, as the Protestant League became a mass organization in imperial Germany, its money, and much of its energy, had already been spent on an integral nationalist project to create a "spiritual Pan-Germany"—on a project that, for all its promise, ended as a failure.

[115] In 1903, a special "war chest" was founded in order to finance the struggle against ultramontanism. Members of the Protestant League were called upon to donate $\frac{1}{2}$% of their income, 1% of their property upon death, and 1% of their inheritance. See AKIEB S185.810.45 "Deutsch-Evangelischer Wehrschatz," Easter, 1903.

[116] AKIEB S185.810.25 "Verhandlungsnachweis über die Sitzung des Ausschusses zur Förderung der evangelischen Kirche in Österreich," 4.3.1907.

[117] Ibid., 28.10.1907. The decision to raise RM 300,000 was taken at a session of the Gesamtvorstand on 3 April 1907.

[118] Ibid. On Meyer's resignation threats, see Otto Everling and Friedrich Meyer to the executive committees of the provincial organizations of the Protestant League, 28.12.1908, in a box with library call number B42.428 in the library of the Evangelische Bund in Bensheim.

[119] See also AKIEB S185.810.25 "Verhandlungsnachweis über die Sitzung des Ausschusses zur Förderung der evangelischen Kirche in Österreich," 28.10.1907, and "Verhandlungsnachweis über die Sitzung der Vertreter der Hauptvereinsvorstände," 5.2.1908.

[120] Even this low level of support was difficult to maintain. In 1912, one year after Meyer's death, the committee was forced to reduce its expenditures further still. AKIEB S185.810.25 "Verhandlungsbericht über die Sitzung des Hauptausschusses zur Förderung der evangelischen Kirche in Österreich," 10.1.1912.

Conclusion _____

ALTHOUGH unified politically, the German empire of 1871 was a deeply divided state. The divisions within Germany—whether between religious groups or social classes—shaped the way Germans imagined their nation and constructed their national identity. Although we are used to thinking of national identity as a relatively coherent body of ideas, sentiments, and prejudices, this study has argued that national ideas made sense to different groups in society not by a generalized notion of what the nation is but by an appeal to the historical memories and experiences of disparate groups within the nation. As a consequence, cultural divisions within the national state influenced not only the formal contents of nationalist ideology but, equally important, the function of German nationalism. In Germany, popular nationalism divided as much as it unified society.

Historians have not always seen German nationalism in this way. In a classic and extremely influential article entitled "The Problem of the German National State," Wolfgang Sauer argued that the "paradox" of "sectional" conflicts in the new national state can be solved when we understand that "the genius of Bismarck" manipulated them in such a way that their effect was actually to integrate society.

> In case the conflict was many-sided (and that was the case in imperial Germany), the majority of the conflicting powers could be rallied around a common flag and led against the minority, assuming that the minority was strong enough to seem to be a danger and yet too weak to really be one. In this way the majority was subject to an admittedly questionable integration process, and even the minority underwent a kind of secondary integration process; for although it was attacked, it was forced to remain in the general community.[1]

Sauer placed conflicts (between liberals and Catholics, Germans and Poles, bourgeois and working class) within the context of nationalism and nation-building. That was the strength of his argument. But Sauer also assumed that conflicts were easily manipulated, turned off and on at Bismarck's will, and therefore ultimately stabilizing. Yet, as we have seen, the myriad affinities and antagonisms in the Kaiserreich were rarely that malleable. The end of the Kulturkampf in 1878 did not lead, as Sauer asserted, "almost without pause" to an anti-

[1] Wolfgang Sauer, "Das Problem des deutschen Nationalstaates," in *Moderne deutsche Sozialgeschichte*, ed. Hans Ulrich Wehler, (Cologne, 1966), 430.

socialist position; for not only did antisocialist sentiment predate 1878, but the confessional animosities that underlay the Kulturkampf persisted well past the preliminary diplomatic peace between church and state. Confessional animosities, more than merely the eccentric apprehensions of a few men who might have been more tolerant, reflected long historical memories, deep social and political conflicts. They were not incidental to German nationalism but the thing itself.

It would make more sense to see the empire's shifting affinities and antagonisms in the context of a slow, unstable process of nation-building characterized by demographic pressures for integration, by state intervention, and by popular mobilization. The demographic shifts that brought Catholics and Protestants into common space prefigured, far more than Bismarck's policy, the recrudescence of confessional conflict in the Kaiserreich. Moreover, the habits of mind, the cultural assumptions, the imperatives of ideology that reinforced confessional antagonism both antedated and outlived Bismarck's strategies of manipulation. This is not to argue that the state did not have an impact. Certainly, the Kulturkampf drastically changed the confessional and political landscape in Germany, creating, among other phenomena, a party system rigidly segregated along religious lines. Conversely, the state could also help heal confessional wounds, if usually at the price of opening new ones. The imperial government's anti-Polish Germanization program did, for example, contribute to the interconfessional cohesion of the German community in the eastern borderlands. Still, this did not happen by a simple sleight of hand. Rather, the most important pressure on the Center party to tolerate certain kinds of Germanization measures came from German Catholic constituents in Silesia, Posen, and West Prussia—from below, not from above—and reflected that constituency's growing animosity toward their Polish coreligionists. Like confessional antagonism generally, ethnic antagonisms in the nationally mixed areas were too rooted in local life to be directed now one way, now another.

A second, equally influential attempt to argue that sectional differences were ultimately stabilizing rests on fundamentally different assumptions. M. Rainer Lepsius, in his essay "The Party System and Social Structure," argued that the German political system revealed a long-term tendency toward stability, and that this stability was a function, not of the malleability of sectional conflicts, but of their deep-rootedness. Lepsius focused on the cultural and political milieu of the major political groups: Catholics, Conservatives, Liberals, and (after 1890) Social Democrats. "The political parties," he argued, "remained fixated on their initially mobilized community of adherents [*Gesinnungsgemeinschaften*] and consequently ritualized and perpetuated conflict, which then shaped and hindered the process of democratiza-tion."[2] Although Lepsius fixed his analytical gaze on political parties and their respective milieus, his insight may also be germane to our problem.[3] Confessional conflict in a modern society could then be explained as ritual activity whose principal function was to shore up cohesion within groups.

Without doubt, anti-Catholic sentiment gave Protestants, otherwise divided, common cause. As Willibald Beyschlag once put it, by wav-ing "the flag of resistance against the Roman flood" one could "awaken the living Protestant spirit in all areas of national life."[4] In the Catholic milieu, confessional conflict served a similar function, papering over differences—economic, social, and political—within the Center party. But was the antagonism merely ritualistic, pre-scribed behavior acted out according to a well-established, long-since memorized, script? I have argued that there was more to it: that con-fessional conflict was dynamic, changing in content as well as in form, and that it implied more than simply the persistence of pre-modern patterns of thought. Rather, I have tried to show that such conflict was a part, an integral part, of the general process of modern-ization, that the people involved, far from possessing an archaic worldview, often perceived themselves as forward-looking, and that the central dilemma—national unity in a polity with a divided memory—posed, and poses, a peculiarly modern problem.

Moreover, to confine religious conflict to a ritual whose purpose was to shore up subcultural cohesion and thus contribute to the main-tenance of an undemocratic social stability denies the disruptive po-tential of this conflict. Imperial Germany, it is true, was not Ulster. Protestants and Catholics may have been suspicious of one another, they may have loathed one another, but Germans religiously opposed did not, as a result, terrorize one another. As a rule, Protestants did not storm Catholic holy sites; Catholics did not desecrate Protestant churches. Yet the import of the antagonism should not therefore be underestimated, for it profoundly influenced social, cultural, and po-litical life. At the community level, it constricted contact between groups, defined whom one married, where one shopped, what one read; culturally, it determined worldviews, constructed, in part, against the "other"; and politically, it predetermined party predilec-

[2] Lepsius, "Parteiensystem und Sozialstruktur" 62. For a criticism of the utility of the milieu thesis for understanding the formation of the Catholic subculture, see Margaret Lavinia Anderson, *Windthorst*, 192–95.

[3] For reflections on the ritualized nature of confessional conflict in an earlier period of German history, see François, *Die unsichtbare Grenze*, 166.

[4] Beyschlag, *Zur Entstehungsgeschichte*, 12–13.

tions (surely as much as class) and informed the programmatic platforms of the empire's political parties. The exigencies of confessional conflict also underlay political Protestantism and political Catholicism.

When focusing on political Protestantism in the empire, most historians have concentrated their researches either on the conservative aspects of the alliance of throne and altar or on the Christian Socialist movement. If the latter has been especially well researched, the former was of considerably greater moment. In imperial Germany, the Protestant churches constituted a pillar of conservative order, buttressing monarchical institutions, upholding authoritarian principles against democratic change and radical thought. Yet neither Christian Socialism nor the alliance of throne and altar exhausted the potential of political Protestantism. The largest lay organization in Protestant Germany, the Protestant League worried more about the Catholic question than about the "social question," and was more concerned with combating ultramontanism than with upholding the deferential politics of the alliance of throne and altar. Although initially bound by sentiment and ideology to the state, the league, by the turn of the century, increasingly embraced radical expressions of popular nationalism. Defining the nation as the *Volk*, the leaders of the Protestant League gave place and priority to the people, conceived of as an ethnic community, above the monarch and his ministers. Consequently, not deference to dynastic interests but dedication and commitment to the national caused defined the politics of the league.

The Protestant League, ostensibly a purely religious organization, pursued politics energetically, if clandestinely, and often against the aims of the imperial government. Where the government attempted to integrate Catholics, the Protestant League resisted; where Conservatives attempted to conciliate the Catholic Center in order to achieve agreement on tax and tariff policies, the league, appealing to Protestant principles, inflamed confessional antagonism anew. Even international relations were not beyond the political purview of the league. Despite being censured by throne and altar in both Berlin and Vienna, the Protestant League lent its ideological, organizational, and financial support to Los von Rom, a radical, even messianic nationalist movement that attempted to create a spiritual Pan-Germany in which national and religious identity would, as Providence demanded, be congruent.

Thus, far from being merely a conservative force, political Protestantism also harbored the potential for radical nationalism. Indeed, for some German Protestants, nationalism was not an ersatz for, but part of, religious belief. Often, religion is conceived as an intermediary loyalty between citizen and nation, as one of a number of concentric rings—self, village, parish, state, nation—each advancing circle defining identity with increasing intensity as modernization occurs.[5] But for many Protestants, there was no necessary contradiction between religious and national identity. Rather, religious belief supported national identity, provisioning it with memory, myth, and tradition. In its antiultramontane inflection, Protestantism not only reinforced national identity but, equally important, radicalized the discourse of German nationalism.[6] It radicalized when it appealed to an exclusive vision of what it meant to be German, when, for example, Willibald Beyschlag imagined German history to be the history of the Protestant half, Germany's future destiny to be the completion of the Reformation.

In a religiously divided national state, based however imperfectly on the principle of religious parity, this was a volatile, potentially disruptive vision. As an appeal to nationalism, it neither unified nor homogenized but rather divided and aggravated tensions within the nation. Hardly a German peculiarity, this internally divisive side of nationalism constitutes a central, if ill-understood, aspect of nationalism more generally. As the anthropologist Katherine Verdery has argued, nation, rather than being seen as something fixed, should be seen as a symbol, and nationalism, rather than being perceived as a singular tradition, should be analyzed "as having multiple meanings, offered as alternatives and competed over by different groups maneuvering to capture the symbol's definition and its legitimating effects."[7] Though drawn from the study of nationalism in eastern Europe, her insight cuts to the quick of the function of nationalism in the German empire. Burdened by a long history of conflict, the tradition of German nationalism bequeathed to the Kaiserreich not only a unifying ideology but also a legacy of contention over the fundamental question of what it meant to be German.

It is in this context that I would suggest that historians place the vexed question of Catholic integration into the national culture of the German empire: not as a gradual assent to a dominant ideology, but as a history of contention over the definition, and the legitimating effects, of the nation. Here, it is especially necessary to measure one's words. Catholics in imperial Germany rarely questioned the legit-

[5] For a critique of this approach in another context, see Peter Sahlins, *Boundaries: The Making of France and Spain in the Pyrenees* (Berkeley and Los Angeles, 1989), 110–13.

[6] On Protestantism and the radicalization of nineteenth-century German nationalism, see Altgeld, *Katholizismus, Protestantismus, Judentum.*

[7] Katherine Verdery, "Whither 'Nation' and 'Nationalism'?" *Daedalus* 122, no. 3 (Summer 1993): 39.

imacy of the national state as it was founded in 1871. From the start, the empire claimed their loyalties and affections. At any time, they would have fought for it and died for it. And at no time did they question their own German national identity. Yet they constructed that national identity differently, appealing to different traditions, separate memories, another history. Moreover, the appeal to an identity differently constructed made sense to Catholics precisely because it was put in the language of a religious culture in many ways distinct from the culture across the confessional divide. Within the parameters of this culture, Catholics combined religious and national identity, and, to a certain extent, wrested German nationalism from its exclusive association with Protestant tradition. Moreover, it would be a mistake to see Catholic integration as a one-sided affair, for it also brought forth a reaction among Protestants in the empire. Radical nationalists and Protestant Leaguers contested the conditions, even the necessity, of Catholic integration, arguing, in some ways correctly, that integration would change the German nation, and that it would attenuate the significance of Germany's Protestant history, identity, and mission. Moreover, the popular nationalist reaction against Catholic integration rendered the process of integration precarious and constituted an important pressure pushing the Catholic Center ever more to the right, ever closer to the government, tying it ever more tightly to official nationalist positions.

From the start, integration was the crux of the problem. Religious division, which Kant once believed would disappear with the passage of time, deepened in nineteenth-century Germany because of, not despite, social and demographic, cultural and political forces pushing for integration. This integration was extremely uneven, marked by disparities in the pace of secularization, by regional differences, by social conflicts, conflicts between city and country and between elite and popular culture. The unevenness of this integration constituted the social background for the renewal of confessional conflict in the nineteenth century. But this conflict would have remained a matter for local quarrels, small-town controversies, and regional rivalries were it not culturally and ideologically bound to issues of national identity and subsumed under the logic of nationalism. For nationalism, as the antagonism between Protestants and Catholics suggests, not only smoothed over conflicts but also sharpened them; it gave groups long existing in tension a new vocabulary with which to explore their differences; and it lent to those differences a new, more modern urgency.

This is not to deny that genuine integration occurred. Between 1870 and 1914, one could, in fact, observe something of the slow, irregular

CONCLUSION   **239**

creation of a common national culture across confessional lines. But
this was not a culture of openness, of tolerance for religious difference. Rather it rested on a rickety structure of limited mutual interests, some fellow feeling, and shared antagonisms. It was also more
advanced between Catholics and Conservatives: both parties wished
to maintain confessional exclusivity in schools, to uphold high grain
tariffs, to protect public morality against the evils of modernity; and
both shared a commitment to the dynastic status quo and to a program of official nationalism that included antipathy toward ethnic minorities and antagonism toward the revolutionary ideas of social democracy. In Germany, then, confessional peace did not happen as a
result of liberal tolerance. Quite the contrary.

Does the German experience therefore suggest a *Sonderweg*, a special path veering from traditions of pluralistic integration and liberal
tolerance that allegedly characterized the histories of western European democracies, in particular England? I would argue the reverse: that German nationalism—precisely because it both integrated
and divided—mirrored a familiar historical experience, though perhaps not that of England. With an eye more to the twentieth than to
the nineteenth century, Clifford Geertz has observed: "Thus, in apparent paradox (though, in fact, it has been a nearly universal occur-
rence in the new states) the move toward national unity intensified
group tensions within the society by raising settled cultural forms out
of their particular contexts, expanding them into general allegiances,
and politicizing them."[8] The universality of such tensions in the
twentieth century among the new states suggests that they should
not be explained in their nineteenth-century German context by an
exclusive appeal to German particularities. It may be, after all, that
imperial Germany reflected stresses and strains typical not of old nations but of new national states.

[8] Geertz, "After the Revolution," in Geertz, *The Interpretation of Cultures*, 245.

Sources

Contents

I. Archives

Bensheim in Hessen

ARCHIV DES KONFESSIONSKUNDLICHEN INSTITUTS DES EVANGELISCHEN BUNDES (AKIEB)
AKIEB PL Private Library. Mitteilungen vom Ausschuss zur Förderung der evangelischen kirche in Österreich
AKIEB S185.810 Los von Rom Bewegung (= Nachlaß Paul Bräunlich)
AKIEB S500.9 Evangelischer Bund. Reichsgeschäftsstelle (1886–1918)

Berlin

ARCHIV DES DIAKONISCHEN WERKES DER EKD (ADW)
ADW CA 2188 Nachlaß Johannes Hesekiel

EVANGELISCHES ZENTRALARCHIV (EZB)
EZB 7/423–24 Los von Rom Bewegung
EZB 7/1843–51 Die . . . Verhandlungen über die Teilungen der größeren Parochien und Vermehrung geistlicher Kräfte, insbesondere in den von Polonismus bedrohten Provinzen, 1883–1928
EZB 7/3690–96 Konfessionelle Verhältnisse in Preußen
EZB 7/3890–93 Evangelischer Bund
EZB 7/3934 Gesellschaft zur Ausbreitung des Evangeliums

GEHEIMES STAATSARCHIV PREUßISCHER KULTURBESITZ (GStAPK)
GStAPK 30, 841–42 Verein deutscher Katholiken

Bonn

POLITISCHES ARCHIV DES AUSWÄRTIGEN AMTES (PAAA)
PAAA R319–25 Die polnische Frage
PAAA R1426–36 Die Centrumspartei
PAAA R2213–21 Die allgemeine deutsche Politik

PAAA R2296–98 Der deutsche Flottenverein
PAAA R2564 Der Evangelische Bund
PAAA R4057–4121 Polnische Agitation, 1886–1914
PAAA R4127–70 Zusammenstellung über die polnische Tagesliteratur, 1892–
  1915
PAAA R8528–45 Allgemeine Angelegenheiten Österreichs
PAAA R8665–71 Kirchen und Schulangelegenheiten Österreich-Ungarns
PAAA R9316–23 Aufhebung des Jesuitengesetzes

Freiburg

BUNDESARCHIV/MILITÄRARCHIV FREIBURG (BA/MA)
BA/MA RM3/v 9914–9919 Deutscher Flottenverein

ERZBISCHÖFLICHES ARCHIV FREIBURG (EAF)
EAF B2/28 Konfessionelle und religiöse Beschwerden

Karlsruhe

GENERALLANDESARCHIV KARLSRUHE (GLA)
GLA 48/6129 Die Wahlagitation der Geistlichen, 1883–1904
GLA 69/ Landesausschuß des deutschen Seevereins
GLA 235/207 Petition gegen die Zulassung von Männerorden, 1902
GLA 235/14901 Wahlagitation der Geistlichen
GLA 236/14880 Wahlagitation, 1887

LANDESKIRCHLICHES ARCHIV KARLSRUHE (LKAK)
LKAK GA/4434 Fronleichnamsprozessionen
LKAK GA/4934 Angriffe gegen die Evangelischen
LKAK GA/Anzeigen und Beschwerden gegen katholische Geistliche

Koblenz

BUNDESARCHIV KOBLENZ (BAK)
BAK NL16 Nachlaß Georg Hertling
BAK NL22 Nachlaß Bernhard von Bülow
BAK NL176 Nachlaß Carl Herold

LANDESHAUPTARCHIV KOBLENZ (LHAK)
LHAK 403/7046–54 Die Aufsicht auf die politischen Vereine, Polenbewegung,
  1895–1909
LHAK 403/8806 Verhalten der Geistlichen . . . bei den Wahlen, 1851–1911
LHAK 403/9661 Deutscher Flottenverein
LHAK 403/16003–9 Wallfahrten und Prozessionen
LHAK 13528–39 Polenbewegung, 1910–14

Köln

STADTARCHIV KÖLN (STAK)
StAK/B1006 Nachlaß Carl Bachem

Ludwigsburg

STAATSARCHIV LUDWIGSBURG (StAL)
StAL E210/305–60 Konfessionelle Streitigkeiten, 1825–1922

München

BAYERISCHES HAUPTSTAATSARCHIV (BHStA)
BHStA GS/1158 Bayerische Gesandtschaft, Berlin
BHStA MA/77693–94 Deutscher Flottenverein

BAYERISCHES HAUPTSTAATSARCHIV BESTAND KRIEGSMINISTERIUM (BHStA MKr.)
BHStA MKr. 774 Deutscher Flottenverein
BHStA MKr. 1124–36 Gesetz über die Friedenspräsenzstärke des deutschen
Heeres, 1892–1913

Speyer

PFÄLZISCHE LANDESBIBLIOTHEK (PLB)
PLB/Nachlaß Ernst Lieber

Stuttgart

HAUPTSTAATSARCHIV STUTTGART (HStAS)
HStAS E14/14344–45 Württembergischer Landesverband des deutschen Flottenvereins, 1900–1918

LANDESKIRCHLICHES ARCHIV STUTTGART (LKAS)
LKAS A26/413 Beschwerden über die Eingriffe der katholischen Kirche in die
Rechte der evangelischen Kirche, 1844–1923

Trier

BISTUMSARCHIV TRIER (BAT)
BAT Nr. 105 Nachlaß Peter Reuß
BAT Nr. 108 Nachlaß Felix Korum

II. Newspapers

Alldeutsches Tageblatt
Allgemeine Evangelische Kirchenzeitung
Amtsblatt des Evangelischen Konsistoriums (Württemberg)
Deutsches Wochenblatt
Deutsche Wacht
Germania
Katholische Rundschau
Kölnische Volkszeitung
Neue preußische Zeitung (Kreuz-zeitung)
Die Ostmark
Posener Tageblatt

Stuttgarter Katholisches Sonntagsblatt
Vaterland

III. Journals

Bonifacius-Broschüren
Broschüren-Cyclus für das katholische Deutschland
Der Christenbote
Die Christliche Welt
Daheim
Deutsche Schriftstellerzeitung
Deutsches Wochenblatt
Deutsch-Evangelische Blätter (DEB)
Deutschland
Evangelische Kirchenzeitung
Evangelischer Bund zur Wahrung der deutsch-protestantischen Interessen. Monatsblatt für die Mitglieder
Die Gartenlaube
Historisches Jahrbuch
Historische Zeitschrift
Historisch-politische Blätter für das Katholische Deutschland
Hochland: Monatsschrift für alle Gebiete des Wissens der Literatur und Kunst
Illustrierte Blätter
Der Katholik
Kirchliche Korrespondenz für die deutsche Tagespresse
Mitteilungen aus dem Verein zur Abwehr des Antisemitismus
Monatskorrespondenz für die Mitglieder des Evangelischen Bundes
Im Neuen Reich
Pastoralblatt für die Diözese Rottenburg
Preußische Jahrbücher
Reden und Vorträge bei der Generalversammlungen des Evangelischen Bundes
Der Scherer
Statistische Mitteilungen aus den deutschen Landeskirchen vom Jahre 1883 bis 1912
Stimmen aus Maria Laach
Theologisches Jahrbuch
Vorstandsblatt des Evangelischen Bundes
Die Wartburg: Deutsch-evangelische Wochenschrift
Württembergische Bundesblätter
Die Zeit

IV. Statistics, Handbooks, and Reference Works

Gesetz und Verordnungsblatt der Evangelischen Kirche in Baden (GVEKB).
Handbuch für die Statistik Württembergs.
Kalkoff, Hermann, ed. *Nationalliberale Parlamentarier 1867–1917 des Reichstages und der Einzellandtage.* Berlin, 1917.
Keiter, Heinrich, ed. *Katholischer Literaturkalender.* Regensburg, 1887–1914.

Krose, H. A. *Konfessionsstatistik Deutschlands*. Freiburg, 1904.

Kürschners Literaturkalender.

Mann, Bernhard. *Biographisches Handbuch für das preußische Abgeordnetenhaus, 1867–1918*. Düsseldorf, 1988.

Österreichische Statistik.

Religionszugehörigkeit in Baden in den letzten 100 Jahren. Ed. Badisches Statistisches Landesamt. Karlsruhe, 1927.

Specht, Fritz. *Die Reichstagswahlen von 1867 bis 1897*. Berlin, 1898.

Statistische Mitteilungen aus den deutschen Landeskirchen vom Jahre 1883 bis 1913.

Statistik des deutschen Reiches.

Statistisches Handbuch für den preußischen Staat.

Statistisches Jahrbuch für das deutsche Reich.

Statistisches Jahrbuch für den preußischen Staat.

Verzeichnis der Haupt- und Zweigvereine des Evangelischen Bundes, 1906. Leipzig, 1906.

Vierteljahreshefte zur Statistik des Deutschen Reichs.

Württembergische Jahrbücher für Statistik und Landeskunde.

V. Other Primary Sources

(Abbreviation: Flugschriften des Evangelischen Bundes = FSEB)

Aktenstücke in Sachen: Evangelischer Bund gegen Bülow (FSEB Nr. 149). Leipzig, 1898.

Altkemper, Johannes. *Deutschtum und Polentum in politisch-konfessioneller Bedeutung*. Leipzig, 1910.

Bachem, Carl. *Zentrum, Katholische Weltanschauung und praktische Politik. Zugleich eine Antwort auf die jüngste Broschüre von Geheimrat Roeren: Zentrum und Kölner Richtung*. Krefeld, 1914.

Bär, Max. *Die Bamberger bei Posen. Zugleich ein Beitrag zur Geschichte der Polonisierungsbestrebungen in der Provinz Posen*. Posen, 1882.

Bärwinkel, Richard. *Aus meinem Leben*. Erfurt, 1904.

———. *Hat der Evangelische Bund politische Aufgaben?* Leipzig, 1904.

Bauer, Karl. *Carlo Borromeo und seine Zeit. Ein Spiegelbild für unsere Gegenwart*. Halle, 1910.

Baumgarten, Hermann. *Historische und politische Aufsätze und Reden*. Ed. Erich Marcks. Strasbourg, 1894.

———. *Römische Triumphe* (FSEB Nr. 2). Halle, 1887.

Beck, Hermann. *Die religiöse Volksliteratur der evangelischen Kirche Deutschlands in einem Abriß ihrer Geschichte*. Gotha, 1891.

Berghahn, Volker R., and Wilhelm Deist, eds. *Rüstung im Zeichen der wilhelminischen Weltpolitik. Grundlegende Dokumente, 1890–1914*. Düsseldorf, 1988.

Betta, O. [Ottomar Bettziech]. *Deutschland und die Juden. Oder der Juda-Jesuitismus*. Berlin, 1876.

Beyschlag, Willibald. *Aus meinem Leben*. 2 vols. Halle, 1896–99.

———. *Der Friedensschluß zwischen Deutschland und Rom*. Leipzig, 1887.

──────. *Zur Entstehungsgeschichte des Evangelischen Bundes*. Posthumous. Berlin, 1926.

Blanckmeister, Franz. *Los von Rom im Königreich Sachsen*. Dresden, 1905.

Blume, E. *Was würde uns ein vollständiger Sieg Roms kosten?* (FSEB Nr. 19). Halle, 1888.

Bodenstein, Wilko Levin Graf von. *Der Evangelische Bund in Frankfurt, 2. Eröffnungsrede*. Leipzig, 1887.

Bodewig, Hartmann. *Geistliche Wahlbeeinflussung in ihrer Theorie und Praxis dargestellt*. Munich, 1909.

Böhtlingk, Arthur. *Noch Einmal. Römisch oder Deutsch?* Leipzig, 1904.

──────. *Die römische Gefahr und die Reichstagswahl*. Lörrach, 1903.

Bolanden, Konrad von [Josef Bischoff]. *Die Reichsfeinde*. Mainz, 1874.

──────. *Satan bei der Arbeit*. Heiligenstadt, 1908.

──────. *Die Sozialdemokraten und ihre Väter*. Mainz, 1894.

Braune, H. *Der Evangelische Bund in der Ostmark*. Leipzig, 1906.

Bräunlich, Paul. *Leo Taxils Teufelsschwindel*. Munich, 1910.

──────. *Meine Ausweisung aus Österreich. Bilder aus den Tagen der Zentrumsherrschaft in Deutschland und Österreich*. 5th ed. Munich, 1910.

──────. *Zentrum und Regierung im Kampf*. Leipzig, 1907.

Brodgut, Lobgot. *Das "wallende Blut" zur Wahrung der protestantischen Interessen. Zu Nutz und Frommen des Christenvolkes dargestellt*. 2d ed. Berlin, 1890.

Brück, Heinrich. *Die systematische Verunglimpfung der Sittenlehre des Hl. Alphons von Liguori*. Mainz, 1901.

Charakterkopf eines protestantischen Polemikers. Berlin, 1892.

Cisar, Ferdinand. *Chauvinismus eine Gefahr für den Österreichischen Protestantismus*. Erlangen, 1909.

Class, Heinrich [Daniel Fryman]. *Wenn ich der Kaiser wär*. 4th ed. Leipzig, 1913.

──────. *Wider den Strom*. Leipzig, 1932.

Controvers-Katechismus oder wahrheitsgemäße und leicht verständliche Darstellung der Unterscheidungslehre. Kempten, 1899.

Cramer, Wilhelm. *Die Erscheinungen und Heilungen in Marpingen*. 3d ed. Würzburg, 1879.

Dahn, Felix. "Kreuzfahrer-Lieder der Deutsch-Herren-Ritter in Preußen. Ein Cyklus." In *Gesammelte Werke*, 2d ser., vol. 6, 296–307. Leipzig, n.d.

Deissmann, D. A., et al. *Beiträge zur Weiterentwicklung der christlichen Religion*. Munich, 1905.

Delbrück, Hans. *Erinnerungen, Aufsätze und Reden*. Berlin, 1902.

Denifle, Heinrich. *Luther und Luthertum*. Mainz, 1904.

Deutscher Protestantismus und Kölnische Zeitung von einem deutschen Protestanten. Halle, 1908.

Diersberg, Heinrich Röder von. *Zur Klosterfrage in Baden*. Lahr, 1902.

Dietrich, Christian. *Kirchliche Fragen der Gegenwart*. N.p., 1887.

Dove, Alfred. *Ausgewählte Schriften*. Leipzig, 1898.

Drache, Richard. *Parität-Imparität. Eine staatsrechtliche Betrachtung* (FSEB Nr. 68). Leipzig, 1892.

Drews, Paul. *Das kirchliche Leben der Evangelisch-Lutherischen Landeskirche des Königreichs Sachsen.* Tübingen and Leipzig, 1902.

Droysen, Johann Gustav. *Briefwechsel.* 2 vols. Ed. Rudolf Hübner. Berlin and Leipzig, 1929.

———. *Politische Schriften.* Ed. Felix Gilbert. Munich and Berlin, 1933.

Egelhaaf, Gottlob. *Lebens-Erinnerungen.* Ed. Adolf Rapp. Stuttgart, 1960.

Englert, W. Ph. *Das Flottenproblem im Lichte der Sozialpolitik.* Paderborn, 1900.

Erzberger, Matthias. *Bilder aus dem Reichstagswahlkampf. Die Agitation der Zentrumsgegner, beleuchtet nach deren Wahlschriften.* Berlin, 1907.

———. *Der Kampf gegen den Katholizismus in der Ostmark.* Berlin, 1908.

———. *Der Toleranzantrag der Zentrumsfraktion des Reichstages.* Osnabrück, 1906.

Falke, Robert. *Fürst Bismarcks Stellung zum Christentum* (FSEB Nr. 160). Leipzig, 1899.

Falkenberg, Heinrich. *Wir Katholiken und die deutsche Literatur.* 4th ed. Bonn, 1909.

Fey, Carl. *Ultramontanismus und Patriotismus* (FSEB Nr. 51). Leipzig, 1891.

Freytag, Gustav. *Soll und Haben.* In *Gesammelte Werke,* vols. 4 and 5. Leipzig, 1887–88.

Generalversammlung der Katholiken Deutschlands. Stenographische Protokolle. Dortmund, 1896.

Gildemeister, J., and Heinrich von Sybel. *Der Heilige Rock zu Trier und die zwanzig anderen heiligen ungenähten Röcke.* Düsseldorf, 1844.

Gottschall, Rudolf. *Die deutsche Nationalliteratur des 19. Jahrhunderts.* 5th ed. 2 vols. Breslau, 1881.

Grassmann, Robert. *Auszüge aus der Moraltheologie des Heiligen Dr. Alphonsus Maria de Liguori und die furchtbare Gefahr dieser Moraltheologie für die Sittlichkeit der Völker.* Stettin, 1898.

Haberkamp, F. *Protestantismus und nationale Politik.* Halle, 1909.

Haffner, Paul. *Göthe's Dichtung.* Frankfurt a.M., 1903.

———. *Göthes Dichtung auf sittlichen Gehalt geprüft.* Frankfurt a.M., 1881.

Harnack, Adolf. *Das Wesen des Christentums.* Leipzig, 1900.

Hasse, Ernst. *Das deutsche Reich als Nationalstaat.* Munich, 1907.

———. *Die Zukunft des deutschen Volkstums.* Munich, 1907.

Hasse, Karl. *Handbuch der protestantischen Polemik gegen die Römisch-Katholische Kirche.* Leipzig, 1871.

Heiner, Franz. *Der sogenannte Toleranzantrag.* 2 vols. Mainz, 1902, 1904.

Hermens, Oskar. *Die gemeinsame Gefahr der evangelischen Kirche und der deutschen Nationalität in der Diaspora der deutschen Grenzmarken* (FSEB Nr. 112/114). Leipzig, 1895.

———. *Professor Harnacks Kaisersgeburtstagsrede 1907 erwogen von einem Mitgliede des Evangelischen Bundes* (FSEB Nr. 254). Leipzig, 1908.

Hermens, Oskar, and Oskar Kohlschmidt. *Ein protestantisches Taschenbuch. Ein Hülfsbüchlein in konfessionellen Streitfragen.* Leipzig, 1903–5.

Hettner, Hermann. *Geschichte der deutschen Literatur im achtzehnten Jahrhundert.* 2d ed. Vol. 1. Braunschweig, 1872.

————. *Schriften zur Literatur.* Ed. Jürgen Jahn. Berlin, 1959.

Die Hexenangst des Evangelischen Bundes vor den katholischen Klosterfrauen. Berlin, 1898.

Hieber, Johannes. *Der Toleranzantrag des Centrums.* Berlin, 1901.

Hitler, Adolf. *Mein Kampf.* Munich, 1940.

Hoensbroech, Paul Graf von. *Der Evangelische Bund und die Politik.* Leipzig, 1910.

————. *Der Toleranzantrag des Zentrums im Lichte der Toleranz der römisch-katholischen Kirche.* 3d. ed. Berlin, 1903.

Höniger, Robert. *Ansprache gehalten auf dem Deutschen Tag des Ostmarkenvereins zu Bromberg am 18. August 1907.* N.p., 1907.

Hülskamp, Franz. *1000 gute Bücher der katholischen deutschen Zunge empfohlen.* 3d ed. Münster, 1882.

Hüttenrauch, H. *Der Evangelischee Bund.* Hamburg, 1911.

Janssen, Johannes. *Frankreichs Rheingelüste und deutschfeindliche Politik in früheren Jahrhunderten.* 2d ed. Freiburg i. Br., 1883.

————. *Geschichte des deutschen Volkes seit dem Ausgang des Mittelalters.* 8 vols. Freiburg i. Br., 1879–94.

Kahl, William. *Die Bedeutung des Toleranzantrags für Staat und evangelische Kirche.* Halle, 1902.

Kant, Immanuel. *Zum ewigen Frieden.* Ed. Theodor Valentiner. Stuttgart, 1954.

Keiter, Heinrich. *Katholische Erzähler der Neuzeit.* Paderborn, 1880.

Keiter, Heinrich [Georg Kampfmuth]. *Konfessionelle Brunnenvergiftung. Die wahre Schmach des Jahrhunderts.* Regensburg and Leipzig, 1896.

————. *Theorie des Romans und der Erzählkunst.* Paderborn, 1876.

————. *Zeitgenössische Katholische Dichter Deutschlands.* Paderborn, 1884.

Ketteler, Wilhelm Emmanuel von. *Sämtliche Werke und Briefe.* Ed. Erwin Iserloh et al. Vol. 1, pt. 2, *Schriften, Aufsätze und Reden 1867–1870.* Mainz, 1978.

Klöckner, Alois. *Die Konfession der sozialdemokratischen Wählerschaft 1907.* Mönchen-Gladbach, 1913.

Klopp, Onno. *Der König Friedrich II. und die deutsche Nation.* Schaffhausen, 1860.

————. *Tilly, Gustav Adolf und die Zerstörung von Magdeburg.* Berlin, 1895.

Kralik, Richard von. *Ein Jahr Katholischer Literaturbewegung.* Regensburg, 1910.

————. *Unsere deutschen Klassiker und der Katholizismus.* Hamm i. Westfalen, 1903.

Kremers, Hermann. *Martin Luther, der deutsche Christ* (FSEB Nr. 125). Leipzig, 1895.

————. *Sammeln und Zerstreuen! Bericht und Rede bei der 44. Versammlung des rheinischen Hauptvereins des Evangelischen Bundes in Bonn am 23. u. 24. Oktober 1933.* Bonn, 1933.

Lange, Friedrich. *Reines Deutschtum. Grundzüge einer nationalen Weltanschauung.* Berlin, 1904.

Lechler, Karl Joh. Friedrich. *Der Evangelische Bund und die kirchlichen Parteien.* Stuttgart, 1887.

Lenz, H. K. *Alban Stolz und die Juden.* Münster, 1893.

Lenz, Max. *Kleine historische Schriften.* 2 vols. Munich, 1922.

Leusche, Georg. "Los von Rom." In *Realencyklopaedie für protestantische Theologie und Kirche*, vol. 29, 20–34. Leipzig, 1913.

Leuschner, Coelestin. *Das deutsche Reich und die kirchliche Frage* (FSEB Nr. 87). Leipzig, 1893.

———. *Römische Angriffe und Evangelische Abwehr* (FSEB Nr. 81). Leipzig, 1893.

———. *Die unserer Kirche gebührende Stellung im öffentlichen Leben* (FSEB Nr. 55). Leipzig, 1981.

Lipsius, Richard Adelbert. *Zehn Jahre preußisch-deutscher Kirchenpolitik* (FSEB Nr. 11). Halle, 1887.

Majunke, Paul, Josef Galland, and Josef Krebs [Freunde der Wahrheit, pseud.] eds. *Geschichtslügen. Eine Widerlegung landläufiger Entstellungen auf dem Gebiet der Geschichte*. Rev. ed. Paderborn, 1893.

Merx, Adalbert. *Über die heutigen Aufgaben des Evangelischen Bundes*. Leipzig, 1892.

Meyer, Elard Hugo. *Badisches Volksleben im 19. Jahrhundert*. Strasbourg, 1900.

Meyer, Friedrich. "Christentum und Germanen." In *Beiträge zur Weiterentwicklung der christlichen Religion*, ed. D. A. Deissmann et al. Munich, 1905.

———. *Heroldsrufe und Hammerschläge. Ein deutsch-evangelisches Vermächtnis*. Berlin, 1929.

———. *Die Sammlung der Evangelischen* (FSEB Nr. 156). Leipzig, 1898.

Mirbt, Carl. *Der Toleranzantrag des Zentrums*. Leipzig, 1901.

Mommsen, Theodor. *Reden und Aufsätze*. Berlin, 1905.

Moulin-Eckart, Richard Graf du. *Deutschtum und Rom*. Munich, 1904.

Münzer, Otto, ed. *Des Landwirths Liederbuch. Ostmarkenausgabe*. Lissa, 1906.

Muth, Karl. *Die literarischen Aufgaben der deutschen Katholiken*. Mainz, 1899.

Muth, Karl [pseud. Vermumdus]. *Steht die katholische Belletristik auf die Höhe der Zeit*. 2d ed. Mainz, 1898.

Naumann, Friedrich. *Demokratie und Kaisertum*. 4th ed. Berlin, 1905.

Nestle, Eberhard. *Meine Antwort an die württembergische Zentrumspresse in Sachen der Fronleichnamsprozession*. 2d ed. Ulm, 1895.

Nippold, Friedrich. *Die Anfänge des Evangelischen Bundes und seiner Pressetätigkeit*. Berlin, 1897.

Nolt, H. von. *Wie hätte es so weit kommen können? Eine kurze Frage und eine lange Antwort*. Berlin, 1892.

Norrenberg, Peter. *Allgemeine Literaturgeschichte*. 2d ed. Ed. Karl Macke Vol. 2. Münster i.W., 1898.

Offenbacher, Martin. *Konfession und soziale Schichtung*. Tübingen, 1901.

Offener Brief an die "römisch-katholischen Erzbischöfe und Bischöfe im deutschen Reich" (FSEB Nr. 40). Leipzig, 1890.

Pachtler, Georg Michael, S. J. [pseud. Annuaris Osseg]. *Der Europäische Militarismus*. Amberg, 1875.

Pastor, Ludwig Freiherr von. *Aus dem Leben des Geschichtschreibers Johannes Janssen*. Cologne, 1929.

Perrone, Johannes. *Der Protestantismus und die Glaubensregel. Dritter oder geschichtlich-sittlicher Theil*. Regensburg and Mainz, 1856.

Pieper, P. *Kirchliche Statistik Deutschlands*. Freiburg i. Br., 1889.

Pollack, Paul. *Zur Entwicklung des katholischen Ordenswesens im Deutschen Reich* (FSEB Nr. 266). Halle, 1909.

Rassek, Richard. *Warum erteilt ein Teil des oberschlesischen Klerus den Beicht- und Kommunion-Unterricht in der deutschen Sprache.* Beuthen, 1902.

Rauter, Gustav. *Studentenschaft und Evangelischer Bund* (FSEB Nr. 84). Leipzig, 1893.

"Das Reich muß uns doch bleiben." Handbuch für Freunde des Evangelischen Bundes. Leipzig, 1896.

Reichensperger, August. *Parlamentarisches über Kunst und Kunsthandwerk.* Cologne, 1880.

———. *Phrasen und Schlagwörter. Ein Noth- und Hilfsbüchlein für Zeitungsleser.* 5th ed. Paderborn, 1872.

———. *Vermischte Schriften über christliche Kunst.* Leipzig, 1856.

Riehl, Wilhelm Heinrich. *Die Naturgeschichte des deutschen Volkes.* 8th ed. Vol. 1, *Land und Leute.* Stuttgart, 1883.

Roeren, Hermann. *Der internationale Kulturkampf insbesondere die Grassmann'sche Schmähschrift.* Trier, 1901.

———. *Der Toleranzantrag des Zentrums.* Hamm i. W., 1901.

———. *Zentrum und Kölner Richtung.* Trier, 1913.

———. *Zur Polenfrage.* Hamm i. W., 1903.

Röhl, John C. G., ed. *Philipp Eulenburgs politische Korrespondenz.* Vol. 2. Boppard am Rhein, 1979.

Rosenberg, Joseph. *Endlich Gelöst!* Leipzig, 1905.

———. *Der polnische Klerus, das deutsche Zentrum und das evangelische Deutschtum.* Lissa, 1908.

Rössler, Constantin. *Das deutsche Reich und die kirchliche Frage.* Würzburg, 1876.

Sammassa, Paul. *Der Völkerstreit im Habsburgstaat.* Leipzig, 1910.

Savigny, Leo von. *Des Zentrums Wandlung und Ende.* Berlin, 1907.

Schäfer, Dietrich. *Aufsätze, Vorträge und Reden.* Jena, 1913.

Schanding, Hilmar. *Glaubensfrühling in Steiermark. Mit einem Vorwort über die gegenwärtige Lage der Protestanten in Bayern von Armatus.* Munich, 1902.

Schell, Hermann. *Der Katholizismus als Prinzip des Fortschritts.* 3d ed. Würzburg, 1897.

Schenkel, Daniel. *Die kirchliche Frage und ihre protestantische Lösung.* Elberfeld, 1862.

Scherenberg, Ernst, ed. *Gegen Rom. Zeitstimmen Deutscher Dichter.* Elberfeld, 1874.

Scherer, Wilhelm. *Geschichte des geistigen Lebens in Deutschland und Österreich.* Berlin, 1874.

———. *Zur Geschichte der deutschen Sprache.* 2d ed. Berlin, 1878.

Schian, Martin. *Das kirchliche Leben der evangelischen Kirche der Provinz Schlesien.* Tübingen and Leipzig, 1903.

Schlechtendahl, G. A. *Ist das Zentrum eine Gefahr für das Deutsche Reich?* Munich, 1909.

Schmidt, Julian. *Geschichte der deutschen Literatur seit Lessings Tod.* Leipzig, 1866.

———. *Geschichte der deutschen Literatur von Leibniz bis auf unsere Zeit.* Vol. 1. Berlin, 1886.

Schmidt, Wilhelm. *Unsre Stellung zur Polenfrage* (FSEB Nr. 203). Leipzig, 1902.

Schmitthenner, Adolf. *"Wisset ihr nicht, wes Geistes Kinder ihr seid?"* (FSEB Nr. 57). Leipzig, 1891.

Schneider, Friedrich, ed. *Universalstaat oder Nationalstaat. Die Streitschriften von Heinrich von Sybel und Julius Ficker zur Kaiserpolitik des Mittelalters.* Innsbruck, 1941.

Schuler, M. *Shakespeare's Confession.* Berlin, 1899.

Schultze, O. *Die "lebenden Bilder" der Alberschweiler Fronleichnamsprozession vor Gericht* (FSEB Nr. 153). Leipzig, 1898.

Spahn, Martin. *Deutsche Lebensfragen.* Kempten, 1914.

Stolz, Alban. *Gesammelte Werke.* Freiburg i. Br., 1875–98.

Sybel, Heinrich von. "Klerikale Politik im neunzehnten Jahrhundert." In *Kleine Schriften,* vol. 3, 376–454. Stuttgart, 1880.

Thönes, Carl. *Der Evangelische Bund und die Toleranz* (FSEB Nr. 24). Leipzig, 1890.

Treitschke, Heinrich von. *Briefe.* 3 vols. Ed. M. Cornicelius. Leipzig, 1913.

———. *Deutsche Geschichte im Neunzehnten Jahrhundert.* 4th ed. 5 vols. Leipzig, 1890.

———. *Zehn Jahre deutscher Kämpfe.* Berlin, 1879.

Troeltsch, Ernst. *Gesammelte Schriften.* Vol. 2. *Zur religiösen Lage, Religionsphilosophie und Ethik.* Tübingen, 1913.

Tschackert, Paul. *Modus Vivendi. Grundlinien für das Zusammenleben der Konfessionen im Deutschen Reiche.* Leipzig, 1892.

Viebig, Clara. *Ausgewählte Werke.* Vol. 5, *Das schlafende Heer.* Berlin, 1905.

Wagner, C. *Die geschlechtlich-sittlichen Verhältnisse der evangelischen Landesbewohner im Deutschen Reiche.* 2 vols. Leipzig, 1895–96.

Warneck, Gustav. *Der Evangelische Bund und seine Gegner.* Güterslohe, 1889.

Warnkönig, Wilhelm. *Joseph von Görres. Ein Kampf für die Freiheit. Dem freien deutschen Volke geschildert.* Berlin, 1895.

Wasserburg, Philipp. *Gedankenspähne über den Militarismus.* Mainz, 1874.

Wattendorff, Ludwig. *Walter von der Vogelweide. Deutschlands größter Lyriker im Mittelalter.* Frankfurt a.M., 1894.

Weber, Ludwig. *Wer soll und muß dem Evangelischen Bund beitreten.* Barmen, 1888.

Weber, Max. *Briefe 1906–1908.* Ed. M. Rainer Lepsius and Wolfgang J. Mommsen with Birgit Rudhard and Manfred Schön. Tübingen, 1990.

———. *Gesammelte politische Schriften.* 2d ed. Ed. Johannes Winckelmann. Tübingen, 1958.

Weitbrecht, Richard. *Redemptoristen und Jesuiten* (FSEB Nr. 64). Leipzig, 1892.

Wentzcke, Paul. *Im neuen Reich 1871–1890. Politische Briefe aus dem Nachlaß liberaler Parteiführer.* Vol. 2. Bonn, 1926. Reprint. Osnabrück, 1970.

Wintzingerode-Bodenstein, Wiko Levin Graf von. *Der Evangelische Bund in Frankfurt. 2. Eröffnungsrede.* Leipzig, 1887.

Witte, Leopold. *Der Kampf unserer Zeit: Ein Kampf zwischen Glauben und Aberglauben* (FSEB Nr. 86). Leipzig, 1893.

———. *Der Protest gegen die römisch-katholische Einstellung des Christentums, eine Pflicht christlicher Frömmigkeit* (FSEB Nr. 36). Halle, 1889.

————. *Welche Aufgaben erwachsen dem geistlichen Amte aus der gegenwärtigen Angriffstellung Roms?* (FSEB Nr. 7). Halle, 1887.

Zottmann, A. *Deutschlands größte Dichterin (Annette Freiin v. Droste-Hülshoff).* Frankfurt a.M., 1897.

VI. Secondary Sources

Albertin, Lothar. "Nationalismus und Protestantismus in der österreichischen Los-von-Rom Bewegung um 1900." Ph.D. diss., University of Cologne, 1953.

Algermissen, K. "Los-von-Rom-Bewegung." In *Lexikon für Theologie und Kirche,* vol. 6, 1154–55. Freiburg, 1961.

Alter, Peter. *Nationalismus.* Frankfurt a.M., 1985.

Altermatt, Urs. *Katholizismus und Moderne. Zur Sozial- und Mentalitätsgeschichte der Schweizer Katholiken im 19. und 20. Jahrhundert.* Zürich, 1989.

Altgeld, Wolfgang. *Katholizismus, Protestantismus, Judentum. Über religiös begründete Gegensätze und nationalreligiöse Ideen in der Geschichte des deutschen Nationalismus.* Mainz, 1992.

Anderson, Benedict. *Imagined Communities: Reflections on the Origins and Spread of Nationalism.* 2d ed. London, 1991.

Anderson. Margaret Lavinia. "Interdenominationalism, Clericalism, Pluralism: The *Zentrumsstreit* and the Dilemma of Catholicism in Wilhemine Germany." *Central European History* 21, no. 4 (1990): 350–78.

————. "The Kulturkampf and the Course of German History." *Central European History* 19, no. 1 (1986): 82–115.

————. "Piety and Politics: Recent Work on German Catholicism." *The Journal of Modern History* 63, no. 4 (December 1991): 681–716.

————. *Windthorst: A Political Biography.* Oxford, 1981.

Anderson, Margaret Lavinia, and Kenneth Barkin. "The Myth of the Puttkamer Purge and the Reality of the Kulturkampf: Some Reflections on the Historiography of Imperial Germany." *Journal of Modern History* 54, no. 4 (1982): 647–86.

Apfelbacher, Karl Ernst. *Frömmigkeit und Wissenschaft. Ernst Troeltsch und sein theologisches Programm.* Munich, 1978.

Applegate, Celia. *A Nation of Provincials: The German Idea of Heimat.* Berkeley, 1990.

Aschoff, Hans-Georg. *Welfische Bewegung und politischer Katholizismus 1866–1918. Die Deutschhannoversche Partei und das Zentrum in der Provinz Hannover während des Kaiserreiches.* Düsseldorf, 1987.

Bachem, Karl. *Vorgeschichte, Geschichte und Politik der deutschen Zentrumspartei, 1815–1914.* 9 vols. Cologne, 1927–32.

Baechler, Christian. *Le partie catholique alsacien 1890–1939.* Paris, 1982.

Balzer, Brigitte. *Die preußische Polenpolitik 1894–1908 und die Haltung der deutschen konservativen und liberalen Parteien.* Frankfurt a.M., 1990.

Bammel, E. *Die Reichsgründung und der deutsche Protestantismus.* Erlangen, 1973.

Banac, Ivo. *The National Question in Yugoslavia.* Ithaca, N.Y., and London, 1984.

Barkin, Kenneth. *The Controversy over German Industrialization, 1890–1902.* Chicago, 1970.

Barth, Dieter. *Zeitschrift für Alle. Das Familienblatt im 19. Jahrhundert.* Münster, 1974.

Baumeister, Martin. *Parität und katholische Inferiorität.* Paderborn, 1987.

Becker, Josef. *Liberaler Staat und Kirche in der Ära von Reichsgründung und Kulturkampf (1860–1876).* Mainz, 1973.

Becker, Winfried. *Georg von Hertling, 1843–1919.* Vol. 1. *Jugend und Selbstfindung zwischen Romantik und Kulturkampf.* Mainz, 1981.

———. "Der Kulturkampf als europäisches und als deutsches Phänomen." *Historisches Jahrbuch* 101 (1981): 422–46.

———. "Liberale Kulturkampf-Positionen und politischer Katholizismus." In *Innenpolitische Probleme des Bismarck-Reiches,* ed. Otto Pflanze, 47–71. Munich and Vienna, 1983.

———. "Luthers Wirkungsgeschichte im konfessionellen Dissens des 19. Jahrhunderts." *Rheinische Vierteljahresblätter* 49 (1985): 219–48.

———, ed. *Die Minderheit als Mitte. Die deutsche Zentrumspartei in der Innenpolitik des Reiches 1871–1933.* Paderborn, 1986.

Becker, Winfried, et al. *Die Verschiebung von Innen- Konfessions- und Kolonialpolitik im Deutschen Reich vor 1914.* Düsseldorf, 1987.

Berghahn, Volker R. *Der Tirpitz Plan.* Düsseldorf, 1971.

Bergsträsser, Ludwig. *Der politische Katholizismus.* Munich, 1923.

Berlin, Isaiah. *Two Concepts of Liberty.* Oxford, 1959.

Besier, Gerhard. *Preußische Kirchenpolitik in der Bismarckära.* Berlin, 1980.

Birke, Adolf M. "Zur Entwicklung und politischen Funktion des bürgerlichen Kulturkampfverständnisses in Preußen-Deutschland." In *Aus Theorie und Praxis der Geschichtswissenschaft,* ed. D. Kurze, 257–79. Berlin, 1972.

Birtsch, Günther. *Die Nation als sittliche Idee.* Cologne and Graz, 1964.

Bischoff-Luithlen, Angelika. "Alte Tröster im Bauernhaus." *Beiträge zur Volks- und Heimatkunde* (1971): 65–66.

Black, Cyril E. *The Dynamics of Modernization.* New York, 1966.

Blackbourn, David. *Class, Religion and Local Politics in Wilhelmine Germany: The Center Party in Württemberg before 1914.* Wiesbaden, 1980.

———. *Populists and Patricians: Essays in Modern German History.* London, 1987.

Blackbourn, David, and Geoff Eley. *The Peculiarities of German History.* Oxford and New York, 1984.

Blanke, Richard. *Prussian Poland in the German Empire (1871–1900).* Boulder, Colo., 1981.

Blessing, Werner K. "Kirchenfromm—volksfromm—weltfromm: Religiosität im katholischen Bayern des späten 19. Jahrhunderts." In *Deutscher Katholizismus im Umbruch zur Moderne,* ed. Wilfried Loth, 95–123. Stuttgart, 1991.

———. *Staat und Kirche in der Gesellschaft. Institutionelle Autorität und mentaler Wandel in Bayern während des 19. Jahrhunderts.* Göttingen, 1982.

Blumberg, Hans. *Säkularisierung und Selbstbehauptung.* Frankfurt a.M., 1974.

Bonhard, Otto. *Geschichte des Alldeutschen Verbandes.* Leipzig, 1920.

Boyer, John. *Political Radicalism in Late Imperial Vienna. Origins of the Christian Social Movement, 1848–1897.* Chicago and London, 1981.

Brock, Peter. "Polish Nationalism." In *Nationalism in Eastern Europe*, ed. Peter Sugar and Ivo Lederer, 310–72. Seattle, 1969.

Brose, Eric D. *Christian Labor and the Politics of Frustration in Imperial Germany.* Washington, D.C., 1985.

Broszat, Martin. *Zweihundert Jahre deutsche Polenpolitik.* 2d ed. Frankfurt a.M., 1972.

Burger, Annemarie. *Religionszugehörigkeit und soziales Verhalten.* Göttingen, 1964.

Büsch, Otto, and James Sheehan, eds. *Die Rolle der Nation in der deutschen Geschichte und Gegenwart.* Berlin, 1985.

Carsten, F. L. *Faschismus in Österreich.* Munich, 1978.

Carter, T. E. "Freytag's Soll und Haben: A Liberal National Manifesto as a Best-Seller." *German Life and Letters* 21, no. 4 (1968): 320–25.

Cary, Noel. "Political Catholicism and the Reform of the German Party System, 1900–1957." Ph.D. diss., University of California, Berkeley, 1988.

Chickering, Roger. *We Men Who Feel Most German: A Cultural Study of the Pan-German League, 1886–1914.* Boston, 1984.

Coetzee, Marilyn Shevin. *The German Army League: Popular Nationalism in Wilhelmine Germany.* New York, 1990.

Conze, Werner, et al. *Modernisierung und nationale Gesellschaft im ausgehenden 18. und im 19. Jahrhundert.* Berlin, 1979.

———. "Nationsbildung durch Trennung. Deutsche und Polen im preußischen Osten." In *Innenpolitische Probleme des Bismarck-Reiches*, ed. Otto Pflanze, 95–119. Munich, 1983.

———. "Zum Verhältnis des Luthertums zu den mitteleuropäischen Nationalbewegungen im 19. Jahrhundert." In *Luther in der Neuzeit*, ed. Bernd Möller, 178–93. Düsseldof, 1983.

Craig, Gordon. *Germany, 1866–1945.* New York, 1978.

Cremers, Hartwig. *Der Toleranzantrag der Zentrumspartei.* Ph.D. diss., University of Tübingen, 1973.

Czaplinski, Marek. "Die polnische Presse in Oberschlesien um die Jahrhundertwende (1889–1914)." *Zeitschrift für Ostforschung* 39, no. 1 (1990): 20–38.

Dann, Otto. *Nationalismus und sozialer Wandel.* Hamburg, 1978.

Deist, Wilhelm. *Flottenpolitik und Flottenpropaganda. Das Nachrichtenbureau des Reichsmarineamtes 1897–1914.* Stuttgart, 1976.

Deuerlein, Ernst. "Die Bekehrung des Zentrums zur nationalen Idee." *Hochland* 62 (1970): 432–49.

Dotterweich, Volker. *Heinrich von Sybel. Geschichtswissenschaft in politischer Absicht (1817–1861).* Göttingen, 1978.

Douglas, Mary. *Implicit Meanings.* London and Boston, 1975.

Düding, Dieter. *Der Nationalsoziale Verein, 1896–1903.* Munich, 1972.

Dülffer, Jost, and Karl Holl, eds. *Bereit zum Krieg. Kriegsmentalität in Wilhelminischen Deutschland 1890–1914.* Göttingen, 1986.

Eley, Geoff. *From Unification to Nazism.* Boston, 1986.

———. *Reshaping the German Right: Radical Nationalism and Political Change after Bismarck.* New Haven and London, 1980.

Elias, Norbert. *The Civilizing Process.* New York, 1978.

Elm, Kaspar, and Hans-Dietrich Loock, eds. *Seelsorge und Diakone in Berlin: Beiträge zum Verhältnis von Kirche und Großstadt im 19. und beginnenden 20. Jahrhundert.* Berlin and New York, 1990.

Engel-Janosi, Friedrich. "The Church and the Nationalities in the Habsburg Monarchy." *Austrian History Yearbook* 3 (1967): 67–82.

———. *Österreich und der Vatikan 1846–1918.* 2 vols. Graz, Vienna, and Cologne, 1958, 1960.

Engelsing, Rudolf. *Analphabetentum und Lektüre.* Stuttgart, 1973.

Epstein, Klaus. "Erzberger and the German Colonial Scandals, 1905–1910." *English Historical Review* 74 (1959): 637–63.

———. *Matthias Erzberger und Das Dilemma der deutschen Demokratie.* 2d ed. Berlin, 1976.

Evans, Ellen Lovell. *The German Center Party, 1870–1933.* Carbondale, Ill., and Edwardsville, 1981.

Evans, Richard J. *Rethinking German History.* London, 1987.

———, ed. *Society and Politics in Wilhelmine Germany.* London, 1978.

Favrot, Brigitte. *Le gouvernement allemand et le clergé catholique lorrain de 1890 à 1914.* Metz, 1981.

Field, Geoffrey. *Evangelist of Race: The Germanic Vision of Houston Stewart Chamberlain.* New York, 1981.

Fischer, Fritz. "Der deutsche Protestantismus und die Politik im 19. Jahrhundert." *Historische Zeitschrift* 171 (1951): 473–518.

Fleischmann-Bisten, Walter, and Heiner Grote. *Protestanten auf dem Wege. Geschichte des Evangelischen Bundes.* Göttingen, 1986.

Fohrmann, Ulrich. *Trierer Kulturkampfpublizistik im Bismarckreich. Leben und Werk des Presskaplans Georg Friedrich Dasbach.* Trier, 1977.

Förster, Stig. *Der doppelte Militarismus. Die deutsche Heeresrüstungspolitik zwischen Status-quo-Sicherung und Aggression 1890–1913.* Stuttgart, 1985.

François, Etienne. *Die unsichtbare Grenze. Protestanten und Katholiken in Augsburg 1648–1806.* Sigmaringen, 1991.

Fredrickson, George M. *White Supremacy: A Comparative Study in American and South African History.* New York, 1981.

Fricke, Dieter. "Der Reichsverband gegen die Sozialdemokratie von seiner Gründung bis zu den Reichstagswahlen von 1907." *Zeitschrift für die Geschichtswissenschaft* 7 (1959): 237–80.

Fricke, Dieter, et al., eds. *Lexikon zur Parteigeschichte.* 4 vols. Leipzig, 1984–86.

Gall, Lothar. "Die partei- und sozialgeschichtliche Problematik des badischen Kulturkampfes." *Zeitschrift für die Geschichte des Oberrheins* 113 (1965): 151–96.

Galos, Adam, et al. *Die Hakatisten. Der Deutsche Ostmarkenverein (1894–1934).* Berlin(o), 1966.

Gatz, E., ed. *Akten zur preußischen Kirchenpolitik in den Bistümern Gnesen-Posen, Kulm und Ermland, 1885–1914.* Mainz, 1977.

———. "Kirchliche Personalpolitik und Nationalitätsprobleme in Wilhelminischen Deutschland." *Archivum Historiae Pontificiae* 18 (1980): 353–81.

Geertz, Clifford. *The Interpretation of Cultures.* New York, 1973.

———. *The Religion of Java.* Chicago, 1960.

Gellner, Ernest. *Nations and Nationalism*. Oxford, 1983.

Gerschenkron, Alexander. *Economic Backwardness in Historical Perspective*. Cambridge, 1966.

Gottwald, Herbert. "Der Umfall des Zentrums. Die Stellung der Zentrumspartei zur Flottenvorlage von 1897." In *Studien zum deutschen Imperialismus vor 1914*, ed. Fritz Klein, 181–224. Berlin(o), 1976.

———. "Zentrum und Imperialismus." Ph.D. diss., University of Jena, 1966.

Grote, Heiner. "Konfessionalistische und unionistische Orientierung am Beispiel des Gustav-Adolf-Vereins und des Evangelischen Bundes." In *Das deutsche Luthertum und die Unionsproblematik im 19. Jahrhundert*, ed. Wolf-Dieter Hauschild, 110–30. Gütersloh, 1991.

Gründer, Horst. *Christliche Mission und deutscher Imperialismus. Eine politische Geschichte ihrer Beziehung während der deutschen Kolonialzeit (1884–1914) unter besonderer Berücksichtigung Afrikas und Chinas*. Paderborn, 1982.

———. " 'Gott will es.' Eine Antisklavereibewegung am Ende des 19. Jahrhunderts." *Geschichte in Wissenschaft und Unterricht* 28 (1977): 210–24.

———. "Nation und Katholizismus im Kaiserreich." In *Katholizismus, nationaler Gedanke und Europa seit 1800*, ed. Albrecht Langner, 65–88. Paderborn, 1985.

———. "Rechtskatholizismus im Kaiserreich und in der Weimarer Republik unter besonderer Berücksichtigung der Rheinlande und Westfalens." *Westfälische Zeitschrift* 134 (1984): 107–55.

Hagen, William W. *Germans, Poles and Jews: The Nationality Conflict in the Prussian East, 1772–1914*. Chicago, 1980.

Hartmannsgruber, Friedrich. *Die Bayerische Patriotenpartei, 1868–1887*. Munich, 1986.

Heitzer, Horstwalter. *Der Volksverein für das katholische Deutschland im Kaiserreich 1890–1918*. Mainz, 1979.

Henning, Hansjoachim. "Kriegervereine in den preußischen Westprovinzen: Ein Beitrag zur preußischen Innenpolitik zwischen 1860 und 1914." *Rheinische Vierteljahresblätter* 32 (1968): 430–75.

Hentschel, Volker. "Wirtschaftliche Entwicklung, soziale Mobilität und nationale Bewegung in Oberschlesien 1871–1914." In *Modernisierung und nationale Gesellschaft im ausgehenden 18. und im 19. Jahrhundert*, ed. Werner Conze et al., 243–250. Berlin, 1979.

Heuss, Alfred. *Theodor Mommsen und das 19. Jahrhundert*. Kiel, 1956.

Heydt, Fritz von der. *Die evangelische Bewegung in Österreich*. 2d ed. Berlin, 1938.

Hiery, Hermann. *Reichstagswahlen im Reichsland. Ein Beitrag zur Landesgeschichte von Elsaß-Lothringen und zur Wahlgeschichte des deutschen Reiches 1871–1918*. Düsseldorf, 1986.

Hirschmann, Günther. *Kulturkampf im historischen Roman der Gründerzeit 1859–1878*. Munich, 1978.

Höbelt, Lothar. *Kornblume und Kaiseradler. Die deutschfreiheitlichen Parteien Altösterreichs 1882–1918*. Vienna, 1993.

Hobsbawm, Eric J. *Nations and Nationalism since 1780. Programme, Myth, Reality*. Cambridge, 1990.

Hobsbawm, Eric J., and Terence Ranger, eds. *The Invention of Tradition.* Cambridge, 1983.

Hohendahl, Peter Uwe. *Building a National Literature: The Case of Germany.* Ithaca, N.Y., 1989.

Hölscher, Lucian. "Die Religion des Bürgers. Bürgerliche Frömmigkeit und protestantische Kirche im 19. Jahrhundert." *Historische Zeitschrift* 250 (1990): 595–630.

———. *Weltgericht oder Revolution. Protestantische und sozialistische Zukunftsvorstellungen im deutschen Kaiserreich.* Stuttgart, 1989.

Hölscher, Lucian, and Ursula Männich-Polenz. "Die Sozialstruktur der Kirchengemeinde Hannovers im 19. Jahrhundert. Eine statistische Analyse." *Jahrbuch der Gesellschaft für niedersächsische Geschichte* 88 (1990): 159–211.

Hroch, Miroslav. *Die Vorkämpfer der nationalen Bewegung bei den kleinen Völkern Europas.* Prague, 1967.

Hubatsch, Walther. *Masuren und Preußisch-Litthauen.* Marburg, 1960.

Hubbard, William H. *Auf dem Weg zur Großstadt. Eine Sozialgeschichte der Stadt Graz 1850–1914.* Munich, 1984.

Hull, Isabel. *The Entourage of Kaiser Wilhelm II 1888–1918.* Cambridge, 1982.

Iggers, George. *The German Conception of History.* Middletown, Conn., 1968.

Jaeger, Georg. "Die deutsche Leihbibliothek im 19. Jahrhundert. Verbreitung—Organisation—Verfall." *Internationales Archiv für Sozialgeschichte der deutschen Literatur* 2 (1977): 96–133.

———. "Medien." In *Handbuch der deutschen Bildungsgeschichte*, ed. Christa Berg, vol. 4, 473–99. Munich. 1991.

James, Harold. *A German Identity, 1770–1990.* London, 1989.

Jaszi, Oscar. *The Dissolution of the Habsburg Monarchy.* Chicago, 1929.

Jenks, William A. *The Austrian Electoral Reform of 1907.* New York, 1950.

Judson, Pieter M. "'Whether Race or Conviction Should Be the Standard': National Identity and Liberal Politics in Nineteenth-Century Austria." *Austrian History Yearbook* 22 (1991): 76–95.

Katzenstein, Peter J. *Disjoined Partners: Austria and Germany since 1815.* Berkeley, 1976.

Kedourie, Eli. *Nationalism.* New York, 1981.

Kehr, Eckart. *Der Primat der Innenpolitik. Gesammelte Aufsätze zur preußisch-deutschen Sozialgeschichte im 19. und 20. Jahrhundert.* 2d ed. Ed. Hans-Ulrich Wehler. Frankfurt, 1970.

Kiefer, Rolf. *Karl Bachem 1845–1945.* Mainz, 1989.

Klessmann, Christoph. *Polnische Bergarbeiter im Ruhrgebiet, 1870–1945.* Göttingen, 1978.

Knoll, Reinhard. *Zur Tradition der christsozialen Partei. Ihre Früh- und Entwicklungsgeschichte bis zu den Reichsratswahlen 1907.* Vienna, 1973.

Kocka, Jürgen. "Probleme der politischen Integration der Deutschen 1867 bis 1945." In *Die Rolle der Nation*, ed. Otto Büsch and James Sheehan, 118–36. Berlin, 1985.

Köhle-Hezinger, Christel. *Evangelisch-Katholisch. Untersuchungen zu konfessionellem Vorurteil und Konflikt im 19. und 20. Jahrhundert vornehmlich am Beispiel Württembergs.* Tübingen, 1976.

Korff, Gottfried. "Heiligenverehrung und soziale Frage. Zur Ideologisierung der populären Frömmigkeit im späten 19. Jahrhundert." In *Kultureller Wandel im 19. Jahrhundert*, ed. G. Wiegelmann, 102–11. Göttingen, 1982.

―――. "Kulturkampf und Volksfrömmigkeit." In *Volksreligösität in der modernen Sozialgeschichte*, ed. Wolfgang Schieder, 137–51. Göttingen, 1986.

―――. "Politischer Heiligenkult im 19. und 20. Jahrhundert." *Zeitschrift für Volkskunde* 71 (1975): 202–20.

Korth, Rudolf. *Die preußische Schulpolitik und die polnischen Schulstreiks*. Würzburg, 1963.

Kotowski, Wojciech. "Die Lage der deutschen Katholiken in Polen in den Jahren 1919–1939." *Zeitschrift für Ostforschung* 39, no. 1 (1990): 39–67.

Kouri, E. I. *Der deutsche Protestantismus und die soziale Frage, 1870–1919*. Berlin, 1984.

Kremer, Hans-Jürgen. "Die Krieger- und Militärvereine in der Innenpolitik des Großherzogtums Baden (1870–1914)." *Zeitschrift für die Geschichte des Oberrheins* 133 (1985): 301–36.

―――. "Der Volksverein für das Katholische Deutschland in Baden." *Freiburger Diözesan-Archiv* 104 (1984): 208–80.

Krieger, Leonard. *The German Idea of Freedom: History of a Political Tradition*. Boston, 1957.

Kruck, Alfred. *Geschichte des Alldeutschen Verbandes 1890–1939*. Wiesbaden, 1954.

Kulczycki, John. *School Strikes in Prussian Poland, 1901–1907*. New York, 1981.

Lamberti, Marjorie. *State, Society, and the Elementary School in Imperial Germany*. New York, 1989.

Langer, Albrecht, ed. *Säkularisation und Säkularisierung im 19. Jahrhundert*. Munich, Paderborn, and Vienna, 1978.

Langewiesche, Dieter, ed. *Liberalismus im 19. Jahrhundert*. Göttingen, 1988.

―――. *Liberalismus in Deutschland*. Frankfurt a.M., 1988.

―――. "Reich, Nation und Staat in der jüngeren deutschen Geschichte." *Historische Zeitschrift* 254 (1992): 341–81.

Langlois, Claude. *Le catholicisme au feminin: Les congrégations françaises à supérieure générale au XIX siécle*. Paris, 1984.

Lehmann, Hartmut. "Martin Luther als deutscher Nationalheld im 19. Jahrhundert." *Luther. Zeitschrift der Luther-Gesellschaft* 55, no. 2 (1984): 53–65.

Lepovitz, Helena Waddy. *Images of Faith: Expressionism, Catholic Folk Art, and the Industrial Revolution*. Athens, Ga., and London, 1991.

Lepsius, M. Rainer. "Parteiensystem und Sozialstruktur: Zum Problem der Demokratisierung der deutschen Gesellschaft." In *Deutsche Parteien vor 1918*, ed. Gerhard A. Ritter, 56–80. Cologne, 1973.

Lerman, Katharine Anne. *The Chancellor as Courtier: Bernhard von Bülow and the Governance of Germany, 1900–1909*. Cambridge, 1990.

Leugers, August-Hermann. "Einstellungen zu Krieg und Frieden im deutschen Katholizismus vor 1914." In *Bereit zum Krieg*, ed. Jost Dülffer and Karl Holl, 56–73. Göttingen, 1986.

―――. "Latente Kulturkampfstimmung im wilhelminischen Kaiserreich." in *Die Verschränkung von Innen-, Konfessions- und Kolonialpolitik im Deutschen Reich vor 1914*, ed. Johannes Horstmann, 13–37. Paderborn, 1987.

Leugers-Scherzberg, August Hermann. *Felix Porsch, 1853–1930*. Mainz, 1990.

Levy, Richard S. *The Downfall of the Anti-Semitic Political Parties in Imperial Germany*. New Haven and London, 1975.

Lewis, Michael James. "August Reichensperger (1808–1895) and the Gothic Revival." Ph.D. diss., University of Pennsylvania, 1989.

Lidtke, Vernon. *The Alternative Culture: Socialist Labor in Imperial Germany*. New York and Oxford, 1985.

———"Social Class and Secularization in Imperial Germany—the Working Classes." *Leo Baeck Institute Yearbook* 25 (1980): 21–40.

Lill, Rudolf. "Die deutschen Katholiken und Bismarcks Reichsgründung." In *Reichsgründung 1870/71*, ed. Theodor Schieder and Ernst Deuerlein, 345–65. Stuttgart, 1970.

———. "Großdeutsch und Kleindeutsch im Spannungsfeld der Konfessionen." In *Probleme des Konfessionalismus in Deutschland seit 1800*, ed. Anton Rauscher, 29–47. Paderborn, 1984,.

———. "Katholizismus und Nation bis zur Reichstagsgründung." In *Katholizismus, nationaler Gedanke und Europa seit 1800*, ed. Albrecht Langer, 51–64. Paderborn, 1985.

———. "Der Kulturkampf in Preußen und im Deutschen Reich (bis 1878)." In *Handbuch der Kirchengeschichte*, ed. Hubert Jedin, vol. 6, no. 2, 28–47. Freiburg, 1973.

———. *Die Wende im Kulturkampf. Leo XIII., Bismarck und die Zentrumspartei 1878–1889*. Tübingen, 1973.

Loth, Wilfried. *Katholiken im Kaiserreich*. Düsseldorf, 1984.

Lübbe, H. *Säkularisierung. Geschichte eines ideenpolitischen Begriffs*. Freiburg i. Br., 1965.

McLeod, Hugh. "Protestantism and the Working Class in Imperial Germany." *European Studies Review* 12 (1982): 323–44.

———. "Weibliche Frömmigkeit—männlicher Unglaube? Religion und Kirche im bürgerlichen 19. Jahrhundert." In *Bürgerinnen und Bürger. Geschlechteverhältnisse im 19. Jahrhundert*, ed. Ute Frevert, 134–56. Göttingen, 1988.

Maier, Hans. "Katholizismus, nationale Bewegung und Demokratie in Deutschland." *Hochland* 57 (1965): 318–33.

Mallmann, Klaus-Michael. "Die neue Attraktivität des Himmels. Kirche, Religion und industrielle Modernisierung." In *Industriekultur an der Saar. Leben und Arbeit in einer Industrieregion, 1840–1914*, ed. Richard van Dülmen, 248–57. Munich, 1989.

———. "Ultramontanismus und Arbeiterbewegung im Kaiserreich. Überlegungen am Beispiel des Saarreviers." In *Deutscher Katholizismus im Umbruch zur Moderne*, ed. Wilfried Loth, 76–94. Stuttgart, 1991.

Marbach, Rainer. *Säkularisierung und sozialer Wandel im 19. Jahrhundert. Die Stellung von Geistlichen zu Entkirchlichung und Entchristlichung in einem Bezirk der hannoverischen Landeskirche*. Göttingen, 1978.

Maron, Gottfried, ed. *Evangelisch und Ökumenisch. Beiträge zum 100jährigen Bestehen des Evangelischen Bundes*. Göttingen, 1986.

Merkl, Gerhard. "Studien zum Priesternachwuchs der Erzdiözese Freiburg, 1870–1914." *Freiburger Diözesan-Archiv* 94 (1974): 4–269.

Mehnert, Gottfried, ed. *Programme evangelischer Kirchenzeitungen im 19. Jahrhundert*. Witten, 1972.

Mommsen, Wolfgang J. *Der autoritäre Nationalstaat. Verfassung, Gesellschaft und Kultur im deutschen Kaiserreich*. Frankfurt a.M., 1990.

———. *Max Weber und die deutsche Politik 1890–1920*. 2d ed. Tübingen, 1974.

Mooser, Josef. "Arbeiter, Bürger und Priester in den konfessionellen Arbeitervereinen im deutschen Kaiserreich, 1880–1914." In *Arbeiter und Bürger im 19. Jahrhundert. Varianten ihres Verhältnisses im europäischen Vergleich*, ed. Jürgen Kocka and Elisabeth Müller-Luckner, 79–105. Oldenburg, 1986.

Morsey, Rudolf. "Die deutschen Katholiken und der Nationalstaat zwischen Kulturkampf und Erstem Weltkrieg." *Historisches Jahrbuch* 90 (1970): 31–64.

Müller, Armin. "Der Evangelische Bund im Kaiserreich. Entstehung, Struktur, Programm und politisches Verhalten einer protestantischen Sammelbewegung, 1886–1914." Staatsexamensarbeit, Universität Hamburg, 1985.

Müller, Leonhard. *Nationalpolnische Presse, Katholizismus und Katholischer Klerus*. Breslau, 1931.

Müller-Salget, Klaus. *Erzählungen für das Volk. Evangelische Pfarrer als Volksschriftsteller im Deutschland des 19. Jahrhunderts*. Berlin, 1984.

Murzynowska, Krystyna. *Der polnische Erwerbsauswanderer im Ruhrgebiet während der Jahre 1880–1914*. Dortmund, 1979.

Nipperdey, Thomas. *Deutsche Geschichte 1866–1918*. 2 vols. Munich, 1990–92.

———. *Religion im Umbruch. Deutschland 1870–1918*. Munich, 1988.

Nolan, Mary. *Social Democracy and Society: Working-class Radicalism in Düsseldorf, 1890–1920*. Cambridge, 1981.

Olenhusen, Irmtraud Götz von. "Die Ultramontanisierung des Klerus. Das Beispiel der Erzdiözese Freiburg." In *Deutscher Katholizismus im Umbruch zur Moderne*, ed. Wilfried Loth, 46–75. Stuttgart, 1991.

Pehl, Hans. "Die deutsche Kolonialpolitik und das Zentrum, 1884–1914." Ph.D. diss., Univ. of Frankfurt, 1934.

Pflanze, Otto. *Bismarck and the Development of Germany*. 2d ed. 3 vols. Princeton, 1990.

Pichl, Eduard. *Georg Schönerer und die Entwicklung des Alldeutschtumes in der Ostmark*. 6 vols. Oldenburg, 1938.

Plessner, Helmuth. *Die verspätete Nation*. In *Gesammelte Schriften*, vol 6. Frankfurt a.M., 1982.

Pollmann, K. E. *Landesherrliches Kirchenregiment und soziale Frage. Der evangelische Oberkirchenrat der altpreußischen Landeskirche und die sozialpolitische Bewegung der Geistlichen nach 1890*. Berlin, 1973.

Puhle, Hans Jürgen. *Agrarische Interessenpolitik und preußischer Konservativismus im wilhelminischen Reich (1893–1914)*. Hannover, 1967.

Pulzer, Peter. *The Rise of Political Antisemitism in Germany and Austria*. Rev. ed. London, 1988.

Rarisch, Ilsedore. *Industrialisierung und Literatur. Buchproduktion, Verlagswesen und Buchhandel in Deutschland im 19. Jahrhundert in ihrem statistischen Zusammenhang*. Berlin, 1976.

Reif, Heinz. *Westfälischer Adel 1770–1860*. Göttingen, 1979.

Retallack, James N. *Notables of the Right: The Conservative Party and Political Mobilization in Germany, 1876–1918*. Boston, 1988.

Rhode, Arthur. *Geschichte der evangelischen Kirche im Posener Lande.* Würzburg, 1956.

Rohe, Karl. "Konfession, Klasse und lokale Gesellschaft als Bestimmungsfaktoren des Wahlverhaltens—Überlegungen und Problematisierungen am Beispiel des historischen Ruhrgebiets." In *Politische Parteien auf dem Weg zur parlamentarischen Demokratie in Deutschland,* ed. Lothar Albertin and Werner Link, 109–26. Düsseldorf, 1981.

————. *Wahlen und Wählertradition in Deutschland: Kulturelle Grundlagen deutscher Parteien und Parteiensysteme im 19. und 20. Jahrhundert.* Frankfurt a.M., 1992.

Rohkrämer, Thomas. *Der Militarismus der "Kleinen Leute." Die Kriegervereine im Deutschen Kaiserreich, 1871–1914.* Munich, 1990.

Röhl, John C. G. *Germany without Bismarck: The Crisis of Government in the Second Reich, 1890–1900.* London, 1967.

————. *Kaiser, Hof und Staat. Wilhelm II. und die deutsche Politik.* Munich, 1987.

Rohner, Ludwig. *Kalendergeschichte und Kalender.* Wiesbaden, 1978.

Rommen, Heinrich Albert. *Der Staat in der katholischen Gedankenwelt.* Paderborn, 1935.

Rosenberg, Hans. *Große Depression und Bismarckzeit.* Berlin, 1967.

Ross, Ronald. *Beleaguered Tower: The Dilemma of Political Catholicism in Wilhelmine Germany.* Notre Dame, 1976.

————. "Enforcing the Kulturkampf in the Bismarckian State and the Limits of Coercion in Imperial Germany." *Journal of Modern History* 56 (September, 1984): 456–82.

Roth, Günther. *The Social Democrats of Imperial Germany: A Study in Working-class Isolation and National Integration.* Totowa, N.J., 1963.

Sahlins, Marshall. *Islands of History.* Chicago, 1985.

Sahlins, Peter. *Boundaries: The Making of France and Spain in the Pyrenees.* Berkeley and Los Angeles, 1989.

Said, Edward W. *Orientalism.* New York, 1978.

Sammons, Jeffrey L. *Imagination and History: Selected Papers on Nineteenth-century German Literature.* New York, 1988.

Saul, Klaus. *Staat, Industrie, Arbeiterbewegung im Kaiserreich. Zur Innen- und Außenpolitik des Wilhelminischen Deutschland 1903–1914.* Düsseldorf, 1974.

Sauer, Wolfgang. "Das Problem des deutschen Nationalstaats." In *Moderne deutsche Sozialgeschichte,* ed. Hans-Ulrich Wehler, 407–36. Cologne, 1966.

Schauff, Johannes. *Das Wahlverhalten der deutschen Katholiken im Kaiserreich und in der Weimarer Republik.* Ed. Rudolf Morsey. Mainz, 1975.

Schenda, Rudolf. *Volk ohne Buch. Studien zur Sozialgeschichte der populären Lesestoffe 1770–1910.* Frankfurt a.M., 1970.

Schieder, Theodor. *Das deutsche Kaiserreich von 1871 als Nationalstaat.* Cologne and Opladen, 1961.

————. *Nationalismus und Nationalstaat. Studien zum nationalen Problem im modernen Europa.* 2d ed. Ed. Otto Dann and Hans-Ulrich Wehler. Göttingen, 1992.

Schieder, Wolfgang. "Kirche und Revolution. Sozialgeschichtliche Aspekte der Trierer Wallfahrt von 1844." *Archiv für Sozialgeschichte* 14 (1974): 141–70.

————, ed. *Volksreligiosität in der modernen Sozialgeschichte.* Göttingen, 1986.

Schloßmacher, Norbert. "Antiultramontanismus im Wilhelminischen Deutschland. Ein Versuch." In *Deutscher Katholizismus im Umbruch zur Moderne*, ed. Wilfried Loth, 164–98. Stuttgart, 1991.

———. *Düsseldorf im Bismarckreich*. Düsseldorf, 1985.

Schmid-Egger, Barbara. *Klerus und Politk in Böhmen um 1900*. Munich, 1974.

Schmidt, Erich. *Bismarcks Kampf mit dem politischen Katholizismus. Pius der IX. und die Zeit der Rüstung 1848–1870*. Hamburg, 1942.

Schmidt, Hans. "Onno Klopp und die 'kleindeutschen Geschichtsbaumeister.'" In *Kirche, Staat und katholische Wissenschaft*, ed. A. Portmann-Tinguely, 381–95. Paderborn, 1988.

Schmidt-Volkmar, Erich. *Der Kulturkampf in Deutschland 1871–1890*. Göttingen, 1962.

Schneider, Michael. *Die Christlichen Gewerkschaften 1894–1933*. Bonn, 1982.

Schofer, Lawrence. *The Formation of a Modern Labor Force. Upper Silesia, 1865–1914*. Berkeley, 1975.

Schödl, Günter. *Alldeutscher Verband und deutsche Minderheitspolitik im kaiserlichen Deutschland, 1871–1914*. Düsseldorf, 1972.

Schulze, Hagen, ed. *Nation-building in Central Europe*. Leamington Spa, 1987.

Schwidetzky, Ilse. *Die polnische Wahlbewegung in Oberschlesien*. Breslau, 1934.

See, Klaus von. *Die Ideen von 1789 und die Ideen von 1914. Völkisches Denken in Deutschland zwischen Französischer Revolution und Erstem Weltkrieg*. Frankfurt, 1975.

Seton-Watson, Hugh. *Nations and States*. Boulder, Colo., 1977.

Sheehan, James. *German Liberalism in the Nineteenth Century*. Chicago, 1978.

———. "Liberalism and the City in 19th-century Germany." *Past and Present* 51 (1971): 116–37.

———. "Political Leadership in the German Reichstag, 1871–1918." *American Historical Review* 74 (1968): 511–28.

———. "The Problem of Nation in German History." In *Die Rolle der Nation in der deutschen Geschichte und Gegenwart*, ed. Otto Büsch and James Sheehan, 3–20. Berlin, 1985.

———. "What Is German History? Reflections on the Role of Nation in German History and Historiography." *Journal of Modern History* 53, no. 1 (1981): 1–23.

———, ed. *Imperial Germany*. New York, 1976.

Shils, Ed. "Primordial, Personal and Civil Ties." *British Journal of Sociology* 8 (1957): 130–45.

Smith, Anthony D. *Theories of Nationalism*. New York, 1983.

Smith, Helmut Walser. "Alltag und politischer Antisemitismus in Baden, 1890–1900." *Zeitschrift für die Geschichte des Oberrheins* 141 (1993): 280–303.

Sperber, Jonathan. *Popular Catholicism in Nineteenth-Century Germany*. Princeton, 1984.

Srbik, Heinrich Ritter von. *Geist und Geschichte vom deutschen Humanismus bis zur Gegenwart*. 2 vols. Munich and Salzburg, 1950–51.

Stark, Gary D. *Entrepreneurs of Ideology: Neoconservative Publishers in Germany, 1890–1933*. Chapel Hill, 1981.

Stegmann, Dirk. *Die Erben Bismarcks. Parteien und Verbände in der Spätphase des*

Wilhelminischen Deutschlands, Sammlungspolitik 1897–1918. Cologne and Berlin, 1970.

Stern, Fritz. *The Failure of Illiberalism.* Chicago, 1971.

———. *The Politics of Cultural Despair: A Study in the Rise of Germanic Ideology.* Berkeley, 1961.

Sutter, Berthold. *Die Badenischen Sprachenverordnungen von 1897.* 2 vols. Graz and Cologne, 1960–65.

Suval, Stanley. *Electoral Politics in Wilhelmine Germany.* Chapel Hill, 1985.

Tal, Uriel. *Christians and Jews in Germany: Religion, Politics, and Ideology in the Second Reich, 1870–1914.* Trans. Noah Jonathan Jacobs. Ithaca, N.Y., and London, 1975.

Tenfelde, Klaus. *Sozialgeschichte der Bergarbeiterschaft an der Ruhr im 19. Jahrhundert.* Bonn-Bad Godesberg, 1977.

Theiner, Peter. *Sozialer Liberalismus und deutsche Weltpolitik. Friedrich Naumann im Wilhelminischen Deutschland (1860–1919).* Baden-Baden, 1983.

Theweleit, Klaus. *Männerphantasien.* 2 vols. Hamburg, 1977, 1980.

Thoma, Hubert. *Georg Friedrich Dasbach: Priester, Publizist, Politiker.* Trier, 1975.

Tims, Richard W. *Germanizing Prussian Poland: The H-K-T-Society and the Struggle for the Eastern Marches in the German Empire, 1894–1919.* New York, 1941.

Trzeciakowski, Lech. *The Kulturkampf in Prussian Poland, 1870–1890.* New York, 1990.

———. "The Prussian State and the Catholic Church in Prussian Poland, 1871–1914." *Slavic Review* 26 (1967): 618–37.

Turner, Victor. *Dramas, Fields, and Metaphors: Symbolic Action in Human Society.* Ithaca, N.Y., and London, 1974.

Verderey, Katherine. "Whither 'Nation' and 'Nationalism'?" *Daedalus* 122, no. 3 (1993): 37–46.

Wadruszka, Adam, and Peter Urbantisch, eds. *Die Habsburgermonarchie, 1848–1918.* Vol. 3, no. 1. *Die Völker des Reiches.* Vienna, 1980.

———. *Die Habsburgermonarchie, 1848–1918.* Vol. 4. *Die Konfessionen.* Vienna, 1984.

Wahl, Alfred. *Confession und comportement dans les compagnes d'Alsace et de Bade (1871–1939).* 2 vols. Metz, 1980.

Walicki, Andrej. *Philosophy and Romantic Nationalism: The Case of Poland.* Oxford, 1982.

Weber, Christoph. *Kirchliche Politik zwischen Rom, Berlin und Trier 1876–1888. Die Beilegung des preußischen Kulturkampfes.* Mainz, 1970.

———. *Quellen und Studien zur Kurie und zur vatikanischen Politik unter Leo XIII.* Tübingen, 1973.

Weber, Max. *Economy and Society.* 2 vols. Ed. and trans. Günther Roth and Claus Wittich. New York, 1968.

Wehler, Hans-Ulrich. *Das deutsche Kaiserreich 1871–1918.* 4th ed. Göttingen, 1980.

———. *Krisenherde des Kaiserreichs 1871–1918.* Göttingen, 1970.

———. "Zur neuen Geschichte der Masuren." *Zeitschrift für Ostforschung* 11 (1962): 147–72.

————, ed. *Moderne deutsche Sozialgeschichte*. Cologne, 1970.

Weidenfeller, Gerhard. *VDA: Verein für das Deutschtum im Ausland. Allgemeiner Deutscher Schulverein (1881–1918)*. Frankfurt a.M., 1976.

Welleck, René. *A History of Modern Criticism: 1750–1950*. Vol. 4. *The Later Nineteenth Century*. New Haven and London, 1965.

Welter, Barbara. "The Feminization of American Religion: 1800–1860." In *Clio's Consciousness Raised: New Perspectives on the History of Women*, ed. Mary Hartman and Lois W. Banner, 137–57. New York, 1974.

Welti, Manfred E. "Abendmahl, Zollpolitik und Sozialistengesetz in der Pfalz. Eine statistisch-quantifizierende Untersuchung zur Verbreitung von liberal-aufklärerischem Gedankengut im 19. Jahrhundert." *Geschichte und Gesellschaft* 3 (1977): 384–405.

Wernecke, Klaus. *Der Wille zur Weltgeltung. Außenpolitik und Öffentlichkeit im Kaiserreich am Vorabend des I. Weltkrieges*. Düsseldorf, 1970.

Werner, Lothar. *Der Alldeutsche Verband 1890–1918*. Berlin, 1935.

White, Hayden. *The Content and the Form: Narrative Discourse and Historical Representation*. Baltimore, 1987

————. *Metahistory: The Historical Imagination in Nineteenth-century Europe*. Baltimore and London, 1973.

Whiteside, Andrew. *The Socialism of Fools: Georg Ritter von Schönerer and Austrian Pan-Germanism*. Berkeley, 1975.

Whiton, Helga B. *Der Wandel des Polenbilds in der deutschen Literatur des 19. Jahrhunderts*. Ann Arbor, 1980.

Windell, George G. *The Catholics and German Unity, 1866–1871*. Minneapolis, 1954.

Winkler, Heinrich A., ed. *Nationalismus*. Königstein/Ts., 1978.

Winzen, Peter. *Bülows Weltmachtkonzept. Untersuchungen zur Frühphase seiner Außenpolitik 1897–1901*. Boppard am Rhein, 1977.

Witt, Peter-Christian. *Die Finanzpolitik des Deutschen Reiches von 1903 bis 1913*. Lübeck and Hamburg, 1970.

Wittmann, Reinhard. *Buchmarkt und Lektüre im 18. und 19. Jahrhundert*. Tübingen, 1982.

————. *Geschichte des deutschen Buchhandels*. Munich, 1991.

Yerushalmi, Yosef Hayim. *Zakhor: Jewish History and Jewish Memory*. New York, 1989.

Yonke, Eric John. "The Emergence of a Roman Catholic Middle Class in Nineteenth-century Germany: Catholic Associations in the Prussian Rhine Province, 1837–1876." Ph.D. diss., University of North Carolina, Chapel Hill, 1990.

Zang, Gert, ed. *Provinzialisierung einer Region. Zur Entstehung der bürgerlichen Gesellschaft in der Provinz*. Frankfurt a.M., 1978.

Zeeden, Ernst Walter. "Die katholische Kirche in der Sicht des deutschen Protestantismus im 19. Jahrhundert." *Historisches Jahrbuch* 72 (1953): 433–56.

Zeender, John K. *The German Center Party, 1890–1906*. Philadelphia, 1976.

Zielinski, Z. "Der Kulturkampf in der Provinz Posen." *Historisches Jahrbuch* 101 (1981): 447–61.

Zillessen, Horst, ed. *Volk-Nation-Vaterland. Der deutsche Protestantismus und der Nationalismus.* Gütersloh, 1970.

Zimmermann, Clemens. "'Die Entwicklung hat uns nun einmal in das Erwerbsleben hineingeführt.' Lage, dörflicher Kontext und Mentalität nordbadischer Tabakarbeiter." *Zeitschrift für die Geschichte des Oberrheins* 135 (1987): 323–58.

Zucker, Stanley. "Philipp Wasserburg and Political Catholicism in Nineteenth-century Germany." *The Catholic Historical Review* 70, no. 1 (1984): 14–27.

Index